PENGUIN

MARY'S
LAST DANCE

Mary Li (formerly Mary McKendry) was raised in Rockhampton, Queensland, the third of eight children. There she was first introduced to ballet by her teacher Valeria Hansen. At sixteen she was accepted into the Royal Ballet School, London. She joined the London Festival Ballet (English National Ballet) in 1977 and was promoted to principal dancer in 1981. In 1985, Mary joined Houston Ballet as a principal dancer. During her performing career, she danced principal roles in all the major classical ballets, including *Swan Lake*, *The Sleeping Beauty*, *Giselle*, *Romeo and Juliet* and *The Nutcracker*, as well as leading roles in contemporary ballets, some created especially for her. She has worked with legendary teachers, choreographers, artistic directors and artists, including Rudolf Nureyev, Margot Fonteyn and Ben Stevenson. She married fellow principal dancer Li Cunxin in 1987, and they have danced together all over the world. Following their return to Australia in 1995 Mary worked with the Australian Ballet as a coach, while raising their children Sophie, Tom and Bridie. For the past ten years she has been ballet mistress at Queensland Ballet where her husband Li is artistic director. Together they have turned the company into one of worldwide recognition and acclaim.

MARY'S
LAST DANCE

MARY LI

PENGUIN BOOKS

PENGUIN BOOKS

UK | USA | Canada | Ireland | Australia
India | New Zealand | South Africa | China

Penguin Books is part of the Penguin Random House group of companies
whose addresses can be found at global.penguinrandomhouse.com.

Penguin
Random House
Australia

First published by Viking, 2020
This paperback edition published by Penguin Books, 2021

Cover photograph of Mary Li and Li Cunxin at Houston Ballet by Ellis Vener
Back-cover photograph of Mary McKendry in *Swan Lake* with
London Festival Ballet by Anthony Crickmay
Typeset in Adobe Garamond by Midland Typesetters, Australia
Colour separation by Splitting Image Colour Studio, Clayton, Victoria
Printed and bound in Australia by Griffin Press, an accredited
ISO AS/NZS 14001 Environmental Management Systems printer

 A catalogue record for this
book is available from the
National Library of Australia

ISBN 978 1 76104 191 4

penguin.com.au

MIX
Paper | Supporting
responsible forestry
FSC® C018684

To my children
Sophie, Tom and Bridie

I can still remember so vividly those last steps I took, led by music that will haunt me forever. I was overwhelmed with sadness, knowing this moment would change my life – knowing the decision I had to make. This would be my last dance . . .

Contents

Foreword
by Li Cunxin

I was born into utter poverty in Mao's Communist China, one of seven sons of hardworking peasant parents in the north-east. It was a troubled period in China's history – tens of millions of people died of famine and disease between 1958 and 1961. My family struggled desperately for survival.

Then, one fateful day, a delegation of Madame Mao's cultural advisers from the Beijing Dance Academy came into my classroom to select students to study ballet. As they were about to walk out, my teacher stopped the last gentleman and said, 'What about that one?' And that one was me.

That magical moment changed my life forever. From millions of children across China, only forty-four were selected. The seven years of harsh training taught me discipline and resilience. Upon graduation in 1979, I was awarded one of the first cultural exchange scholarships to study in America. This opportunity propelled me to become a ballet star. I danced all around the world, in front of presidents, prime ministers and royalty, and on the most prestigious stages.

In 1985, Mary McKendry, a principal dancer of London Festival Ballet (now English National Ballet), came into my life when she joined Houston Ballet. The chemistry and magic that ignited between us was immediate, and we became favourite partners on stage and fell in love away from the spotlight. Mary was a dream to dance with.

Her artistry, passion, work ethic and pursuit of perfection matched my own.

Although her childhood in Rockhampton, Queensland, was vastly different from the childhood I experienced in Communist China, there were similarities. Both of us were part of large, loving families. Mary was one of eight children born to a talented architect father and an artistic mother. She was trained by a brilliant ballet teacher in Rockhampton, and was subsequently accepted into the Royal Ballet School in London at the age of sixteen. Like me, she had to overcome homesickness, self-doubt and heartbreaking setbacks but was helped by some special, gifted mentors.

In each other we found our soulmate, both on stage and in life, and we chose to share our lives together. When our first child, Sophie, was born, she became the joy of our lives. Our world was blissful and perfect. Then something unexpected happened that knocked Mary's life and career completely off course. I was heartbroken for her as I knew how much she loved ballet, which had been her deepest passion since she was an eight-year-old girl. Suddenly her beloved ballet was no more, and our perfect world crashed down. The road we travelled was full of difficulties, heartaches and shattered dreams, and we needed all the courage, determination and strength we could muster to overcome those challenges.

After many years devoted to the care of our family, Mary finally reconnected with ballet. She began working with leading dancers at the Australian Ballet and is currently principal *répétiteur* and ballet mistress at Queensland Ballet. She is a highly respected teacher and coach who is thrilled to continue her journey in ballet by helping the stars of today and tomorrow.

Mary is an incredible mother to our three children, Sophie, Tom and Bridie. Not only is she the bedrock of our family, but she has also changed me completely as a man. Her sophistication, joy of life, passion for ballet, strength of character, and love for me and our children have shaped me into the man I am. She is the strength behind my success.

In 2000 I started writing the story of my life, which became *Mao's Last Dancer*. Little did I know then that it would touch so many hearts. To my surprise it became a bestseller, and then a celebrated film.

Ever since the publication of my book and the release of the film, people have been intrigued to know more of Mary's story. She has been pursued by publishing houses but declined all approaches until Sophie encouraged her and volunteered to help. It has been fascinating to see their roles reversed from when our daughter was younger – Sophie is actually helping her mother now! Piecing together Mary's story has been a special bonding experience for them.

It's so gratifying to see Mary giving voice to her own story. I laughed and cried when I read the first 100-page draft manuscript. Her story is not only a companion to *Mao's Last Dancer* but a sequel to it. So here is Mary's story, and what happened next in our lives . . .

Li Cunxin
August 2020

BEFORE

PART ONE

Rockhampton
1958–75

*I was the most unlikely candidate to be
a ballerina if ever there was one . . .*

1

Sometimes, even the most impossible dream can come true. When I look back on my childhood I wonder how I managed to get from that wild and wonderful town called Rockhampton to the Royal Ballet School in London. It seemed so unlikely. Back then, Rocky was a town where there was nothing much to do besides family and friendship, and nothing much to think about except the idea of stepping out into a bigger world.

I took that step, and I have my mother, Coralie, to thank for that. Oh, my mother, dear Coralie. She was so refined. She married my dad, Neil George McKendry, and then having eight children in eleven years made refinement and gentility somewhat difficult.

Coralie Tighe grew up with her older brother, Hugh, and much younger sister, Anne, in 1930s and 1940s Kalinga, a humble suburb of Brisbane. She was taught by nuns at Corpus Christi College, Nundah, where she played piano and developed a great love of music, dance and art, which was part of her mother, Bridie's, family heritage. Coralie learned ballet when she was younger, but the nuns didn't think that was very ladylike. Instead, she was encouraged to spend more time on piano and music theory, which she continued right up until her Licentiate in Music.

After attending St Rita's College, Clayfield, Coralie worked for the Australian Broadcasting Commission as a stenotypist in the centre of

Brisbane – a job she adored. She was genteel in nature and would go off to work on the train every day, beautiful and stylish, showing off her 22-inch waist in the latest fashion. Perhaps this was what caught Neil George's eye when they had a chance meeting on the train one morning.

They say opposites attract, and Coralie quickly fell for Neil George's confident personality, Irish sense of humour and sparkling blue eyes. She learned that he was from Allora, a tiny town of 200 people two hours west of Brisbane. He and his brother, Jack (affectionately known as Jock), were brought up by Josephine, their widowed mother, who owned the local pub. After graduating from Nudgee College, Brisbane, Neil George studied architecture at Queensland University – an unexpected choice for a country boy back then.

Coralie and Neil George began their married life in 1955. Back then young married women had to give up their work and attend to house duties, so that was the end of Coralie's much-loved career. They rented a run-down cottage in the inner-western suburb of Rainworth. Neil George started his day at four in the morning to do a milk run to help with the finances before heading to uni for the rest of the day. He would return to paint the rooms at night and work on fixing up the place.

It wasn't long before Coralie became pregnant. Contraceptives were never mentioned in those days so Catholic couples were encouraged to use the rhythm method of birth control, but surely that is one of the Catholic mysteries given how many continued to have numerous children quite happily. By the time she was twenty-five, Coralie had three children. I was the third, and the first girl, born on 7 September 1958.

For a young woman in the 1950s, life with three children under the age of three was a struggle, so Neil George, ever the dreamer, talked about moving to India where they could have all the children they wanted and as many *amahs* as were needed to help. Of course it was his fascination with India's incredible architecture and history and his indomitable sense of adventure that had a lot to do with this. I don't think Coralie quite knew what she was getting into by marrying my father. Although the India dream didn't transpire, Coralie was certainly in for an adventure for the rest of their married life.

Upon graduating from university in 1960, Neil was offered a job with an architecture firm in the central Queensland town of Rockhampton. He had never much liked big-city life with its stuffiness, so he jumped at the chance. This would still be an adventure! He and Coralie had been five years married; Gerry was four, Michael was three and I was two. There had been a miscarriage after me, and another baby was on the way. The plan was to move to Rocky where he would earn a decent salary, build a nice house, and the children would have a safe, happy and carefree childhood in a small town where everyone knew and looked out for each other.

So Mum, Dad, Ger, Mick and me – along with Mum's bump – moved to Talford Street, not far from the centre of Rockhampton. Our rented home in Rocky was a little blue weatherboard cottage with a small porch at the front and steep back stairs leading into the garden. It was hardly big enough, with its three tiny bedrooms and small family space, but it would do until Dad could build us our great big family home.

Back then, Rocky had a population of around 30 000. Many hailed from down south, having moved there to join the gold rush. Situated on either side of the Fitzroy River, Rocky was a major port for the region and in the mid-1880s serviced one of the biggest gold-mines in the world, Mount Morgan, 39 kilometres to the west.

The town had a colonial feel with its broad walkways and wide ornate verandahs, providing much-needed shade. The main street was called East Street, and it consisted of two small department stores, a few cafes, some banks, and a grand stone-and-brick post office with a clock tower built in Rocky's heyday in the late nineteenth century. Also built during the gold rush was the beautiful Customs House on Quay Street. Made of local sandstone, with a huge copper dome and semicircular portico, it sat elegantly overlooking the river. Dotted around town were numerous pubs and churches, including the impressive St Joseph's Cathedral.

The city boasted beautiful botanic gardens, which also included a zoo full of chimpanzees, crocodiles, koalas, kangaroos, wombats, echidnas, dingoes, native Australian birds, and a snake house. Past the zoo enclosure was our favourite: a simple playground including a whirly-girdy. You couldn't get on it unless you were fast and fierce, because the boys would make it spin so furiously. But I always managed. I loved it. There was also a slippery slide, which all the children jumped on, no matter how many. It was made of steel, so on the many hot Rocky days it burnt your bum on the way down, but we didn't care – it was all part of the fun. I can't remember how many children ended up with broken teeth, arms or legs. My brother Ger broke his wrist on the whirly-girdy once. It seemed all the parents expected their children to have something broken at some time.

~

Matthew was born soon after we arrived in Rocky, and before long Ger, Mick, Matt and I became 'the top gang'. After Matt then came the little ones: Brigid, Josephine, Patrick and, finally, Dominic. By the time Coralie was thirty-three, she had eight children under the age of eleven.

I was not the quiet, obedient daughter that my gentle and ladylike mother had hoped for. I was born wild – so I'm told – and then of course I had to keep up with Ger and Mick. I was often tipped out of the pram when I was a baby, and as soon as I was able to walk I followed them, as they leapt across our beds and out the front door, though sometimes one of us would end up on the porch with a split head.

The boys also loved to kick a football in the big backyard, and I'd often join in. They were very physical, so it was inevitable that I became strong and physically competent too, just to keep up. There wasn't much traffic, and the wide street was another playground for us. I followed the boys everywhere. Later, when they went to a kindergarten at least a kilometre away, I would follow them there, too. Sometimes I wandered off on my own, only to be collected by my frantic mother, who would have received a call from a neighbour who'd spotted me somewhere on the street.

At first Mum would worry. However, she soon got used to it as she became far too busy with the other children or being pregnant to wonder where her eldest daughter had got to this time. In any case – and a blessing for my poor mother – Rocky was for families. So many children everywhere. I didn't have to ask my mum's permission. I just climbed over a few fences to check if anyone was home and invariably stayed for dinner, as one or two extra mouths to feed was nothing in large families.

Mum couldn't always cope. She just did the best she could to carry on. Grandma Bridie would have loved to come up and help, but grumpy Grandpa Tom wanted her to stay home and look after him instead. So after Matt's birth, when I was three and Mum was at her wits' end, she decided to put me on a plane for the first of my stays with Grandma Bridie in Brisbane – hoping that some of Bridie's refinement would rub off on me. I remember walking onto the tarmac and up the stairs of the plane by myself and waving goodbye to Mum.

Grandma Bridie was smart, charming and intelligent. She was the fourth of five children. Her father, a dairy farmer in northern New South Wales, drowned in a flood when she was a teenager, which changed the family's fortunes. Her two elder sisters went to Sydney University, but her family couldn't afford for Bridie to go. She had a love of literature and music and read a lot of books; she always gave me books to read.

Bridie was beautiful-looking, had a gorgeous figure and she was a lot of fun. I adored her from the moment we met, and loved my annual week-long visits. She always planned those visits carefully and would often make special trips to the movies with me, or together we would walk around the neighbourhood, looking at houses and people.

Back at home I had so much energy that I rarely wanted to go to sleep. 'Mary, you're impossible!' Mum would rail at me when it was past bedtime and I was still racing around. Once, she decided to take me to a doctor to find some relief. The doctor prescribed something, but Mum gave up on the idea after one night. She thought better not to rely on medication to dampen my rambunctious spirit.

It was a chaotic life and we needed home help. Jocey, the sixteen-year-old sister of a woman from Dad's office, came to live with us after Patrick was born. By then we had moved into the big house Dad designed for us in Little Kellow Street. Jocey and the accident-prone Patrick, who we called Paddy, were joined at the hip until she left to get married when he was about six. We all adored her and missed her like crazy. Next came Faye, but that didn't work out as she was disco mad and determined to have a baby, which was a great worry to Mum. Then we had Joy, who was quite large and couldn't bend down easily; when Joy got hot and sweaty, Coralie would make her a cup of tea and finish the work herself. Joy loved us, though, and she particularly loved ironing. She would stand at the ironing board for hours, even though we didn't think the job should take that long. She was slow, but Mum never had the heart to let her go.

Meanwhile, Dad, our brilliant Dad, was unstoppable. He reckoned he could do things better if he did them himself, and decided to leave his employer to start his own firm. Together with Peter Cheney, a fellow architecture student from uni, he set up McKendry and Cheney Architects, which was pretty amazing for a 28-year-old from Allora. The firm's name quickly became synonymous with many of the significant buildings erected in Central Queensland, including the Pilbeam Theatre and the Rockhampton Art Gallery. Their large office on the south side of the river had glass walls and you could see all the drawing boards laid out with draftsman's drawings in progress – everything was done by hand back then. In time Peter went on to what is now the Queensland University of Technology to be one of its principal lecturers, and Neil George then formed a new partnership with his senior architect, Robert Buckley.

As a successful architect, Neil George was always in demand, and it was hard for Mum when the long hours and the statewide travel to places like Longreach or Emerald and new coalmining towns such as Blackwater kept him away from home. He also devoted a lot of time to supporting the Liberal Party in Central Queensland. In 1966 Neil George ran as the federal Liberal candidate for the historically safe Labor seat of Capricornia. On one occasion the whole family went to the airport, scrubbed clean and hair combed, and stood in line, in order of age, to meet Prime Minister Harold Holt and his wife, Zara, when they came to campaign in Rocky.

We kids stood in the back of Mum's blue Hillman to go delivering how-to-vote leaflets for Dad. The first thing Dad did when he bought the Hillman was to remove the rear seat so that five of us could stand in the back. It was the only way we could all fit! There were no seat-belts either so it was bad luck if you couldn't hold on. We'd hang on for dear life to the front seat with every bump and dip in the road.

Gerry would be sitting in the front seat holding one of the babies. Mum was hugely pregnant with Dom. She couldn't have done the leaflet delivery without us as she could hardly get in and out of the car. Instead, Mum drove from letterbox to letterbox and we would hop off from the back and run out to drop off leaflets to as many houses in Rocky as we could manage. Mr Gray, the Labor nominee, eventually won with an increased majority, but Dad never gave up his political beliefs, especially about the power of the individual. 'The Lung' was a common term for the government bureaucracy – a play on the saying 'Wouldn't work in an iron lung'. Dad would often talk about 'Lungers'. 'Listen, kids,' he used to say, 'the Lung sucks everything out of you, the Lung does the breathing for you and there are no returns for the people.' We'd laugh and roll our eyes, but today we all have similarly cynical views about politics and government bureaucracy.

Despite all of his outside commitments, Neil George was the most wonderful father and always found ways to make life better for us. Innovation should have been his middle name. The amazing house he designed and built for us was our saviour. He bought a steep sloping piece of land at 42 Little Kellow Street, in the centre of Rocky, close to the hospital and the grammar school. Half of the block was rock face, which looked like a cliff to us kids. 'What a very ordinary piece of land,' stated Coralie when she first saw it. She had yearned for a big Queenslander home with sweeping verandahs, floral wallpaper and pretty things, but Neil George was just too practical, and it was all they could afford at the time. With his usual foresight Dad could see that being in the centre of town would be important for eight children growing up.

The elevated house had to be built into the rock face. I was eight when we moved in – such an exciting day for us all. However, it was a work in progress, with alterations done as Dad made more money and the babies kept coming. It was a fibro construction, built in two sections, with separate buildings linked by a walkway. The section at the top of the block was two-storey. Upstairs was a huge open-plan living space, very modern for the time – with floor-to-ceiling glass doors that opened to a balcony with views of the town centre. In time, the space included a lounge room with a fireplace, where Mum would read and play piano, and an elegant dining area for special occasions. Downstairs were the kitchen, laundry, carport and greenery, although the latter didn't last long as we kids soon managed to wreck it. You accessed the house via a long, steep driveway. Only one car at a time could drive up, and it was best not to reverse down. A family friend did at one time and accidentally ran over baby Paddy, who was playing by the clothes line. Coralie heard the screams, and scooped him up and immediately headed to the hospital. Luckily he was only badly bruised but the tyre marks stayed for months, we were told.

The second section, with a main bedroom and a bathroom, was situated towards the front of the block, close to the road. The bathroom floor was painted speckled cement — non-slip commercial grade. Coralie had wanted nice white tiles, but Neil George was thinking of children's injuries, and no one would slip on this cement. We had enough emergency dramas as it was. Next to the bedroom was a large sleepout that became the boys' and girls' 'dormitories'.

The dorms were separated by a thin partition wall with gaps at the top and bottom for airflow. The boys had their two sets of double bunk beds and on the girls' side was another set of bunk beds and a single bed. I slept alone on the single bed and my younger sisters, Brig and Jo, slept in the bunks, usually in the same one. They were inseparable. We could all crawl underneath the partition, which led to lots of pranks that often ended in tears. During games of chasey, we could escape by scrambling under or jumping over and landing on the top bunk beds. Balls, pillows and profanities were also hurled over the partition.

Neil George was always chasing the breeze. As air conditioners were not affordable then, he installed glass louvres everywhere so there was always a cross-breeze somewhere to keep the house cool. On hot summer nights we slept under mosquito nets as mozzies came through the louvres too. Since there were also no blinds on the windows, we always woke up with the sun — there was no need for an alarm clock. In any case, Dad would never put up with us lying around in bed.

The two buildings were connected by a 10-metre-long cement walkway with grass on either side, leading from the bedrooms to the kitchen. At night-time we would run frantically between the two buildings, squealing as we sprang over huge, ugly cane toads. The walkway was covered with an aluminium roof for shade so we wouldn't burn our feet. However, we would happily run barefoot on the scorching hot roof and jump down onto the nearby trampoline — often five of us at the same time.

The night of the Catholic Ball, a fundraiser for the parish, Mum was all dressed up. She was so excited because she hardly ever went out. Paddy didn't want her to go and was lying on the trampoline, whining, when the boys started jumping from the roof onto the trampoline. Paddy flew up into the air and hit his face on the metal trampoline frame, knocking out his front teeth, with blood pouring everywhere.

'Mum, Mum!' we all screamed.

'What's happened now!' Mum, dressed in angelic white, called as she rushed to Paddy.

Coralie immediately drove him to emergency and called Uncle Alan. Paddy had lost all six front teeth.

After that night, Coralie always said it was a master stroke of Dad's to have our home situated in a 'medical triangle', which included our GP, Dr Tommy Nutley, Alan Agnew, the surgeon, Gerard Dowling, our dentist, and the general hospital smack bang in the middle. But sadly, I don't think Mum ever did get to the ball that night.

The Hills hoist to hang washing was at the top of the driveway away from the house, and all of us children were known to swing on it at times. It was usually covered in cloth nappies to dry. There were no garden beds but there were big shady poinciana trees to climb. The yard was basically a jungle, perfect for wild kids.

There were large sliding glass doors between the kitchen and the yard. We would all try to jump the three steps from the yard up to the kitchen, but after most of us had hit the glass doors not realising they were shut, and poor Paddy frequently knocking himself out, Dad eventually added a stick-on danger strip to the door at child's eye level.

Later, Dad had a slab floor poured under the lower section so we could put a table-tennis table in there. He also added on to the kitchen and replaced the barbecue area with an entertainment room and an impressive floor-to-ceiling library brimming with books. Coralie came to adore this room.

To cater for our large family, Dad bought an oversized industrial stove. It had two ovens, six burners and ran the length of one entire wall in the kitchen. We also had three fridges, with one dedicated to meat: Neil George would make a trip down to the butcher to buy half a beast that would feed us for eight weeks. He also saw another problem with all eight children going to one fridge to get water. That poor fridge was never able to keep up with the number of times it was opened, and the contents were ruined in the Rocky heat. Dad quickly solved this problem by installing a commercial water cooler near the kitchen. He put a rock beside it so the smaller children could step up to get a drink. Now there was no excuse for any of us to be opening that fridge.

It probably took eight years all up to finish the house. I think it was the finest and most practical house Neil George ever designed. It worked so well with eight rampaging kids, and we loved it.

~

Home life was very boisterous and chaotic but wonderful. We might not have had fancy clothes or the latest gadgets, but we had love and food. On a typical day Mum and Dad would be up at 5 a.m., with Dad heading off to work early and Mum doing a load of washing and hanging out all the nappies, wearing a large hat to avoid the scorching sun. She was never without a full-brimmed hat, and we girls were introduced to anti-freckle cream very early. She would then start on breakfast, usually with one baby on her hip and another around her ankles. She'd cook pan-loads of bacon and eggs and I'd be on toaster duty with two loaves of bread while the other children promptly arrived at the table, Dom in the highchair. I would be either holding or feeding a baby.

Every day, Mum had the task of feeding eight children morning, noon and night. She did this three times a day, almost every day, for twenty-five years! She got a brief respite for a few years when another helper, Conway, came on Wednesdays and Fridays. On those days she would cook breakfast and play the piano for us if we helped her with the tidying up. Often on Sunday nights, Dad would make a damper, which we would eat straight from the oven spread with butter and jam. It was a perfect, simple meal to have at night. On special occasions,

he would come up with a delicious oxtail stew. We would sit on the
benches at the long table in the kitchen. Dad insisted on benches
instead of chairs so we could not lean backwards, fall off and break our
neck or any other body part – there was enough broken furniture and
broken bones in our home already.

After breakfast, we'd get ourselves ready for school, brush our
teeth if we could find a toothbrush. Toothbrushes, towels and
pillows always went missing, and likewise no one could ever find
a hairbrush in the general chaos of family life with eight children.
Unlike all my siblings, who had wavy brown or straight blond hair,
I had huge bouffant hair filled with knots that would send the local
hairdresser into despair. The only way to control the knots was to
have them cut out at monthly visits. By that time, the knots were
already the size of ten-cent pieces. Sometimes in between visits, I
would just lightly brush over the top layer to hide the rest of the hair
and hope for the best. It wasn't my fault – I often couldn't find the
hairbrush!

With Mum completely overwhelmed by the laundry, cleaning,
cooking and looking after small babies, some days she wouldn't have
time to make our lunches for school. 'I'll bring them over at noon,'
she'd promise, waving us off. Sometimes she said she'd buy us something from the famous Melbourne Fish Bar or pick up some Cranston
Pies, which suited us. Whatever it was to be, occasionally she would
forget. Starving, we'd eagerly wait at the gate for her to bring our
lunches in her blue Hillman, but if she didn't turn up, we knew we'd
have to go and knock on the nuns' convent door. This didn't sit well
with any of us.

'Sister, Mum forgot our lunch. We're hungry.' We would try to
downplay this as we didn't want to make our poor mother look bad.

With kindness, the nuns would always share their food –
invariably hot, stale sandwiches and room-temperature green milk.
They must have added green cordial just for us, thinking that children
would like flavoured milk. Milk made my stomach churn at the best

of times, so I would quickly hand my glass to Ger, who also went green at the sight of green milk.

After walking back from school I would help Mum with the dinner. 'Mary, darling, peel forty potatoes for me,' she would say, then call out, 'Brig, get the boys out of here!' Dinner was always a frantic time for her, the children hungry and wanting food, especially the boys. The little ones demanded her attention, but Coralie was simply too busy trying to get dinner on the table. Often she was seen wielding a wooden spoon to stir the food and also to smack any random child who came too near the hot ovens.

Despite the chaos, Coralie was a fine cook. Dinner was typically meat and three veg, all beautifully presented on a white plate. We would stand in line behind the counter, tallest to smallest, holding a plate, and file past Mum. She would stand on the other side of the counter in her apron in the sweltering heat, smiling while carefully serving the food. Everyone was fed the same. It was a military operation as Coralie was determined to bring some civility to dinnertime. If we wanted seconds, we would hide under the table and eat quickly, then pop up to pretend that Mum had forgotten us. Poor Dom, being last in line, always missed out on things like pork crackling, and one year when he was asked what he wanted for his birthday, he said he'd like to be served first.

While we ate, Coralie would sit in her rocking chair with a glass of Scotch in hand and watch us devour what was on our plates. Other times she'd read a book, waiting for Neil George to come home so they could have their dinner together. Dad would normally appear when all the dinnertime mayhem was over. He would have had a beer or two at the Brunswick Hotel after work, discussing politics and general business. In a country town like Rocky, this was how people got to know and trust you – the pub after work was where business contacts were made. 'What splendid children you are! What a queen your wonderful mother is!' he would say when he came home. He was always happy to be with his brood and his darling queen.

He would change into a singlet and boxer underpants, smoking, and, with a 'tallie' (longneck) of beer at his elbow and a full glass, he'd sit at the table, happily looking over his family.

In spite of the chaos, table manners were enforced: 'Pass the salt, please.' We had to hold our knife and fork properly and weren't allowed to elbow whoever was sitting next to us. However, we were encouraged to speak: there was no adherence to the notion that 'Children should be seen and not heard'. If one of us looked like stepping out of line, Dad would make up nonsense to make us laugh. He had sayings like 'Stand by for a karate farty', or he'd tell us about his mate Tommy Tit who wanted to change his name to Edgar.

Sometimes there was a race to sit next to baby Dom, because if you didn't like the meal that had been served you could just put it on his plate; he usually flicked his food on the floor anyway. The other ploy was to sit near one of the louvred windows and throw any unwanted food into the neighbour's yard. We would often put peas in our pocket, leave the table with an 'Excuse me' and empty them into the bin.

With ten people eating every day, Dad was all about the rubbish. Somebody had to take it out to the bins at least twice a day, after breakfast and after dinner. The weekly council collection was not sufficient: we had to drive to the dump at least once a week to empty our bins, and then we'd start again, to escape the maggots. This was how Dad taught us what maggots were.

Paddy was a big boy, and clumsy. We eventually found out he needed glasses, but every night at the dinner table we would wait for him to knock over his drink or something. Every single night . . . We were waiting for it. And over it would go.

'Don't say anything!' Mum would warn us, worrying Paddy would get an inferiority complex, which was the mental health buzzword of that era. So we would just wipe it up and pretend it hadn't happened. Then we could relax and eat after that.

Afterwards, while all of us children had our baths – water puddles everywhere – Dad would help with the dishes and then join Coralie for a beer and a smoke. We were supposed to do our homework, but we spent most of the evening distracting each other.

One time we had an unwelcome guest living near the downstairs bedroom under the walkway where we often played hide-and-seek. We all knew the big, scary, lethal brown snake was living there, but we couldn't catch it, until one day Dad spotted it and got a rake, managed to trap it against a wall and squished the life out it. It was around 5 feet long, but to us kids it was triple the length! We talked about that snake for a long time.

Another time when we were swimming at Lammermoor Beach with our friends, Dad grabbed a baby shark by the tail and began smacking it onto the sand while yelling at us to get out of the water. It was only a couple of feet long, but it seemed much larger to us. Dad was worried about us in the water in case other sharks were close.

Coralie's night off was Friday, when we went to the Melbourne Fish Bar, famous for its fish and chips wrapped in newspaper. The whole package was placed on the table, with Dom sitting alongside it. I had never tasted anything better. No plates, no lemon, no tomato sauce, and it was our favourite meal of the week. This is where 'the top gang' really had to learn to share and look after the young ones to ensure they actually got a piece of fish and some chips.

On Sundays, we would go to church and then to the pub for Coke and potato chips. Coralie would have a shandy and later a Scotch, while Dad would have a beer. There weren't many places you could take eight children, so we adored the Brunswick. It had a very lush lawn where we could play touch footy using someone's shoe as the ball, or run races. After this treat, we would go home for a roast lunch.

～

We had a great network of friends within walking distance of our home. The Agnew clan, with five children, lived just up the road near the hospital, where Alan was the surgeon. We called him Uncle Alan, and his wife was Auntie Shirl. Shirl and Mum were great friends and she often came to Mum for advice because Mum was always so calm, despite everything.

Nella and Jack Gillogley and their three children lived behind us. Jack was the hospital's radiographer and Nella was the organiser of neighbourhood Friday drinks. Nella loved a party and was very generous. Often on a Friday afternoon Mum would tell us she'd had enough and walk out. We collectively knew that she was going for drinks at Nella's, and that, sadly, we children weren't invited. Instead, Nella's son, Peter, would jump over the fence and stay with us.

At Christmas time, we would go to a church service before we were allowed to gather around the Christmas tree. One present was handed to each of us, usually from youngest to oldest. I might be given a skipping rope or a pogo stick, while my sisters Brig and Jo would receive cute dolls. Even though I didn't like dolls, I remember feeling a little jealous. Once I found the scissors and cut the dolls' hair – I was desperate to be a hairdresser then. I was in pretty big trouble after that incident.

It was also not unusual to have seventeen children in the house for Christmas, as the Agnews or the Gillogleys, or both, would join us. Mum would set up the big table upstairs in the 'good room' for all the kids, with a table for the adults next to it. Mum adored Christmas and always looked calm and serene on the day. She would put on her apron, excited for Christmas lunch. The table would have been set the night before with a white tablecloth and Christmas crackers. Our friends would soon arrive and the parents would help the children settle with a traditional Christmas lunch, including roast pork and veg, plum pudding and custard. We ate with gusto even though it felt like it was 100 degrees in spite of the ceiling fans.

After lunch, the children would play Monopoly and the game could go on for hours. We all had a competitive streak, and often there would be screaming, the board would be upended and money, dice and counters would fly into the air and scatter across the floor.

~

As children, we were not a particularly disciplined bunch, but we always knew the rules of the McKendry clan: no dobbing on each other; always stick up for family members in any confrontation or fight outside of home; no punching, kicking or slapping, unless Coralie decided to smack someone; and lastly, always look out for the baby.

As I got older, I refused to have friends over because it was such chaos at our house. You just didn't know how messy it was going to be, and I found it really embarrassing. As Mum was such a calm and proper lady, she was a total misfit in the McKendry household. With that many of us under one roof, I quickly learned the pecking order. Part of the responsibility of being the eldest girl meant being old enough to feel sorry for my poor gentle mother. I believe this is where I learned about empathy. I would try to help her clean up the house, only for my unruly siblings to devastate the place in seconds. I would make the bunk beds in the dormitories, but the boys were always jumping on them and messing up the blankets and pillows. With Joy gone, I did the best I could ironing all the boys' shirts on a tall ironing board that was at my shoulder height.

I also took it upon myself, at age nine, to look after seven-month-old baby Dom. He always wanted to be part of the group, so someone had to mind him to make sure he didn't jump off the roof onto the trampoline or do anything else dangerous. I often had him on my hip or in the highchair. All in all, he was a pretty good baby. I fed, bathed and changed him until he started school, and as a result we became very close.

As I matured, I started to see that my mother was the Australian definition of a sweetheart. In her slow, soft voice she would end phrases with 'my love' or 'my darling'. However, as we children were unruly at the best of times, we often saw her holding a wooden spoon or a coat hanger – whichever happened to be in her hand at the time – thin-lipped and threatening to spank us if we didn't behave. Rarely did she carry out the threat: she was too much of a gentle soul. It's no wonder that we loved being home sick with Coralie. She would feed us spoonfuls of flat lemonade in bed and spoil us with rare undivided attention.

In those days, we kids did whatever we needed to do to survive, even though there were constant hazards. Sometimes one of us would fall and split our head open, and Neil George would call out to Coralie, 'Is everyone still alive, or do we need to go to emergency?'

Coralie would answer with her usual calm demeanour, 'No, my love. They'll live,' and Neil George would get back to whatever he was doing.

One time we decided to build a small tree house in the backyard. Naturally, nails were left lying around, and that day ended with Neil George taking all of the children to the hospital for a tetanus shot after spotting various scratches and cuts on arms, legs and feet.

I came to love the huge library of books Mum and Dad had. The first novel I read was *Girl with Green Eyes* by the Irish novelist Edna O'Brien and I loved it. There was also a local municipal library in Rocky, but any books we brought home would invariably get lost, stolen or torn. Between the eight of us, everything got wrecked. When I was about twelve, Mum and Dad got very excited about ordering a set of encyclopaedias, but we weren't allowed to touch them except when doing homework.

We could never keep a record-player because it would get broken. We would often joke that whatever we seemed to touch would break. This was why Dad, who loved art, didn't spend money on furniture or pretty ornaments, although he and Mum occasionally bought paintings when they could afford it. The next breakdown of the washing machine was always on Dad's mind.

They had at least managed to purchase a piano when Dad and his firm began making money. It was a revelation for us, as we hadn't known that both of our parents could read music and play the piano. The piano was very precious to Mum. How she managed to play it with so little spare time, I'll never know, but to have music in the house was special. I think it's what helped her stay calm in the daily chaos.

Unfortunately, I did not share Coralie's gift for piano. I didn't have a light touch and found it torturous to sit still. The only time I cheated in my life was when I once lied to Sister Magdalene by copying Coralie's signature to say I had practised piano for thirty minutes each day.

Mum's 'good room' upstairs was designed as a parents' retreat, and she loved entertaining friends there. We children went up there to open presents on Christmas Day, and occasionally when it was really cold we sat on the warm rug and Dad lit the fire. I remember seeing him and Mum play a piano duet.

Except for church and school, we ran barefoot and wore T-shirts and shorts or swimming togs. That way, it was easy to run under the hose while Mum, with her hat on, squirted us with water. She always got a good chuckle out of that.

When we needed to dress up and look smart, such as for church, Mum went to a dressmaker. It was difficult to purchase nice clothes in Rockhampton. She would buy some fabric and design us all different outfits from it. She enjoyed picking out the fabric and having the dresses made. I was never really interested in clothes or dressing up, but Mum had great style and it was a novelty for her to do something 'girly' in our household of rowdy boys. Mum also loved to go to Sydney or Melbourne with Dad when he had a conference because she could shop to buy material, and visit galleries. Later our parents would take us all to Sydney, Melbourne and Canberra to explore some of Australia's history and they always insisted we look at the architecture. In Sydney we discovered museums, the Sydney Opera House,

Vaucluse House and many others. We didn't care much for the history then, though – we just wanted to go to the beaches and Luna Park. In hindsight, how lucky we all were.

Church was a big part of our lives. Every night we would climb into bed and together, through the partition we would say the rosary: one Our Father led by Dad, then us joining with ten Hail Marys and a closing prayer, but we usually fell asleep before we could finish. We could easily hear each other as there were no doors. That was another thing Neil George didn't allow – doors. If we didn't have doors, there could be no slamming and no accidents, he reasoned.

We rarely missed Sunday Mass. We attended St Vincent's Church, right next door to our school, St Joseph's Wandal primary school. Dad had designed the church in 1974, replacing a 1912 wooden building. Inside the church our family would take up a whole pew, except for Ger and Mick, who had to serve at the altar in red-and-white gowns. At the other end of the family there was Paddy, who couldn't keep still and would crawl up the aisle, grinning, to be with his older brothers. We kids would try not to laugh, but Mum and Dad were silently mortified. Usually it fell to me to try to snatch him before he got to the altar – cue his screaming and carrying on as I dragged him back to his place in the pew. Church was meant to be sacred and peaceful, but we never once managed to stay quiet for a whole service. Instead, we would just try to survive without wetting ourselves with laughter.

Eventually Paddy and Dom replaced Ger and Mick as altar boys. Paddy, still clumsy, once set his tunic alight with dripping wax from the candle he was carrying. He quickly patted it out, but he wore that singed tunic for the rest of his time at the altar. Another day, Paddy and Dom looked down and were surprised to see our black dog, Nellie, on the altar with them, just as she'd wandered into our home years earlier. Paddy, not knowing what to do, had to move quickly to get her out after she snapped at a devout old woman who always sat in the same spot at the front of the church.

As Mum was the saintly one, she insisted we were confirmed as well as baptised. I was confirmed when I was eight, and chose St Bernadette of Lourdes as my patron saint: I was fascinated that she had a spring whose water could cure diseases. Every large Irish Catholic family in the 1950s was encouraged to produce a nun and a priest. I tried to be saintly like Mum to please the nuns at school and walked a few miles to church each morning, there and back, before my confirmation, but it didn't last. However, Mum must have thought I was angelic for that period. Once we were confirmed, we went to weekly confession. I was given the same prayers for penance again and again and my brothers and sisters and I realised, when we compared notes, that all of us were given the same thing. Two Our Fathers and three Hail Marys was the standard.

We sang at most parish funerals and cried at every one, which is how I learned to be dramatic. The church taught me theatre: Sundays with the bishop in his ceremonial robes, the kissing of the ring, the arches of waving palms on Palm Sunday, watching and listening to people walking down the aisles to view a coffin – it was all in front of you. You have to go to drama class these days, but back then the church was real theatre.

~

St Joseph's Wandal primary school was a small school with one grade in each year level, all made up of local children. Most of us came from Mrs Flemming's kindergarten or St Vincent's Church. Basically, the Agnews and McKendrys and two other large Catholic families, the Murphys and the Pearsons, made up a big proportion of the school. The only negative for our family was that sometimes my brothers and their friends got into trouble and were called up at morning assembly. One day Ger and Mick were both named and we had to watch them each put out a hand to be smacked with a metre-long piece of cane. I felt so sorry for them. It was hard to hold back the tears.

I loved school and enjoyed my lessons, but there was always drama at home. When I started school in 1964 there were already six of us children, and the biggest accomplishment was finding – among the laundry – underpants that would stay up so I could at least walk to and from school and play during lunchbreak. I was lucky if I could find a pair big enough to cover my bum, or where the elastic wasn't completely worn out. Otherwise, I would have to sit down at the edge of the playground, decline playing with other kids, and wait until it was time to return to class. Then after school, I had to walk home discreetly trying to hold up my knickers. It was another victory if I found matching socks. It was no wonder that I couldn't be bothered with my hair, which always resembled a bird's nest – there were more important things to do to survive around the home.

When I was in Grade 4, a new nun called Sister Zita came to the school and put on a musical. She gave me the main part and I danced a little on stage in the school hall. After the success of this performance, Sister Zita encouraged my mother to let me stop learning the piano and concentrate on dancing instead. She said to Mum once, 'Mary sounds like an elephant on the piano, but dances like a fairy.' I was elated when I was allowed to give up the piano.

Our little school punched above its weight in sport: St Joseph's Wandal seemed to win almost every sport carnival. With all the boys in the Pearson and McKendry families, no one else had much chance. We McKendrys were very involved and competitive. Ger and Mick excelled in rugby league. During our lunch hour we organised rounders. Anyone could play, and we were sorry when the bell rang and the game was over. We were good swimmers, too, because Rocky's public pool was just down the road from our house and we were taught to swim at an early age. For us, the top gang, Mum or Dad always came to our games and recitals. The younger ones missed out a bit, as there were just too many of us by then.

Transport was always a challenge for our family. We soon grew out of the Hillman. Once we'd got to seven children with another baby on the way, Dad had invented a people mover by upgrading to an old dry-cleaning van. Now he and Mum could take the whole family in one vehicle. It was perfect, especially after Dad had it customised with rows of seats and plenty of standing room at the back. You could even fit an entire football team in there if you wanted to. Often we would have the Agnews or Pearsons as well, and we would just climb onto the lap of another child if necessary. No instruction was needed: we understood what you had to do with the younger brothers and sisters. When one of the little ones did something stupid, they were all in trouble and we would sing in unison, 'Embarrasser! Embarrasser!' Then we would weep with laughter.

After my brothers finished primary school, sadly, they went to boarding school in Yeppoon, 15 miles east of Rocky. Ger went first, then Mick a year later and Matt a couple of years after that. I missed them. We would often drive to visit them on weekends. In summer the sand on the beach in Yeppoon was too hot to walk on, so we had to be up very early if we wanted a swim. Mum and Ger each carried two babies, one on each hip, while Mick and I followed with the towels and bags. On the way back, we had to run as the sand burnt our feet. Ger said later, 'Mum, please don't have any more babies. I can't cope.'

Most of our school holidays were spent on the beach at the Gold Coast. It was our favourite spot. Blue skies, white sand, fantastic surf breaks, milkshakes, fish and chips, long carefree days – unforgettable. To this day, as a family we come together at the beach each year.

~

By the time I was fifteen, in the early 1970s, many things were changing. Dad repurposed the dorms so I could have some privacy in my own room. I cared what I looked like and started skiving off church. Other things were becoming more important: television, movies, boys, clothes – especially the hotpants and purple velvet flared trousers that Mum bought for me in Sydney. I loved them, and kept looking at myself wearing them in the mirror.

Occasionally, Mum would let me go to the movies on Friday nights. Annoyingly, before the movies even finished, she would send the four little ones – Brig, Joe, Paddy and Dom – in their pyjamas to find me and ask, 'What time does the movie finish?'

Really? I knew perfectly well that Mum had sent them to check if I was meeting boys. Of course I was. Flushed with embarrassment, I would try to discreetly get rid of my siblings. Mum would pick me up in our second car, a Valiant, wearing her nightie, which was just mortifying. Occasionally I would skip the movie completely to meet boys at the pub instead.

I could feel myself growing up and my ties to the family were loosening. My siblings didn't need me like they used to. Paddy would soon be joining the older boys at boarding school. Brig and Jo were still inseparable, doing ballet and just about everything else together. Dom – dear Dom – was still the baby of the family. Mum was able to spend more time with him than she'd ever been able to give the rest of us. Dad's buildings were also garnering him plaudits and earning him his place in the history of Rockhampton.

To me, school was incidental. My parents were considering a possible move for me to boarding school. I thought this idea had merit but by that time I had developed a passion for something else altogether – something you couldn't take me away from no matter what.

2

Seven years earlier I had fallen into ballet quite by accident. Mrs Murphy, a family friend, called Mum to ask if she was interested in sending me along to Saturday morning ballet lessons with her daughter, Marise. Mum loved all forms of art but was too tired and busy to take me herself. She agreed for me to go with Marise. On that hot Saturday morning, Dad drove the boys to football as usual and Mrs Murphy took Marise and me to our first ballet lesson at Buffalo Hall. I was excited and Marise was a little shy.

When we went into the studio, I was shocked to be greeted by a roomful of little girls in white dresses. Both Marise and I were eight and the little girls were five. Some of their mothers had dutifully tied pink satin sashes around their daughters' waists with big bows in the back, and each girl had her hair in a perfect bun with a hairnet and pretty flowers. Marise also had her hair in a bun finished off with a pink bow. Very prim and proper, while my wild nest of hair was uncontrollable as usual. Marise and I were in black leotards. Mum had also bought me a big pair of black ballet 'boats' – shoes with thick black soles. Definitely not the right shoes, by the looks of it. In that respect, my first class was a disaster.

The hall had two floors and Miss Valeria Hansen rented the top floor for her studio. Mothers and children gathered on the upstairs landing before class. The studio room was nothing fancy, but it had a small stage, a piano and timber floors, and one wall lined with a long wooden ballet *barre*. The sun was pouring in and it looked like a very hot place to do exercises. On Miss Hansen's table at the front was a small tin box for fees, though I was sure she never counted what went in or out. We couldn't see out the windows, but as we grew taller we could see railway lines and cattle trains.

I took to Miss Hansen immediately. She wasn't wearing a habit and appeared non-threatening compared to the nuns at my school. Instead, she exuded elegance. She sat with a straight back, perfect black hair shaped around her pale face and an immaculately pressed dress, silk stockings and low-heeled black shoes. She shepherded us towards the *barre*. All the little girls looked so perfect, standing daintily at Miss Hansen's instructions.

I was immediately mesmerised. 'See how high you can jump,' said Miss Hansen in her quiet voice, and we all jumped. When the little girls started jumping to the music, I thought, *I can do better than that!* I had a lot of practice at home on the trampoline, and as I jumped higher than the little girls in front of me, I was in heaven. I loved the feeling of being suspended in the air, hearing the music and jumping to the beat. Miss Hansen must have thought, *What is this girl doing?* I was the most unlikely candidate to be a ballerina if ever there was one. I had buck teeth and then there was my untameable hair and my big black boat shoes.

Yet despite my embarrassment I adored my first ballet class, because I could feel myself soaring in the air. I loved the music played on the piano. I knew from the first time I stepped through the studio door that this was it. My world had transformed instantly and my love for dance was born. From then on that studio was the only place I wanted to be. I had discovered the world of ballet at the age of eight.

~

Every Saturday I would wait at the bottom of our driveway for Mrs Murphy to pick me up. We were only ever just in time for class, which was too late as far as I was concerned. I often thought I would get there faster if I walked. Soon, all day, all night, all week, I was uncontainable until I got to ballet, and even though I was three years older than the others in the class, it didn't matter to me. At one time I even went to ballet with my arm in plaster after breaking it when I fell off the trampoline at home – yet another trip to emergency.

It took me until I was ten to catch up to the others, who had been dancing since they were four years old. Dad often picked up me and my ballet classmates afterwards, always greeting us smiling, 'Hello, darlings! How was class?' It was a joy to see him waiting there.

I also loved both of our pianists. The main one, Ms Veronica, was a marvellous player who had been trained at the Queensland Conservatoire. She played for our exams, concerts and competitions. She would often bring her knitting to class for quiet moments. Our other pianist, Mrs Veretennikova – or Mrs V, as we called her – played for our regular ballet classes and Saturday-morning Scottish dancing. She had two daughters at my school – Anna, who was older, and Nina, who was my age. Nina and I became very good friends as we got older.

I learned that Miss Hansen was always serious and the work in class was strenuous. I guess dance can be quite competitive – much like running and swimming, but with less order and so much learning. I think from the very first day I was good at it, possibly because I was more mature than the other kids. I had no idea there would be a life or career in ballet – I just knew it was the only thing I wanted to do. It was also a sanctuary for me from the chaos of home. In the studio, it was time for *me*.

Little did I know Miss Hansen was a renowned ballet teacher, widely respected for her excellent results. She rarely got off her chair to demonstrate. Instead, she verbalised exactly what she wanted. You had to listen hard. She demanded complete concentration and quality, never apologised if class went over time. As soon as we were dismissed, we would say in unison, 'Thank you, Miss Hansen,' and leave the room on our toes, quietly, as the next class was due to start.

I could tell she liked me and thought I had promise, but I was definitely not destined to become a ballerina. Often she would call me 'the Wild Woman from Borneo'.

'So wild, Mary! So careless!' she would often say after one of my many attempts to get the ballet steps right.

I had no idea who the wild woman was or where Borneo was, but it would make me mad when she called me wild, which was often. Later on, I came to understand that she was looking for refinement. Growing up with five brothers, refinement for me was a long time coming. But I would push aside the bubbling emotions as I just adored the music – and I could really jump.

Miss Hansen would first set exercises for us at the *barre*, starting with *plié*, which is bending from your knees at the *barre* with your feet turned outwards – the idea being hips over knees and toes in turn-out position. 'Turn-out is one of the most basic yet most important foundation disciplines in ballet,' Miss Hansen kept telling us.

At every class I couldn't wait to move from the *barre* to the centre to start jumping. We began with small jumps and followed with medium and big jumps, which were my favourites. All the steps had French names like *jeté* and *changement*. The big jumps were so satisfying and exhilarating. I felt like a bird soaring through the air, and the sense of freedom made me happy.

~

After six months, I was ready for my first ballet exam. Miss Hansen had prepared us well. I was very excited about the dress rehearsal. I put on a white tunic with a pink sash and pink ballet shoes and was all set to go apart from my messy hair. Mum took me to her hairdresser, Jan, who put a pink headband on my head, teased the rest of my hair around my face covering my ears, and arranged a small bun at the back.

'Sorry, Coralie. That's about all I can do with it,' she said, as she hairsprayed the bun into place.

'That's lovely,' said Mum in her usual sweet way. 'I'm sure Miss Hansen will think it's a big improvement.' It was the neatest I'd ever looked, but I resembled a doll in a pink and white costume with its hair puffed out. I knew it was way too puffy because as soon as I walked into the studio Miss Hansen took one look and immediately directed me over to one of the stern mothers, who proceeded to pull apart my new hairdo quite violently, without a word. Mum nearly started weeping in embarrassment. She was mortified. Mum wasn't one of those bossy 'stage mothers' always there doing everything with their daughters just perfectly. The other mother rearranged my hair in a tight classical style and I went in to join the other girls for the rehearsal. We did exactly what we would do on exam day, including a curtsey and thanking the pretend examiner. My scalp was still stinging from the trauma but my hair stayed in place, which was all I cared about.

At last, the exam day came. As we drove down the driveway we saw the boys had started a fire. It looked like their tent was about to catch alight. Mum stopped the car, wound down the window and calmly said, 'Darlings, put out the fire. I am very late to take Mary to her exam.' Without further ado, we drove off.

The examination was in our upstairs studio and only four students could enter at a time. We knew there was to be no speaking and no mothers in the room. Our ballet shoes had to be brand new with not a speck of dirt on them. While we were waiting for our turn, Miss Hansen appeared cheery and often looked in through the peephole to check her students' progress. I had a few butterflies in my stomach, and then suddenly it was our turn and we walked in as elegantly as we could to the *barre*. The examiner and pianist were the only ones present in the room. We were assessed on our skills and ability at the *barre*, centre, turns, jumps and choreographed dances, in that order. Everything was performed as a group until the last part: our solo dances were assessed individually. In the end, it felt like the exam flew past. We thanked the examiner as we had practised with Miss Hansen the day before and ran down the stairs to our mothers, who treated us to ice-cream.

We had to wait weeks for our report cards. Then, at class one day, Miss Hansen called us up individually to hand us each our results in an envelope. We accepted it with a curtsey and a 'Thank you, Miss Hansen' and returned to our place to continue class. Luckily, we had been trained by a most wonderful teacher and nobody received less than honours.

~

In the early years ballet can be very slow and tedious, but after the first year Miss Hansen wanted to move me up more quickly so I could join my age group. I did Grade Two and Three together and Grade Four and Five together, and finally, when I was about ten, I caught up with the girls in black leotards who were my age and height, including Nina Veretennikova and Sharon Hamilton, my friends from school. I then had a whole new routine.

'Wake up, beautiful,' were the words I heard at 5.30 a.m. as Dad stroked my cheek softly to wake me up for my ballet class. The rest of the household would still be asleep and Dad would cook me a steak or lamb chops for breakfast. I treasured this rare time together with my Dad. Class started at 6.30 but Dad was always ready to leave the house at six so I could get there twenty minutes early. We had early classes because it was impossible to work during the sweltering heat later in the day. The sun would beat down through the windows and you could barely stand outside by ten o'clock. The heat also meant we didn't need much time to warm up before class as it was already so hot.

I adored the early-morning classes and never once regretted being there, no matter how strenuous the class was. Miss Hansen was ruthless on our technique. The steps were taught meticulously, and we repeated each one again and again until we had perfected it. After two hours of class, Mum would pick me up to take me to school. I would change in the car and got it down to a fine art, ducking for cover each time another car went by. I'd put on my school uniform and shoes and give her my leotard and tights, still dripping with sweat. 'Mum, can you please wash these and bring them back this afternoon?' I'd ask.

I always reminded her, but occasionally she would bring back the tights and forget the leotard or vice versa. She seemed to always get confused or forget. I would then walk into the studio with my uniform still on and apologise to Miss Hansen. 'Never mind, Mary, take your tunic off and go to the *barre*,' she'd say. With my white blouse tucked into my blue school knickers, I was silently turning red with embarrassment as I lined up at the *barre* beside the others in their black leotards. Nevertheless, I would never dream of missing a class, leotard or not. After enduring a few of these mishaps, I never sent my ballet stuff home with Mum again. My poor mother just couldn't keep up. She had seven other children to look after. I was thirteen when I finally decided to kick Mum out of my ballet world and took responsibility for my clothes and shoes – and especially my hair – by myself.

~

My new life was in full swing. I was rarely at home, I worked hard in ballet, I was organised and I was as happy as could be. I loved Miss Hansen. She wasn't just a teacher, she was every bit a choreographer too, creating compositions, arranging dance steps, movements and patterns, and many of the dances for our competitions. We danced pieces from stage musicals such as *Mame* and *Oliver*. She had once choreographed a dance to Nikolai Rimsky-Korsakov's famous *Flight of the Bumblebee*. I remember being astounded at the cleverness of the music, which sounded exactly like a swarm of bees. We were around ten years of age and there were eight of us. We then learned about patterning, staying in line and working as one. Learning to work in groups was wonderful. We danced in Scottish groups, character groups, modern groups, tap and classical ballet groups, according to the talents in the school.

The costumes were also superior. For Scottish dancing, authentic kilts and velvet vests were ordered directly from Scotland, along with brooches and big safety pins to hold the kilts together. We also had proper Scottish socks that were so thick they had to be held up with garters. It was as though through the experience of dance, Miss Hansen introduced us to the whole world.

I was thirteen when I did my first competition. Miss Hansen understood competing was necessary. Having stage experience was essential if you wanted a career in ballet. For my solo, I danced a Norwegian piece wearing a black skirt with a ribboned edge, a white blouse, a black velvet jacket trimmed with silver brocade and a square hat with ribbons flowing from it. I didn't know where Norway was, and no one explained it to me either. All I knew was that the costume was very heavy and hot for the Queensland climate and that my mother bought it from an older dance student. I came away with a 'highly commended' award from the judges. I was elated.

We competed against students from all over Queensland. For some competitions afar, where we had to stay overnight, Mum would drive me and my classmates the night before and we would find a nice motel nearby, do the competition the next day, stay another night and then return home the following morning. I adored the whole experience! Although I don't think anything was ever a holiday for Mum, these short escapes to a nice quiet motel must have been close enough for her.

Dancing one of Miss Hansen's ballet solos was such a privilege. You always knew you were good enough to go on stage after working with her. She came to watch all of our performances and never missed a competition. I quickly learned that most dancers were terrified of competing against her girls as we usually won. Interestingly, she never said anything about the competitions back in the studio – not a word.

So I suppose she was very discreet because the competitive world of ballet can inspire nastiness and she did not tolerate that. There were no favourites with her, we just got what we got in the competition and that was it. Instead, Miss Hansen was more concerned about the quality of the performance than who was going to win. She was very clear about that: she was training dancers for long professional careers. As a result, Sharon, Nina and I never fell out over a competition – we were just glad for whoever won, and our friendship and camaraderie developed. Then, sadly, Sharon moved to Melbourne shortly after. I continued to be inspired during these competitions because I got to see other dancers from different dance schools.

However, mishaps can happen in competitions. At one competition, our group was performing a contemporary move called contraction – a curling of the spine and pelvis to make a shape like a barbecued prawn. We wore funky hot-pink tops with flared pants and bare midriffs. Our hair was supposed to be in a sleek, long ponytail, so I had to get a fake one to clip onto my head. As I flipped my head forward towards my toes, I was mortified to see my fake ponytail suddenly on the floor! I had to quickly pick it up and keep dancing, otherwise someone might trip on it. Miss Hansen praised me afterwards for my quick-witted reaction. It was a good lesson that no matter what happens during the show, you must continue at all costs!

There were always a lot of mothers fussing in the dressing room during these competitions, but my mother would just stay quiet in the background. The only input she gave during the whole competition was 'That's lovely, darling' when it was finished. I believed that was the correct response for a mother.

The following year I had my first tutu made. Mum bought the material in Sydney on an earlier trip with Dad. The tulle was pink and the bodice was in pink and gold. Mum also bought me a tiara from Brisbane. Unlike my hair, I never worried about my costumes as Mum had great taste. I knew this tutu would be stunning without being too over the top.

All of my family came to watch me at Rocky's Municipal Theatre
for my next competition. This time, I was competing in my first classical solo competition and was very excited to be wearing my beautiful
tutu. Mum had a bucket ready beside her in case she was overwhelmed
with nerves. Even Dad came. Mum always kept him in the dark about
this kind of thing in case he got too excited.

Once everyone had danced, we waited at the side of the stage
for the winners' numbers to be called. I loved that solo, but it wasn't
as difficult as some others. The third-place girl was really good, so I
didn't believe I had placed. Thinking I wasn't going to get anything,
I was a little disappointed and started walking back to my dressing
room when I heard someone call 'Number eight!'.

My head snapped up. 'That's me! That's me!' I said to the other
disappointed girls who were also walking backstage. I rushed back
quickly in my tutu and then stopped at the wing. Remembering grace
and posture, I glided onto the stage to receive a crystal bell for first
prize. Even though I had only been *en pointe* for a short time, the
judge said I had an unusual quality. She had decided to give the prize
not to the most difficult solo but to mine. I was beside myself with
happiness and couldn't stop smiling!

The crystal bell was small and delicate. It meant everything to me.
Dom liked it, too. Sometime later at home, no one could find it. It
was a mystery for weeks, and I cried, devastated. I was suspicious and
sweetly convinced Dom that if he confessed to taking the bell and
returned it, there would be no punishment. He eventually admitted
he had accidentally broken it and hidden it in his chest of drawers.
I promptly told Mum. Dom was mortified at the betrayal and hid
under his bed, but Mum was furious and found him. He rolled from
side to side to avoid the wooden spoon while Mum got on the bed
and went from side to side determined to punish him! Dom threat-
ened to run away and disappeared for a few hours, but we found
him later hiding in a bedroom wardrobe. Nothing was ever safe in
that household!

~

My life at fourteen revolved entirely around ballet. I got to see the Australian Ballet perform *Giselle* with Grandma Bridie in Brisbane. It tells the love story of a noble count and a village girl, with music by Adolphe Adam. As it was my first ballet, I was transfixed and will never forget the experience. The performance ignited my great passion for theatre. On another one of my visits to my grandparents, I saw the great Dame Margot Fonteyn and Rudolf Nureyev in *Swan Lake* at Her Majesty's Theatre. That was incredibly special and I will always remember how the audience stood up to roar at the end. Grandma Bridie and I were so excited that we waited at the stage door hoping unsuccessfully to get a glimpse of the stars. Never in my wildest imagination would I have believed that these two superstars would come into my life in the years ahead.

It was also around this time when Miss Hansen called Mum to see if I could help her after school by teaching the little ones. In return, my fees would be taken care of. I liked the idea. I was quite at ease with children, having five younger siblings. I am not sure if Miss Hansen wanted me to teach because she thought I would one day be a good teacher, or if she was concerned that as a teenager I might lose interest in ballet as so many of my classmates had started to drop out of it. She not only taught me how to dance, but also how to teach. She obviously believed in me, and that gave me enormous confidence. I enjoyed teaching and felt I was good at it. The little girls looked up to me and I loved seeing them improve each week.

By the time I was in Year 11, I was doing school part-time. Ballet training went for four-and-a-half hours in the morning – 6.30 to 11 a.m., I'd go to school after that, and then back to ballet for another few hours. Miss Hansen was one of those teachers who thought nothing of keeping us for another hour and a half at night class. As a result, the other girls always wanted to be driven home by my father because he didn't get cranky. Other parents would be impatiently pacing up and down on the landing, but Neil George would simply wait in the car and, when we emerged, greet us with the usual, 'Hello, beautiful girls! Do you want a Coke?' And he'd stop at the corner store and get each of us a Coke. What a treat!

During one summer holiday Dad picked me up but we couldn't join the family at the beach as we had planned to because there was a cyclone looming. All we could do was drive home and shut all the windows and stay there. I wasn't too worried because we were used to cyclones, but this time the wind was more ferocious than before. The iron roof was banging and threatening to blow off, the palm trees outside were bending so low to the ground in the sheeting rain, and the trampoline was upturned against the back fence. It was the year Cyclone Tracy demolished Darwin at Christmas time.

After that, I stopped going on family holidays over summer. Miss Hansen insisted that we go to the Scully-Borovansky summer school in Sydney. 'Girls, the school break is too long for dancers,' she told us. 'You've got to keep your bodies in good shape. I also don't want you out in the sun. No freckles or burnt skin, please.' The 'English rose' is what Miss Hansen was aiming for. Her own skin was like milk powder and the colour of peaches and cream. So we all tried to have that type of skin in the stinking heat in Rocky.

The three weeks in Sydney quickly became a great time of my life. Three extra weeks of nothing but ballet! I couldn't believe my luck. I couldn't wait to get to Scully's to dance. Each year I went there, I stayed at a hostel under the Sydney Harbour Bridge and had to wash my tights in the shower. I kind of missed my family but I loved the program – I just couldn't miss ballet for the world. Miss Hansen joined us and would sit watching us for the whole three weeks, taking notes about corrections and music.

~

My last year with Miss Hansen was 1975, when Sharon and I were both sixteen. Sharon returned from Melbourne to continue her training. Nina had left to accept a position with the Australian Ballet School in Melbourne and all my other classmates had dropped out long ago. Ballet was getting more and more difficult. Together Sharon and I would study Solo Seal, the Royal Academy of Dance's highest graded exam. After two years away, Sharon's training had been neglected and her mother hoped Miss Hansen could get her up to standard and that she could go to the Royal Ballet School in London. To my sadness, I discovered that our friendship wasn't the same any more. We had simply grown apart. In spite of this, I admitted to myself that it was good to have a classmate during this final exam. As I was the only other one doing the exam, the intensity of the training was very difficult to manage on my own.

Miss Hansen had English heritage and over the years we came to understand that she believed that London's Royal Ballet Company and the Royal Ballet School were the epitome of classical ballet. So it was her dream for her best dancers to train at the Royal Ballet School and have a career in dance. Some students before us had already succeeded. What were the odds . . . from Rocky!

I knew Miss Hansen thought I had some potential – not that she ever told me as much. I just worked really hard every day, not expecting anything, so I never anticipated what was to happen at home one night after dinner.

With the dishes done and my brothers and sisters dispersed, Dad said he wanted to tell me something. He poured Mum a Scotch, himself a beer and me a Coke, then looked at me with a twinkle in his eye and said, 'Mary, Miss Hansen rang your mum today.'

'What for?' I asked, with butterflies in my stomach.

'She talked about the possibility of you auditioning for the Royal Ballet School.'

'Really?' I tried my hardest to contain myself.

I looked at Mum and she nodded with her sweet smile. 'Yes.

Miss Hansen thinks both you and Sharon have the potential to be accepted.'

'Please, can I go?' I asked eagerly.

'Well, Miss Hansen said that you have to go through the audition process,' Mum cautioned, seeing how I could not contain my excitement. 'If you are good enough to get into the Royal Ballet School, we are able to send you there.'

'Can we afford it?' I inquired, feeling uneasy, knowing it would be very expensive.

'Yes. We have saved enough money to send you for one year,' Neil George replied.

'Really, Dad?' My eyes lit up. I could not believe what I was hearing. I looked from Dad to Mum and then back to Dad.

'Mary, are you sure you want to go?' Dad asked.

'I'm going, Dad! I'm going!' I blurted. Did he even need to ask me?

Dad smiled. Mum was just happy to see that I was happy.

I could hardly sleep that night. Both Sharon and I were so excited. It was very unexpected, beyond my wildest dreams. From then on I did all I could to help Miss Hansen with my application and to prepare for my Solo Seal exam. I had to attach my most recent results from my ballet exams. My average mark was mostly highly commended or honours. I had photos of myself in various ballet poses for the judges to assess my skill. The Royal Ballet School already knew the quality of Miss Hansen's students – she had built a reputation for training strong dancers. Finally, my application was sent in the mail: it was now a waiting game.

I went back to practising for Solo Seal. It is still the most difficult and prestigious of all the Royal Academy of Dance exams: a true test of a dancer's ability. It takes two years of practice to conquer because the exam is so technical. All dances are *en pointe* and have to meet a certain standard of musicality, artistry and performance quality. It is graded either a pass or a fail. There is nothing in between.

I practised whenever I could. The nuns would let me leave school early and miss certain lessons because I needed to be at the studio as much as possible. I was often back in the studio to teach the younger ones and then to start my class later in the evening. On Tuesdays, I would sometimes finish as late as 9.30 p.m. My legs were constantly sore and my feet covered in blisters, but all I wanted was to get better. Though Miss Hansen no longer called me the Wild Woman from Borneo – she had tamed me, to a degree – she continued to be tough. I became exasperated when she made me do things over and over and over.

Sunday was my day off, and I mostly spent it with my boyfriend, John Hancock. I had met John some months back through Nina's ex-boyfriend, Wayne. John was very sweet on me and I liked him a lot. He was fun to be with and interesting, too. He was studying at university and had a car, so that gave us a lot of freedom to go out on our own. On Sundays we would go to the beach if I was allowed.

One particular Sunday we were having a great time. I knew it might be the last day like this for a while as my Solo Seal was approaching. We were all laughing as we drove between beaches on a small dirt road. Unfortunately, I was sitting in the middle in the front, without a seatbelt, when we took a bend too wide and hit another car head on. Luckily, we were going slowly so we barely grazed the other car. John was okay but I hit my right eye on the rear-view mirror and blood was pouring everywhere. I started to panic because I thought I'd damaged my eye from the broken glass. I couldn't afford for anything to go wrong with my Solo Seal coming up so soon!

Fortunately, John's car only had minor damage and he was able to drive to the nearby Yeppoon Hospital emergency department. We had to wait for ages but eventually I had eight stitches put in – three across my eyelid, with five more extended out to the corner of my eye. John was full of apologies and looked ashen. He kept saying, 'You'll be fine, Mary. Don't worry. You'll still be able to do your Solo Seal.' He didn't sound very convinced. John was also upset about the damage to the front bumper of his car. I was more worried about how I would look than anything else.

Mum and Dad drove 25 miles to the hospital. They were beside themselves when they saw me: I looked terrible! The little hospital hadn't done a great job, in their opinion. They took me straight back to Rocky to Alan Agnew, but Uncle Alan determined that if he redid the stitches, he would only make it worse.

I was in bed for two weeks afterwards because my eye was so black and swollen. Mum had called Miss Hansen to tell her that I had been in an accident and damaged my eye. Miss Hansen came and looked horrified when she saw my face. She then pulled up a chair beside my bed. 'Oh dear, Mary. What did you think you were doing by going to the beach?' she said, a little less calmly than usual.

I couldn't say anything, as I was ashamed. All I wanted to do was to hide my face under the covers. I hated to disappoint Miss Hansen.

She then said in a softer tone, 'I hope this doesn't take too long to heal. We'll see you back in the studio soon.'

I was worried that I had screwed up my exam and my chances of going to the Royal Ballet School, and about letting Miss Hansen down. I also knew there was nothing I could do now, so I focused on enjoying Mum looking after me for the next two weeks. She was so tender, helping me to keep still while my eye healed, she taught me to crochet. I loved it, because I ended up with a blanket the size of a double bed. I didn't go outside during that time, and promised myself that I would never again be in a sickbed.

All this time I was still waiting to hear whether I had been accepted to the Royal Ballet School. I didn't think I would get in, but I couldn't help myself walking down to the bottom of the driveway every day to check the postbox, hoping the letter would come. Finally, one miraculous day, the envelope was there. *Royal Ballet School London* was stamped on the envelope and it had a blue airmail sticker in the corner. I held my breath as I ripped it open right there on the street. It said, 'ACCEPTED'!

I was elated and went running back up the driveway, knowing somehow that my parents would manage everything. I would soon be on my way! Mum and Dad were delighted for me, so was my whole family. Sharon had also been accepted. We would leave in late August, the day after my Solo Seal exam in Brisbane, a mere five weeks away.

I practised every day and every night until the night before the exam, when I had my final rehearsal. It would be my last time dancing with Miss Hansen at Buffalo Hall and in Rocky. All night, Miss Hansen was relentless. The rehearsal was particularly tough that night and she frustrated me more than usual. *I was doing my best, wasn't I? What more did she want?* I started fuming silently as I went to the back of the studio to once more perform my classical solos and virtuoso beats, turns and *manèges*. I'd just had it. I went off in a temper. Miss Hansen followed me to the bathroom.

As I turned around to face her, she looked straight into my eyes and said in a calm, quiet voice, 'Mary McKendry, you will fail your Solo Seal if you perform like that.' She paused for a moment. 'Now, pull yourself together and do it again properly!'

I didn't say anything but returned to the studio one last time. With great resolve, I was more determined than ever to prove that I could pass the exam. *Right, I'll show you, Miss Hansen!*

~

Before leaving for Brisbane I had to say my goodbyes to my boyfriend, John, and my ballet friends, who were so happy for me. I had felt nothing but excitement until the whole family arrived at the little Rocky airport to see me off. Then I started to feel wobbly, my heart clenched tightly in my chest. Our family life wasn't disciplined or organised, but everyone knew their place in it. My beloved siblings organised themselves in a line as they did at home, from tallest to smallest, and I hugged each of them individually, long and hard: Ger, Mick and Matt, Brig and Jo, Paddy and my dear little Dom. It was the first time we would be broken up by such a distance, and everyone looked sad – especially Dom, who was only seven at the time.

The Agnews had come to see me off too. All their children lined up behind Uncle Alan and Aunty Shirl, and I said my goodbyes to them one by one as well. We were all broken-hearted. At the same time I was desperate to go. Everyone waved goodbye with tears running down their faces, but I knew they were happy for me too.

Everything started to happen very fast. Suddenly, Mum and I were bound for Brisbane for the exam of my life. Dad would join us after the exam, and they were both coming to London to help me settle in while the siblings back in Rocky were billeted out to different friends and families. As I sat on the plane, I thought how I would miss them all and felt a little teary – but not for long, as I had to concentrate on the exam.

Miss Hansen's warning during my disastrous dress rehearsal the night before had shaken me up and made me more determined not to fail. She knew how difficult the Solo Seal was to pass. I was sixteen and it would be my last exam – the last exam in the Royal Academy of Dance syllabus. There was no higher exam you could take, and you had to pass all the criteria perfectly and to the highest standard in order to achieve the Solo Seal. Miss Hansen had pushed me to think a bit more about details, and this filled my head on the rest of the journey to Brisbane.

Mum and I stayed nearby at Lennons Hotel in the city and the exam was at the Queensland Ballet Studio. I was really nervous. I knew friends who had failed Solo Seal before – sometimes it just wasn't possible to excel at all those difficult steps and do them with ease, musicality and expression. The exam room was not ideal: it had a lot of posts in it, and I knew it would be even more difficult having to dance around them, adjusting to a different kind of performance space.

Miss Potts and Miss Daintree from Scully's in Sydney were the examiners. They were very English and very proper, but I knew they had a high regard for Miss Hansen's students. Reassuringly, Miss Veronica was there, too. She was to play for both me and Sharon. Miss Hansen had to stay outside this time, not peer in through the door like she did back in Rocky.

In the dressing room beforehand, I did my own hair and make-up, and put on my black tutu. It was the first time I'd worn a black tutu in an exam and I absolutely loved it. I felt so sophisticated and elegant. What you wear can impact your performance. I had two pairs of pointe shoes, one softer pair for the adage section and a harder pair for the classical solo and the four codas.

Although I was nervous, I felt I did my absolute best in the exam. I had to concentrate because what I was doing was hard. The classical solo was very long and incorporated many difficult dance combinations, so it was technically demanding and exhausting. The exam took one hour, and it finished with reverence – a bow with the music to give thanks to the examiners and pianist. I was relieved and happy when it was over.

The official results would arrive by mail, and Miss Hansen was quietly confident that both Sharon and I would pass. And she was right.

After the exam, Mum and Dad organised a dinner for Miss Hansen and me to celebrate and say goodbye. Dad hired a private room in the hotel where we were staying and we all dressed up. Grandma Bridie joined us, too. It was a special, memorable night and a fitting farewell to my teacher. That evening I formally thanked her for all she had done for me. Her eyes were slightly moist and it was the most emotional I had ever seen her. I could tell she was proud of me, but I also knew her high expectations of me.

I didn't know it then, but Miss Hansen's training had not only held me in good stead for that difficult exam, it also provided the foundation for the rest of my dancing career. Ballet isn't a competition. It's a long, hard journey that requires stamina, determination and tenacity. Performing show after show eight times a week is a test of resilience and endurance. I was grateful to Miss Hansen for her tough, disciplined training that set me up for the future.

I promised myself that night that I would try my hardest in London to repay her for all the care, hard work, hope and expectations she had invested in me over the years. No matter what, I was determined not to fail.

PART TWO

London
1975–85

There was no question about it – if I wanted
to dance, London was where I needed to be.

3

Mum, Dad, Sharon and I boarded the plane to London late at night. It was a very long journey – about thirty-two hours, including fuel stops at Sydney, Singapore and Bahrain.

I had no idea what to expect. I was filled with excitement, and focused on looking ahead. I couldn't wait to dance with dancers from all over the world. Rockhampton was a small town in Central Queensland but soon I would be in the centre of the world, a melting pot of people and cultures. I was going to learn so much. Sharon and I were desperate to get started on our new lives. In our eyes, the Royal Ballet School (RBS) was the pinnacle of the ballet world. We were enthralled by the Royal Ballet, especially their stars Margot Fonteyn and Rudolf Nureyev.

When we finally landed at Heathrow Airport very early that August morning, I was jumping out of my skin, tired but so eager, pushing my luggage trolley through the crowds. Eventually we were outside in the fresh morning air, lining up for a black London cab. As the cockney driver pulled out, I had to pinch myself.

The journey to the hotel was exciting, especially as we passed Buckingham Palace with its smart guards in their red jackets and black busbies. Soon we arrived at St James's Hotel, an ornate building dating from 1857, when the English were still sending convicts across the world to Australia. Mum told us about some of the famous people

who'd stayed there – Winston Churchill, Michael Caine, Elton John.
I could hardly believe it. Dad was already talking about the architecture to anyone who would listen.

We were shown to our luxurious rooms, with views over a green
and beautiful St James's Park. After showering and unpacking, we
wandered the streets soaking up the atmosphere and identifying sights
like Trafalgar Square, the Tower of London and Big Ben. Coralie and
Neil George loved history and architecture, so this was the greatest
adventure in their lives so far. In between preparing me for my new
life in London, they 'choofed off' to museums and churches, and
Coralie spent a great deal of time at Covent Garden markets.

I adored listening to the distinct English accents – I was a real
colonial in the middle of London with my broad Australian twang!
My mother had tried to teach me to speak in a more cultured manner,
but it was a hopeless cause. 'There is no such word as "gunna" or
"youse", Mary,' she would say with her best elocution. 'Please refrain
from using words not in the dictionary.'

Something of what Coralie had tried to teach me would eventually sink in: by the end of my first year, 'dance' would become 'dahnce'
and 'Mum' would become 'Mummy'.

~

Before we left Rocky, Coralie and Neil George had rather audaciously
written to request an interview with Miss Barbara Fewster, the head
of the Royal Ballet School, and we went along to meet her on our
second day. Miss Fewster was a grand schoolmarm with an imposing
slim frame, huge dark-rimmed glasses and a rather large bun on the
top of her head. I was quite intimidated. Mum and Dad went into
her office to meet with her alone. I became very concerned about the
size of Neil George's stomach, his classic Australian beer belly, and
wondered what Miss Fewster's reaction might be. I had grown up with
it and never thought twice about it before that moment. In fact, our

family adored Dad's belly and all eight children would at some stage lie and float on it in the ocean. He loved his beer and had earned his belly. I was relieved when Mum and Dad came out smiling after the interview.

We headed out to Talgarth Road, that noisy main thoroughfare between Hammersmith and West Kensington, and walked one block to our new digs at Mrs Woolf's. She ran two big terrace houses with rooms converted into bedsits, almost all of which were let out to RBS students. We walked up the small flight of stairs and rang the bell. Mrs Woolf answered the door and led us into her sitting room for tea. She did not seem particularly welcoming. In fact, Sharon and I were terrified of her and her heavy German accent, but the following day we left the hotel and moved in.

Our room was the smallest, at the top of four flights of stairs. It must once have been the attic. Mrs Woolf walked us up with Dad lugging our suitcases. The stairs were very narrow and Neil George was a large man. The room had a sink, a single hotplate, a table, a small chest of drawers and two single beds. The four of us could barely fit and we could hardly stand up straight without our heads touching the ceiling. We had to walk around the table sideways so we didn't bump into the beds. Mrs Woolf showed us the bathtub, up another five stairs on another landing, which needed 50 pence for hot water, and a small fan heater that also took 50 pence. There was no refrigerator, so Sharon just left her milk outside on the windowsill. We could make reverse-charge calls on a phone on the wall downstairs.

Neil George put our suitcases on the table and then backed out to the landing while Coralie did a quick glance around the room to see what we might need.

While Sharon and I went to the ballet school, Coralie and Neil George hit Selfridges in Oxford Street to buy a kettle, a toaster, plates, knives and forks, cups and blankets, enjoying the history along the way as they passed Kensington Palace, Buckingham Palace and Marble Arch. I didn't even know you had to have that stuff, but Mum was good at organising a household and happily purchased what I needed. She enjoyed the art of living well and worked at it. Having survived all the children and chaos, she adored making any home beautiful.

Coralie also supplied us with food – mainly eggs, milk, Ryvita biscuits and tomatoes. There was a little fruit shop next to Barons Court tube station, a butcher and a newsagent across the road. It took Sharon and me quite a while to find a large supermarket, as they weren't common in the 1970s.

I didn't have a coat or boots for the harsh English winter as I had never needed such things in Rockhampton, so the next day my parents took me to buy a coat. It was a soft greeny-grey, warm and stylish, and doubled as a raincoat.

~

Finally, I was at the Royal Ballet School. It was a plain brown-brick building on Talgarth Road, a short walk from our bedsit.

My first day was full of butterflies in the stomach. Sharon and I were there at least an hour early, anxious for class to start. We went to a small dressing room crowded with almost forty new students, all nervously changing into pink tights and black leotards for our first class. We were shepherded into the studio and began quietly stretching, awaiting the appearance of our teacher. To my relief Katherine Wade seemed to be the complete opposite of Miss Fewster: young, charming and kind. I liked her from the beginning. She had just retired from professional dancing at Sadler's Wells Royal Ballet.

The class was full of international students, including a girl named Summer-Lee Rhatigan from the USA, Desney Severn from Newcastle, Australia, a New Zealander, a few Canadians, two very well trained girls from Zimbabwe, and some English girls from the north. Within a month we were all quite friendly.

After the nerves eased off that first morning, I felt comfortable, and each day's routine just rolled on. I was in my element, dancing all day and making new friends, meeting boys in *pas de deux* classes. I loved my parents dearly and appreciated everything they were doing for me, especially paying the high fees for my tuition, but I was becoming desperate to see them go. Like when I left Miss Hansen, I just wanted to get on with my new life.

When the month was up, we went back to Heathrow and kissed goodbye at the departure gate. As I watched them walk away, for the first time I felt reality kick in. The tears started and I knew I was really going to be here, in London, all alone. *I hope I can do this*, I thought. I knew London was my future and that Rocky would never have been enough.

~

Now I was on my own, I had to acquire a few life skills, and quickly. I soon learned how to boil an egg and do my laundry. I also tried hard to budget. I was living on £11 a week, and often ran out of money on the sixth day. In the first month or so we woke to a weak autumn sun, but soon after that we were waking and coming home in the dark. The heater was either useless or we couldn't afford it. Sometimes I would wear my leotard and tights (and sometimes my dressing gown, too) to bed so I didn't have to change in the freezing cold in the morning.

I often went without breakfast or stopped at the local shop to buy fruit for the day. My walk to school took me past the few Barons Court shops and some elegant flats with a green garden that felt like a slice of home. We had classes from 9 a.m. to 5 p.m., so most shops would be closed when we finished for the day. Getting food was not an easy task as they were also closed on weekends. The local Indian-owned supermarket was the only thing open on the weekend, and it wasn't well stocked and was expensive. I spent half of every Sunday for the next six years at the laundromat.

One of the things I liked best about the school was walking past its fishbowl studio. This was primarily used by the graduate class:

mainly made up of the school's subsidised White Lodge or junior English students. Us older ones and the overseas students paid high fees and had to find our own lodgings. The White Lodge girls were terribly English – soft, pale and delicate like roses. If you could get into the class with them, then you had a strong chance of getting into the Royal Ballet afterwards.

I was discovering how to grow as a dancer. There were multiple classes with twenty girls in each: we had ballet, Spanish with castanets, *pas de deux*, *repertoire*, music appreciation and Benesh notation – where we had to write dance steps in a special shorthand style. The notation class was terribly dull to me. I just wanted to keep moving.

A *pas de deux* is a duet where the boy keeps the girl *en pointe* and on balance, helping her turn and lifting her into the air. For some seventeen-year-old boys who were yet to develop muscle strength, this class was quite a struggle. We girls were nervous about being dropped and some of the boys were quite hopeless, but it was still fun.

The Royal Ballet rehearsed upstairs. Occasionally we peeked through the little window in the door to see Frederick Ashton or Kenneth MacMillan rehearsing one of their ballets with Antoinette Sibley, Anthony Dowell or, if we were lucky, Margot and Rudolf. Other than Fonteyn and Nureyev, I didn't know who these stunning dancers were – only that they danced superbly. I soon discovered they were English ballet royalty. They showed me a glimpse of the future and what might be possible.

The excitement over my new-found independence didn't last long. By Christmas I was very homesick, despite the beauty of Piccadilly Circus and Trafalgar Square covered in lights like a fairyland. Going to Covent Garden to see *The Nutcracker* for the first time was a magical experience. Little did I know that it would figure in almost every Christmas for the rest of my life.

Miss Wade invited the international students over for Christmas lunch. A group of around seven of us went – the South Africans and Australians, plus a couple of Canadians. It was freezing cold and I wore almost every piece of clothing I owned. Miss Wade's home was warm and inviting, with a small kitchen and nice dining room, but my strongest memory of the day is the food: delicious roast beef and Yorkshire pudding. It was the first home-cooked meal I'd had in London since my parents left. I remember taking a small gift for Miss Wade and will never forget her kindness.

When I returned home I made a collect phone call to Mum and Dad. Neil George answered, 'Hello, beautiful.'

It was a relief to hear his familiar voice. I spoke to some of my siblings and heard about everything they were doing. I could visualise all the familiar chaos and I missed them terribly.

~

During that first winter break, some of the girls, including Sharon, were rehearsing for a famous competition called the Adeline Genée, where they performed at Sadler's Wells Theatre. Unfortunately I had already turned seventeen, so I was too old to compete. I watched some of the rehearsals and was thrilled when girls from the RBS won gold, silver and bronze.

We didn't have many days off, and it was soon back to ballet classes. I was chosen to perform the waltz solo in *Les Sylphides* in front of the whole school. I was quick to pick up the choreography and good at interpreting the music. This solo required musicality and a big jump. I felt my teachers thought this solo would suit me as I had both. It's well understood that the Royal Ballet valued highly the perfect body, including long legs, arms and neck. I didn't have all of that. Not then, anyway. I was given a bit of coaching for the difficult solo and felt I performed it well. I wasn't crippled with nerves like some dancers – I thrived on the adrenaline of a performance and actually felt lighter. If nerves and stress provoke the fight-or-flight response, it was 'flight' for me. I felt like I was literally flying. It was my first taste of performing in the company studio and I loved it.

Repertoire classes were my favourite because we were introduced to so many different ballets. They were taught expertly by Maryon Lane. Later we did these classes with Lynn Wallis, who went on to become artistic director of the Royal Academy of Dance (RAD). I would manage to cross paths with both of them again in later years. I so enjoyed learning the big ballets – thirty dancers standing in line in the *corps de ballet* learning to be swans and being transported by the great Tchaikovsky music. This was more like music appreciation to me!

That London winter seemed to go on forever, especially for someone from sunny Queensland. Temperatures below freezing during the day were new to me, as were the endless months of darkness. The days were so short, and we were always inside. By February I thought, *It can't still be cold*, but soon learned that February was usually the worst month. How I longed for the hot Australian summer!

At this time the RBS was organising a trip to Russia for the upcoming Easter break. I knew I couldn't go home to Australia for Easter and could hardly bear the thought of staying in London by myself. I didn't know anyone there except Mum's distant Irish relation Roisin Kearns. I didn't have any money, and I badly wanted to go with the school group to visit Moscow, Leningrad and the famous Bolshoi Ballet. I begged Mum and Dad to let me go and, happily, they agreed. The trip would be a good opportunity to meet other students from different year levels. It was to be a small group with just a few teachers.

Soon I was on the plane to Moscow, where it was even colder and fully snowing. I was seventeen years old when I saw snow for the first time, in Red Square. St Basil's Cathedral was one of the most magnificent works of architecture I'd ever seen, with its gold, yellow, blue and red domes. Dad would have loved it. I remember Moscow vividly – the cathedral, the snow, no food, and the greyness. Grey people, grey weather, grey cabbage and grey sausages. Grey everything. No one spoke English, and the Russian language sounded aggressive to me. The city was strange, so dark and different. Russia was very foreign then. The communist government and the KGB meant that you didn't dare wander out and you didn't go to shops. In fact, there wasn't anything in the shops to purchase and there wasn't much to eat, either. Only vodka was widely available. It was pretty depressing.

The most exciting thing on the trip besides going to the Bolshoi and sightseeing was the overnight train trip from Moscow to Leningrad. It was a thrill to visit the Vaganova Academy of Ballet, one of the most famous ballet training academies in the world. We were allowed to watch a senior girls' class. It was fascinating to compare their training with our own. This was where Rudolf Nureyev had trained before he defected to the West, and I was reminded of how lucky I'd been to see him dance in Brisbane. He was already a legend – the finest dancer of his generation.

The trip inspired me to read one of Russia's most famous books, *Anna Karenina* by Leo Tolstoy. At home, Neil George had talked about communism, and this trip opened my mind to Russia, the history of ballet and the magnificent Russian music. For me, real-life education was much more my thing than learning in class. I yearned to travel and learn more about the world. I was determined to work harder than ever before, to never miss a class and to grasp every opportunity that came my way.

~

In the summer of 1976, our character teacher, Nancy Kilgour, picked me out for the lead village girl role in the RBS's performance of *Coppélia* at the Royal Opera House in Covent Garden. She thought the role was perfect for me. There was no big announcement: we all just lined up and checked the cast noticeboard in the hallway. It was a big deal to be chosen over a White Lodge student to perform this soloist role, and I was surprised and excited. I didn't know the ballet or that we were going to be performing it at Covent Garden. Nothing was ever explained, you just turned up for rehearsal. As RBS students we were regularly treated to the company's dress rehearsals, but I couldn't believe I would be performing on the same stage as them. The Opera House stage was enormous, and I never imagined as a student in the audience that I would ever be on the other side of the curtain.

I had no idea that the annual RBS performance was the highlight of the school's calendar. Everyone interested in ballet, including choreographers and directors of ballet companies, came to see the emerging talents.

In the story, the character I was playing had to flirt with the main character, Franz, played by a handsome young dancer, Stephen Sheriff – 'Cher' for short – and dance with him while his fiancée, Swanilda, became furious with jealousy. This was easy for me, as all the girls were in love with Cher. He had curly black hair and a cheery disposition, and he became a very fine dancer.

I danced well. I wasn't overwhelmed and knew I just had to do what we'd rehearsed. It was only one show, but it was my first public performance in London and I understood that my teachers were really happy with me. 'Well done, Mary!' Nancy said. There was never any effusive praise given, so a 'well done' was a good sign.

I was relieved, but something was missing and I felt sad. I realised it was because no one close to me had been there to watch – no family or friends. How I wished my parents and Miss Hansen could have been there to see me in my first major role, on stage at the Royal Opera House in Covent Garden – Mary McKendry from Rockhampton, dancing solo on one of the most prestigious stages in the world! I could hardly believe it had happened. I knew Mum would have been there if she could, but I understood how costly it was, and they had already organised for me to fly home in August.

I didn't know then that Betty Anderton, ballet mistress with London Festival Ballet, had been in the audience that night and that she'd noticed me.

～

During third term, my parents phoned to say I had been offered a second year. Ballet students were constantly being assessed and nearly half of my class weren't offered a second year. Sharon was one of them. She was devastated. I felt sad for her, but I had my own future to think about. Despite the expense, Mum and Dad had agreed that I would stay on. I hoped I would be able to get a job to relieve the costs for them once I finished my training. I was desperate to work as a dancer, but it was very difficult for any dancers to get a job in a professional ballet company as contracts were scarce.

I was still homesick when the English summer break came in 1976. I couldn't wait for August so I could go home and be with my family. My longing to see them was becoming quite physical and I was counting the days. When the plane finally touched down in warm old Rocky, I felt overwhelming relief.

Although Ger, Mick and Matt were away, at university or working, it was wonderful to be home again. I had a marvellous time with Mum and Dad, Brig and Jo, Pat and Dom. The bookshelves were full, so I helped myself to a month of reading. *Gone with the Wind* was a favourite – I adored Scarlett O'Hara with her strong will and independence. I also read novels by great authors such as Charles Dickens, Charlotte Brontë and George Eliot.

Having home-cooked food was special – delicious local steaks, fresh fruit and salads, and Mum's wonderful creations. She was no longer cooking for eight, so could take her time. Sometimes Dad came home for lunch, or Mum and I would meet him in town for a pub counter lunch. Neil George was still prolific in his architectural design work and was busy preparing for the biggest project of his life: the Pilbeam Theatre and the adjacent art gallery in Rocky.

Mum and I visited Miss Hansen, who had lots of questions as she was intending to send more students to the RBS. My friend Nina returned from her Australian Ballet School studies in Melbourne, so we caught up for a *barre* session and went out for a few drinks. I spent a bit of time with Mum and her close friends, including Nella Gillogley,

Shirley Agnew, Keir Nutley and Jill Benjamin, over long lunches filled with interesting conversations. I'd left home as a rather naive girl and returned a young woman who relished their adult company.

Mum and I also visited Grandma Bridie in Brisbane and did some shopping before I left again for London. Sadly, Grandma Bridie had been diagnosed with cancer and I wondered if it would be our last goodbye.

I loved the warmth of family, but by the end of the break I had become agitated not dancing and was ready to return to England. After that trip I never got really homesick again. There was no question about it – if I wanted to dance, London was where I needed to be.

~

In September 1976 I started my second year at the Royal Ballet School. I changed to a new, larger room at Mrs Woolf's – it had a view of the park and I no longer banged my head on the ceiling.

Although I was lucky to live across from a park and could see the seasons changing, children playing and buses passing, I didn't notice too much of those things. My mindset and focus were totally on my dancing. Dancers aren't really aware of their surroundings: their focus is on their body. You look at your body and think, 'Well, I can fix that arm today, and I need to make that line appear longer.' You stare at yourself in the mirror and concentrate on how you can improve. That's it. That's every day for over eight hours.

Sightseeing was not really in my budget, but I did get on the tube and go to Leicester Square. You went up the escalator and wow – all the theatres and restaurants were just waiting for you. Occasionally I'd go to a movie with a small group from the RBS and we'd then have a drink in Soho or Chinatown. By springtime in 1976 I knew London like the back of my hand.

One day, Mum's Irish relative Roisin Kearns called to ask if I'd like to see a Sunday matinee of *Billy*, a musical that was showing at the Theatre Royal in Drury Lane. It was kind of her to think of me and I accepted her invitation immediately. I lived for anything that involved acting and singing and dancing, and had never seen musical theatre before.

I pulled on my cleanest tights, warm pants and my one and only woollen jumper and headed off. The atmosphere at the Theatre Royal was buzzing. It had magnificent chandeliers, steep tiers of seating, red velvet and gold ornamentation, and all around the walls balconied boxes for patrons who didn't want to sit with the crowd. The musical tells the story of a Yorkshire boy who dreams of making it big in London showbusiness. I loved the lead actor, Michael Crawford, who subsequently became famous for the role, and Elaine Paige, who was at an early point in her career. Crawford could really dance and sing. I walked out of the theatre on a high. I thought the show was the most mind-blowing experience I'd ever had in the theatre. I adored spending time with Roisin and her wonderful Irish lilt. She later took me to see *A Chorus Line* and *Sweeney Todd*, opening the door to the world of musical theatre.

Theatre just connected for me – the music, the storytelling and the talent of the storytellers, whether actors, musicians or dancers. I always had an interest in people, and theatre was alive with their stories. After seeing *Billy* I decided to go to every show I could afford, in as many London theatres as possible. Tickets were much more affordable in the seventies. I was inspired by seeing actors such as Judi Dench, Anthony Hopkins and Ben Kingsley, who all rose to even greater stardom later. I admired what these stage actors could do, and they inspired me to bring more story, more drama, to my dance performances.

~

All through 1976 I was helped enormously by my second-year teachers at the RBS: former stars Miss Julia Farron and Miss Pamela

May, and principal dancer David Drew. All three were now character
artists with the Royal Ballet while also teaching at the school. I liked
Julia especially. She had a great personality and was still performing
character roles such as Lady Capulet in Kenneth MacMillan's *Romeo
and Juliet*. David choreographed a small piece for three of us as the
three witches from *Macbeth* and as a result the Royal Ballet became
a little more interested in me. But contracts with the company were
limited. They would most likely take British dancers before someone
like me.

I never assumed I'd be offered a contract. You had to be a
particular type to get into the Royal Ballet Company, and I wasn't
the English rose they were looking for. At the same time, I was
conscious of the high fees and financial burden on my parents. I'd
danced well in *Coppélia*, and the feedback I'd received gave me a
lot of confidence, so I began to think that perhaps I *could* have
a career in ballet. Putting it all together, I decided it would be best
if I tried to get a paid job as a dancer instead of seeing through the
three-year course.

Getting a job is the most difficult part for a dancer. The RBS
didn't offer assistance or advice regarding auditions. They were
focused on the White Lodge dancers who they had trained since
they were eleven years of age, and were mostly British. Studying
at the RBS was a very cloistered existence. The only companies we
saw were the Royal Ballet and Sadler's Wells. While I heard about
a few other companies in England and Europe holding auditions,
I knew nothing about those companies and nobody in the RBS ever
talked about them.

I was always able to make friends across the boundaries, whether
White Lodgers or foreign students or English students in our own
class. I became friends with one of the White Lodge girls Jane Scott,
nicknamed Scottie. During *The Nutcracker* season in 1976 she told
me she was going to audition for London Festival Ballet. I didn't know
anything about the company but immediately my ears pricked up.

I pushed Scottie for more information. She didn't know how many places were available, but I decided to try out anyway.

~

When the time came for the audition, it was freezing cold and I was quite nervous. I had no experience of auditions and fairly low expectations that I would get an offer. I wrapped up in my big grey coat and found my way on the tube to Waterloo station.

Despite its stature in the arts world and its fabulous location on the River Thames, the Royal Festival Hall was hard to locate. Eventually I found it by following some girls with hair in ballet buns who looked like they knew where they were going. The outside of the building was pretty dark and depressing. I walked through the stage door and up the lift to see over 200 dancers milling around in the foyer. I began to realise what a big deal this audition was and how significant Festival Ballet was as a company. Dancers had come from all over the world to audition.

I had my pointe shoes in a bag and my ballet clothes on already, underneath my coat. My hair was neatly tied up in a bun – I'd finally mastered that art. This was my first big audition. I didn't know anyone, and couldn't see Scottie anywhere. No one spoke and the atmosphere was tense. We were given a number to pin on our leotard and were called to the stage in groups of twenty.

The panel of judges sat a few rows back from the front. I felt very nervous. It wasn't like performance nerves. It was intimidating and I felt sick. I knew the panel was made up of important people, but I didn't know who they were until later: Dame Beryl Grey, once an English child prodigy and now Festival Ballet's artistic director; Betty Anderton, ballet mistress; and Australian virtuoso Vassilie Trunoff and his wife, Joan Potter, who were ballet master and mistress respectively.

You could feel the competitiveness in the air. We were all looking sideways at each other, trying to make comparisons and see whether we looked good and mature enough to be a professional. I focused on my technique, on perfecting every step. Towards the end of the audition we put on our pointe shoes. The floor was slippery and I could feel the back of my pointe shoe coming off as I completed a set of diagonal *piqué* turns. I asked if there was any resin (we used to dab this on our shoes to provide some hold and prevent them from slipping off). Unfortunately Beryl Grey said in her high-pitched English voice, 'Oh, no, no.' Nothing felt quite right after that.

After the audition was over, we waited in the foyer to see if our number was called and whether we'd made it. While I had done some good jumps and turns, I felt flat. I heard there were only three spots available. I did the maths and thought I didn't stand a chance. So I waited with a sinking heart and soon discovered I was indeed not among the chosen ones. I headed home with my heart as leaden as the sky above. It was my first major setback.

I returned to the RBS as motivated as I could be, but the disappointment lingered. I wondered if I was really any good, whether I'd ever make it as a professional dancer. Perhaps being a bold Australian and not an English rose would go against me all my life. I tried to explain the audition to Mum and Dad, but it was difficult. They didn't really get it. 'Never mind,' said Mum. 'Keep working hard, beautiful,' said Dad.

The fact that they were so ignorant of the process and my job prospects was actually a blessing. They didn't question me about what was next or what I might need to do differently, and didn't put any pressure on me to find a job. That was a big relief. It was also comforting to go home to my new apartment and housemates Bess and Chenca.

They were dancing with the Royal Ballet Company and Sadler's Wells. Both of them understood how hard it was to get a job in ballet and did their best to console me. 'There are other companies and there'll be other auditions,' they assured me. 'This is just the beginning.'

And so it was the beginning for Scottie, who had auditioned and landed one of those three jobs, and I was so happy for her. Although I hadn't succeeded, this audition was a turning point.

~

The new apartment was large, comfortable and warm, with carpet on the floor, and I had access to a fridge and a stove. (I did boil an egg occasionally.) But more important was that I was with friends. I missed my family, and this felt more like home.

I became very friendly with Summer-Lee Rhatigan, who, like me, never skipped class. She was an amazing dancer, even at sixteen. She lived with her mother in a neat terrace house in Barons Court, around the corner from the ballet school.

Moving into the apartment meant I now had a small social life. Chenca was very popular and had lots of boyfriends. Often we would go to the Fox pub, just up the street in West Kensington. It was a classic cosy London pub, with a red carpet, a long wooden bar, and as many ales on tap as you could think of. Not that I drank any of it: to me, warm beer was peculiar to the English. We would meet for drinks only as we were too poor to afford a pub meal. We'd sit huddled together, drinking rum and Coke or vodka and orange, thinking we were very grown-up. I remember one handsome Irish boy with a charming accent we were all in love with.

Chenca and her friends were older and she was touring a lot, so I would hang out with Bess's younger sister Angie, along with my other friends, including Summer-Lee. We would often go to watch the Royal Ballet perform – standing-room only, of course.

About three weeks after my failed audition, Chenca called to me from the other room: 'Mary, you've got a phone call.' I looked at her inquisitively but she shrugged, uncertain.

'Hello, this is Mary,' I said, puzzled.

I heard a classic English voice on the line: 'It's Betty Anderton from Festival Ballet here.'

My stomach jumped. 'Oh, Miss Anderton. Hello.' I was beside myself, wondering why on earth she was calling.

'I remember seeing you perform the role of the village girl in *Coppélia* at the Royal Ballet School last summer. We would like you to come in and take class tomorrow. We want to take another look at you.'

'I-I-I-I'd love to!' I stammered.

'Come to Donmar Studio in Covent Garden. Could you come in the morning for ten o'clock class?'

'Yes. Yes, I can be there. Thank you, Miss Anderton!' I said breathlessly.

'Fine. I'll see you then,' she said, hanging up and leaving me stunned and speechless. To say I was excited was a gross understatement, but I wondered what I'd do about my RBS classes. My flatmates were buzzing around me and there were squeals and hugs when I told them what had happened. They helped me search through my leotards to find the best one to wear.

Despite the short notice, I felt prepared, determined and excited. Somehow I'd heard that Miss Anderton had been involved with the Australian Ballet and its 1970 production of Rudolf Nureyev's *Don Quixote*. I instinctively felt she liked Aussies and this filled me with hope and confidence. For once, being a bold Australian might be an advantage.

The Donmar Studio was in a dismal grey building down a narrow street in Covent Garden. I climbed the stairs and felt my heart pounding as I walked across the empty studio space to the one female dressing room – everyone got changed together, whether principal or *corps de ballet*. I was early, of course: only a handful of other dancers had arrived. I was nervous of taking someone else's space, which was just not done. I avoided eye contact and felt out of place. It was quite intimidating. I noticed that the other dancers were older and there was no chatter like I was used to at the RBS. These were serious professionals, and I felt the grown-up atmosphere.

Once I was finished in the dressing room, I had to find a spot on the *barre*, once again without taking anyone's place. I looked for an inconspicuous spot and sat and started stretching. I discreetly observed other dancers, and then I saw a man striding across the studio in a woollen hat, fur coat, boots and scarf. I instantly knew it was Rudolph Nureyev! *Oh my God! Was I going to do my audition class with this famous star?!*

I wasn't going to let nerves interfere with my dancing this time. I knew this was a second chance. I thought Betty would be on my side, as she'd asked for me. What I didn't know, at the time, was that Rudolf needed more dancers for his new production of *Romeo and Juliet*. This would be serendipitous for me.

The studio was big, but with over sixty dancers it was very crowded. I tried not to be too conspicuous. Betty was teaching. Her exercises were wonderful and I liked her instantly. She had exotic looks and dark, wild hair that reflected her vibrant, open and outgoing personality. She was certainly no English rose.

The class began with about thirty minutes of *barre* work. Then we moved to the centre of the studio to practise balances, turns and jumps before finishing with work in pointe shoes. This is what I had trained for. We moved across the room in groups of five or six, waiting our turn. I felt positive rather than overly nervous. I just focused and showed what I could do, fully aware that I was being assessed. I felt lucky to be given this opportunity. Beryl Grey arrived halfway through and I could feel her gaze on me. I asked Betty afterwards if I could stay and watch Rudolf rehearse with Patricia Ruanne: his *Romeo and Juliet* production was then at the beginning of the creative process. This was a new experience for me. A ballet was being created before my eyes!

They asked me to return for a few more classes that week, so I went to my second-year RBS teacher, Julia Farron, and told her I'd been invited to take classes with London Festival Ballet. She was thrilled for me and said that would be fine.

I was inspired by the classes at Donmar Studio. After the final class that week, to my astonishment, Beryl Grey asked to see me.

'We like you, Mary, and we'd like to offer you a contract in our *corps de ballet*,' she said.

I was over the moon with happiness. I was speechless, and barely managed to respond. 'Thank you, thank you so much, Miss Grey.'

I couldn't believe it. The feeling was beyond anything I'd ever felt before. I floated all the way home. *Brilliant!* I thought. *I have a job!* I was in heaven. It was all I'd ever wanted, to be a professional ballet dancer in a prestigious ballet company. Finally, I'd be getting on stage and being paid to dance. I told myself I would be content even if I was just in the back line of the *corps* for the rest of my life.

I no longer needed to feel guilty about my parents having to pay for another year of RBS tuition when there were seven other children at home. Mum and Dad couldn't have been happier.

I wouldn't be starting for a few weeks, so I decided to go back to the RBS and do my classes with renewed focus and energy until it was time to leave. It was a gutsy move – you just didn't leave the RBS before finishing your course. When I notified Miss Fewster, she remained prim and uncommunicative, but that didn't matter to me. I continued to work hard, to show what I was capable of.

~

It was early spring, 1977, when I finally started at London Festival Ballet, and the first week went quickly. It was a real adult, professional ballet company environment, with a fascinating mix of different personalities, nationalities and ages. The place was inspiring, buzzing with energy, music and sheer physicality. Compared to the freezing wintry temperature outside, inside the studio it was steamy, sweaty and wonderfully exuberant. I worked as hard as I knew how and never wanted to leave when the day ended – I couldn't get enough! Scottie was a familiar face, as of course was Betty Anderton. And there were so many new people I couldn't wait to get to know.

Then, suddenly, devastation. On the Monday of my second week, just after class, I saw Beryl Grey walking towards me with a stern expression on her face. She was always slightly intimidating with her tall, elegant figure and a tight ballerina hair bun, and this time I was more than a little scared. 'Mary,' she said in her clipped speech. 'I'm very sorry to have to tell you this.'

My stomach lurched.

'I'm afraid you can't work with Festival Ballet after all.'

My mouth fell open and my eyes asked why. All the colour must have drained from my face, because she then softened a little.

'Unfortunately, you don't have a working visa.'

In that instant, my world came crashing down. I didn't know what to do. I looked around for help, but no one could help. I went quickly to the dressing room, shaking, threw my stuff into my bag and walked out onto Kensington High Street. I walked and walked. I don't know how long it took. It didn't matter. Nothing mattered. When I got home I was still sobbing. I had lost my first job – the only job I wanted.

4

My dream had gone up in smoke, my chance to tour the world, work with international stars – all gone. I was devastated. I couldn't believe this was happening to me. I had no idea how I would get a working visa.

London Festival Ballet had scheduled the Nureyev Festival for that summer, only four months away. Was I not to be a part of it? And there was the plan to tour Australia in July – the possibility of performing in my home country, for family and friends.

Technically, I couldn't work in England at all. I knew nothing about other European companies and their repertoires, and wasn't keen to work in a place where I didn't speak the language. Adjusting to London had been hard enough. Besides, I had missed the European audition season and would have to wait until January the following year to audition again – and even then, a job wasn't guaranteed. Nor could I go back to the Royal Ballet School.

I didn't call my parents as I didn't want to worry them. I cried to my flatmates instead. We were sitting in the apartment throwing ideas around when Bess said, 'Don't worry, Mary. I've got an idea.'

'What?' I said between my tears.

'My brother Ben is going to Paris to see some friends next weekend. You should go with him. It's just for a weekend,' Bess said.

'Paris? Why? How can that help?' I asked.

'Well, you go with him and just have a fun weekend. You'll love Paris! It's such a glorious city. Then when you come back through customs they will ask whether you are travelling for business or pleasure. Just tell them you're going to work *in a bar*. They'll give you a visa for six months.'

I was desperate enough to try anything. Ben kindly agreed to the plan and I flew with him to Paris. He and his friends were very kind to me but they did their own thing. I had no money and just wandered along the Seine, around Notre Dame and the Eiffel Tower. Yes, it was a magnificent city, but it was also very cold, and always at the back of my mind was the worry about whether the scheme would work.

When I arrived back in London, I told the customs officer I was 'going to work *at a barre*' – a small twist of words as I didn't want to tell a complete lie. He casually stamped my passport and suddenly I had a working-holiday visa.

The next day I hurried back to London Festival Ballet and handed my passport to the company manager, John Smith, with the new visa, hoping the company would want to keep me on. I knew I had to convince him, because we'd be touring Australia in July. So I said very confidently, 'My father will get me a working visa when we go on our Australian tour. He will have the right one organised by the time we come back to London.'

Mr Smith looked at me a little uncertainly. I quickly added, 'Trust me. My father will know what to do.'

'I hope you're right,' Mr Smith replied. 'But for now, you have your temporary visa and can stay with us until the end of the Australian tour. Now, go on – get to class.'

I skipped out of there on a high, ran to the dressing room and took my place in the studio at the *barre*. Everyone looked at me in surprise, smiling. That evening I called my parents at last to explain.

'Don't worry, darling. We'll sort this out by the time you get here,' Neil George said. 'We can't wait to see you, by the way. Everyone will be coming to see you dance!'

I felt like a great weight had been lifted from me – for now, anyway. Dad had influential contacts in Queensland, and I had faith he could do it. In my mind, Dad could do anything.

~

The next five weeks of rehearsals went by in a flash. Life with London Festival Ballet was a whirlwind of excitement compared to the RBS. I loved Betty's classes. She had a wicked sense of humour. She'd sing tunes from old musicals or operas with terrific abandon. 'Mary McGregor,' she'd drawl at me, or 'Mary MacKillop'. I knew Mary MacKillop was an Australian nun in line for sainthood, but I never asked her who Mary McGregor was, and I didn't care either, as long as she liked me. I knew I could learn a lot from her. She demanded we attend optional Saturday classes and I was never going to miss one. She rarely had a weekend off.

One day she said to me, 'Do you want to improve your footwork, McGregor?'

'Of course!' I replied.

'Then take that crap off your ankles,' she said, looking down at my ankle warmers with a grin. Of course, quick smart, I did.

There was no one like Betty. She had a marvellous relationship with Nureyev, and with all the senior dancers. Sometimes I watched their rehearsals, listening to her critiques and tuition. Tell any classical dancer you worked with 'Betty' and they know who you are referring to. She was at every performance, and was always on tour with us. She was single all her life but we were her family, and she was like a surrogate mother to me.

In the two years before I joined Festival Ballet, Beryl Grey had commissioned Nureyev to stage a new interpretation of *The Sleeping Beauty* in 1975. This led to some big London seasons with him for the company, which often showcased popular classical ballets and drew large crowds. The next ballet Mrs Grey had commissioned from Nureyev was the *Romeo and Juliet* that had led me to audition for London Festival Ballet in the first place. This production was to be part of the Queen's Silver Jubilee celebrations and, lucky for me, required a huge cast.

Soon after I rejoined the company I read the casting for *Romeo and Juliet* and was thrilled to learn I was to be one of the four servant girls in the Montague family. I was only in the *corps de ballet* but it was an important role. I think I'd shown my teachers and now Nureyev that character dancing was my strength. I was a natural actress, and there was good opportunity to show that in *Romeo and Juliet*.

In addition, I was also covering one of Juliet's friends and a court lady, so I was busy from that day forward. We were in a new studio at Jay Mews in Kensington and it was an exciting time to be at London Festival Ballet, with Nureyev as guest star as well as the choreographer. I'd heard so much about this talented man – his charisma, his passion, his sensual style – and I was now seeing it for myself. The fact that he was a Russian defector made him seem even more daring and mysterious. The whole company was alight with anticipation. *Romeo and Juliet* was set to open on 2 May 1977 at the London Coliseum as part of the Nureyev Festival, and the whole world would be watching.

Rudolf was funny, hardworking and brilliant all at the same time. He had a larger-than-life vision. His dancing, of course, is legendary, and seeing him in action was awe-inspiring. In *Romeo and Juliet* there were spectacular sword-fighting scenes that required weeks of rehearsal. A specialist sword expert was brought in to coach the dancers, and occasionally there were minor accidents. A few times, Rudolf would get frustrated and had the foulest mouth I'd ever heard. He wanted the scenes to be intense and realistic, and one day when the boys weren't paying enough attention, he let rip at them and threw a chair at a mirror, which cracked.

His temper aside, Rudolf was a creative genius. Some rehearsals involved huge, long silk flags carried by the boys who were acrobats. The flags were thrown a long distance across the studio and caught, in a realistic recreation of the famous flag-throwing in Siena, Italy. We dancers had to dodge them. In true Rudolf style, the flags he commissioned for our production were even larger than real life!

We would watch Rudolf in rehearsal with Patricia Ruanne, who had the role of Juliet, and Betty as Juliet's nurse. It was truly special and formative to be surrounded by such inspiring artists.

Scottie was playing a Capulet servant, so we were both involved for the whole ballet. We were fitted with the most sumptuous and colourful costumes of heavy velvet, even for the servants. I'd never seen anything like them. My wig for the court lady was close to a foot high.

Rudolf got to know me very early on. His big Italian masseur, Luigi Pignotti, became interested in me and flirted outrageously in an innocent but hilarious way. His infatuation became a running joke in the company. He was always running after Rudolf with cups of tea or massage oil, and I would sometimes chat to him in the wings.

On opening night, I was nervous but excited. We had been screamed at regularly by Rudolf and were very well rehearsed. I stood near the stage manager calling the show, waiting to go on, and when it was our turn, we just burst out of the wings. Our piece was pretty physical and there was a lot of strenuous dancing, partnering with four boys, and then the huge fight scene. Our change from servants to court ladies was very quick, so we had to do it standing in the wings, and then on we went again. While we weren't in pointe shoes, our deep-red velvet dresses had a very long train which you had to take care of. Every time we turned, we had to grab it with a full fist and yank it around, using our shoulder, and hope no one was standing on it. Often one of the clumsy boys was, so you'd have to swoop your neck back elegantly, glare at the boy and mouth, 'Off, off, you!'

I always stayed in the wings to watch the famous balcony *pas de deux*. As the orchestra played the wonderful Sergei Prokofiev score, my heart would swell. At interval we had to run up three flights of stairs to the dressing room and get back on stage ready for the opening of the next act. We sat and watched with the curtain closed as Rudolf warmed up on stage for the next scene. I would cry watching the death scene with him and Patricia every time. *Romeo and Juliet* became my absolute favourite ballet, and this production was a great learning curve at a pivotal time in my career.

While we danced, Rudolf would sit in the wings with Luigi and watch every step. We dared not put a foot wrong. I didn't feel intimidated though: I just knew to do my best. I revelled in the hard work and the constant demands to improve. You had to be tough around Rudolf – no crying, though that was his effect on some dancers. Luckily, I'm not a crier. I'd learned very early from my brothers that if you cried, you got left behind.

Rudolf's performances were electric. He was a master in the studio, but once he stepped onto the stage it was like a thousand-watt light switched on inside him. He was luminescent and magnetic. We all watched from the wings and bathed in his glow. He and Patricia were stunning together. Patricia was a wonderful actress and made her role fresh every night. What energy! To keep up with Rudolf for that mammoth season, which included twenty-five performances within three weeks plus rehearsing other ballets. She was an inspiration to me.

We performed *Romeo and Juliet* every night of the week except Sunday. Each day started with class at ten o'clock in the morning and finished with that night's performance. The dancers became my family. We needed stamina to keep up with Rudolf and learned a good work ethic, not to mention high standards of artistry. We were given a wonderful foundation for life in ballet, though we didn't know it at the time. And I was being paid for this joy! Money began appearing in my bank account, which was quite a novelty.

Giselle was to be performed the week after we finished the *Romeo and Juliet* season. *Giselle* is about a peasant girl who dies of a broken heart when she finds her lover is royal and betrothed to another. A group of spirits called the Wilis, who force men to dance to their deaths, summon her from the grave in order to kill her lover. On the cast board I saw I was to be a court lady and a Wili, as well as covering for one of the villagers. This ballet later became one of my favourites, though I never assumed I'd be anything but a peasant or a Wili.

I was too busy and tired to go out at night much, but one Saturday a couple of us went to a club. I bumped into a guy I recognised from the Fox, and got chatting. Kevin was a tall, dark, handsome New Zealander. He was twenty-five years old – six years older than me – and very kind. He had been working in Europe for about five years and seemed very grown-up. He lived upstairs at the Fox.

Kevin became my first real boyfriend, although we never really had time for traditional dating. He worked long hours as manager of the Fox, and I was always dancing. He wasn't free until after 10 p.m. and that didn't suit me as I needed to be up early. After a couple of months of trying to grab time here and there, we decided I should move into the pub and live with him. We still didn't get to see each other a lot, only having breakfast and the occasional dinner together. With access to the pub kitchen I didn't have to worry about cooking, but the fare was typical English pub food so I had to be conscious of my figure. I was dancing all day, touring and performing around 180 shows a year. I would come home and be in bed, exhausted. On weekends, I had to sleep to recover, and I had to do my laundry for the next week. Sundays were relaxed. We often went for a drive into the country in Kevin's BMW to enjoy lunch at a quiet pub. But I was soon touring constantly, and we became like ships in the night.

~

In August 1977 my first big tour took me away for five weeks. *Romeo and Juliet* had been a huge success and now we were taking that production, along with *Giselle*, to Australia – to my home! I was excited at the prospect of dancing in front of my family and friends. But my excitement was bittersweet. I was sad not to have had my beloved Grandma Bridie there, as she had passed away. She was the one who introduced me to my first ballet productions here in Brisbane, and she would have been so proud to see me take the stage.

After a long flight, we touched down in Perth. It was the middle of winter, but about as warm as the London summer. It was so good to feel the Australian air and smell the eucalyptus trees. There were over seventy company dancers plus crew and support people, so just booking into our hotel was a logistical exercise. The tour was sponsored by show-business promoter Michael Edgley, a true impresario. He really turned it on for Rudolf and even invited us all to a lavish party at his palatial home overlooking the Swan River.

The day after we arrived was a day off, and I met Mum and Dad at the hotel. It was wonderful to see them. After big hugs, in her thoughtful way, Mum suggested, 'Darling, you really are going to need a very warm coat for the London winter and touring. I've found a little boutique I'd love to take you to.'

Only Coralie could find a place in hot Perth that sold warm fur coats. In those days, real furs were still very popular – particularly in Europe, and particularly among ballerinas. Even Rudolf had a fur coat. While we dancers weren't paid much, we were expected to look smart and stylish. This shop had all types of furs, but a warm fox fur caught my eye immediately. 'That looks young and fun, Mary,' Coralie said.

The coat was exquisite. I remember being a bit stunned by the cost, but Dad was finally getting paid for some larger projects and I knew the fur would be good for me in England during my touring years. He was happy to pay for the coat, his head no doubt full of how to get my visa. I had faith in him and had handed over my passport as soon as we met. Everything depended on him succeeding.

'Dad, my visa . . .'

'Put it out of your mind now, beautiful girl!' he said before I could finish my sentence. And I did.

Coralie and Neil George came to one of the *Romeo and Juliet* performances in Perth and were truly impressed. They hadn't seen anything on that scale before. With her eye for beauty, Coralie was thrilled with the richness of the costuming and the strength and grace of Rudolf and Patricia. 'Darling, you were beautiful and the whole production is just breathtaking,' she said. 'What a feast for the eyes!'

'It is just splendid!' Neil George chipped in with his usual big grin.

We toured all the major capital cities. Rudolf had been to Australia before – I had my own fond memories of seeing him with Grandma Bridie – and had a huge following. After a sold-out week at the Entertainment Centre in Perth, we continued to the Festival Theatre in Adelaide, the Palais Theatre in Melbourne, the Regent Theatre in Sydney, and finally Festival Hall in Brisbane.

In Adelaide, Rudolf took us on an outing. Two buses were hired to drive the whole company to a winery in the Adelaide Hills. I didn't drink wine in those days, but I enjoyed the delicious food. It was very special to share an evening together away from dancing, particularly with Rudolf. I thrived on the wonderful atmosphere of having the entire multicultural company together. It was good to see everyone having such a great time in Australia.

Our schedule was intense, but thankfully I had no injuries and I never missed a show. We were all exhausted and often laughed deliriously from sheer tiredness. Performances began on Tuesday and ran every day until double shows on Saturday, then we travelled on Sunday to the next venue, with Monday off to settle in and explore. Everywhere we went we had to find food and any other essentials we needed. Life was fairly simple, and everyone shared.

By the time we got to our final destination, Brisbane, all my family and friends wanted to come and see me dance, including Miss Hansen. I knew I had to perform to my very best to make them proud. I was a little bit proud of myself, to be honest.

During that last week of the tour, I had an idea and worked up the courage to approach Betty.

'Miss Anderton,' I said. 'This is the first time my whole family has been able to come and see me dance, and some of my old friends and my ballet teacher are also coming to the performance on Saturday night. Dad has bought so many tickets, and they're all flying down from Rockhampton.'

'That's lovely, Mary. I'm delighted for you all,' she said.

'I'm wondering whether it would be possible for me to dance as one of the village girls instead of the court lady . . .'

'I'll see what I can do,' she said, giving me hope.

It meant that someone else would need to do my court lady part, and a senior dancer would have to give up her spot as a villager – a part that had quite a lot of dancing that I hadn't even rehearsed. But I knew the role and was confident I could do it. I left Betty with all my fingers and toes crossed.

After class, she told me I had permission to dance the village girl. I was so excited!

Everyone was there to cheer me on, and I danced like never before. There was a huge contingent from Rocky in the audience, and a special announcement at the beginning of the performance about my role change. It was exhilarating to dance as a village girl in Act 1 and a Wili in Act 2 on the same night.

Afterwards, my family and friends were waiting for me at the stage door. 'Congratulations!', 'Splendid!', 'You were so beautiful!' they all exclaimed, hugging me tight. My smile was a mile wide. I walked with my family back to Lennon's Hotel, where they'd had to take three rooms because everyone was there – Mum, Dad, Ger, Mick, Matt, Brig, Jo, Pat and Dom. They'd all grown up, including baby Dom, who was now ten. He was entranced by *Giselle* and the magic of the storytelling. They were very happy for me, and thrilled to have seen Rudolf dance.

We gathered in one of the hotel rooms and yelled and jumped up and down on the beds. Mum, as always, was hoping no one ended up in the emergency room or got us kicked out of the hotel. I lay on the beds with my brothers and sisters and laughed deliriously about nothing, just happy to be together again for a short time. We knew that tomorrow I would be flying back to London. It was the perfect reunion.

The tour had been wonderful, but after this special time with my family I was feeling ready to go back to my life in London and see Kevin again. There was just one thing to sort out before I got on the plane to Heathrow: my visa.

Dad had managed to pull strings. 'Mary,' he said during our family celebrations. 'You don't need to know the details, but here is your visa. It's a working visa and will cover you for the next two years.'

I gave him the biggest hug. I was so relieved to be able to continue my dream. Mum and I embraced too, and all the siblings lined up just as they had always done – but it was smiles this time, rather than tears.

~

It was autumn when I arrived back in London, 1977 – just two years since leaving Rocky for the first time – and the tree leaves were starting to turn. Kevin and I were pleased to be together again and fell comfortably into our old routine, except that now I would be away touring for even longer periods, performing show after show across Britain and beyond.

My first provincial tour through England began in October, performing *The Nutcracker, Swan Lake* and *Romeo and Juliet*. Life on the road was tough – really hard work, and freezing cold. There was never a minute to spare. We boarded the overland train at Waterloo station on Monday morning, got off in Cardiff, went straight to the New Theatre to unpack our skips (where we kept our make-up and dance gear), did a full rehearsal in the afternoon, and then opened the show that night.

I shared accommodation on tour with Scottie, and new friends Johanna Adams, assistant stage manager, and Jackie Barrett, another dancer. Summer-Lee was now in the company as well, and sometimes a group of us would get really good digs or we'd rent a room from a local woman and go home to a meal she'd prepared. Some meals were better than others. Sometimes we'd go to a 'naff caff' – a local cafe where the food was pretty naff. There were no lattes back then. Occasionally we'd spend a bit more money and stay in a nice hotel, but we had to book it ourselves. Companies now would never dream of operating that way, but in those days we had to organise everything ourselves and pay for it with our per diem allowance.

After the last show at the end of the week we boarded the bus for the next town, Norwich, and did it all again. From there we headed to Birmingham, then Blackpool, Leeds, Newcastle, Liverpool and finally down to Bristol.

I was exhausted every day. Working as a professional dancer was relentless. Your intensity wasn't allowed to wane or you could lose your job, so that became another discipline. I worked on it as I went to sleep every night, visualising the work planned for the following day in my brain and preparing for it mentally.

The performing was constant. We would head out at 5 p.m. to find food somewhere nearby, be back in the dressing room at 5.30 p.m. for make-up, and then warm up at 7 p.m., half an hour before the orchestra started.

We didn't earn much as dancers, but when we went on tour we got around £5 a day extra, for meal allowance and accommodation. This meant we could actually save our salary. In London we earned around £36 a week, which was hard to live on. I tried to save money but it was impossible. I rarely looked at my pay packet, but knew I had to be careful with my spending.

That first UK tour lasted eight weeks. Some of the dancers were weeping with exhaustion by the end of it, and many were nursing injuries. The senior dancers had been doing this for years and seemed disenchanted. Not me, though. I couldn't have been happier. I was learning so much, making new friends – friends I would have for life. I honestly loved every minute of it.

When you dance so much on stage as distinct from in the rehearsal studio, it's easy to sustain injuries. We would try to put up with them as no one wanted to miss a performance. My physical strength meant I was less prone to injury and could endure the demanding schedule. I was often called upon to step in for another dancer who had torn her calf or a hamstring. In this way I learned rather quickly how to become a performer. I didn't know it then, but this would lead to a fast-track career with the company.

~

After that first tour, Dad and my sisters came to visit. Kevin kindly put them up in the pub, so we could spend more time together, as I was busy doing two shows of *The Nutcracker* a day. We were on a high from then on. So happy to be in London together.

I wanted to show them London, meet my friends and, most of all, see me perform. Brig and Jo were still doing ballet back home, though Brig was doing less because her final years of high school were taking over and Miss Hansen's classes were very demanding. She also had issues with her knees.

Living above a pub! They thought it was fun and a bit crazy. Dad liked it because he could just walk downstairs in the afternoon and talk politics with everyone. First on the list for him was to buy my sisters warm coats. I had to leave them to go to work every day and they had to get themselves around, but Dad was thrilled to do it. Kevin was on hand to answer all their questions and direct Dad to trains, buses, high streets and the closest tourist spots.

It was the girls' first overseas trip. They were in awe of London at Christmas time with all the lights, double-decker buses and decorated shopfronts. *The Nutcracker* opened at Festival Hall on Boxing Day, as was the tradition. I didn't feel like I could eat much on Christmas Day as I had to get into my tutu the next day.

The Nutcracker is a magical show, at a magical time of year.

People flocked from all over the country to see this most family-friendly ballet complete with snowflakes, Christmas tree, toys that come alive, sweets galore and the famous Sugar Plum Fairy. There were festive lights in and around the theatre and all along South Bank, lifting the dark winter days and nights, and snow fell quietly as if to order, which made the experience extra-special for my sisters.

Dad didn't offer an opinion about my living with a guy above a pub: he and Mum never questioned my choices. Kevin was very mature and looked after us wonderfully. He took us for Sunday drives and traditional roast meals at quaint little pubs with fireplaces, and doors so low we had to duck to get in.

By the end of the *Nutcracker* season it was time for Dad, Brig and Jo to return to Rocky. I was sad to see them go but relieved that I was finally able to collapse, as the company gave us a precious week off. I was exhausted. Sometimes, I didn't even have enough energy to be nice to Kevin, and we saw very little of each other due to our different schedules. I came to realise we didn't actually have that much in common. We were growing apart.

~

The next year, in early spring 1978, we started the tour in Bradford, where Scottie's parents lived. That was a complete treat because I went with her to stay with her family instead of in the usual digs. Their house was warm and her mother cooked us delicious food, including the most wonderful chilli con carne and the best banana bread I ever had. I was very grateful for their kindness.

After Manchester, we headed back down the country to Wolverhampton, Eastbourne and Oxford. Soon the days grew longer and warmer, and the world seemed full of possibilities. Oxford in springtime was picturesque with its charming historic buildings, open parkland, river with painted narrowboats, and smart undergraduates everywhere. Our Sunday off that year coincided with the famous

Oxford and Cambridge Boat Race and we watched it from a bridge across the Thames.

After the long tour we were back in London, preparing for an overseas trip to New York and Washington with Rudolf and his *Romeo and Juliet*, as well as a whole suite of other ballets, including *Giselle*, *The Sanguine Fan*, *Le Conservatoire*, *Le Spectre de la Rose* and *Scheherazade*. New York! I couldn't wait to dance at the Metropolitan Opera House. I would be away for three weeks and realised this would be the end of my relationship with Kevin. We both knew it. We had drifted apart over the winter, especially after my family left. I wanted to be as free as a bird; he was the salt of the earth. In another life our complementary relationship could have worked, but not at this time. And I was still only twenty.

I moved in with Chris Mercer and John Carney, two boys from Festival Ballet, quite far from central London. It was challenging as late at night I had to get the tube, then an overground train, and walk through the suburbs to get home. The trip took over an hour. Eventually, my friend and fellow dancer Anthea Neal offered me a bedroom in her parents' apartment in Marble Arch, just around the corner from the ballet. She was living with her boyfriend in a little cottage mews house. Anthea's parents had a stately home in Wales and only used the apartment when they came to London. It was spacious and gorgeous, with four bedrooms, a long hallway and tasteful decor, and I stayed there by myself. Occasionally Anthea's parents came to visit. They were the loveliest people. Anthea's mum also invited Coralie to stay with me. They subsequently became good friends and enjoyed catching up with each other on what became Coralie's annual visits.

Mum or Dad would come most years during the five-week London season and stay with me, cooking and looking after me. They were divine. Some years they came together and had the best time. Only in their forties, they were still young, full of curiosity and energy – on one visit they travelled on the *Orient Express* to Italy. Dad adored the architecture in Italy but not the food – he just wasn't a pasta type of guy. He was able to work a holiday around some of the bigger projects he was designing in Central Queensland, including the library at the Capricornia College of Advanced Education (now Central Queensland University) and regional hospitals.

They were always generous when they came. Coralie would set me up with more stuff – things like rugs and lamps that put homely touches to my decor and that I didn't have the time or interest to shop for. She'd cook and help with the laundry – bliss! – and made my life very easy. Their generosity was extended to my friends too: they would take us out to dinner and pay for everyone. They were delightful company. Coralie was always so charming that everyone loved her, and Neil George was funny and brilliant. He was always in such good humour.

~

Before long it was time for the New York tour. No digs on this trip: we were staying at the famous Mayflower Hotel on the Upper West Side. We'd never seen anything like it. Each room had its own little kitchen and sitting room and it was true New York, with a concierge at the door and views of Central Park. It was only a walk around the corner to the iconic Metropolitan Opera House (the Met) at the Lincoln Center, where we were to perform. The Lincoln Center was home to the New York City Ballet, and the Met was home to the American Ballet Theatre, where Mikhail Baryshnikov was a star. Here, we were experiencing it all.

Our first day in New York was the only free day of the tour. We walked around the city, pointing at landmarks as we ate bagels and waffles. I didn't know food like this existed! It wasn't great for a dancer's figure. Then it was straight back to rehearsals in the theatre.

The Met is truly remarkable. It's one of the biggest theatres in the world and seats nearly 4000 patrons in the stalls and five levels above. It is decorated luxuriously in red velvet and gold, with beautiful, enormous chandeliers hanging from the ceiling. The grand lobby also featured many levels and chandeliers, and huge Chagall murals adorned the walls. The stage is huge, as is the orchestra pit, and the acoustics are so good that even quiet music can be heard anywhere in the auditorium. This is where Rudolf's *Romeo and Juliet* would open on 18 July 1978.

We were thrilled to be bringing it to an American audience. Once again I was to play one of the four Montague servants in the first half. As a group, we understood the momentous occasion of performing at the Met and wanted the season to go well for Rudolf. Once on stage I didn't have time to think, because halfway through I had to do that quick change in the wings to become a court lady. Again I battled with the foot-high wig and changed into the long velvet gown and velvet shoes.

At the end of our first performance, the theatre erupted. We received a standing ovation and took something like nineteen curtain calls. The applause hit us like a physical thing and we looked up into the five tiers of seating and let it wash over us. We just kept beaming at each other, incredulous.

I'm sure Rudolf and the stars had a big afterparty, but as members of the *corps de ballet* we just took off our make-up and walked out the stage door into the steamy New York evening. The fans were waiting to catch a glimpse of Rudolf or get his autograph. We called in at one of the little bars on the way to the Mayflower. After a performance like that, it is nearly impossible to go to bed and sleep. We were on such an adrenaline high – but tomorrow it was back to class, then to the theatre for the evening performance.

During the week-long season, we took New York by storm. The tour marked Rudolf's American choreographic debut and the *New York Times* reviewer acknowledged how much the audience loved the ballet, saying it was 'greeted like the Second Coming'! Being part of something so special was an unforgettable part of my career.

On this tour, we were able to afford to eat in some fabulous places. Unlike in England, here our accommodation was paid for, so our allowance went a little further. New York – my God! It was incredible. There was a coffee shop, diner or bar on almost every corner serving hamburgers, of course, but the city also had restaurants with every cuisine you could think of. Such places didn't exist in England.

We looked around the Lincoln Center and I found the famous Juilliard School, the School of American Ballet, and a professional dance studio called Steps. I was very curious about the ballet scene in New York.

Rudolf's masseur, Luigi, invited me and Scottie to go with Rudolf and a few others to Studio 54. It was a night I'll never forget. Studio 54 was the epicentre of 1970s hedonism, the lavish Manhattan playground of people like Liza Minnelli, Cher, Truman Capote, Bianca Jagger and Jackie Onassis. Entry was highly restricted, and we would never have been allowed in without Rudolf. The building had once been a radio and TV studio and some of the lighting and sets had been retained to evoke a movie set. The atmosphere was electric. Disco music was at its height and the beat was deafening. None of us were big drinkers – we were just wide-eyed at all the glamorous people having fun under the wild disco lights to the pounding music. That night was a glimpse into the world of high celebrity.

After New York, we had another successful week at the Kennedy Center in Washington, DC and then returned to London to rehearse for the Festival Hall season. There was no time to reflect on the enormity of what we'd done in America, but I had already decided that I wanted to go back and take classes in New York.

During our three-week summer break Jackie Barrett and I did just that. The teacher we liked most was Robert Denvers at Steps. I had somehow heard he was highly respected, and my sixth sense for opportunities wasn't wrong. He was young, charismatic and knowledgeable about the Danish technique, which fascinated me. The footwork was very fast and I relished the opportunity to develop my technique.

By the end of the year we were preparing for the season's tour of *The Nutcracker*. We were in Norwich and I was still in the *corps de ballet*. I had a group role as a snowflake, with white tutu and silver crown. The choreographer, Ronald (Ronnie) Hynd, had also put me down as an understudy for one of the leading snowflakes. There was no time set aside to rehearse the role as it was not expected I would perform it.

But then it happened. One of the leading snowflake soloists got injured and I was put in her place. I had to think on my feet – literally. The role was very difficult, with fast steps. It is danced to Tchaikovsky's famous 'Waltz of the Snowflakes' and includes a set of fast *piqué* turns on the diagonal. I was terrified, but before I knew it I was whirling down through the snow on the floor and flurries in the air. I could feel myself getting closer and closer to the four snowflakes standing beside me, so close that I could see the anxious expressions on their faces. Then bam! I knocked two of them over. They bounced up and continued dancing. I hadn't seen it coming: I literally couldn't see because of my nerves and the swirling snow. Luckily, no one was injured.

I panicked. It wasn't funny and no one said anything to me until I heard Ronnie Hynd coming upstairs to the dressing room during interval. A choreographer does not go into the dressing room in the middle of a performance unless it is serious. I was mortified by the angry look on his face and could almost hear him screaming, 'What on earth were you doing, girl?' But nothing came out of his mouth. He must have seen my petrified expression and thought better of it. He just walked off in a huff. I had a lucky escape – but I will never forget that particular performance of *The Nutcracker*!

~

London Festival Ballet was in an exciting place in the late 1970s and early 1980s, not only because we toured all over the world with Rudolf, which was extraordinary in itself as people didn't travel as much then as they do now, but also because the company was a cultural melting pot. We learned about the world through our fellow dancers, who came from everywhere. I was among Argentines, South Africans, French, Belgians, Italians, Scots, Americans and Canadians. The French dancers were meticulously trained, and I remember an Argentine called Liliana Belfiore being a wildly passionate dancer. Later, I danced many *Don Quixote pas de deux* with Raffaele Paganini, an Italian who didn't speak a word of English. He was a marvellous partner and would throw me into the air and hold me on one hand until the audience clapped. The Belgians were blue-eyed, handsome, and also good partners. As Rudolf was fluent in French, he had no trouble cursing at us in that language as well as in Russian and English.

I felt lucky to be a paid dancer, but as I improved I began to think, 'I could do some of those solo roles.' And then my first big opportunity came: the Queen of the Wilis in *Giselle*. It's a demanding role that requires a strong technique, big jumps to create the illusion of floating in the air, and a lot of stamina. There was little fanfare for this important change in my career. During my annual interview, Beryl Grey had simply said, 'Well done, dear. You've worked very hard and I'm promoting you to junior soloist.' Just like that, here was my first important promotion.

I was thrilled and relieved that I didn't have to go to the Home Office to renew my visa. As a soloist I was considered to have specialist skills and that meant I would only have to renew my visa every two years. My name began appearing on the all-knowing noticeboard as a soloist. It was not star billing as a principal, of course, where I would be lead dancer for the entire performance: it would be a matinee, and fourth cast. Even so, it was my first soloist role. My rehearsals now included working on my role as Queen of the Wilis as well as my *corps de ballet* work. I learned the role standing behind the other principals and senior soloists, which I'm sure annoyed them. Much of my rehearsal I did myself, but the choreographer, Mary Skeaping, worked with me. Her production is still performed today and is widely considered one of the best incarnations of *Giselle* in the world.

Other opportunities then came my way, including the Mazurka from *Les Sylphides*. We were lucky enough to have the famous and enormously talented Alicia Markova rehearsing us. She was Britain's first prima ballerina and, with Dame Margot Fonteyn, one of only two English dancers to have been recognised as a prima ballerina assoluta – a title bestowed on the most outstanding dancers of their generation. I still remember her saying to the *corps* in her soft voice, 'See the moon, see the moon' as we *bouréed en pointe* in fifth position with our arms to the side and eyes gazing up. She was so pale and ethereal that it really looked like she could see that moon.

~

Danish phenomenon and global superstar Peter Schaufuss regularly performed with the company also. He was a guest star with top companies all over the world and was very involved with London Festival Ballet from his early career. I was nearly twenty and in my third year with the company when, without fanfare, it was announced that we would be touring China in May and Peter would be joining us. Beryl had been trying to get the company to China since the early 1970s; she had danced in Beijing and Shanghai herself in the 1960s. Our visit was part of the Great Britain–China Centre's initiative to open up dialogue between the two countries after Mao's death and a political hiatus of some years. The centre had donated £38 000 towards the tour, and the British Council was also involved.

We got to work following the announcement. It was very exciting to be one of the first foreign ballet companies to perform in China since the Communist Party rose to power in 1949. We were to go to Beijing to perform in the wonderfully named Theatre of Heavenly Bridges, and then to the very communist-sounding Hall of the

Revolutionary Committee in Shanghai. We were also to see Chinese ballet performed by students at the Beijing Dance Academy.

We'd prepared two programs for that tour: a triple bill and *Giselle*. The triple bill program would consist of three works: the Danish-styled *Études*, a technically brilliant one-act ballet in white and black tutus that is seen as a homage to classical ballet training; the American contemporary choreographer Glen Tetley's new ballet, *Greening*, which mixed modern and classical dance and was very avant-garde for the time, especially for a Chinese audience; and Ronnie Hynd's particularly English twist on *The Sanguine Fan*, with music written by the composer Edward Elgar. I had danced *Giselle* many times by then. I was especially thrilled that I'd be dancing a soloist role in *Études* and one of the four solo roles in *Greening*.

I hadn't mixed with any Chinese people at that stage, and didn't know much about China except that it was a poor and communist country. We were given no cultural preparation and were simply asked to hand over our passports so the company could arrange our visas.

We arrived at Beijing Airport on a pleasant spring night in early May. The air smelt completely different from anywhere else we'd been. We were met by Chinese officials mostly in grey Mao suits and taken to our hotel. It was difficult to see much because there was minimal street lighting. The hotel was very plain with little ambience. I fell into bed. I had to be rested for the performances that were to begin the next day.

Breakfast was a strange and suspicious-looking rice soup, and vegetables we'd never seen before – no cereal, toast or jam in sight. We were met by our Chinese guides and bussed to the Theatre of Heavenly Bridges. The roads were long and straight, and full of people on bicycles wearing Mao suits. Everyone looked alike to us, and there were so many of them. People everywhere!

The trip was an eye-opener, the performances included. The seats in the theatre were made of canvas and the audience would cough and spit loudly into spittoons at the end of each aisle, even during the show. 'Watch out for the guy in the front row,' we'd tease each other backstage. We thought it was hilarious.

The morning after our first performance, we had a bit of time to ourselves. However, there weren't any shops nearby – at least none that made sense to us – and we weren't allowed out by ourselves. We were taken to the Friendship Store, which was the only store where foreigners were allowed to shop. It had a special currency designed for foreigners and some Western-branded things, including bread, butter and cigarettes. Jackie was crazy about sweets and found some Chinese ones. 'Found something! Found something!' she screamed with delight, and we all went to look. One was an orange sweet and sour, and the other was a milky chew. We survived mostly on these for the rest of the trip. If we wanted something else to eat, it had to be rice, because the pig's intestines and sea slugs on offer didn't appeal. 'Dreadful!' we all agreed, pulling faces. There seemed to be very little food for all those people. All of us lost weight on that trip.

At the Beijing Dance Academy, we watched students perform Chinese dances to traditional music in their little theatre. I was mesmerised by the delicate hand and eye movements of the dancers, and one particular number danced by three boys. It was so foreign – their movements were so different, especially the way they moved their eyes and arms in perfect unison. The music, to our ears, sounded jangly and disturbing. To represent us, Peter Schaufuss and principal dancer Elisabetta Terabust danced the *Don Quixote pas de deux*. Our hosts were particularly impressed with Peter's technical skills.

After our week of performances in Beijing, we had a day off to climb the Great Wall. It was hot, but we were very excited. While the wall was rough and worn in places, the vast scale and majesty astounded me. I learned that it took more than 2300 years to build and extends for more than 21 000 kilometres. It was constructed in sections in mountainous terrain by different dynasties to protect their borders and trade, and is dotted with military fortifications. We heard that some of its millions of workers are interred in the wall. It is an awe-inspiring and mysterious place.

We flew on to Shanghai and stayed at the Peace Hotel on the famous Bund, in the British Quarter. With its grand, run-down rooms and wonderful location on the Huangpu River, it was much more atmospheric than our dreary hotel in Beijing. We still couldn't venture out without our Chinese guides, so we just stuck to the tours organised for us – except when we went on a quest to find chocolate! There was a reception after our opening-night performance and we were well looked after, though still wary of the exotic food. Little did I know how China would come to figure in my life in years to come.

~

After our tour to China, Beryl Grey invited Peter to create a new *La Sylphide* for Festival Ballet. Based on August Bournonville's choreography, the new production was Danish-style and demanding, with difficult footwork and ethereal upper body movements. Peter chose me to be one of the three sylphs. I'd never seen the ballet and had no idea what the role entailed. He created the lead sylph role on me, the first time in my career someone created something on me, which was an honour. I loved it. Peter worked with us diligently for weeks. We had never had such in-depth coaching, and I revelled in it. The music by Herman Severin Løvenskiold was especially romantic. It was the beginning of my understanding of the Romantic style, which would become one of my favourite genres.

Peter also chose me to perform the role of Effie, the Scotsman James's betrothed, which required some dramatic acting. As Effie, I also led the challenging reel dance with the rest of the company. So in Act 1, I was dancing Effie, and in Act 2, I was a lead sylph in a different cast. It was a transformative experience, given the amount of focus required on footwork and style.

The ballet was a triumph. It went on to win two major British theatre awards – an Olivier and the Evening Standard Award – and was filmed for television. The company rose to new technical heights. I had settled into the demands of professional life and I was loving it.

We had a three-week break after *La Sylphide*. With Scottie and a few others, we went to get some sun in Barbados – a rare treat. While we were away things changed at the company. We heard on the grapevine that we were going to have to farewell our director, Beryl Grey. After her illustrious career as a classical ballet dancer and ten years as artistic director of London Festival Ballet, she had decided to retire. Like everyone else, I was shocked as she had been such an important part of my journey. Before long, there was talk among senior dancers and all of us were curious as to who would fill her shoes.

~

During the summer break, I returned home again. The car accident in my teens had left me with a bump on the bridge of my nose and I had spoken to Mum about getting rid of it. Initially Coralie was opposed to the surgery, but she eventually understood that I needed to do it to improve my chances of being selected for bigger and 'softer' roles. I wanted to dance roles like Giselle, where looks mattered, and this would soften my appearance. Mum arranged everything, finding the best surgeon and booking the operation in Brisbane. I didn't tell anyone at the company, and they were quite surprised when I came back without my bump.

When John Field was appointed as the new artistic director of London Festival Ballet in 1979, we were very excited. He had danced with many legendary ballerinas including Margot Fonteyn and Beryl Grey. He'd gone on to become the founding artistic director of Sadler's Wells Theatre Ballet (which later became Sadler's Wells Royal Ballet) and co-director of the Royal Ballet with the brilliant British choreographer Kenneth MacMillan, and had also directed La Scala Theatre

Ballet in Milan. He was leaving his position as director of the Royal Academy of Dance to come to us. So he came with a wealth of experience and gravitas.

John was in his late fifties, a big man who wore heavy black-rimmed glasses. As soon as he arrived I knew he liked me. He was a charming gentleman, and he spoke directly to me, which was unusual. Directors in those days were quite remote figures, whereas John was more approachable. I didn't find him intimidating. Initially he took a more directorial role than a teaching one, so we didn't have much to do with him early on. He wasn't in the studio much until he did his brand-new *Swan Lake* in 1982.

The gruelling eight-week domestic touring schedule continued, but more soloist roles were coming my way. I was recognised as one of the hardest-working dancers in the company and I gave 110 per cent every day. John watched me closely all through the next year as I continued to perform soloist and leading roles. On the summer tour, I was rewarded by being cast in soloist roles in *The Sleeping Beauty*.

Touring was intense. I focused on surviving and learning as much as I could about theatre. What made this tour even better was that I fell in love with Matz Skoog, a handsome Swedish dancer who had been with the company for a year or so. He'd been in another relationship, but when that ended we became close. It was much easier to have a relationship with a person in the company, and nice to have someone on tour who cared for you. Matz and I were never paired together as he was too short for me. Being with Matz, and the close friendships I had formed with Jackie, Scottie, Johanna Adams and Janey Devine, made the gruelling work schedule enjoyable.

During the next season of *Romeo and Juliet* at the London Coliseum I suffered a pretty bad injury. When the boys threw me up in the air one night, one of their knees hit my tailbone as I came down, resulting in immediate, excruciating pain. I could hardly dance, but luckily it happened at the end of the act and the performance didn't require much more dancing after that.

It was terribly bruised. I went to the physio, and he told me there was nothing to do but to allow it heal. For a while I couldn't sit down easily. I brushed it off, believing the pain would eventually go away, but it was still sore months later. Every time I did an *arabesque* or moved my legs from front to back quickly, a pulling sensation would start at my tailbone and hurt for minutes after.

I described my pain to a few other dancers and some thought I would need to have surgery. I'd heard some horror stories about operations and the idea terrified me. Most dancers had foot, calf or knee niggles from time to time. Summer-Lee had been dropped during a lift and had to have a knee reconstruction; it was a difficult injury to come back from. I realised deep down that I wanted to avoid surgery at all costs as the risk involved was high and the recovery was long – too long for a ballet dancer to return to the stage.

Just as I began to panic, I heard of a London osteopath called Demetri Papoutsis, who had dealt with many dancers' serious injuries. Dr Papoutsis was a short Greek fellow in his mid-fifties. He looked experienced and, to my relief, was very gentle. I felt sick when he manipulated my tailbone back into place, but the relief was instant. Despite it taking only a few minutes, I couldn't get off his table fast enough. To this day, I can't thank him enough for saving and prolonging my career. I continued to see him for treatment of occasional injuries such as hip and back strains.

We had to be very careful with our toes and try to avoid blisters, but sometimes they were inevitable. If I did get a blister it could hinder my performance, so I would buy a cheap steak and cut it into thin slices to bandage around the affected toe to act like a second 'skin'. The cool, wet feel of the raw meat was immediate relief for the pain. Eventually, a specialised product came onto the market and now all dancers use it, which means blisters are no longer such a problem to manage.

It was wonderful to spend time with Mum when she came to visit. We often shared a glass of wine in the Lemon Tree pub right outside the Coliseum door in St Martin's Lane. She enjoyed meeting my friends and fellow dancers, and was kind and generous, genuinely interested in their lives. London was a shopping mecca for my stylish mother. Freed of London, the dance apparel store across the road from the Coliseum, was where dancers longed to shop, and when Mum visited she treated me to tights and leotards from there. But it was the old Covent Garden markets she loved the most. She couldn't stay away. She was a collector of antique lace and found pieces there she couldn't resist. For years she kept them in a bottom drawer, until Dad encouraged her to open a shop in Rocky where she could sell them. It was called Linen and Lace, and over the years collecting lace became even more of a passion for her.

All too soon Mum would leave. Her visits were good for us both. She would get insight into what my life was like now. Although she wasn't one for effusive praise, I knew she was proud of me.

~

John Field had settled into his role as director and at my annual review in August 1981 he promoted me to soloist, and a year later to senior soloist. This was where I thought I would stay, because leading international stars normally came in to do the big principal roles.

During our summer tour that year John stopped me in the hallway of the theatre and said, 'Mary, could I speak to you privately?'

'Of course!' I said, a little surprised.

'Shall we meet at my hotel lounge tomorrow for tea at 4 p.m.?'

'Yes, I will be there,' I replied, and off he strode.

It was quite an official request, and highly unusual. *What does he want to talk to me about?* I wondered.

The following afternoon I put on my one nice dress that I always took on tour with me and walked from the theatre to the hotel. The suspense was killing me. John had a kind face and gentle manner and I sat down opposite him, waiting as he ordered our tea, desperate to hear what he was going to say.

'I've been very happy with your dancing, Mary,' he said. 'What I like about you is your work ethic.'

'Thank you, Mr Field.'

'I'm very pleased with your performances as Sugar Plum, Queen of the Wilis – and the Swan Queen in particular. You really rose to the occasion.'

I was moved to hear his compliments, but there was more to come. John smiled and, looking straight at me through his heavy-framed glasses, said, 'I'm going to promote you to principal dancer. How do you feel about that?'

I couldn't believe what I was hearing. I hadn't expected it at all. Was I hearing him right?

'Are you sure?' I asked, feeling a little trepidatious.

'Yes, I'm sure,' he assured me, standing up. 'Just keep doing what you're doing.' He came around the table and gave me a big hug. 'Congratulations, Mary.'

I was shaking with excitement and left the hotel walking on air. *How did I feel about that?* As if he needed to ask. It was all I'd ever dreamed of!

I walked back to the studio for rehearsal, looking for Matz. I didn't want everyone to hear, so I called him aside and told him the good news. He was so happy for me. I was reticent to tell the other dancers, even my friends, for fear of seeming too superior. Everyone knew that only a few of us would ever make it to the top. But I decided to tell my friends Jackie and Johanna. 'Congratulations, Mary! You so deserve it!' They were so thrilled for me.

On my way out, I passed Betty Anderton in the hall and she gave me a wink. I knew she was happy for me too.

As soon as I got home I rang Mum and Dad. 'How wonderful, darling! Well done!' they exclaimed, and I knew I'd made them proud.

Promoting from within was John's agenda. Being one of the first dancers he promoted to principal, I was determined to prove that his faith in me was justified. It really did seem that I was on my way.

This promotion motivated me to work even harder, to be even more focused.

My continued hard work began to pay off, and later that year saw me preparing for my first White Swan Odette and Black Swan Odile in *Swan Lake*, at the age of twenty-three. It was a real milestone. I was young to be dancing this kind of leading role. John had made a gutsy decision in selecting me so early in my career. He obviously believed in me.

As a professional dancer you can never learn enough about *Swan Lake* – it's one of the hardest of all the classical ballets. I knew I would perform the role of the dramatic Black Swan well, because it required excellent technique, which was my strength, but I would have to work hard to develop softness and vulnerability for the lyrical White Swan. It was going to be a challenge.

John paired me with the most wonderful dancer and partner in the company, Jonathan Kelly – an internationally recognised Australian principal who was tall, handsome and princely. We would look good together on stage. Luckily for me, he was knowledgeable and had danced the role of Siegfried before. He and I would have to carry *Swan Lake* between us. Was I up to it? I thought so – I hoped so! I worked very hard on the two roles, especially the White Swan. Jonathan helped me a great deal. We practised on our own and he coached me all the way through. He was caring and encouraging, which gave me confidence.

When John put me on a Saturday night at the Coliseum I felt added pressure. It was a big deal to be trusted to carry off a full-length ballet on a Saturday night, which was also the closing night of a season. Closing nights are as important as the opening nights. On top of preparing the White and Black Swans, I had to perform the demanding jumping solo in Act One and one of the two big swans in Act Two throughout the whole season. Both were very taxing roles. And I would have to do them the night before my first *Swan Lake* lead role. It was a killer week!

During my final run-through rehearsal Friday afternoon, both of my calves started cramping so intensely that I could barely walk. I started to panic that I wouldn't get through the evening or, worse, would not be able to make my debut in the principal role the following night. My parents had come to London especially to see me dance – it was very important to me that they be there for my first *Swan Lake* as principal. I tried to continue the rehearsal, but ended up in tears. The pressure was obviously getting to me, too. My friend Jane Devine's masseur boyfriend managed to come to my rescue, massaging my calves for over an hour to relieve the pain.

The next morning I woke up and tenderly checked my calves. To my immense relief, the muscles felt much better. In fact, I felt refreshed and ready to go. I was performing my first principal role in *Swan Lake*! To say I was nervous would be an understatement: I was petrified. I caught a black cab in to the theatre feeling sick. I'd worked so hard – especially on the White Swan's very first step on her entrance, which I'd practised at least 100 times just in that week. It's a dramatic *jeté*, a leap with legs in full splits, that requires you to look like you've flown in from the sky. And I needed to then hold it together for three poses in *arabesque* until frightened by the entrance of the prince and his bow. I'd analysed the exact number of steps needed to land my correct foot in the centre of the stage.

Suddenly, it seemed, I was standing in the wings ready to enter. 'Hail Mary, full of grace . . .' I prayed, and off I flew! Once I'd started, I just did what I'd practised, with Jonathan to support me. Everything went nicely, but I was a little disappointed that I didn't manage to complete all thirty-two of the famous consecutive *fouettés* as I had easily done in rehearsals.

Before I knew it, it was over. For the first time I walked out alone, centre stage, to take my bow and receive the applause and adoration. It was wonderful! I could actually feel the applause like live music against my skin. More important to me was that I knew in my heart I had performed well. I was filled with pride and happiness.

My wonderful partner Jonathan joined me on stage, and then the rest of the company. Once the curtain came down for the last time, Jonathan hugged me tight and said, 'I'm so proud of you. Well done, Mary!' The other dancers crowded around in a blur of hugs and congratulations.

John brought my parents backstage and Neil George said to me excitedly, 'You were splendid, darling.' He gave me a huge hug that I'll never forget. Mum was ecstatic and relieved. 'It was just sublime,' she told me, with her gentle smile.

'Were you nervous for me, Mum?'

'I had to calm my nerves with a couple of Scotches beforehand,' she replied.

I arranged to celebrate with them at the Lemon Tree. We were surrounded by dancers, musicians and members of the crew, spilling out onto the street in the pleasant night air. Many came to congratulate me.

I went to bed that night exhausted, but sleep eluded me. I couldn't stop thinking about what John Field had done for me. To work on something as big as *Swan Lake* was a gift. I thought about how wonderful it had felt to dance both lead swans, how the music had got into my bones and into my blood, how light I had felt, how open, how in the moment, how Jonathan had lifted me as though I were weightless. I thought about the curtain calls and the applause, and my parents sitting there watching me.

The main roles in large ballets like *Swan Lake* can take a whole career to master. They are challenging for both body and mind, and they force you to be resilient and courageous. In subsequent years I had the opportunity to perform *Swan Lake* many more times, and my skills in tackling the major roles grew. I became more and more confident in being able to perform the lead in a full-length ballet.

~

I decided to move into a flat in Hammersmith Road with Chris Mercer, one of the boys I'd shared a flat with previously. It was a small place on the second floor of a plain three-storey building. There was a pub on the corner, a Pakistani-run supermarket and a little Italian restaurant, which became a regular haunt. It was close to the Royal Albert Hall and Kensington Palace, and also close to the studios in Jay Mews and Festival Hall. So I had a better commute, and it was fabulous living without the distractions of a share house. Everything seemed to be a little easier, and my career started to take off.

Matz hadn't been happy with the level of principal work offered to him at the company. He was a virtuoso dancer but a bit shorter than most of the girls and it was hard to match him with dance partners. So I wasn't totally surprised when he told me he planned to audition for the Nederlands Dans Theater.

After the audition he told me with excitement, 'I got in!'

I cried, knowing he was determined to go. 'I'm happy for you,' I assured him, but my heart was breaking.

In the first months after he left London I felt like half of me was missing. On a few weekends I flew to Amsterdam and caught the train down to The Hague to spend time with him. He was working with Jiří Kylián, one of the best choreographers in the world at that time. I was always excited to hear how well he was doing, but was often lonely without him. So it was wonderful to see Brig and Jo, who each came to visit me a few times. On one visit, Jo and I, with Matz, took a trip to Paris and Brussels, and then to Amsterdam. My brother Matt and a friend of his also came to London and stayed with me for a few weeks.

Ballet was broadening my horizons and I had a thirst for more. I went to the theatre whenever I could and read as much as I could. When we toured internationally, I read the most famous authors of that country to provide an insight, and on Sundays at home I'd go to Leicester Square with friends to see the latest films – movies that offered a window to the world and to key events in history, like *Gandhi* and *Chariots of Fire*. We'd go to see symphony orchestra performances and stage plays. I saw *Children of a Lesser God*, Mark Medoff's play about the hidden world of deafness, at St Martin's Theatre. I was struck by the impressive lead character played by Elizabeth Quinn. I would learn a lot more about that hidden world in the years to come.

~

While Rudolf Nureyev was a part of London Festival Ballet between 1977 and 1984, he took his production of *Romeo and Juliet* all over the world. He was such a superstar that he could choose which company he wanted to perform with. The company's international touring took me to places I had only ever seen on a map. After our sold-out shows in Australia and the USA, we went to France and Italy, then South America and, lastly, Turkey. The experiences I gained from these tours were so educational.

Rudolf was riding high. His brilliant standard was influencing ballet, particularly male dancers. Yes, he was tough and demanding and a stickler when it came to perfection, and sometimes you would weep, thinking you would never achieve what he wanted. But he did recognise our efforts and always tried to show us a good time when we were away, as if to say thank you for giving every performance our best.

In Paris, after we danced *Romeo and Juliet* at the Palais des Sports, he took some of us, including Scottie and me, to Maxim's, once considered 'the world's most famous restaurant'. Many celebrities had dined in the Art Nouveau building on rue Royale, including Maria Callas, the Duke of Windsor, Brigitte Bardot and Barbra Streisand. And there we were, the dancers of Festival Ballet, with none other than Rudolf Nureyev! The restaurant had red velvet everywhere and little seating alcoves – very sophisticated and very French.

In Italy we went to Macerata, an ancient walled city on the east coast across from Rome, to perform in the Sferisterio di Macerata outdoor arena. It was a unique setting but the performances didn't start until nine o'clock after the summer sun had gone down. It was still very hot on the stage even late at night. We couldn't believe how fast our pointe shoes got soft in the heat. We would be groaning with tiredness as we performed *The Sleeping Beauty*, which was rather a long ballet. By the time we finished it was well past midnight.

Rudolf took us to see a Wagnerian opera at the same venue before our performances. It was a treat to experience the atmosphere, and invaluable to get an idea of what the audience could see when we were performing.

In Turkey in late 1982, we performed *Giselle* in the outdoor amphitheatre Cemil Topuzlu in the centre of Istanbul and Rudolf asked me to be Myrtha, the Queen of the Wilis. It was a bigger role than when I'd danced in the group of Wilis back in my first two years with the company. Rudolf was dancing the lead role of Albrecht, with Eva Evdokimova as his Giselle. She was delicate in her sorrow, and they were brilliant together. Afterwards, Rudolf hosted a party for us overlooking the Bosporus Strait. The next day, we had time off to go to the markets – a wonder of colour and noise, and tourists haggling over bargains.

The role of Tatiana in John Cranko's *Onegin* was another break-through moment in my life orchestrated by John Field. We were one of the first companies to perform the ballet outside Stuttgart, where it had originated. I was unsure whether I would get the chance to perform the role, as it was usually given to a much more experienced ballerina. I was a young woman of just twenty-five playing a much older woman with a huge range of emotions. John believed in me and I was grateful for the challenge. The reviews were rewarding: 'Mary McKendry was brilliant as Tatiana,' wrote internationally renowned dance critic Ann Nugent in *The Stage*.

~

In 1984 Houston Ballet happened to be performing at Sadler's Wells at the same time as we were performing at the Coliseum. Ben Stevenson had been their artistic director for eight years by then. John Field had an ongoing relationship with Ben Stevenson, a former Sadler's Wells Royal Ballet and Festival Ballet dancer. Ben had moved to the USA in 1971, where he became co-director and choreographer first with Washington's National Ballet and then with Chicago Ballet. Since being appointed artistic director of Houston Ballet in 1976, he'd been doing some exciting things: expanding the company's repertoire by acquiring the works of the world's most respected choreographers, commissioning new works, staging the classics and choreographing original works. As soon as I heard he would be in town, I decided to go and watch the company rehearsing.

I had to sneak out from the Coliseum at lunchtime so as not to create suspicion – loyalty to the company was everything. It wasn't far from St Martin's Lane to Sadler's Wells in Islington, and I was able to get into the auditorium while they were rehearsing. I sank low in my seat as I didn't want anyone to know I was there. It was magic. I saw straightaway that the company had a wonderful energy and artistry, led by a Chinese principal dancer. During their break, to my surprise, he came and sat beside me. I thought he looked familiar and I wondered whether he was one of the three boys I saw in China who had mesmerised me with their eyes and arms when they did their traditional dance.

'Hello, Mary. I'm Li.' He extended his hand and I hesitantly shook it. So much for going incognito. 'I really enjoyed your performances in *Cinderella* and *Four Last Songs*,' he told me.

'Thank you,' I replied.

He tried to strike up a conversation, but I was having none of it as I was so nervous at having been discovered. Finally, he left. He struck me as a bit overly friendly, although he did have a lovely smile. I hoped he didn't think me rude.

I got back to rehearsals just in time. I'd missed my lunch, but no matter: I'd seen what I wanted to see and that was the most important thing.

I had the opportunity to work with Ben in 1984 when he was invited back to London to stage his *Cinderella* and *Four Last Songs*. He took an interest in me and gave me corrections, which I loved. With his cultured English accent and razor-sharp wit, some dancers found him quite intimidating, but I took to him straightaway. He chose me to do one of the most exquisite *pas de deux* of my life in *Four Last Songs*. It was a defining time, during which I refined my technique and body line. Ben was very artistic and talked a lot about emotion. He had flair and I found him incredibly inspiring.

Mum was in London for that season, and I invited Ben to dinner. 'Would you like to come to my place for dinner after work?' I boldly asked him. 'My mum's visiting, so it won't be me cooking.' He turned up with the best wine and beautiful flowers, and Mum adored him from then on. She cooked traditional English fare for him – sausages and mash – and we all got to know each other.

~

Later that year it was announced that John was to leave the company at the end of the season and they would be looking for a new director. We were all shocked and had many questions. He had been one of the most important guiding lights in my career, and the careers of many others. I was very sad to lose him as my director. He was a kind and caring gentleman who had given me so many opportunities and I felt I owed him a lot. We were left feeling insecure and anxious about the future.

Peter Schaufuss was named the new artistic director. We were surprised because he was at the height of his dance career. It would be quite difficult for him to undertake both roles simultaneously, but his stature as a superstar would help our box office.

Peter was trained at the Royal Danish Ballet School from a young age and debuted in the *Don Quixote* grand *pas de deux* as a teenager.

He'd had a long association with London Festival Ballet, having worked as principal, guest star and choreographer, and he had danced with companies all over the world.

I had worked quite intensely with Peter on *La Sylphide*, and our relationship had continued to build when he had come to guest with the company. Despite my sadness about losing John, I felt relieved and excited that the new director was to be someone I knew, and who knew me. And to my surprise, when I looked at the casting for the upcoming season of *Don Quixote*, I found I was going to be his partner in the grand *pas de deux*. I would be dancing with my boss!

Don Quixote is a famous ballet, with athletic roles for both women and men. It transports audiences to a bright and enchanting Spain, with colourful gypsy dances and fandangos, matadors and windmills. The Act III grand *pas de deux* is very technical and uplifting. I found dancing with Peter a struggle to start with. I didn't feel quite ready, as our rehearsals were often disrupted due to his other commitments as the director – and I felt nervous dancing with him. Nevertheless, this *pas de deux* always brought loud applauses and enthusiastic responses. One could never feel totally confident with such a challenging *pas de deux* and I worked hard to lift my game to meet Peter's astounding standard. The good thing was that I had lots of opportunity to improve over the eight-week tour, and got there in the end. I also mastered my thirty-two *fouettés* in this ballet.

Eventually I started to do *Don Quixote* with Raffaele Paganini because I was a bit too tall for Peter. Matching the sizes of dancers is very important for aesthetic reasons – the girl is not supposed to be taller than the boy when she is *en pointe*. Peter gave Raffaele and me the opportunity to dance for the King and Queen of Holland in a televised gala performance in Amsterdam. There were many curtain calls for us that night, which was surprising as we were relatively unknown, and there were many stars on the bill, including German ballerina Birgit Keil and some well-known Russian dancers.

Under Peter's leadership, London Festival Ballet continued to tour the world. I was thrilled that Matz had decided he missed the classical *repertoire* and wanted to return to us. We hadn't seen much of each other in the last six months, but we easily slipped back into being a couple again. We took *La Sylphide* to an atmospheric outdoor theatre in Nervi, Italy; to Denmark in the renowned Tivoli Gardens; and then to Monaco, where we had to dance on a very small raked stage. What's more, in Monaco we did the very difficult ballet *Études*, in which I danced the lead. My role involved entering from the top wing, doing a line of turns *en pointe* that got faster and faster, and finishing very still at the bottom wing in an *arabesque* on *relevé* (on the toes). I had to do all this on the sloping floor but control the speed while getting faster and be able to stop and hold the *arabesque*. I managed it somehow, but was terrified the whole time.

~

Quite early in my third year as principal dancer, I began to want more of a challenge. Peter was a dancer with strong technique and had challenged us more technically, but I wanted more artistically. I was starting to get itchy feet.

I wasn't feeling as inspired by Peter and his direction, where he had less time for the dancers' development and artistry. It seemed to me he was overstretched being both our director and our top dancer. He had been a great influence on my technique, especially my footwork, but I was beginning to long for someone who could help me in the next stage of my artistic development. Instinctively, I knew I had to move on.

I had no idea how to approach this with Peter, so I spoke to Matz about my feelings.

'There are lots of other opportunities out there, Mary,' he said. 'Something will come up.'

'Maybe America? Why not look elsewhere?' Mum suggested when I confided my feelings to her.

Dad agreed: 'Don't limit yourself, beautiful. Think big.' I was grateful for their understanding and support.

Ben Stevenson and Houston Ballet came to mind. We had just started working with Ronnie Hynd on a new *Coppélia*. I was learning the lead role of Swanilda and also the difficult Prayer solo. I liked working with Ronnie. Coincidentally, right at this time when I was thinking of leaving London Festival Ballet, Ben was looking for a principal dancer. Houston Ballet's general manager, Jeannot Cerrone, left a message for me at the stage door. I was excited, and called him as soon as I could. He wanted to meet that evening, so after the performance at the Coliseum I hurried to the little Italian restaurant round the corner.

Jeannot was very French and very charming. After we ordered our drinks, he said, 'Mary, Ben would like to offer you a two-year principal contract with Houston Ballet. Would you like to think about this?'

'I don't need to think about it,' I said. 'Yes, I will accept!'

'That's wonderful!' He was both surprised and delighted with my quick answer. 'You'll need to provide us with your good reviews, because we need to establish that you have special skills to qualify as an exceptional talent as part of the visa qualification process in America,' Jeannot added.

God, here we go with the visa issue again! I thought.

Matz was very happy for me. 'That's exactly what you've been looking for, Mary!' he said.

A few days later, a confirmation phone call from Jeannot sealed it. My contract arrived in the mail soon after and I didn't hesitate to sign. I knew it would be shocking news to Peter and the company, and I didn't know how they'd react. I suspected I would be emotional and didn't want to be alone with Peter when I told him. With trepidation, I went to him after a class and said, 'Hi, Peter. Can I speak to you, please?'

He just looked at me.

'I've accepted an offer to dance for another company, and I've decided to leave at the end of my contract,' I told him.

'Where to?' he asked.

'Houston Ballet.'

He was totally shocked. 'What?' he exclaimed.

Without another word, Peter walked away.

He took the news very hard. I guess he felt betrayed – I understood that. He had supported me as principal for the last four years. The relationship of a director and their principal dancers is crucial to the success of a company, and it wasn't a common thing for a principal to leave. He was so furious that I was put back to solo roles instead of the leading roles for the remainder of my contract.

The last three months were really difficult, working under the dark shadow of Peter's displeasure. Betty was obviously upset with me, too. She didn't say anything, but I could tell she was disappointed. I felt gutted by her cool reaction – she was such an important figure in my life. But it was a decision I had to make: I felt it was right for my career.

My friends were gobsmacked at my bravery in telling Peter and my audacity in leaving London. 'Oh my God!', 'Please don't go!', 'I know why you need to go,' and 'I wish I had your guts!' they all said.

My friend Jackie, a great organiser, seemed to know what was involved in moving across the globe. I was grateful for her help as I had no idea. Between her and Matz, things got done.

A crowd came to my apartment for a farewell party. Then, after my last matinee, the company got together in the studio and we said goodbye officially, with lots of tears. They gave me a high-quality suitcase, which I desperately needed. It was such a thoughtful gift. Betty presented me with a book, Sir Thomas More's *Utopia*, which I came to treasure more and more as my life unfolded. Peter did not attend.

Friends had bought my furniture and the decor items so lovingly selected by Coralie. I wouldn't be taking anything with me to the USA except a beautiful silver trunk given to me by Matz, and the suitcase from the dancers.

It was a late summer morning when I finally left. I hugged Matz and went to the airport alone. It didn't feel like the end for us, even though we'd be so far apart. I was sad to leave him and my wonderful ballet family, but I had to spread my wings.

At twenty-seven, after ten years in London, including eight years at the Festival Ballet, I was off to live and work on the other side of the world for the second time. London had been such an important part of my life, but I was looking forward to a new beginning.

PART THREE

Houston
1985–91

*As soon as we stepped onto the stage we were in
that other place, with room only for the music
and the movement and each other . . .*

5

Ben Stevenson was an enormously gifted choreographer and teacher. I adored his choreography and the way he rehearsed. There was so much emotion and musicality in his coaching, which brought out the best in me. I'd had eight incredible years with London Festival Ballet, working my way from *corps de ballet* to principal dancer, and I would never forget those talented, inspiring people who had believed in me and taught me so much. Now I could hardly wait to start working with Ben.

When I walked out of the luggage area with my one suitcase and silver trunk, there was Ben waiting for me with his big smile and warm embrace. Outside the sky was blue, and it was hot. How I loved seeing those blue skies after the grey skies of England!

'Mary, you must join me for dinner tonight,' Ben said as we were walking to his car. This made me feel so welcome. It was a first – no director had ever done that for me in England.

'I've arranged for you to stay with Rosie Miles,' said Ben. 'She's English and was trained at the Royal Ballet School. She is a soloist here. You'll like her. Her apartment isn't far from our studio.'

'You're so thoughtful, Ben. Thank you!'

'You're welcome. It's just till you find your feet, Mary. I'm sure you will settle in quite quickly,' he said.

We set off in his big American sedan and drove along the wide, multi-laned highways, cars and billboards everywhere, skyscrapers' windows glinting in the sun, until we arrived at an apartment complex in midtown Houston, not far from Ben's townhouse.

I knew of Rosemary Miles. She was one of the dancers Ben had hired when he became artistic director of the company. The London background we shared would provide common ground. Rosie was there to meet me, vivacious and welcoming. She was a bit older than me, with dark hair and a pale English complexion. She very kindly showed me around the apartment and the complex. With a spacious living room, separate bedrooms, huge glass windows looking onto a swimming pool, it was a far cry from Mrs Woolf's boarding rooms. I was absolutely delighted.

I unpacked and got organised for the next day. I chatted with Rosie and she drove me to Ben's place for dinner. A few other dancers were there, including the Chinese principal dancer, Li Cunxin, who I'd met briefly in London. It was good to meet some of the people I'd be working with. Also there were Ben's friend and ballet mistress Carmen Mathe, another Brit, and her Scottish husband, Gerry, who taught Latin at a private secondary school. The conversation flowed freely that night. Ben had a wicked sense of humour and we laughed at his endless jokes.

Rosie drove me to work every day. The studio stood on Grey Street, opposite a big bread factory that welcomed us with the delicious aroma of baking bread each morning. There were a couple of shopping centres close by, with a 'drugstore' and a large supermarket. Everything was large and the distances seemed vast, as Houston is quite spread out. The Houston Ballet studio was a newly renovated two-storey building, fairly bland to look at from the outside, but I was amazed to find six studios within – a significant facility for a smaller company. The studios were spacious and bright. You could look out the vast windows and see the blue sky.

On that first day I met again with Jeannot Cerrone, who was very happy to see me. Carmen introduced me to another female principal,

Janie Parker, who showed me to the dressing room, which had plenty of space. I had replaced principal dancer Suzanne Longley following her tragic career-ending injury, so I simply took her spot in the dressing room. Janie was a country girl from the South, with a broad accent. After we got dressed, she then took me to the studio.

Most of the company dancers were American but a few had come from other parts of the world. Li was there at the *barre* and he came over. 'Hello, Mary. You sleep well?' he asked in his Chinese accent, with that big smile of his.

'No, I didn't really,' I replied honestly. I hadn't slept well on my first night, in a foreign country, on a foreign bed, jet-lagged and uneasy with anticipation for the following day. 'Jet lag, I think.' I shrugged my shoulders. Li nodded.

By this time, I could see that all the dancers in the studio were looking at me with interest. They must have been wondering what Ben's newly recruited principal dancer would be like. I was getting a little uncomfortable under all those glances, and was keen to find a suitable spot on the *barre*, quickly. As though Li could see what I was thinking, he pointed at the *barres* and said with his gentle accent, 'Mary, you stand anywhere.'

Rosie told me later that Li had defected from China when Ben brought him to the US as a scholarship student in 1979, with the help of none other than Vice-President George Bush, whose wife, Barbara, was on the Houston Ballet board! It made me think of Rudolf defecting from Russia. How incredible. I thought *I* was far from home, but at least I could see my family whenever I liked. Could Li go back to his family in China whenever he wanted to? There was obviously much more to his story, and I hoped I'd learn about it later on.

Ben introduced me to the company. Everyone was very friendly – especially the American dancers, who didn't have that English reserve that I'd become so used to – it was refreshing. We did class with Ben, then my dance partner, Ken McCombie, and I went straight into rehearsals.

I knew Ken from London Festival Ballet, where he'd been a principal dancer before he joined Houston Ballet. I was very pleased to see him. He was Scottish, older and more mature, and somewhat reserved. We were on a very tight timeline: I had to learn every step of the full production of *Swan Lake* in five weeks with Ken as my new partner. I also had to learn Ben's *Peer Gynt*, which I'd be dancing with Li. Another new partner to get used to. And then we would perform in New York. So I switched on, focused, and worked and worked.

Although I had danced *Swan Lake* before, I had to learn Ben's choreography, which was full of his renowned flair and drama. In one part I had to throw myself off a three-metre-high rock. To achieve this, I had to run up to the top of the rock, do an *arabesque en pointe*, fall into the arms of four strong male dancers and then onto a mattress (all hidden behind a raging lake), and roll off quickly because the prince was diving right behind me. Years spent jumping on the trampoline with my brothers was going to pay off.

The tour to New York City would be historic. Houston Ballet had been invited to perform at the City Center Theater. For a small company from Houston to be invited to New York to perform *Swan Lake* was thrilling. There'd been a lot of work behind the scenes to make the tour affordable for the company. I was beyond excited. *I've really landed on my feet here*, I thought. I hadn't danced in *Swan Lake* since 1983, and to perform it again in New York would be a dream.

Houston Ballet was really making a name for itself under Ben's direction. He was committed to training local talent, but also brought in exceptional dancers and choreographers from around the world. By the time I arrived, he was already world famous for several full-length ballets he had created there, winning gold medals for his choreography at international ballet competitions. He was also widening the company's repertoire by adding world premieres of his original works. Working with Ben was going to offer me lots of new opportunities to learn and grow.

Houston Ballet had a totally different feel to London Festival Ballet. One of the first things I noticed was that the dancers were all quite young. I'd become accustomed to working with experienced artists like Rudolf Nureyev, Patricia Ruanne and Eva Evdokimova. I realised with a jolt that I was now one of the more mature dancers in the company. My artistry would carry the lead roles and guide others. I had to really open up to all these responsibilities and possibilities.

But initially, after rehearsal on that first day, I attended to basic things with Ben's assistant, like pointe shoes, photos for marketing, and bank details so I could get paid.

'How many shows does the Houston Ballet perform each year?' I asked.

'It varies, Mary. Fifty, sixty or maybe seventy sometimes – it very much depends on how much we tour.'

I was shocked. At London Festival Ballet, we performed over 180 shows a year. I was used to dancing eight shows per week; Houston Ballet only did five shows a week, with fewer seasons. And being a principal, I would be sharing these shows with Janie and other dancers, so I would have to get used to being on stage much less. This would be difficult for me, as performing on stage lifted my standard of dancing and energised me.

After the first few weeks, I began to miss London, my friends and the life I was used to. I started to have second thoughts about my decision to leave London Festival Ballet, but then remembered that at twenty-seven, I didn't know how to live a normal life because I had been touring and performing so much. Perhaps now I would find a better balance, with a decent salary and less touring. Finally I felt like I had a job and could afford a good lifestyle. *You just need to come to terms with all the changes*, I told myself.

What saved me was the busy schedule. I had little time for anything except rehearsing, sleeping and eating. Peggy and Patrick Oxford from the Houston Ballet Board hosted a welcome barbecue for me. Matz had flown over to visit, and I was so happy to have him with me. Peggy and Patrick were fun people and had two small daughters. Peggy had been a fashion model and Patrick was a partner at a prestigious law firm, and they lived in a huge, beautiful home. They were both very glamorous, and I warmed to Peggy immediately, with her wonderful Southern drawl and charm.

It was a joy to return to *Swan Lake*, and Ben's production was beautiful. I enjoyed this rehearsal period with Ken. He was a quietly spoken and gentle person, and partnered me with care. The main *pas de deux* and solo parts were similar to the version I'd danced in London, except the Act Four *pas de deux*. It was so tender and sad that it made me weep even rehearsing it. However, the best part was Ben's coaching. He was incredibly inspiring and knew exactly how to pull the best out of me emotionally, technically and dramatically. It was exactly what I was looking for. This time, I really got to understand the story and enjoy the breadth of musicality and storytelling. My technique was now strong enough that I could focus on my artistry. This was exactly why I had come to Houston.

Peer Gynt would be performed in New York in the week after *Swan Lake* closed. Li Cunxin would be my partner, which I was looking forward to. I liked him immediately – his open face, his wide smile, his enthusiasm. I hoped we would be a good pairing, and I soon discovered that he was an incredible partner. In dance terms I felt we were made for each other. He was the perfect height for me and we were matched in maturity and experience as well as musicality and work ethic.

Li was familiar with *Peer Gynt*, and was very patient with me as I learned it. Based on Henrik Ibsen's 1867 play, with beautiful music by Edvard Grieg, *Peer Gynt* is such a romantic story. Li was Peer, the village boy, and I was his love interest, Solveig, the pure and innocent priest's daughter he meets at a wedding. Peer falls in love with Solveig but then leaves her to go on an adventure. When he finally returns to her, she is old and blind. Solveig has never given up on him and the lovers are reunited. There are two amazing *pas de deux* in the ballet and a romantic and heart-wrenching parting at the end of the first act that involves a kiss. I loved this story.

~

It was fall when we arrived in New York City, and the trees in Central Park blazed with delightful autumn colours. The air was crisp and so refreshing after the intense heat of Texas. Our hotel was close to Central Park, within walking distance of the theatre. It was a treat to walk around the theatre district, past Carnegie Hall and the Russian Tea Room. The Art Deco City Center, where we were to perform, was a beautiful theatre but the stage wasn't large.

I got unpacked at the hotel and enjoyed having a room to myself. Coralie was to arrive the following day – I was excited. She made her own way to the hotel as I was rehearsing. When she arrived, Ben took her under his wing. Somehow, he still had time to be a wonderful host and presented her with tickets to the ballet. Ben had bought me a glamorous red evening dress shimmering with sequins for opening night. Just stunning! Coralie and I watched that performance together – Janie and Li were performing the Swan Queen and the Prince; Ken and I would perform the leads the following night. Ben had created his *Swan Lake* in 1977, an update of the much-loved classic. It combined Acts One and Two, and Three and Four, to create a shorter, more condensed ballet with greater emotional impact. David Walker's design looked expansive, elegant and magical, and Ben's choreography flowed effortlessly with Tchaikovsky's sublime music. The dramatic dive from the high rock at the end created a tragic yet satisfying emotional climax. I loved it.

After the show, we went to a club. That night we saw the famous English singer Cleo Laine – a good friend of Ben's – perform, with her musician husband, John Dankworth, leading the band. What a voice. I remember being concerned about how long we might stay out, as I had to dance *Swan Lake* the following night. As a dancer, the next show was never too far away and you couldn't afford to let your guard down.

Coralie enjoyed coming to New York City and was keen to see how I'd settled in. She looked as elegant as ever. We laughed for days when she discovered a live mouse in the rubbish bin of her fancy hotel room. 'New York! New York!' we sang.

While I was doing my morning stretches, Mum headed downstairs for breakfast – it was a treat for her to have someone else cooking for her, and she always looked forward to a buffet breakfast. When she returned to our room she told me she'd had the most interesting conversation with Li. 'That Chinese dancer, Mary. Li. He is very friendly. He saw me sitting by myself and came over and introduced himself, and asked if he could join me for breakfast. We had such a lovely chat.'

'Oh, yes. He's very nice.'

'Somehow he guessed I was your mother, Mary. How could he have known that? Did you tell him I was coming?'

'Oh, I told quite a few people you were coming, Mum.'

'Li spoke very highly of you, too, which was wonderful to hear. He is a charming young man,' she said. 'And handsome, too!' she added, looking intently at me.

Li and I had developed a strong connection dancing together. I had no intention of forming an intimate relationship with a dancer, particularly one of my partners – it would be a recipe for disaster. In any case, we were both in relationships. Matz was planning to visit again when we returned to Houston. Li also had a girlfriend: Linda, a flautist in the orchestra. But Mum seemed to have sensed something. I quickly tried to change the subject.

'He's an incredible dancer, Mum. Wait till you see him in *Peer Gynt*. He has so much artistry and athleticism – and I feel so safe in his hands.'

Without knowing it, maybe there was a twinkle in my eye or something in my voice when I talked about him. Maybe Mum knew more than I did at that stage, because she then said, in her charming voice, 'Be careful with the Chinese. They're very different.'

I thought she seemed very wise. I suppose thirty years ago, her generation wouldn't have had much association with Chinese people. I knew Li was very charming, and didn't read anything else into it.

When Ken and I danced on the second night, I was beyond excited as I remembered admiring Rudolf and Patricia dancing *Romeo and Juliet* from the side of the stage in this city eight years ago. And now I was actually dancing a leading role in front of this audience. It was truly surreal, but knowing how big the occasion was, I had to focus on the character and music. I couldn't afford to allow my nerves to get the better of me.

The performance went very well. I was thrilled that my first show had gone without a hitch. I was surprised to hear the audience clapping in the middle of my *fouetté* turns in Act Three. What an enthusiastic reception! Ben was happy with my performance, and Coralie was beaming with pride, 'Darling, you are now dancing with much refinement and lovely maturity,' she said to me. This was the best compliment of all – Mum had always yearned for refinement.

Then came the performances of *Peer Gynt* with Li. Our partnership was electric – I hadn't felt this way on stage with any other partner. It is quite difficult to find the perfect partner in ballet, just as it is in life, but with Li there was no need to talk, no need for explanations, just physical intuition. In the dance world, you know instantly if you are simpatico, and we were. I hoped so much that he would become my regular dance partner.

In between *Swan Lake* and *Peer Gynt* we had a Sunday off. Mum and I went shopping and shared a lunch at the Russian Tea Room. She enjoyed giving me advice on the dresses that I bought at Bloomingdale's – an apricot, a blue floral and a navy blue. It was the first time I had paid quite a bit for clothes. I needed cool summer dresses for the Houston heat. I loved those dresses and wore them for years. I hadn't needed anything like this in London, but here as a principal dancer I was expected to socialise, and I was going out more, too.

Too soon, it was time for Mum to go. We were used to these farewells by now and I knew that she needed to get home to keep an eye on Dad, who wasn't so well these days. She had enjoyed her visit to New York and spending time with me.

~

Once I returned to Houston, and the pace and rehearsal schedule slowed, I began to feel quite lonely. Houston was very different to the hustle and bustle of London. You didn't bump into other dancers on the street or on the tube. I couldn't just pop into M&S for a salad. Rosie was busy with her own schedule and relationships, and I really had to find my own way of doing things. There was a phone in the apartment, but it was very expensive to call overseas; nevertheless, I still rang my parents a few times when I got desperate, and they promised to come to visit me again soon.

I wrote love letters to Matz telling him how much I missed him. I knew a number of things were contributing to my sense of isolation. I'd grown up with the *corps de ballet* crowd in London and we'd been together for eight years. They were like my family. I didn't have that support here. It wasn't as easy to make friends as a principal dancer – it was lonelier at the top. I was on my own much more. I soon worked out that I needed to make the first move. I called Peggy Oxford and we started to become friends. I had also felt a connection from the beginning to our publicity person, Kate Crady, and we developed a good friendship over time that later extended to our families. As principals, Janie, Li, Ken and I were expected to greet people after every show, which I enjoyed. It extended my circle.

Geographically, Houston is spread out. There is no subway system and public transport is non-existent. Everyone had a car. Having to get cars or taxis everywhere was quite alienating, but I needed a car to get to work. So I bought one, even before I could actually drive. Some of the male dancers kindly taught me to drive over the next few months. 'Best not be on the road with Mary!' they warned jokingly. I had never been behind the wheel of a car before.

I went for my driving test and did terribly. I should have failed but I wept and begged the examiner, 'I just have to have the licence or I can't get to work.' I knew I couldn't really drive as I was terrified to drive on the freeways, but the tears somehow worked – the examiner passed me. I managed to avoid the freeways for at least a year. People are driving at sixteen in Texas. I think they were happy to give a driver's licence to anyone. Later I came to love the independence of driving – it revolutionised my life in Houston.

~

With time I started to feel at home, despite the cultural shift. Streets in Houston are very wide and set out in grids. Downtown Houston, like the whole of the city, is very flat and hot, with towering glass skyscrapers but no real heart, as at the time no one lived in that area. The city felt strange, and was a ghost town at night. Cars were king – there were no footpaths to get around. There was a Mexican flavour, with restaurants everywhere, and an arts district taking shape, but as I had come from London it all seemed very disjointed to me.

There were drive-throughs for everything, even banks and fuel stations, which could be found on virtually every block. I was introduced to Thanksgiving at Ben's. Then there was Halloween, which I didn't much care for, and of course Christmas. The fuss! It was all about shopping and presents. It was endless.

A lot of women in Houston had big hair. At least that suited me! The clothes were far more colourful than in London, and there seemed to be an abundance of money on show – as demonstrated by the jewellery, the vastness of people's homes, and everyone owning three or four cars. Now at the ballet I was being introduced to oil barons in tuxedos and their glittering wives and daughters with double-barrelled names such as Betty Lou and Ava Jean.

Real estate was actually affordable, so when a one-bedroom apartment in my complex became available for rent, I took it. It was the first time I'd ever lived by myself. I bought a mattress and slept on it on the floor. In fact, I never did get a bed. Then I bought an old table and chairs at the neighbourhood shopping strip. A few months later, I added a nice sofa. I still wasn't a good cook, so didn't need much kitchen equipment. Luckily I was often invited to Ben's or other people's places for dinner. Ben always had a posse of people with him. His friends Preston Frazier and Ava Jean Mears became my friends too. Ben also took us to a Chinese restaurant called Dong Ting that served delicious dumplings. He was a foodie and knew all the best restaurants, but I had to watch my figure carefully, which required strict self-control. I always spent Christmas with Ben, along with all the senior dancers who didn't have families in Houston. We became a close group – I had found a ballet family again.

And Li and I really loved working together. The chemistry between us lingered beyond the stage. To be honest, my connection to him had been instant, and I had the impression it had been the same for him. Mum had definitely detected something! I quickly put such thoughts out of my mind though – we were only becoming good friends, I told myself. He was just very friendly and approachable.

We didn't spend much time together outside the studio, but I was fascinated by Li and his Chinese background. Although his English was imperfect, which made conversations challenging, it was not a problem in the studio because we communicated through physicality and French ballet terminology. Ben had told me that Li came from a very poor peasant background and a large family but had been taken away from his village by the authorities to be trained as a ballet dancer at the Beijing Dance Academy, miles away, when he was only eleven.

How sad! But I had another piece of the puzzle and was to learn more as time went on.

Meanwhile, Matz and I were drifting apart.

~

We were back in the studio, preparing for the winter and spring seasons. Li and I were paired for *Giselle*. I had done the role of Giselle before, but never like this, dancing with Li as Albrecht. *Giselle* is such a beautiful love story. So many of the ballets Li and I performed together were romantic ones, providing an allure, an environment, where real love could flourish. It was so good to dance with a partner for whom I actually felt something.

In January 1986 we headed to Washington, DC with *Swan Lake* and a new ballet created by Ben, *The Miraculous Mandarin*. I was looking forward to revisiting the Kennedy Center where I had last been with Rudolf, and now I was going to be there dancing as the lead in *Swan Lake*. And my sister Brig was coming to visit me!

It was during this tour that I had another lucky break, but it was due to another's misfortune. Janie Parker had injured her ribs badly in that high dive from the *Swan Lake* rock, so I was thrown in at the last minute to partner with Li in *The Miraculous Mandarin* and perform the lead character, Mimi, against the very difficult Béla Bartók score. I only had a weekend to learn it, and I hadn't even been in the studio during the creation. Not only that, but it was Ben's new ballet, premiering at one of the best showcase venues in the US. Ben loved the music and thought it would be a great vehicle for his very own miraculous mandarin – Li!

The Miraculous Mandarin is an exotic and intense one-act ballet. The Mandarin is robbed, attacked, strangled and hanged by three thugs, but won't die, until at last, Mimi is moved by his unquenchable passion for her and kisses him. It is only then he starts to bleed, and then dies in her arms. Very dramatic!

I still didn't really know the music and the choreography well enough by the time I got on stage, but my acting and interpretive ability got me through. Mimi is a prostitute and had a stunning costume – even if I didn't *know* the part, I looked the part. The dress was by a New York designer – a yellow mini-dress with sequins all over it – and I wore a red wig, black fishnet stockings and black pointe shoes.

We shone as the leads that night, and the show was a triumph. I remember stepping forward during the many curtain calls and hearing the cheering audience. I was relieved and elated. The reviews were excellent, and I was so happy for Ben. Any new work is like having a baby, and you don't know how it will be received until it hits the stage.

The Kennedy Center season was a huge success, but something tragic happened on the opening night: the space shuttle *Challenger* exploded, killing all seven on board. We cancelled the planned post-performance reception as a show of respect. NASA's Johnson Space Center was part of the Houston landscape, and would be the site of a huge memorial service later that month.

Brig had dinner with me after the show instead. 'There are a few younger dancers in the company I'm friendly with, but Li is becoming one of my best friends here. I like him a lot,' I told her.

'Yes, he's a marvellous dancer, and so nice,' Brig agreed, with a knowing look.

Our friendship – or was it more than that? – continued to grow. We dancers were always pretending to fall in love with our partners in ballets, but that love rarely went beyond the stage. It just wouldn't work, and Li and I were aware of that.

I could see, though, that he would be very easy to fall in love with.

∽

Soon after, as part of the spring program, Li and I were dancing *Giselle* together. While in Houston in the Act One solo on the last diagonal series of hops *en pointe*, I felt a pull in my groin. I didn't want to stop so I kept going. Afterwards I could barely lift my leg. There was pain in my hip, too. An injury has to be really bad, such as a broken foot, for a dancer to stop mid-performance, as it's not easy to replace a dancer quickly, and I knew this well. It had happened to me in *Swan Lake* in London when I had to step in for Elisabetta Terabust mid-performance, changing quickly from a Russian dance costume to the Black Swan. You simply have to step up, and there's no stopping the show – the audience have paid for their tickets and expect a great ballet. With only a few shows left, I didn't want to worry Li, so I kept the injury to myself and hoped it would go away. I wasn't going to give up my *Giselle*.

Somehow I managed to finish the week of performances and no one seemed to notice. There wasn't an in-house physiotherapist at the time, so I had to make a booking and go to a physio clinic to get treated. Li eventually found out that I was in pain and suggested I give acupuncture a try. He swore by it. I was open to everything, but was terrified of needles at the best of times. The Chinese acupuncturist was very gentle and caring but when she put a long needle in my groin, I quietly screamed. The worst part was that the needle had to stay in my groin for twenty minutes. Li was having acupuncture at the same time and I looked over to see he had fallen asleep! If I'm honest, I don't think the treatment helped much.

However, Li's incredible masseur, Charles Webster, did help me. He was born in America to a German father and American mother. He was so proud of his German lineage that he tried hard to speak English with a German accent! After a performance, Charles would be available at all hours to give Li a massage. We called him 'Mad Charles', because he was eccentric and brilliant. He was a strong man who just seemed to sense which parts of our bodies needed extra attention. At last I could afford things like this that could really make a difference.

So with good management of my injury, I was able to push through and continue to dance in physically demanding lead roles.

I couldn't believe my life now. All I wanted to do was dance, and I was doing exactly that – with Li.

During another performance of *Giselle*, I came back to the wings to find Li lying on the floor unable to move.

'Help me roll over,' he said. He got up slowly.

'Are you injured, Li?' I was concerned.

'I'm fine,' he simply replied.

'Are you sure?' I asked. He didn't look it.

He just nodded. I could tell he was in a lot of pain, but I also knew from his stern expression that he wanted no fuss made. So we continued with the second act. He lifted me above his head just as effortlessly as he had always done in rehearsal, but I knew he must be in excruciating pain. I found out later that he'd had a bad fall and injured his back at the Moscow International Ballet Competition the year before and he must have exacerbated that injury. I couldn't believe he had finished the show with all the partnering work! After that, I pretty much knew that this man could do anything he set his mind to. I was in awe of his determination, strength and professionalism.

During this tour Li and I became much closer and he told me about some of his problems with his girlfriend, Linda. I instinctively knew their relationship wasn't going to work, based on what he told me, but he was determined to keep it going. Maybe because he already had a failed marriage. I'd learned that his marriage to Elizabeth Mackey, also a dancer, at the time of his defection, hadn't worked out. He had been devastated by the marriage break-up. They were both just too young and came from different cultures, had different dreams and also a language barrier.

The more I got to know Li, the more I discovered what a kind, gentle soul he was. His integrity and sunny nature, and his unguarded and unassuming charm, moved me. I even found his broken English and unfashionable clothes charming. Of course, there was also the ballet side of things I liked about him. My heart went out to him when he was blaming himself for his failed marriage, and for the challenges in his relationship with Linda.

'Li, I see how you treat people every day and I see all your relationships with friends. I can't believe *you* could be the problem,' I told him. I stopped myself saying, 'You are the most beautiful person I have ever met.'

I knew I was falling for him at this point. I knew deeply who he was because I'd danced with him for a year and been with him on a daily basis. I knew this man was special. I wanted to make him happy and I sensed that to do so would make *me* happy. I knew at the bottom of my heart that I would love him if he felt the same about me, which I wasn't entirely sure of yet.

A couple of days later, we were having dinner alone. Our conversation flowed effortlessly, despite his imperfect English. We had no trouble understanding each other. We shared stories about our respective families, laughed and were having a great time. Li asked me many questions about my family that night and about my time in London. Of course, I had a lot of questions for him too.

'How is your family, Li?' I asked.

'They're okay, but I'm worried about them all times,' he replied.

'Why, Li?'

'They are too poor. Not enough food. Not enough clothes. Winter is too cold. No heating.'

From his expression and the way he spoke, I could clearly see his love and worry for his parents and six brothers. I could feel his pain. Before I could say anything to comfort him, he continued: 'I dream about them. I feel guilty.'

'Why is that?'

'I have more than them. They have nothing.'

'But you can help them,' I said.

'No. I will never be allowed go back see them. I can't help them. I feel hopeless,' he replied.

I was heartbroken for him. I couldn't really comprehend the depth of his turmoil and emotional suffering. I desperately wanted to help him but I didn't know how. I tried to make him laugh. 'I was right about why people defected. You did it because of the dried yams, right?' I teased. He had told me earlier that he and his family virtually survived on dried yams and he'd be happy to never see yams again as long as he lived.

I hated seeing him upset, and tried to comfort him. Maybe it was because I loved him so. Maybe it was because of how lovingly he spoke of his brothers and his beloved mother and father, or Niang and Dia, as he called them. The defection had been incredibly difficult for him. While his parents had been allowed to visit him in America the year before and had finally seen him dance, it had been over eight years since he had last seen the rest of his family, and he feared he would never be allowed to return to China.

'Of course you will!' I reassured him, unable to even contemplate never seeing my own big, noisy family again. Li's ability to push forward despite that big dark cloud showed me the quality of this man yet again. 'Li, I'm sure you will be allowed to see them soon.'

He shook his head. 'No, I don't think so.'

'Why are you so certain about this?' I asked.

'Chinese government hate defector, just like Russian Government. Just look at Baryshnikov and Nureyev. They have never been allowed to go back to Russia.'

I knew he had a point, and I was at a loss as to what to say next.

'I don't think I can help them as I dream,' he continued, and gulped a big mouthful of his beer as if to wash down his sorrows.

I was so sad for him. What a torturous situation. I wondered how he could even get up and go to work every day with this kind of suffering. What strength it would have taken him to just survive. He wiped the tears from his face. It would have taken so much for him to let his guard down. I felt such compassion and sympathy towards him. I was getting very emotional too. I desperately wanted to comfort and help him. I reached across the table and grabbed his hands.

'You'll go back and see them again. You will,' I told him.

Li responded by squeezing my hands, but then released them to wipe more tears. 'I hope so. I will never give up my hopes.' Then, quickly, he said, 'I want this a happy night. Let's not talk about China any more.'

'Okay. What do you want to talk about?' I asked.

'You like books. I see you read all times.'

The unexpected topic and the imperfect grammar made me smile. 'You should say, "I see you reading all the time", not "all times".'

'Oh, thanks,' he replied earnestly. 'Please correct my English, Mary.'

'Are you sure?'

'Yes. Yes. English very difficult . . . very different.'

The rest of the evening became lighter and happier. I could sense the rhythm speeding up and thought I saw Li's eyes sparkle across the candlelight. *Could he be feeling this way too?* I asked myself.

Then Li asked a question that took me by surprise: 'Are you and Matz together still, Mary?'

Ever since I'd arrived in Houston and my feelings for Li had grown, I had repeatedly questioned my feelings for Matz. I thought carefully before I answered: 'I have deep feelings for Matz, and he's a wonderful man, but to be totally honest I don't think he's *the one*.'

From that moment I knew that Li was interested in me, and that our feelings for each other were mutual. At the end of that night as we said goodnight, I told him, 'It is probably inevitable that we'll be together.' Li drew me to him and we kissed – our first kiss, but neither of us said another word.

We tried hard to keep our relationship secret. It was both thrilling and agonising. We both felt guilty. Li was trying to break it off with Linda but she was still in love with him, and I was still in touch with Matz in London. Matz and I were very fond of each other, but in my heart I had known for a while that he and I were never going to be lifelong partners. Falling in love with Li finally ended my relationship with Matz. We didn't actually speak about it. I wasn't going back to

London and he wasn't coming to Houston. We both realised we had grown apart, and simply remained friends.

Li and I also knew Ben didn't like dancers from the company forming close relationships with each other. It posed too great a risk – if one of the dancers wasn't happy within the company, the director could potentially lose both dancers. If Ben came to suspect that was a possibility, when Li was his star dancer whom he couldn't afford to lose, things could become quite difficult for everyone. I often sensed, too, that Ben felt Li was like a son to him, and that Li saw Ben as a surrogate father.

'I would hate for our relationship to cause Ben any angst,' I told Li.

'Yes, best keep secret for now,' he agreed.

So we continued to keep our relationship hidden as best we could. In the studio rehearsing together, we shared lots of expressive eye contact. Afterwards, we would go and have a meal together quietly, in restaurants where we didn't think anyone from the company would be. Sometimes we would meet at our own places. Li convinced me to try his favourite Japanese restaurant, but unfortunately for him I didn't like fish in those days, which was the main thing on the menu. Li loved fish because seafood was a speciality in his hometown, Qingdao, and he hadn't enjoyed much of it in his childhood as his family were too poor. I ended up eating meat and tempura vegetables instead.

While secrecy made our relationship even more exciting, the stress of keeping it to ourselves was starting to show. It was a tumultuous time and I became frustrated with Li's guilt and indecisiveness with Linda. She didn't know about us and was planning a holiday for the two of them. Under pressure, Li decided to give their relationship another chance and began to push me away. 'Mary, in my heart I feel I need to have one more try with Linda,' he told me.

I was devastated, and beyond hurt. His decision seemed crazy when we both felt the inevitable force pulling us together. I came to the realisation that I had to let him go, but gave him a rather cold shoulder after that. Even though we were together every day in a very physical way in the studio, I held back emotionally. It was incredibly draining.

So he's dumped me, I thought. *Right!* I started seeing more of Randy Lombardo, a cardiologist-in-training I'd had a few dates with when I first arrived in Houston. I was trying to move on from Li. I also decided that the next person I was going to have a relationship with would be the person I would marry. *Otherwise*, I said firmly to myself, *the only other option is to stay single. I can't do dating — I don't have the time!*

Randy came to the ballet to watch me perform. Li didn't like this, which I relished! The ball was in his court now. We didn't talk about it, and I didn't ask what was going on with Linda.

Back in Houston after being on tour, we both attended the annual Houston Ballet Ball. Neither Linda nor Randy was invited, so Li picked me up. We were at the same table and I wore the beautiful glittery red dress Ben had bought me. Throughout the night, I noticed that his eyes kept darting over to me. I intentionally avoided him, which drove him crazy. Of course, it was killing me too. I was certain that we still loved and cared for each other.

After the ball I told him straight: 'You're not in love with Linda. You're in love with me.'

But then I backed off to let him think about that. How I wished that he would get with the program!

The following couple of weeks were excruciating. Li was struggling to end his relationship with Linda and tried to hide his feelings at work. He was known for his positive attitude and focus, but I could sense his unhappiness. He confided to me that Linda was making extra efforts and he felt guilty for not loving her back the same way. He was even reading books and listening to audiotapes on self-help. Although I was frustrated with his indecisiveness, I fell in love with him even more seeing how hard he was trying to make it work with Linda, and how serious and sincere he was.

Even though I tried to give him space to work through his feelings, we still had to work with each other every day in the studio and on stage. It seemed the more we pushed away from each other, the more we were drawn closer and closer. I sensed an inevitability that we were meant to be together one day, but sometimes I wondered if Li would ever wake up.

One day after rehearsal, I asked him if we could go for a drink and he agreed. We drove out of town and went to a quiet bar where people wouldn't recognise us.

'How are you doing, Li?' I asked him as soon as our drinks arrived.

'Okay,' Li replied.

'Really? I don't think you're happy,' I probed.

He gave me a meek smile and shook his head. 'No, I'm not happy. My relationship with Linda is not going well. We both try hard . . .'

'Li, do you still love her?' There was no need for small talk. I had to get to the point. 'You need to be honest about this. This is the most important question you need to answer.'

Li turned and gazed away from me. He was silent for a while. He frowned and took a mouthful of beer, then looked at me and said, 'No, not any more, Mary. I think I love you.'

My heart leapt. I knew it! And now he'd said it. And then we started laughing.

'What are we going to do, though, Li?' I asked him, thinking about how our colleagues might react.

'Well, I don't want this affect relationship with Ben,' he said. 'Better let him know soon, I think!'

I knew Li was right but thought him very brave, as Ben could be quite intimidating. But our relationship was solid: it was built on a strong friendship and trust. Li and I had known each other over a year now and had been in close contact every day – in a way, it was more intimate than a marriage, which is exactly why we'd been reticent to get involved with each other. But it wasn't just dating now – it was a serious relationship and we were both ready.

'I talk to Ben tomorrow, Mary,' Li said with determination as we got back in the car. Though I was a little afraid too, inside I was dancing on air.

The next day Li spoke to Ben. He told me Ben was quite shocked at first, but then was reassured when Li insisted that we planned to prove to him we could make it all work. 'And that's what we must do, Mary. Make it work.'

'We will, Li,' I assured him. 'We will.'

~

Our first real opportunity to be together openly came the following month. It was June 1986, at the end of my first season with Houston Ballet, and we were touring to Singapore and Jakarta. We danced *Swan Lake* and a triple-bill program. It was a fabulous trip, not only because Li and I were openly together and dancing better than ever (which made Ben happy), but also because we had time to explore.

We drank cocktails at the famous Raffles Hotel in Singapore, and did all the touristy things we could fit in. How different from China this Asian city was! It felt so much more Westernised with its busy centre and futuristic skyscrapers alongside elegant colonial buildings, exotic temples surrounded by lush tropical greenery, and the smell of wonderful food everywhere.

In Jakarta, we met a couple of Li's friends from Houston for dinner. It was interesting to see how they lived. We were picked up by their chauffeur and taken past some very poor areas to their house, which was part of a gated community for Western expat families. They had amahs (maids), gardeners and drivers. 'Neil George will love to hear about this,' I thought, remembering his dream of an Indian adventure for the family, including lots of amahs to help Coralie.

From Jakarta, I flew straight to Perth. It was winter and much cooler than Indonesia. Beryl Grey was staging *Giselle* for the West Australian Ballet, and the director, Barry Moreland, had asked me to dance the lead role. I had previously worked with Barry in London where he had created a ballet for me, *Sir Lancelot and the Round Table*. We had a good relationship. I was excited to see Beryl again. My partner was a famous Australian dancer, Kelvin Coe, who was called out of his retirement to do six of the twelve shows. During rehearsals I was delighted to discover he was a truly magical artist, and he became one of my favourite partners. What an opportunity, to dance my favourite role in one of my favourite ballets with such a partner!

It was the first time I had danced in Australia as a principal. Mum, Dad and Dom came for opening night, and stayed in the same hotel as me. We saw each other at breakfast and sometimes for dinner, but really, I was busy with the performances and sleeping in when I could. I had a couple of media interviews while I was in Perth: 'Aussie ballerina comes home'.

After the Perth performances I went to Brisbane to spend time with my family. We had a gorgeous week. Mum and Dad had moved from Rocky to Brisbane after Dad retired. They had bought in the inner suburb of Windsor, with fantastic views to the city. Dad had been diagnosed with diabetes and emphysema, so he had quit smoking and had taken up walking, which enabled him to enjoy the old and new architecture all over Brisbane.

Because all the kids except Ger and Mick were still at home, Mum and Dad had bought two units on the top floor of a six-unit block. This meant you could just walk across the landing into the next unit, which had the kids' bedrooms and a second bathroom and lounge. Dad had convinced Ger to buy the other top-floor unit and Matt and Pat to invest in one on the ground floor. So the McKendrys had the majority of votes on the body corporate!

It was so good to get to know my brothers and sisters as young adults. Ger was in the police force; Mick had started working in insurance; Matt, a carpenter, was working on major performances backstage at the Queensland Performing Arts Centre; Brig was a teacher; and Pat, Jo and Dom were at university. Dad would still hold court, sitting at the top end of the table with a beer in hand, discussing the events of the day with anyone who'd listen.

Above all, I remember the constant talking and laughter. As much as I adored the ballet, my time with my family was always a wonderful break from the ballet world. But Li was never far from my mind. I wondered if he was having a nice break in Bali, where he had gone for a week's holiday at the end of our Asian tour. I knew he was looking forward to massages on the beach. I missed him and was keen to get back to our life in Houston. I was always sad to say goodbye to my Australian family, my Australian home, but I had started to see my life as being made up of two families, two homes.

~

Around September, Li and I had a real setback. We were preparing Ben's newly designed production of *The Sleeping Beauty* with that wonderful soaring Tchaikovsky score. I was paired to dance Princess Aurora with Li as my Prince Florimund, who awakens me with a kiss. Ben had brought focus to the storytelling, and with his choreography and Li beside me, I was looking forward to performing this production. The *Sleeping Beauty* tutu was the most beautiful I have ever worn – cerise pink, with long flowing sleeves, a rose in the middle of the bodice and a rose crown. When I came onto stage, I really felt like a princess.

One day, when we were practising the three 'fish dives' (fast turns), with Li wrapping me into his body and then putting me head down to centimetres from the floor and my legs fishtailed up into the air. All of a sudden, Li's back injury flared up again. He was grimacing with pain, and we had to stop the rehearsal. It seemed more serious this time.

Back injuries can be career-ending for a dancer. I was so worried for him. Li went to a specialist, and an MRI scan showed he had two herniated discs in his lower back. He was told he had two choices: to have an operation, or stop dancing for six months. I just knew that the operation would be too risky and could spell the end of his career. Li insisted on continuing as he didn't want to let me down, but I told him: 'Don't even think about it. It will be a disaster.'

Of course I was no expert, but the thought of back surgery filled me with foreboding. We had to stop ourselves from thinking about the worst-case scenarios: 'What if he can never dance again? What if he can't work?' And I didn't even want to think about dancing if Li wasn't in the studio with me.

Li had bought a small wooden bungalow with a verandah in a neighbourhood called the Heights. It had two bedrooms and a central bathroom. He had renovated it from scratch, proudly telling me that he and his friends had done nearly all the work, from levelling the foundation to plumbing and electrical wiring, learning skills and trades as they went.

So Li lay on his back for over three months in his bungalow. People brought him food, and movies to watch. I would visit him almost every day. He was only allowed to get up to go to the bathroom, shower and eat. He even ate most of his meals in bed and had regular massage and acupuncture treatments at his home. When I finished work or was free for the weekend, I would take books to read to him. Larry McMurtry's *Lonesome Dove* – in keeping with our Houston location – was one of his favourites.

When I first met Li, his reading of English was limited. I started to give him small newspaper articles I knew he'd be interested in, and he soon became a fervent reader. Then off and on I would give him spelling tests. 'English is such a hard language. Just keep trying!' I would tell him. He kept a Chinese–English dictionary beside the bed. He went from reading the sports pages in the *Houston Chronicle* to the business section, and then he found the *Wall Street Journal* and never looked back. This taught him to read well and fast, and gave him an education in the world outside of ballet.

I really missed Li in the studio. He was my best friend and, I was beginning to realise, my soulmate. I mainly paired with Ken McCombie, who was a very fine artist. But there was always that lingering question that would affect both of us, in ways we couldn't imagine: *Would Li ever dance again?*

Well, of course he would. How could I have doubted it? His comeback was hard and tedious. It took a total of six months of rest, therapy, rehabilitation and training. He was positive and determined throughout. I've never seen anybody work harder, or with more tenacity.

Li's discipline and persistence enabled him to return to ballet even stronger and better. I was thrilled to have him back to dance with me in Ronnie Hynd's *Rosalinda* in March 1987. The ballet required some very tricky partnering, especially with *pirouettes* and lifts. He was incredible.

6

Six months before my arrival in Houston, Li's parents had been to visit for the first time since his defection. They were now preparing for a return visit, and excitement spread among the entire ballet community as they had left a big impression on many people. Li had told me how emotional their reunion was on their first visit, when they were secretly rushed into the theatre by Li's friends without him knowing. I heard there'd been a lot of teary eyes in the audience that night, and Li's mother had just sobbed and sobbed. It was a dream-come-true moment for them all.

The first time I met Li's parents was at Ben's for dinner soon after their arrival. They didn't speak a single word of English, and Li had to translate for them. They were nice and polite but I could tell they were overwhelmed. There were many questions thrown at them all night. I wondered what they would think of me, their son's new girlfriend.

I came to know Li's parents over a few home-cooked dinners at his place – delicious dumplings and other traditional Chinese dishes. Li's mother was small, had a bright personality and laughed a lot, and she was an excellent cook. His father was handsome and more reserved – a man of few words. I asked Li what I should call them and he explained it would be impolite to call them by their given names because they were elders. So we agreed it would be best to call them what Li called them: Niang and Dia. I was relieved and overjoyed when Li told me one day, 'Mary, my parents like you.'

Niang and Dia were staying for two months. When Li had to go to Pittsburgh for a couple of weeks to guest-perform, he asked me to look after them. I would call in after work to see if they needed anything. One night when Li and I were chatting on the phone after I'd had dinner with his parents, he suddenly said, 'Mary, I miss you. I want ask you something . . .' I could hear him fumbling with words, which I thought was odd.

We had talked before about the fact that I didn't want to move in with him. I had made a promise to myself that if I was to live with a man again, it would be in marriage or not at all. Li continued mumbling by saying something like I was the most beautiful person in the world and the most special person in his heart and I was a better person than him . . . By this stage I was getting impatient with him and just wanted him to get on and spill out what he really wanted to say. Then he muttered something about whether I would still love him when he was old and grey.

Where is this heading? I wondered. His English was even more halting than usual.

'What are you trying to say, Li?' I asked him. 'Are you trying to tell me you want to spend the rest of your life with me?'

'Yes! Mary, you think we can be happy together for rest of our lives?'

'Li, you are the dearest person in my life. I will love you always, and I *know* we can be happy together for the rest of our lives,' I replied.

'Will you marry me?' he finally asked.

I was so surprised. *Oh my God! Where has this come from?* I thought. But then, deep down I should have known Li would have the courage to actually ask me. That was the happiest moment of my life. We both started laughing deliriously. Such joy!

When Li returned from Pittsburgh, he told his parents. And the next time I saw them, they both gave me a tight hug and chatted in

Chinese to me – particularly Niang, who was a great talker. In his reserved manner, Dia nodded to me approvingly. He was a decent and good man, and so kind to Niang. Their relationship was an inspiration. I felt they were slightly hesitant about our engagement, but I also sensed they liked me, even if I wasn't able to understand them. Li assured me that they approved, so we were all very happy.

It was a tricky thing to tell Ben about our forthcoming marriage. He'd just got used to the fact that we were dating. Li wanted to make the announcement quickly so Ben wouldn't hear it from any other source. He decided it was better to break the news in a social environment, so he organised a dinner party with close friends. Once everyone had had a few drinks and had eaten, Li stood up.

'My wonderful friends, thank you for coming,' he began. 'I have an announcement to make. You all know that Mary and I are together, but what you don't know is how much we love each other. We have made an important decision and we want you, our dearest friends, to know first. Mary and I are getting married!'

There was complete silence. Everyone was stunned. I had only been at the ballet for eighteen months and officially with Li for about eight months. On top of that, dancers in the same ballet company didn't get married that often. I think Li's friends were also worried because they had seen him through his failed marriage a few years earlier.

I was proud of the way Li handled himself under pressure. When things are difficult he just faces it and gets it done with integrity. His friend Richard stood quickly and proposed a toast, and Ben congratulated us along with everyone else. Li and I were just relieved it was over.

Coralie and Neil George were soon coming to see me perform *La Sylphide*, and I decided that would be the best opportunity to tell them about our engagement. I was very excited to be doing this ballet, especially as this was the first time I would be dancing the main sylph. But first I had to share our news with my parents. I wasn't nervous, but I knew it would be an important conversation.

I met them off the plane and they were terrified to be riding in a car with me at the wheel, giving them the odd fright when I slammed on the brakes, but that's just how I was. *Best to get on with it*, I thought to myself, so I said casually, 'By the way, I'm getting married.'

'Who to?' they asked.

'To Li,' I replied, and that was all I said.

'Li is Mary's Chinese partner in the company. He's a charming young man,' Mum told Neil George.

'Congratulations, beautiful!' he said. 'The Chinese are a marvellous race. I can't wait to meet him.' I caught his big smile in the rear-view mirror.

'Have you decided on a date yet?' Coralie asked.

'No, not yet,' I said.

They didn't ask much more right then – let's face it, I'm sure they were in shock.

They were very tired after their flight, so we had a cup of tea together. 'Our friend Ava Jean is throwing a party tonight for their son Andy's engagement,' I told them, 'and you're invited, if you feel up to it. I have to go back to rehearsal, so Li and I will go to their place straight from work. Our friend Peggy will pick you up and we'll meet you there,' I added, knowing they'd be relieved I wasn't driving.

'That's fine,' said Mum. 'But we might just have a rest this afternoon.' I still only had my mattress on the floor, so they would sleep on it and I would have the sofa.

As Li and I drove to the party, Ava Jean called us on Li's car phone. 'Hello, Mary. Herb and I think it'd be extra special to have a double celebration of your and Andy's engagement tonight. How do you feel about that?' she asked.

'Oh, Ava Jean. You're so generous! But how will Andy and Kathy feel?' I asked.

'We'd all be delighted. We've spoken with Andy and Kathy and they're thrilled for you to celebrate together,' she replied.

What could you say to such generosity and enthusiasm? I looked at Li and he nodded. I said, 'Yes, Ava Jean. We would be so honoured. Thank you!'

I turned to Li. 'Well, I've told Mum and Dad about our engagement, but you'd better ask Dad for my hand in marriage before you get inside the party, because they'll all be congratulating us.'

'What should I say?' asked Li nervously.

'Just tell him that you love me and ask him if he will give you his blessing to marry me.'

We parked outside and waited for Coralie and Neil George beneath a tree in the front yard. As soon as they got out of the car, Li asked, 'Mr McKendry, can I talk to you?'

I walked off with Coralie and we waited at the front door. This was something Li had to do for himself. From where we stood I could see curiosity and then smiles. Then Neil George and Li shook hands, so I knew everything was all right. Li rushed to us, beaming with happiness. He gave Coralie a hug and said, 'Thank you, Coralie!'

'We're very happy for you,' Coralie smiled to us. We went into the party with grins on our faces.

Ava Jean's was a beautiful home with spacious rooms ideal for entertaining, lush green lawns, and a wonderful pool out the back. It was an idyllic lifestyle. Her husband, Herb Mears, was a well-known artist, so the walls were covered in his paintings. They had three grown children and it was their second son, Andy, who was celebrating his engagement that night – along with us.

I introduced Mum and Dad to everyone. Li had so many friends who adored him that it was staggering. When I was touring all the time with London Festival Ballet, it was only really possible for me to form friendships inside the company – but here you could dance, tour and still have a life outside the ballet. My parents were in their element. I never had to think twice about leaving them to chat with people they'd only just met.

Guests wandered through the house, where an abundance of

delicious food was spread across numerous tables. Ava Jean and Herb were gracious hosts. These wonderful people were the epitome of America's old South – well dressed, generous and always looking for what they could do for you. Everyone toasted Andy and his fiancée, Kathy, and then also toasted Li and me. Neither of us had ever felt happier, and as we left at the end of the night I thought that I must be dreaming.

Mum had never been too fussed about my other boyfriends. With each of them she had asked me whether I'd be happy sitting across from him in forty years' time and left it at that. But now I could sense that she and Dad were pleased.

'You've made good decisions about your life so far, and we trust that this is another good one. You're old enough and mature enough to make your own decisions,' Dad said.

'If you're happy, we're happy,' said Mum.

How I loved my parents! I guess I'd always known they would be all right about it. They'd let me lead my own life all these years, and had only ever been supportive.

Neil George was fascinated by China, and Mum would have filled him in on Li's background. In fact, that night Mum did her homework on Li, as I found out the next morning, when she said, 'Mary, Li was married before. This means that you won't be able to have a Catholic wedding.' I could clearly see the disappointment in her eyes. I knew this was very important to her, but I hadn't thought about it. Both Li and I only ever thought about dancing and each other.

Although I was brought up in a country town, my parents were quite educated. Even though they had never been to China – in fact, few people had been to China in the 1980s – they weren't worried about Li or the fact he was Chinese. Marrying in the Catholic Church was the most important thing to Coralie because she believed that marriage was sacred and the commitment was for life. That was how I'd been brought up. If you weren't married in a church, it wasn't considered a marriage.

This was the one thing I wanted to do for my mother. I didn't really care if we got married in a church or not, but it was the only thing that mattered to her. For this to happen, Li would have to have his marriage to Elizabeth annulled.

~

One lunchbreak, I told Li, 'You know how Mum's disappointed that we can't get married in the Catholic Church? This upsets me. It's the last thing I want to do – to make my parents sad, especially for our wedding. This is something I want to do for my mother. She has never asked for anything, only given.'

'I know, darling,' Li assured me. 'I will do everything that you ask, you know that.'

God, I loved this man. He'd never been part of a religion or inside a church as a parishioner. I had absolutely no idea what, if anything, he could do about this. Mum was doubtful that anything could be done, but I had faith in Li. He always had a friend with a solution, and he was never frightened to ask. 'I'm going to talk to Mike. He's Catholic,' he said. Mike Stude and his wife, Anita, were big donors to Houston Ballet and Li knew them quite well.

My parents stayed on in Houston for another couple of weeks and caught me up on family news. My brothers Ger and Mick had both been married the year before. I was always disappointed that I couldn't go home for these special events, but that's what you give up for a theatrical life. You couldn't just miss a show and be away, even for a week.

Dad loved Americans and was fascinated by the country. He and Mum saw that now, thanks to Li's huge circle of friends and acquaintances, we had a very full life. This time when they were due to go home to Australia, I sensed they were more comfortable leaving me behind. 'It will be an interesting life for you here, Mary,' Mum said. Dad knew that the fast-paced American lifestyle would suit me just fine.

All the while, Li was working on his marriage annulment. Mike had spoken to Father Francis Monaghan, the highest-ranking Catholic priest in the city. A meeting was set up and we knew that Father Monaghan would ask some hard questions of Li. I had tried to give him a quick overview of Christianity and the Catholic religion, but it sounded ridiculous when I tried to describe it!

'Jesus was born to the Virgin Mary,' I told him.

'What?' asked Li in surprise.

'And no heaven for you if you're not baptised. Babies who die before baptism end up in Limbo.'

'What's that?' Li asked, wide-eyed with suspicion.

I threw my hands up and said, 'That's it! I can't explain any further. I'm sorry!' I realised Catholicism was a lived experience that becomes entrenched in who you are. It was all based on a faith that I didn't question. 'Li, my beliefs and values, and my relationship with my big family, were all influenced by my Catholic faith. But you'll have to ask Father Monaghan about the rest.'

Father Monaghan was a plump, jovial man, very approachable and wise. Li told me how Father Monaghan asked him whether he believed in God, and Li had to think about it for a bit but came to the conclusion he'd often asked for help from a God – during hard times, when he was locked up in the Chinese consulate fearing for his life, and when he was struggling with his separation from his family and fearing for their lives. He'd sometimes felt the force of a higher power in his life.

'Yes, I do,' he told Father Monaghan, 'but in China I never allowed have religion.'

Then came the hardest question: 'Are you willing to become a Catholic so you can marry Mary in the Catholic faith?'

'Yes,' Li said emphatically.

So Li started to read the Bible and his five catechism lessons. I think he actually enjoyed them. Father Monaghan was very patient with his many questions, such as, 'Why Jesus born to a virgin? How you sure Mary was virgin?'

After many more questions, on just the third lesson, Father Monaghan declared, 'Li, I think you're ready to be baptised.'

The baptism was held at a simple little Catholic chapel on the campus of the University of St Thomas. Mike was Li's godfather and Anita the witness. Mike had to promise to guide Li in his faith. It was a sweet ceremony and Li was serious. He said later it was very emotional for him. It was for me too, to see him doing this big thing for me.

I'm not sure what Father Monaghan proposed to the Vatican regarding an annulment of Li's first marriage, but somehow, just a few months later, it was annulled by Rome! I called Mum immediately.

'Oh, darling, this is most unbelievable,' she said. 'I never thought it would be allowed. Those friends of Li's are just amazing!' I could hear the elation in her voice.

～

The date for our wedding was set for 24 October 1987, which was during the ballet's lay-off period. We asked Father Monaghan to marry us, and then made another big decision – to buy a new house. While Li was proud of his first house, with the eye of an architect's daughter I felt it lacked character. Furthermore, we felt it would be a good idea to invest in something bigger.

We found a house near Downtown Houston in a neighbourhood called Woodland Heights, which was the only area Li and I could afford close to the studio. It was an old timber Victorian house with character, a bit like a Queenslander, and that appealed to me. The wraparound cast-iron verandah caught my attention. It was a two-bedroom bungalow in Euclid Street, quite run down, and it smelt mouldy, but with its 4-metre ceilings and huge rooms, the house had 'good bones', as my father would say. Li pulled up a piece of the ugly green carpet and we saw a beautiful old oak floor underneath. 'Mary, it won't take much for us fix house,' he said confidently.

We decided to have a small wedding right there in the front yard, and every free hour for the next three months we worked on the house. The paint was peeling off everywhere inside and out. There were hurricane shutters on the windows, plus security bars. Although a couple of windows were very old and would need replacing, there were mosquito screens throughout, which delighted Li, who loathed flies and mozzies. The big bay window in the living room was lovely, and looked out onto the front yard. There was also a two-car garage with a two-room storage shed attached out the back. The backyard had three beautiful, big and shady pecan trees. We knew that after some freshening up, this little house would become a happy home for us.

We didn't have the money for a new kitchen or bathroom, but Li was almost as excited to buy paintbrushes and other bits and pieces. With help from some workers, he sanded and varnished the floors and painted the verandah railing. We pulled down the filthy lace curtains, but after a wash they were nice and we hung them up again. With some convincing, Li agreed to tear down the hurricane shutters and suddenly the house was bright and welcoming. We moved in his furniture and my sofa, table and chairs. We were so excited! Finally, with the heating and cooling installed, we had a beautiful home ready for our wedding.

Houston Ballet opened its 1987–88 season in September in a stunning new theatre, the Wortham Theatre Center. It was a huge building with large, spacious studios. Culturally, this new arts complex was a real milestone for Houston. Houston Ballet and Houston Grand Opera had been instrumental in the fundraising effort, and it was incredible that the theatre had been built during one of the worst-ever oil price slumps. It was only five minutes from our new home in Woodland Heights, so we could dash home before a show if we needed to. As principal I had my own dressing room with private toilet and shower, hanging closet, mirror and dressing table, located right near the stage. But I missed sharing a room and the excitement

generated as dancers prepared for shows or enjoyed post-show celebrations together.

We didn't have much money left for our wedding, but a big
wedding wasn't my style anyway. I hated the ostentation of the few
venues I looked over – huge, blank conference rooms with no atmosphere. I went shopping a few times searching for a dress, but I thought
the pouffy dresses and long veils that were popular at that time were
awful. Despite wearing tutus and wondrous costumes on stage, my
everyday tastes were much simpler.

In one store, the assistants finally got me to try on a dress. It looked
enormous, with leg-of-mutton sleeves and a bell skirt. 'See how tiny it
makes your waist look!' they exclaimed.

But then I looked in the mirror. 'I look like a crocheted toilet-
roll cover,' I told them. They smiled at me blankly, with no idea what
I was talking about! *It must be an Australian thing*, I thought.

'No, it's no good. It's hideous,' I said, and couldn't wait to rip it off.

I rang Coralie. My mum with her fabulous taste would help me
out. Unbeknown to me, she had already solved it. Within the week
I was the owner of a divine size 6, embroidered cream silk dress by the
Australian designer Prue Acton. It had a mandarin collar (a lovely nod
to the Chinese connection), a cinched waist, and a narrow skirt that
came halfway down my calves. I tried it on and looked at myself in
the bedroom mirror. *Hmm . . . not bad*, I thought. It was the perfect
fit. All I had to do was buy a pair of shoes to go with it, a bouquet and
something for my hair.

We were to have fifty of our closest friends and family at the
wedding. The reception would be held on our front lawn. Mum
was horrified that we hadn't hired a marquee in case of bad weather,
and promptly got on to it. Thank goodness she'd arrived the week
before the wedding to help us get organised. I hired a woman to do
the catering and make the cake. Li bought the champagne, wine, beer
and soft drinks, which we would serve on ice from an antique bathtub
Coralie found in the backyard.

Word about the wedding leaked, and television stations wanted to broadcast our special day. Although that meant it would be paid for, I immediately responded, 'Absolutely not.' Li agreed. So much of our life was about performing in the public eye. We wanted our wedding to be intimate and private.

The big day was fast approaching. Brig and Matt flew from Australia together. Jo was now in New York working as a contemporary dancer, and flew in later. Dad sent his love – his fear of flying and failing health meant he couldn't make the trip this time. Matt would walk me down the aisle. My best friend, Jackie Barrett, arrived from London a week before and joined in all the parties and festivities. She would be my bridesmaid. Nella and Jack Gillogley, two of my parents' best friends in Rocky, came over for the wedding as well.

My family liked the house. We sat in the bay window seat and laughed and laughed while flowers just kept coming through the door, filling the house. Gifts were delivered too – Li had many generous friends. Together with Mum and the girls, we took great delight in opening them. They included expensive dinnerware and glassware, crystal champagne glasses, jugs and a silver tea set – even an antique American side table. Ben bought us four beautiful white wicker chairs for the porch. Neither of us had ever owned anything like this before. And still the flowers and gifts kept coming.

There were suddenly seven of us staying in the house. Brig and Jo shared a bed, and we got a single bed and mattresses for the others to sleep on the floor. What an ad hoc wedding. I was no bridezilla, that's for sure. I wasn't concerned about the details, except the person I would be marrying. It was just the happiest time – wonderful chaos!

Li and I discussed how we needed to somehow include the friends who couldn't come to the wedding, and decided to have a pre-wedding party for them at our favourite Chinese restaurant Dong Ting in downtown Houston. Mum and Dad generously paid for the party. We booked out the entire restaurant for around 100 guests. It was truly fabulous – friends, family, colleagues all sharing in our special night. Li looked divine in his traditional dark-navy Mandarin gown, while I wore a black velvet dress that he had bought for me. Mum looked as gracious and elegant as ever. The food was delicious and the champagne flowed. Many people made speeches, and I did get teary when Matt read out a speech Dad had written. There was so much love and pride in his words. That was the sad part of the evening for me – my wonderful father was missing, and Li's Niang and Dia weren't there either. We weren't quite complete.

We had a wedding rehearsal in the chapel, the same little chapel where Li had been baptised. He and I thought the idea of a rehearsal was absolutely hilarious. All I had to do was walk down a very short aisle – no pointe shoes, no dance steps, no partner, no lighting, no conductor with orchestra. It was the easiest thing I'd ever had to do. A rehearsal just to do that?!

Apparently Li had to have a bucks party a couple of nights before the wedding. Of course he had absolutely no idea about these Western wedding traditions, but he went along with it nevertheless. The group was a mixture of old friends like Charles Foster, Li's best man. Charles was the immigration lawyer who'd prevented the Chinese Consulate officials from taking Li back to China against his will all those years before. Then there was John Grensback, his close friend from the company, and some other friends and dancers. Mum was nervous about what might happen. My brother Matt went with Li, and I'm sure was equipped with instructions from Coralie to get him home safely. I heard the next day that the party started at an Irish pub where Li and his dancer friends often played darts on the weekends, and then moved to a black-tie party being held in honour of Hollywood star Isabella Rossellini, hosted by a friend of Li's. They then headed to a club for more drinking and fun until well into the early hours. Matt drove Li home but unfortunately forgot that he needed to drive on the other side of the road in America. Li has never forgotten that journey, drunk as he was at the time.

The day before the wedding, while Li was still in bed recovering from his hangover, Mum asked me, 'Have you organised your licence?'

I said, 'What licence?'

I had no idea. I hoped Li had already done it, but when I woke him and asked the question, he looked as puzzled as I was.

Coralie was very upset with us. 'You are both so hopeless!'

I could see she was livid and this was the first time Li had seen sweet Coralie so cross. We had to rush to City Hall and appear before a county clerk to take an oath to prove that we really were who we said we were. It was a bit scary actually, doing it at the last minute.

That night, Li and I parted. He was to stay with Charles that night. 'See you tomorrow, darling,' he whispered in my ear as we kissed goodnight.

We were all up early on the big day, Mum organising breakfast for those who wanted it. The ceremony was at 11 a.m. and everyone was queuing up for the shower. The girls were putting on their outfits and Matt was polishing his shoes. People were starting to feel flustered, but as always my calm mother held it all together. Jackie did my make-up and found a cream ribbon and some flowers for my hair. She just made it all up on the spot and I was so impressed at how she managed to tame my wild hair and make me look presentable. And then I put on my beautiful Prue Acton frock and simple court shoes and it was time to go.

Mum and the girls took their seats in the chapel while Matt and I drove around the block one more time. As I entered I saw Li waiting at the altar, and I caught my breath. It was really happening. We were about to be married. He looked so handsome standing there. The re-tailored beige suit from his godfather, Mike Stude, set him off to perfection.

The chapel was very simple – white walls, and only ten or so pews lining the short aisle. I held on to Matt's arm tightly as the music sounded, and off we went. There was my mother, my sisters and Jackie, Ben, Charles and other ballet friends, Anita and Mike, Ava Jean and Herb, and even Chinese Consul Ding Wei and his wife accepted our invitation.

It was not a full nuptial Mass, but our vows were traditional and heartfelt. It was a moving, simple ceremony – exactly what we wanted. We both knew that each of us took our vows seriously. Li didn't have his family with him. Now he would become part of my family. He already felt accepted and I knew he would be one of us. We all gathered on the grass for a group photo.

Afterwards we went back to our house on Euclid Street. Li carried me over the threshold and our family and friends showered us in confetti. It was such a happy afternoon, the reception in our front yard nicely catered. Tables and chairs were set up under the marquee, with a small vase of white flowers in the centre of each table. Brig and Jo had cleverly put these together from the many bouquets delivered that morning. It was quite modest, and I was proud that I hadn't needed to ask my parents for money. The speeches were spontaneous and heartfelt. Ben and Charles spoke beautifully about Li, and Nella talked about the McKendry family. Li told the guests how much he wished his family could be there. When it was my turn, I said, 'I wish my father Neil George was with us. I know he would be proud.'

At around 5 p.m. we had waved off the last of our guests. We said goodbye to my family, who were staying at our house, and drove ourselves to Warwick Hotel, one of Houston's finest, overlooking Hermann Park. We were so tired that we didn't even feel like dinner. So we had a quiet first evening together as husband and wife, reflecting on the day. It had been perfect.

The next day, my family and a few close friends met us there for brunch, which was a highlight of the celebrations. Everyone was relaxed and now we had time to laugh and digest the week of parties that had just seemed to happen spontaneously, thanks to the generosity of our friends. We'd had no idea what was normal for weddings in Houston, or much about weddings at all – except on stage. What a whirlwind it had been.

Now it was time to start our married life. We had a week off and went to Acapulco, Mexico, for our honeymoon, staying in a four-star hotel. Li drove me around in a small pink Jeep called 'the Mosquito', up and down the hills with the wind in our hair. We had no rehearsals or schedules to keep, just pleased ourselves. We chartered a boat around the coast, swam and lazed in the sun, bought food and headed off to a secluded beach for the day. We swam and swam together, knowing it was a great way to keep in shape because soon enough we'd be back on stage. Mexico was wonderful, and it was only a three-hour flight from Houston. Li booked a celebration dinner in a fabulous restaurant overlooking Acapulco. When the sun went down, the lights on the coast made it look like the stars in the sky continued right down to the earth. We toasted our new life together with champagne and watched the moonlight glint on the ocean.

~

When we got home, there were some exciting things happening. Celebrated choreographer Ronnie Hynd had returned to create a brand-new ballet, *The Hunchback of Notre Dame*. I was to be Esmeralda and Li would play Quasimodo, the hunchback. We both thought how strange it was for Li to be the ugly one instead of the handsome hero. He was in a huge red wig and ugly make-up, with a big bump on his back, and he had to move very clumsily with a limp. He had to maintain this character for hours. There was more acting than dancing for Li in this role, but I had a lot of dancing. The role of Esmeralda was a wonderful experience for me to show my emotional range and acting abilities.

Ronnie was followed all through the next year by other guest choreographers in what was an exciting time for Houston Ballet. Christopher Bruce, the highly lauded British choreographer, came and staged his chilling *Ghost Dances*, and Glen Tetley staged *Le Sacre du Printemps* (*The Rite of Spring*) by Stravinsky, a contemporary ballet in which Li and I danced lead roles.

Romeo and Juliet was next. I had waited all my life to dance the role of Juliet! It was the ballet I'd grown up with – with Rudolf. Every ballerina wants to dance Juliet. The music is so stirring. Ben was creating a new production – including costumes and sets – so it felt even more special. Many times I'd watched from the wings, Rudolf and Patricia as Romeo and Juliet, never assuming I'd be Juliet myself one day. Ken was my Romeo; I was very comfortable with him by now. My time to dance Juliet had come. It was a shame that Li and I weren't cast as the star-crossed lovers, but I did get to do the *pas de deux* later with him at a gala in South Carolina, which felt so natural that it didn't feel like dancing at all.

~

Li continuously talked about his family and I knew his separation from them broke his heart. A few months after we were married we decided to do something about it. I encouraged Li to organise a meeting with Consul Tang at the Chinese consulate in Houston. He was new and we had met him and his wife at one of our performances.

Li was nervous and quiet when we arrived, but I saw it as an opportunity to make things happen. We had heard that China had opened up considerably under their paramount leader Deng Xiaoping's Open Door Policy. 'Don't worry. It'll be fine,' I said, but I knew Li was remembering that this was the same place where he had nearly lost his life when he defected in 1981.

After providing identification, we were led into a small reception room and given Chinese tea. I felt Li stiffen. Unknown to Cultural Consul Mr Tang, who soon joined us, this was the very room where Li and his ex-wife, Elizabeth, had been detained.

Mr Tang and Li spoke in Chinese and I didn't understand what was being said. Things seemed to be dragging on. So when Mr Tang turned to me, I quickly said, 'Mr Tang, it would make Li so happy to be able to visit his family. Do you think it's possible for him to go back to China to visit his parents?'

Li grabbed my hand. The look on his face was saying, 'Don't, please don't.' I guess it wasn't the Chinese way to deal with things head-on, but that was my way. I thought, *What's the beating around the bush for? He's been waiting nine years. They can only say no.*

I continued to hold Li's hand tightly, but I saw his face change. Something positive was happening. Mr Tang's response surprised him: 'Mary, China has opened up. I can't promise you anything, but I'll look into it.'

A couple of months later, Consul Tang called Li and informed him that we had been given permission by the Chinese government to visit Li's family in China. We were overjoyed, and I could almost see that dark cloud lifting from Li's shoulders. Soon, we received the visas and booked our flights for the June summer break.

I was thrilled to be returning to China, this time to see Li's parents and meet the rest of his family. The language barrier didn't really bother me. As I always did when I travelled, I started reading about China and books by Chinese authors, including Nien Cheng's *Life and Death in Shanghai*, and *The Good Earth* by Pearl Buck, which Li bought me. I went on to read lots more, especially anything about the Cultural Revolution, which was so important to Li and his family's life. But I didn't really know what I was in for in China until I saw it firsthand. Then the questions started and didn't stop.

Before we left home, Li tried to teach me the names of all his brothers. I learned them from one to seven, oldest to youngest, and Li was the sixth of the seven boys. He showed me a photo of them when they were children. I particularly remembered his oldest brother, Cuncia, who was really handsome. As the firstborn, he had a lot of responsibility and was almost like a second father to his younger brothers.

'Second Brother, Cunyuan, is different and cheeky!' Li told me. Cunyuan had an arranged marriage, like his parents. Third Brother,

Cunmao, had been given away to his fourth uncle and aunt who couldn't have children. This horrified me, but Li explained that having a male child was very important for survival – you needed a son to look after you in your old age and to continue the family bloodline, and it also meant one less mouth to feed in Li's family and a better life for Cunmao. Later, having seen how little the families had, all this made more sense to me. Fourth Brother, Cunsang, was a former naval soldier, now turned farmer. Fifth Brother, Cunfar, worked for a transport company. Li's youngest brother, Cungui, was known as Jing Tring, which means 'coming the group', because Li's mother couldn't think of a name with lucky meaning for him initially and thought that seven sons certainly made a group. I learned to say hello, goodbye and thank you, and to count from one to ten in Li's hometown dialect, which is similar to Mandarin.

Li tried to prepare me, saying, 'My family live in a commune. It's very poor. There's no running water, and the electricity cuts out all the time. There's no phone at the house. The whole village shares one phone and any calls are announced over the loudspeaker.'

But nothing would prepare me for the poverty – and yet the conditions were now much better than they had been when Li was growing up.

In the weeks before we flew out, Li went on a buying spree. 'Gift-giving is a tradition in China,' he told me. *But how on earth are we going to fit all this stuff?* I thought.

Li bought presents for everyone we were going to meet, as well as spares for someone he mightn't have thought of, so he bought lollies, cigarettes, lipstick, make-up, perfume and children's toys. We had as many suitcases as we were allowed, packed full. On top of that, Li bought not one but two refrigerators for his family, as they couldn't buy whitegoods in China then.

Finally, we flew to Beijing and Li's blood brother, 'the Bandit', his wife, Marji, and his violinist friend, Fengtian, and his wife, Jiping, were waiting for us. They never left our side from the moment we landed. I had been so looking forward to meeting the Bandit. Li had been telling me stories about him since we first met. He and Li had met at the Beijing Dance Academy. Li had told me they had a rare and special friendship that developed during the hard times separated from their families. At the academy, they supported each other and their friendship helped them survive those tough years there – they were like true brothers. The Bandit was China's junior martial arts champion before he joined the Beijing Dance Academy and was now a soloist at the Central Ballet of China. He was incredibly resourceful and just seemed able to conjure up whatever was needed – stuff like extra food that couldn't be found in the shops or medicine for Li when he was sick.

The Bandit was over six feet tall, strongly built and handsome. He had a more angular, chiselled face than Li and Li's other Chinese friends. He and Li hugged each other hard, with tears in their eyes. Li introduced me to the Bandit and Fengtian, and then introduced us to their wives. The Bandit gave me a passionate hug, which took me by surprise as Li had told me that the Chinese are rather reserved and they don't do hugs. Marji whispered, '*Xiao xin dian, ye su ren jia bo si huan yin bo na.*' The Bandit laughed sheepishly and looked embarrassed. I asked Li what Marji said. Before Li could answer me, Marji told me in English, 'Mary, I told him that he needs to be careful, you may not like hugs.'

'Tell him, I do like hugs,' I said to Marji.

After Marji translated, the Bandit nudged her gently and said, '*Ni kan, ni kan.*' You see, you see.

I liked him from the beginning. He never spoke a word of English but we got on fantastically.

The Bandit and Fentian grabbed the suitcases, and off we went in a van. All the way from the airport to our hotel, they seemed to speak at 100 miles an hour. I looked out the window. There were people on bicycles everywhere, many carrying huge loads on their backs, sometimes even whole families on one bike. There didn't appear to be any road rules. Cars would swerve into other lanes and back again. It was terrifying – but Li wasn't taking any notice.

'Mary, the Bandit says Chinese secret police already know we're coming. They are waiting for us at hotel.'

I could see his face had tightened with worry, but within minutes the Bandit was making him smile. The Bandit had booked us into one of the best hotels in Beijing at the time, called Front Gate Hotel. By Western standards it was more like a three-star hotel. It was named for the first gate of many that people had to pass through before they could get close to the Forbidden City and the emperor. This hotel was famous for its food.

But the tension returned soon after we checked in to our room and three Chinese officials knocked on the door. One of the men was three times Li's size.

Li said they wanted me to leave the room. 'Absolutely not,' I said. 'Tell them I don't understand Chinese anyway and there's no way I'm going to leave my husband.' As if I would leave Li alone with the Chinese secret police!

They were surprised by my firm reply – I don't think there would have been many occasions when their orders were disobeyed. I could see Li was apprehensive, but I knew they wouldn't force me to leave. Not a Westerner. And they eventually relented.

They stayed for over three hours and asked Li many questions in Chinese. The room was full of smoke as two of the secret police kept smoking one cigarette after another. I just sat beside Li on the sofa. He told me later they had asked all sorts of questions about his defection to the USA. He was exhausted and relieved when they finally left with the parting message: 'We will be watching you while you're in China – for your safety.' Of course, we knew exactly what they really meant. We were just happy to get on with our visit.

Li's friends returned with drinks and snacks. They tried to catch up on all the years apart. It had been nearly ten years since Li had last seen them. To me, the rapid Chinese language sounded quite harsh, like they were arguing. I'd occasionally ask, 'Are you fighting?'

'No! No! It's all fine,' Li would laugh. When he translated what I'd said, his friends laughed too.

Li had to get used to riding a bike again with millions of people fighting for an inch of space on the road. It was a zoo – just mayhem! There were four lanes of bicycles, not even in actual lanes. I rode on the back of the Bandit's bicycle. I didn't mind, as he was very capable. We started on our adventure. The most important thing was that Li was finally back in his country as a free man after a decade of not being able to return. In fact, he was no longer a citizen of his country, but a foreigner on home soil.

Li and the Bandit took me to his old academy. We met some of his teachers, including his ballet teacher, Teacher Xiao, who had been such an important influence on Li. They asked Li to demonstrate and share his knowledge. As he warmed up I could see how nervous he was. He had danced many performances in front of dignitaries, even royalty, and won medals in international competitions, but I could tell that this small audience meant very much to him. It was almost like doing an important exam in front of his teachers.

Li first danced the Prince solo from Act Three of *Swan Lake*, and then, upon request from one of his teachers, he danced two contemporary solos, one from Bruce's *Ghost Dances* and the other from Tetley's *Le Sacre du Printemps*. I could see that Li's teachers were thoroughly impressed with the versatility and standard of the dancer he had become, especially Teacher Xiao, whose eyes became moist as he watched.

Teacher Xiao was now a professor at the Beijing Dance Academy, in charge of the choreography department and widely considered one of the best teachers in China. He was a small man, full of life – funny and smart. I thought how lucky Li had been to have him in his early life, a brilliant teacher who had inspired his passion for ballet. As more requests and endless questions poured in, he intervened. 'All right, all right, let's not kill Cunxin off.' He then invited us to his home for lunch. He had a nice apartment compared to the Bandit's one room. His charming second wife, who was a model, cooked us a delicious meal. I could clearly see just how proud Teacher Xiao was with all of Li's career success, and he told Li that after his defection, he could only dream of ever seeing him again – let alone seeing him dance – and that he was so proud of having been his teacher. Li told Teacher Xiao how grateful he was for the inspiration he had given him, and that he would never have had such a successful career without his love and care. Both of them were very emotional.

After the lunch, we visited the Bandit's small room at the Beijing Dance Academy, and met up with Fengtian. The Bandit was still living in the old dormitories where he and Li had slept, so they showed me Li's old room. Just as Li had told me, the room was tiny. I couldn't picture eight students crammed into such a small space to sleep. Not in a million years could I imagine that this was where Li had grown up and spent his formative years in such primitive conditions.

Everyone who lived in the building had to cook in the dormitory hallway on small gas cooktops, so it smelt strongly of food. It was dark and smoky. There was a bathroom down the hallway, and the smell from it was so foul that I just turned around and decided to hold on. Li had warned me about the challenging conditions, but even with my very low expectations I was shocked by the living standards. Li explained that it was vastly improved since he had lived there, and that not many people in China today could enjoy even this standard of living.

The Bandit then took us to a Peking duck restaurant. It had five floors, with large rooms and round tables, traditional wood carvings of dragons and phoenixes, and lanterns hanging from the ceiling. True to its name, it seemed every dish was duck – roast duck, duck liver, duck tongue, duck feet and duck soup, plus condiments of plum sauce, spring onions and cucumber, and pancakes to wrap. So delicious! I'd never had Peking duck before, and later craved that particular Peking duck each time I was pregnant.

People we were with were happy, and there was lots of drinking. I found out about a custom called *gan bei*, the Chinese version of 'Cheers' or 'Bottoms up', where you have to scull a whole glass of alcohol – it is considered rude if you don't. Luckily I was let off the hook most times because I was a Westerner, but poor Li had to *gan bei* all the time! All the talk was about planning the next party, the next meal, and all the people they were going to meet. Parties always included a dinner, and restaurants didn't always provide alcohol, so it had to be taken with you. There were very strong Chinese spirits, beer and one main wine called the Great Wall, which was pretty dreadful.

I was learning how many good friends Li had, and how marvellous he was at expressing his gratitude to them. He spent as much time as he could entertaining them.

Li wanted to thank all his teachers and friends, so on our last night in Beijing he hosted a dinner for over forty people in the famous Front Gate restaurant. The Bandit had helped Li organise it, contacting fellow classmates, academy officials and teachers. Li sat beside me at dinner, happily translating when he could – it must have been exhausting! The head of the academy spoke and said how proud everyone was of Li and all he'd achieved. We were congratulated again and again on our marriage. The food just kept coming, along with fancy Chinese wine that was a treat for them all. Others made small toasts and of course we had to do a lot of *gan bei*. Many *gan beis* later, everyone became cheery and I could hear the laughter grow louder and louder.

Finally, Li thanked his teachers and academy officials, then raised his glass to his friends. He told them how important they had been during his time at the academy. He said being with them now was a dream come true: 'Over those seven years you taught me and cared for me and befriended me. You have given me things I can never repay. I don't know where I would be today without you.'

This dinner was a really important thing for Li to do, to thank and recognise all these people who had been so instrumental in his life. It was a special moment in time for everyone in the room – a bittersweet reunion.

When the bill arrived, we couldn't believe it – it was something like a couple of hundred dollars to feed more than forty people for the whole night! Everyone walked away happy, if rather wobbly.

~

Being with Li in his own country was so different to our life together in Houston. With every passing day that I spent with him, he revealed the generous type of person he is. Not once did he hesitate to translate so that I could be involved in the conversations. Soon, I would discover where he got his generosity from.

Before long it was time to say goodbye to Li's Beijing friends. We boarded the plane for Qingdao, his hometown, and Li could hardly breathe the entire flight, especially when we were landing. I held his hand and we walked out. 'There they are, Mary!' he said, and I saw a group of people waving madly – all of Li's brothers except his fourth brother, their wives and children. (Li's fouth brother, Cunsang, had to stay home to prepare the welcome feast.) They were not allowed inside the airport and I will never forget the row of faces pressed to the glass wall and the children jumping up and down with excitement. Two stern soldiers with guns were guarding the doors as we walked through.

'Cunxin! Cunxin! *Jing Hao. Jing Hao!*' the family called out. Then Li was surrounded by bodies, all talking at the same time. He had tears in his eyes as he greeted his brothers and was introduced to his sisters-in-law and children he had never met. He introduced me and then I was greeted by each of them, one by one. I had attracted a lot of attention in the airport and people were standing staring both at the reunion and at me. It was still not common to see foreigners in

Qingdao, particularly young blue-eyed women. Several people asked Li's brothers who I was, and they proudly told them that I was their sister-in-law.

The brothers took us to two trucks they had borrowed and we drove to the village. The traffic again was insane. I was sitting in the front seat of one truck and Li was in the other, both with no seatbelts. There was a lot of happy chatter coming from the wives and children in the open bed of the truck. It was another perilous journey in the traffic, with a lot of old bikes and tractors, and very few cars. No one seemed to be worried except me. It was a pretty stark environment, with old buildings. There were lots of communes – little clusters of low, tile-roofed brick buildings with mazes of alleyways between them. These villages were punctuated by fields and I could see men and women working in them, some wearing traditional conical bamboo hats. We passed the occasional group of shops, with market stalls where women were stirring large woks of food and people were milling around shopping. I gazed out of the window, fascinated.

We slowed in one village and had to walk the rest of the way as the trucks were too big to squeeze through the narrow road into Li's village. I noticed that there were deep concrete gutters down the edges of the dirt laneways – open sewers. You wouldn't want to trip and fall into the mess of rotten eggs, garbage, leftover noodles and human waste. The smell wasn't pleasant.

Finally, we arrived at the last row of houses. 'This is it!' Li said excitedly. 'We're home!'

I jumped as firecrackers started going off and children came running out of houses everywhere. Faces with big smiles were peering out of the doorways and windows. The whole village knew that Li was coming home and they were keen to catch a glimpse of him. We turned down a laneway and I saw Niang and Dia standing by a gate. His mother went straight to Li and threw her arms around him. Li's eyes filled with tears once again. He took both his father's hands, then the hands of his fourth brother and his fourth uncle. A tall, grey-haired lady pushed through and shouted loudly, '*Shi Jing Hao ma? Zen shi Jing Hao ma?*' She gave Li a big hug, and he told me, through tears, 'Mary, this is my fourth auntie. She asked me whether it was really me. She was the one who saved my arm when I was little and it got badly burnt and infected.'

We stepped through the door into a shady little courtyard. A ceramic teapot was on the table and we all sat and had tea. Niang then showed me the rest of her home. The Li family house consisted of four small rooms. You walked through a doorway covered by long ribbons of plastic to stop the flies and mozzies, into a space that had a pantry cupboard and a small table with short legs pushed up against the wall. A large wok was built into a countertop. Doors on either side of the room led into bedrooms. Each bedroom was only just the size of a double bed. The beds, made of mud bricks, were all built against the walls. The floors were cement – an improvement since Li's time, he told me.

Our bedroom was tiny – standing room only. Two walls were decorated with floral paper, another with red and gold cigarette packets. There was no such thing as plaster, paint or even cladding. The bed was hard but covered with colourful soft quilts. The pillows were filled with straw. It was summer so it was very hot, even with a window. Li told me his family felt very lucky to have glass panes in the windows and that with the little bit of electricity available we could use fans at night, provided the electricity was on. It was pretty intermittent.

My head was beginning to spin with all the emotion and Chinese language swirling around. Also, I was beginning to wonder where I would be able to have a shower. 'Third Brother has a detached house known as the "army general"-style house, where they have a shower and a toilet,' said Li. I later discovered the shower was really just a hose attached to the wall.

There was a little shed outside for cooking in the summer, which gave the family more space in the house, and then further outside was the toilet. The toilet was the dreaded hole in the ground. It was just a hole, with two concrete patches either side for your feet. You had to squat right down to the ground, very close to the hole. As the waste stayed in the hole, you can imagine the stink over many years, and God knows what kind of creepy-crawlies were living in there. I said, 'I can't go there, Li. I just can't. I'm thinking that a creature is going to come out and grab me. I'm not used to relaxing in a squat.'

Li just laughed. After all, I was a ballerina completely used to Western amenities and comforts. I was so bloody precious, so used to an ordered, scheduled life, going from home to studio to stage in my pink tights and pink ballet shoes. What an experience this was for me! Needless to say, I had all kinds of problems with my bowels during my time in China.

Late in the afternoon, Dia said, 'Li, everyone is calling for you on their way home from work. You must go and say hello.' So out we went. There were children everywhere and they sang and danced together, and I clapped for them, laughing.

'They are much nicer, sweeter tunes than the revolutionary songs I learned when I was growing up,' Li said.

Villagers popped in to see Li and to check out his Western wife with the big nose, blue eyes and curly brown hair. They told me I was the first Westerner to visit their village since 1949. There were many questions for Li to answer. I got busy with the gifts for the children. I loved having so many of them around. They were easy to communicate with using gestures and lollies, and were a joy to watch. But the biggest hit with everyone was Li's Polaroid instant camera. They couldn't believe that it could spew out images instantly. Every villager wanted a Polaroid photo of themselves. The American ciggies were very popular, as many people in China smoked. Li had been panicked about running out of gifts, so they were ideal, perfect for anyone.

Niang, Li's fourth brother, Cunsang, and the sisters-in-law were busy making dumplings, a traditional welcome-home meal. They were sharing all the jobs – chopping, filling and folding – which was amazing to watch, and such a skill. I got to know all the brothers and their wives and the children.

Inside was like a hot oven, so dinner was served outside. Two small tables were brought into the courtyard and we squatted around them on little stools that had magically appeared from under one of the cupboards. I was asked to sit with the men, and all the women and children sat at another table. I felt quite uncomfortable sitting at the main table. 'Mary, Niang said you need my translation,' Li told me.

On the second day, the local police arrived at Li's family home and took away our passports, which I thought was criminal. You could only buy one-way domestic airline tickets at the time, so we had no return plane tickets out of Qingdao, which frightened me even more.

'Why are they taking our passports? They can't take our passports!' I said to Li, in alarm.

'Yes, they can,' Li said. 'But don't worry, Mary. They'll return them.'

'Well, how can you be so sure?' I was thinking, 'What if we get stuck here?'

'Relax, darling,' Li said. 'All will be fine. There's nothing we can do. It's China. Just think of it as being the same as handing over your passport at a foreign hotel. It just takes longer to get them back here. Don't worry.'

But I wondered if he really knew what would happen.

I wanted to enjoy the family reunion. I always tried to help cleaning up. The family liked this, and laughed and said I was like a true peasant. Li's third brother, Cunmao, joined us for dinner although he was still with his adoptive family. It wasn't until years later when Li's fourth uncle and auntie – Cunmao's adoptive parents – passed away that Cunmao was able to welcome his biological parents as his own parents again. Cunmao had quite a serious personality compared to fourth brother, Cunsang, the farmer. They all knew their places. Respect was given from the younger ones to their elders.

Li's eldest brother, Cuncia, was my favourite. He was the quietest of them all, but had such presence. He had a beautiful, moon-shaped face and was very handsome.

I learned that Li's great-grandfather on his mother's side had been an acrobat with a travelling circus. I also noticed a strong physique in Li's second uncle, also on his mother's side. He would bounce up seven flights of stairs to his city apartment like a young man, even though he was in his late fifties. I could see a physicality through the family, the strength from his father's side and agility from his mother's side. Second uncle also had a lovely vivacious personality.

We visited Li's maternal grandparents, and fourth uncle who had adopted third brother. Incredibly, fourth aunty had tiny, crumpled feet. They had been traditionally bound for many years. She now mostly wore soft slippers but I could still see her poor tortured feet.

As our visit progressed our luggage got lighter by the minute, as we distributed our gifts – ties, suits (bought second-hand from thrift shops in Houston) and the best Chinese liquor, Maotai. I realised cash was the best gift. We had brought as much cash as we could afford to, and gave it all away.

The brothers played a popular card game with four packs of cards. They were very serious. The loser had to give away his precious cigarettes or be penalised with alcoholic drinks. They played all night. *Li was back where he belonged*, I thought.

Soon after our arrival we had to visit Li's father's ancestors' graves – a sacred trip. Li's family carried stacks of coin-imprinted rice paper, water and incense, which represented the gold bars and money of olden times. 'We need to take gifts of money, water and food so they are not hungry, thirsty or poor in their afterlife,' Li told me.

First Dia knelt, and then one after the other the brothers knelt in order of their age. When it was Li's turn, he said, 'Kowtow with me, Mary,' so I knelt beside him and we bent our heads to the ground three times. Li was overcome. I think he finally realised he had come home and was surrounded by his extended family and their history – and with me there to share it, his two worlds had come together. He had thought it would never happen. I was so happy for him. It was a very emotional time.

~

In the last few days of our stay, Li's youngest brother, Jing Tring, was getting married, so I got to experience a traditional Chinese wedding. He was marrying a beautiful girl, Xiao Zhu, who was the youngest sister of one of Li's good childhood friends. The bridal party arrived in two cars decorated with flowers and ribbons. We stood in the laneway as the bride was carried from her car by two male family members. This was so her feet didn't touch the ground until she got onto the bed where we had been sleeping at Niang's house. It's considered bad luck if your feet touch the ground. Xiao Zhu wore a frilly white dress with a veil, and Jing Tring wore a cream suit. They sat on the bed and were given wide noodles 'to widen your hearts' as part of the wedding tradition.

Meanwhile, two brothers were busy at a house down the road, killing chickens, cleaning fish and cooking food for the guests. They cooked outside on two little coal burners, and tables were set up in the courtyard. There were two sittings of fifty people each, so an enormous amount of food had to be cooked on the two little burners. I couldn't believe this was possible without any refrigeration. The two fridges Li had bought hadn't yet arrived.

Dia made a speech and included lovely wishes for Li and me, Li told me later. It was a long speech for this very quiet man. I didn't understand what he was saying, but I could tell it was heartfelt. Li said he spoke about the importance of values and family, integrity, dignity and pride, and loving your wife until the end. When Li told me this I walked over and gave his father a kiss on the cheek. Then I offered a toast to Li's parents. Everyone clapped and cheered. It was not really the done thing to kiss in public in China, but Li explained to everyone that I had kissed Dia because I was so happy to hear his affectionate words, which were so much a part of my own family values. And I got away with it because I was a Westerner. I could see the happiness in Li's eyes.

Traditionally, Chinese brides have more than one dress. And Li's family insisted I wear one of Xiao Zhu's wedding dresses to celebrate *our* wedding, even though it had happened nearly a year earlier. It was a frilly pink dress – not at all to my taste – but they all clapped when I came out. There were fireworks going off and it was lots of fun. We walked with the bride and groom, who held a tray of drinks, and every person who took a drink had to offer a lucky or funny toast. Then that person had to *gan bei*. So the groom was told, 'May you have happiness until your silver beard touches the ground.' The more toasts, the drunker everyone got and the sillier the wishes became. There was constant laughter.

At the first session, one of the uncles said, 'We want to see you dance!' Luckily we hadn't *gan-beied* too much. I had no ballet gear or shoes with me, but Li said, 'Just put on your shorts and a shirt and we can do it.' We performed the *Giselle pas de deux* for the family in their tiny courtyard with both of us humming the music. They clapped every time Li lifted me in the air. *What a universal language dance is*, I thought.

Word of our little impromptu dance spread quickly, and we ended up performing as we walked through the village, the children begging us to dance for them. Again and again, Li would lift me above his head and their little faces were full of wonder. I asked Li to have the children perform something for us in return. This request always resulted in them bursting into song, with one hand on their hip and the other hand waving in the air with military-style precision.

'What are they singing, Li?' I asked.

He laughed. 'It's a popular song, "We Love You, Chairman Mao"!'

I began to realise how amazing it was that Li had managed to escape such a stringent regime. Nothing meant more than freedom – of thought, of education, to move and travel, to live the life you chose and to have your own thoughts. I felt sad that a whole generation of people were denied a proper education, because during the Cultural Revolution between 1966 and 1976 the educated class were all taken away to work on farms or to jail, or simply disappeared from the face of the earth. Some historians have estimated that tens of millions died – mostly due to poverty, but millions were murdered. It just blew my mind.

I could see that Li's family was doing well, in part because Li could send them money. Others didn't have that. I was seeing first-hand the damage of the Cultural Revolution. If not for Madame Mao wanting to see ballet and realising that all the teachers had been sent to communes in the countryside (supposedly to 'cleanse their filthy minds'), working on pig farms and in other harsh environments, Li would not have gone to Beijing and learned ballet, or travelled to Houston and met me. So many times during that visit my mouth was agape at the reality of it all.

Since Mao had imposed the one-child policy in China, some women got pregnant a second time and the child would have to be aborted – all enforced by the state. Women were encouraged to have hysterectomies to avoid ongoing abortions. We were told stories of babies birthed and abandoned. They would be 'unauthorised babies' and couldn't be registered for education or medical benefits. Some parents were even jailed for breaking these rules.

Second brother, Cunyuan, had found a baby girl, Jie Jie, abandoned in a field in northern China and brought her home. There was a note from the mother, hoping that luck would see a kind person find and care for her daughter. Second brother was in an arranged marriage and always blamed Niang and Dia for his unhappiness. Adultery was a real no-no in China and an unwanted pregnancy was a disaster for the mother. Cunyuan had been caught between the old traditions and the new regime. He and his wife cared for and loved the baby girl as their own two daughters – but what a start for the little toddler I now saw before me. And it had not been easy. Just weeks before we arrived, she had pulled a pot of hot soup onto her face. One side of her perfect face had been burnt and blistered. I feared she would be scarred for life. However, she was still the cutest thing I'd ever seen!

Finally it was time to say farewell. I had fallen in love with Li's family. I was so sad to say goodbye and I could see Li's sorrow too. Thanks to some manoeuvring by the brothers, we eventually got our passports and return tickets a couple of days before our scheduled departure to Beijing. I suspected many packets of cigarettes had changed hands.

We bid a teary farewell to Niang and Dia at home while the rest of the family came to the airport. His younger brother and his bride would come with us to Beijing for their honeymoon. All the brothers, wives and children cried and everyone was very emotional. We had no idea when we would be allowed to come back again. Li's brothers were all in Dia's mould – strong, proud, dignified and loving men. And it was clear how much they loved each other.

As I looked back at their teary faces through the glass departure door, the tears started to roll down my face. I turned to Li and he was crying, too. We held hands and walked slowly to the plane, glancing back one last time to catch a final glimpse of the family.

Back in Houston we were enjoying making our house a home. Li got stuck into the garden and we renovated the garage apartment for his friend John Grensback and his new wife, Megan, to rent. While they were living there, Megan became pregnant. Li and I had talked about having children ourselves. We both knew it was something we wanted, but we hadn't made any firm plans. We were simply too busy with our ballet careers, and we both knew that children did not really fit into performers' lives. However, after some agonising discussions, we finally agreed that there was never a perfect time to have a child and decided to bite the bullet and go for it. But as fate would have it, we had to put this plan on hold for a while after all.

Christopher Bruce was returning to Houston Ballet to create a new ballet. Li and I were amazed and honoured when we learned that he wanted to choreograph it using the two of us as leads. The ballet would be based on the life of Buddha, with the possibility of filming it in India. Here was yet another exciting new opportunity – India and a film! I was thrilled to be cast as Buddha's wife, and Li was Buddha.

'I'd really like to do this ballet, Li, so let's think about a baby later on,' I told him.

'Fine, darling. Whatever you want. It will be wonderful for us to work with Christopher, and to go to India!'

Christopher was coming in a few weeks' time, but in the meantime we had to rehearse for Ben's *Swan Lake*. He had invited his good friend Dame Margot Fonteyn – one of the world's greatest ballerinas – to coach us. Unbeknown to me at that time, Dame Margot had been diagnosed with cancer. She had shared with Ben that she was coming to Houston for treatment at the city's world-famous MD Anderson Cancer Center. She was a graceful and elegant woman. She was so knowledgeable and quite straightforward, which I loved. She was around seventy and still very beautiful. She had a wonderful aura, an inner radiance and calm. You felt quite at ease in her rehearsals. I had met her when she performed *Afternoon of a Faun* with Rudolf at London Festival Ballet. I'd had the privilege of being one of the five nymphs and been able to watch her perform at close quarters. Now she was coaching me as a principal dancer, along with Li, Janie and Ken. It was such an honour.

Margot adored Li. She had actually spent quite a lot of her youth in China – living in Tianjin for a year when she was nine, then Hong Kong and Shanghai. Her early experiences had given her a familiarity and fascination with China, so she was very interested in Li and his story. It was in Shanghai that she'd started ballet lessons with Vera Volkova, who had herself studied directly under renowned Russian dancer and teacher Agrippina Vaganova. She was considered one of the greatest ballet teachers in the world and the famous ballet academy I'd visited in Saint Petersburg was named after her.

I was dancing the Swan Queen once again. Margot helped me discover more about the nuances of the enchanting Tchaikovsky score. Something of Margot's essence just slipped into me. Simplicity and music were the focus of her coaching. She pushed us to deliver on artistic interpretation and technique, even in the studio. The role of Swan Queen was huge, requiring a great deal of stamina and strength. I felt Margot was pleased with my improvements, and I really enjoyed the performances as a result of her coaching.

After *Swan Lake*, Christopher arrived and it was time to start choreographing *Gautama Buddha* immediately. It sounded exciting but it could be a slow process. Christopher began with an idea of what he wanted to explore, but he wouldn't be able to finalise the choreography until he saw us move, and move together. It could be a magical experience when things came nicely together, but it could also be frustrating if he didn't get exactly what he was after. It was a privilege to have a whole *new* ballet choreographed on Li and me, only so recently married, felt like a dream come true.

Li and I had agreed to talk about a baby again once *Gautama Buddha* was over. And that was the plan – only we were a little too late. Just a few weeks later, I discovered I was six weeks pregnant. Peggy Oxford recommended a doctor downtown and I went to see him between rehearsals. 'Well, Mary, you are pregnant,' he announced. 'Congratulations!'

I didn't say anything. I was shocked and didn't know what to think or feel. I walked out in a daze. All I knew was that I had to get back to the studio to tell Li.

I stood in front of the circular window that allowed viewing into the studio. Li was working with Christopher, but when I caught his eye, I nodded – slowly but emphatically. He couldn't stop working so just turned back to Christopher, but I had glimpsed the shock on his face. I waited for Li. He had a break coming up.

When he came out of the studio, he grabbed my hand and led me to a private area.

'Yes, I'm pregnant,' I said. 'What are we going to do?'

'What do you think?' Li asked me back.

'I'm not really sure, but I want this baby,' I replied.

'Well, we'll have to tell Ben and Christopher, then,' Li said.

The unexpected pregnancy had thrown my life into chaos as we were in the middle of the *Gautama Buddha* creation. We both knew that I couldn't continue as I wouldn't be able to perform it in six months' time. Christopher would need to have another dancer involved in the creation process. I was bitterly disappointed.

That night I remember crying into my spaghetti, not knowing

what the future would bring. Our life was about to change and we didn't know if I would be able to keep working after a baby. All these things were going through my head. I could see that a million thoughts were whizzing through Li's head too. We were both naive about babies and the reality of life outside the ballet. We had been cloistered in the ballet world. I was only thirty, and probably had another five years of dancing left in my career. But now I had to think about the probability that I wouldn't be dancing again. Would I get my body back in shape and still perform at top level? Would Ben still want me? It was all so unknown.

It took us a while to adjust, but what I knew with certainty was that I wanted our baby and I couldn't do Christopher's new ballet. Together we shared the news with Ben. He was shocked but genuinely happy for us. 'Congratulations!' he said with a big smile. He assured me that there was no question that my job would still be there for me after the baby. He was very generous and loyal.

I called Mum, just days after one of our regular calls. 'Is everything okay, darling?' she asked.

'I'm pregnant!' I blurted.

'Oh, darling! How lovely. Congratulations!' she cried.

'Thanks. I'm still getting used to the idea. We're a bit shocked,' I told her. She knew about *Gautama Buddha* and how excited I'd been, but she also knew a lot about babies.

'Babies don't know about schedules, darling,' she said – something I was just beginning to learn.

Li called his parents and they were over the moon and wished for a boy to carry on the Li family name. They only had one grandson so far. Li found out that his fifth and seventh brothers' wives were also pregnant and their babies would be born around the same time as ours.

I had an easy pregnancy, except I was constantly starving. Being so slim and muscular while trying to grow a baby was hard work for my body. For the first twelve weeks I had to be careful with my food intake as I still had to dance. Then I found out I was very iron deficient, so I ate a lot of steaks and Li made me roast duck with pancakes, which I craved. I finished *The Nutcracker* that year when I was about twelve weeks pregnant. It was a relief – my tutu had started to get tight around my waist and I was getting heavier for Li to lift. Now I could enjoy the pregnancy – and food!

I embraced my new condition and watched my stomach grow bigger by the day. I was now able to do many normal things that I hadn't had the time to do previously. I visited friends like Peggy and we went shopping for baby things. I started reading about pregnancy and birth, and attending appointments with the obstetrician.

'I really want to have a natural birth,' I told him. 'A caesarean may damage my stomach muscles and make returning to work difficult – even impossible,' I explained.

'Don't worry. You're a young, healthy woman. You'll be fine,' he assured me.

I continued to do *barre* each day to keep myself involved and in shape. So I still took my place beside all the other dancers, except my belly was growing while all the bodies around me remained lithe and straight. I was determined to retain some tone so I could return to work more easily.

~

John's wife, Megan, had her baby in March. She had a difficult labour and ended up having a caesarean, so her recovery period was hard. Their son, Austin, was such a handsome baby. I visited them in the garage apartment almost every day and reacquainted myself with holding a baby.

The weeks started to drag and I thought our baby would never come. Towards the end my stomach grew huge. I could feel the baby moving around and sometimes could see its little feet pushing out the skin of my stomach as if it were a punching bag. 'Dancing feet!' Li would say with delight.

I was actually bored and fed up with all the waiting. I just wanted to get on with it. It was June in Houston, very muggy. 'It's too hot, Li,' I would moan. 'I can't stand it.'

'Hang in there, darling. Not long to go now,' he'd reply sweetly. 'Let me give you a massage.'

Our publicist friend Kate Crady's mother, Pat, offered to host a baby shower at her home. I was overwhelmed by the number of gifts we received from our generous friends – Li could hardly fit everything in the car when he came to pick me up.

Coralie flew to Houston to stay with me the week before the due date and that made a big difference. 'Darling, you look beautiful,' she said. 'Glowing!'

Of course she came with an extra suitcase full of things for the baby. She always thought of everything. I oohed and aahed over the tiny clothes – could there ever be a person that small? How would I cope with such a tiny person in my arms? I couldn't imagine it, and yet I'd done it so many times before, helping to look after each new sibling as he or she came along. Now it was my turn to bring a new life into the world.

Mum and I went shopping. She was a star shopper and loved it, and she enjoyed getting to know Houston. Thank God! I hate shopping. I find it boring after the first hour and just want to go home. We bought a nursing chair – Mum insisted it be a rocking chair. We found it at one of the many antique shops that Mum adored visiting. She cooked steaks for us to help with my iron levels. Li had discovered a place where he could buy seaweed, which was full of iron, so he just sliced it up and added it to the other vege-tables in his stir-fried dishes. And much to Mum's surprise, I was eating that as well.

Dame Margot was continuing to visit Houston for her cancer treatment, and of course Ben had told her that I was having a baby. During one of her trips, Ben invited us to dinner and I was heavily pregnant. Margot was very excited about the baby, which was due any minute. Mum was thrilled to meet this legend of the ballet world, and I was very grateful for such a wonderful distraction from my seemingly never-ending pregnancy.

There was such a lot of hanging about, especially once I'd passed my due date of 25 June. I wasn't a patient person. The days were long and Mum was getting anxious – she could only stay a month. To help pass the time and take our mind off things, she taught Li how to play bridge. He took to it like a duck to water. They would play well into the night and really got to know each other over cards. It was lovely to watch.

The baby didn't want to come out, so eventually I had to be induced. We drove to the hospital with my bag on 12 July at 7 a.m. and I was put on a drip to induce the labour. After a while the drugs kicked in and I soon knew what it meant to feel contractions. My God! I thought ballet injuries were painful, but they were nothing compared to this. My labour was long and I had hours of contractions but nothing was happening, so my obstetrician decided to break my waters to hurry things up. Once that happened, there was a time limit for the baby to come out or there was a risk of infection. I had an epidural for the pain. 'God, please let me have a healthy baby!' I was praying.

Li was with me, but I could see that he was nervous and scared. Even so, he was talking calmly, encouraging me: 'You're doing great. You can do it, Mary.'

Coralie waited outside the room. She was frantic because the delivery was taking too long. Li kept going out and reassuring her. At around 8 p.m., the baby was finally ready to come out. The doctor had to use forceps to pull her down. He was brilliant – there was not a mark on her.

Her. A baby girl. We were shocked. We hadn't wanted to find out the sex beforehand, and everybody had guessed our baby would be a boy. After all, Li was one of seven boys, and I had five brothers of my own. Even the experienced Niang and Coralie had agreed our baby would be a boy just from the way I carried the child. Now, here was this precious little girl. I was stunned by her beauty – she looked just like her father. I felt quite emotional as I took her in my arms for the first time. Li had tears in his eyes too: 'A girl, Mary! I can't believe it. She's so beautiful!'

'Yes, she is!' I said. I put her to my breast straightaway. And she was calm. She was 7 pounds 7 ounces with glossy black hair, and nicely chubby. Definitely ready to be born. We just gazed and gazed at her. *Is there a bit of me in her?* I wondered, not taking my eyes off her.

'Oh, darling, she is so beautiful,' said Mum, as she wiped her eyes.

'What are we going to call her?' Li asked. We had a lot of boys' names ready, but hadn't really prepared names for a girl.

'I don't know.' I said.

'I don't know either, but I'm sure the right name will come when we get to know her better,' Li said.

I was exhausted after the long labour, and our baby was taken away so I could rest, but not for long. Thankfully our daughter took readily to the breast, and Mum was there while I breastfed, with a glass of water and a pillow to support me.

I stayed in hospital for the next three days, and during that time many friends came to visit. My little room was overflowing with flowers. Ben arrived with the biggest pink teddy bear I've ever seen. Everyone who came made suggestions for girls' names. It was Charles Foster's eldest son, John, who mentioned he liked the name Sophie.

'Sophie!' Li and I responded together. 'That's lovely!' Sophie was not such a common name in Texas in the 1980s. And I had always liked the name Catherine – Catherine the Great, so strong. That was that. Sophie Catherine Li was born on 12 July 1989.

We went home as a family of three. Li and I were in total awe and wonder. We were shocked at the beauty of this baby, and fell in love with her from the moment she arrived. She had a similar tanned skin colour to Li's, as well as his deep brown eyes. 'She's perfect,' I said to Li as we gazed at her sleeping in my arms.

He just smiled, holding us both close.

Sophie was such an easy baby. She was more like my mother than me in temperament, I decided – so calm. Definitely not my nature!

Mum made sure I had snacks to keep up my milk, cooked meals and tried to get me to have naps. She was just as happy as I was to discuss Sophie – her nappies, her feeds, her skin – all day long. But soon it was time for her to return to Brisbane.

'Sophie is a wonderful baby, Mary. So easy. And you're a wonderful mother,' she told me. I was teary, but it was time to get on with our life as a new family.

~

Our family life was busy but not hard, as Sophie was so little trouble. We would often comment on how good she was. The midwife said that too. We felt blessed. And to my surprise I discovered I was maternal. I adored her and couldn't get enough of her. Her beauty, her fragility, took my breath away. I gazed at her all day and stroked her precious head, and my heart leapt when her tiny hand squeezed around my finger.

Li was so capable it was fantastic. He was comfortable around babies. As soon as he arrived home from work, he would scoop her up into his arms. He could do everything – he bathed her, changed her, fed her and played with her. When it was cooler at night, we would often put her in a baby pouch strapped to Li's chest and walk around the neighbourhood. On one of our walks, I met a neighbour, Maria Myler, who also had a new baby called Cara. She knew a couple of other mothers in the neighbourhood, so we decided to meet up each Monday morning. I met some other lovely friends through Maria – Becky Houston, Anne Cullotta and Liz Gianini. We called ourselves the Mad Mothers.

Lots of our friends from the ballet were keen to visit us, so we decided to have an afternoon tea. For almost all of our dance friends, a baby was a totally new experience. Sophie was such a novelty.

Li and I couldn't believe our luck in settling Sophie to sleep each night. We had heard horror stories of new parents who struggled night after night, but that wasn't a problem with Sophie. I constantly pinched myself. Life was still a dream, and yet it was real. Sophie, Li – my own family.

When Sophie was six weeks old I started to detect little smiles on her cute face. Li went to the Edinburgh Festival with the company, dancing *Swan Lake* and *Gautama Buddha*, which in the end had been performed in Houston but had not been taken to India. I decided not to go as Sophie was still too young and I was slowly trying to get back to some regular classes. I was on a schedule to get back into shape for a guesting role in *The Nutcracker* in Hong Kong with Li in early December. It was going okay, and breastfeeding helped me lose my baby weight. I had a babysitter organised each day so I could have that time away. Sophie was usually asleep anyway.

We had discussed how I would manage going back to work. 'I don't want to put Sophie in child care, Li,' I told him.

'I agree. I've been thinking about this. What if we bring my parents to Houston for a while? We'd have to ask John and Megan to move out, but I'm sure they'll understand. Niang and Dia would want to help us with their granddaughter. They're her *nana* and *yeye*,' he said, using the Chinese terms for grandma and grandpa.

I felt bad about John and Megan and baby Austin, but they were happy to move into a house in the same neighbourhood. Li's plan made so much sense and Niang and Dia didn't even need time to think. They relished the chance of actually living with Li again after so many years apart. They arrived when Sophie was a few months old.

They were incredibly excited. It was going to be a special time for Li, too, as he had not seen much of his parents since leaving for Beijing at the age of eleven. This would make up for some lost family time. I was happy for him, for all of them – and for me, as I could increase my time at work. I felt lucky.

The first day back at the ballet, I cried at being parted from my baby. However, I also felt comforted that Sophie was in the best of hands – Li's parents completely doted on her. And Sophie was happily contented with them and didn't have separation anxiety at all.

Niang and Dia enjoyed having their own little home next to us. Eventually, Li installed a satellite dish so they could watch some Chinese television, and they created a vegetable garden, picking out all the weeds and planting Chinese vegetables. Delicious! They did all the cooking for us, which was wonderful and healthy, and so good for helping me get back into shape. They were incredible.

I was now able to do a full class with the company. I started putting on my pointe shoes and doing more strengthening exercises. I was still breastfeeding and was always desperate to get back to Sophie after class. I managed to communicate with Li's parents quite well despite only having a few words of Chinese. If I needed to convey something important, I'd just call Li to translate. As long as Sophie was happy, I was fine with whatever they were doing.

Niang was the most sparkling and adorable woman you could ever imagine. She had personality plus and was full of fun. Dia was quiet and thoughtful. It was so lovely to see him with Sophie. He adored her and carried her proudly everywhere. If she was awake, she was in their arms. I am sure he had never had that time to hold his own babies back in China. Dia made her a little swing and put it up under one of the big pecan trees in the backyard. They would often take Sophie for a walk in the stroller, and soon discovered a love of garage sales where Niang bought old dresses and curtains and made amazing patterned dresses and quilts for Sophie. We still have one of the quilts, which is quite a work of art. She also made a puffer jacket and bib for Sophie, but it was a pillowcase that Sophie became very attached to. She sucked her thumb and held onto her *nana's* handstitched silk pillowcase at the same time. It became her security 'silkie' – her comforter.

I knew how much they loved Sophie and they were fond of me, too. I did learn some basic Chinese – things like 'How are you?', 'Is it time for her milk?', 'Let's eat' and 'Good morning'. I was excited that Sophie would learn Chinese too, and probably more quickly than me, considering her grandparents spent all day chatting happily with her. Then, when she got a bit older, she could help me learn to speak the dialect and translate between the two cherished languages in our home.

I continued to meet with my Mad Mother friends each Monday morning. It was a happy time with the other babies and mothers – they all had such interesting and fun personalities. We enjoyed chatting together as we watched our babies. It was a chance for me just to be a mother. Li got to know their husbands as well. Ours was a friendly neighbourhood. If I needed to pop in and see someone, I just had to walk down the street to their home.

Every Sunday we went shopping with Li's parents. It was quite a drive to the Chinese supermarket in Chinatown. We'd arrive home with big bags of rice and gallons of soy sauce. Sometimes we'd go with Charles and Lily Foster. They had a baby boy, Zachary, around that same time and Lily's Chinese parents were staying with them as well, so we'd take Li's parents and meet up with them, and all go to yum cha and on shopping expeditions. Sunday night was often dumpling night – everybody's favourite.

Soon Sophie was four months old. The only difficulty we had was feeding her. She wasn't interested in food at all – not regular baby food anyway. Niang would dip little bits of her homemade steamed Chinese bread into tasty sauce from a vegetable dish, and peel the skin off grapes, before popping them into Sophie's mouth.

Sophie liked the royal treatment at mealtimes. She didn't care for bottled baby food and had already demonstrated quite a strong will. Almost every time I gave her a spoonful of nutritious baby food, her face would cringe at the bland taste and texture, then she would turn her tiny head to the side and spit it on the floor. Niang would just laugh and say, '*Ta tai chong min la!*' She is too smart!, and would then give her the same food the rest of us were eating. It didn't matter what I thought – Niang would just keep on laughing and exclaim, 'Sophie only wants to eat *my* food!' It was hilarious to watch and I let them be. My in-laws were the best thing for Sophie.

Niang was such a good cook. She would produce the most delicious food almost every night: rice, Chinese bread, noodles, stewed chicken and baby pork ribs, broccoli, asparagus, fish and even pig's head and trotters sometimes, and of course delicious dumplings. We rarely went out to restaurants because there was such variety at home.

Niang and Dia delighted in Li. As soon as he walked through the door each night, he was the centre of their universe. They had waited for him all day. The chatting never stopped. They had lots to tell us about Sophie and their day, and what might be needed the following day. They weren't huggers. They showed their love by doing everything they could for us – cooking, cleaning, washing and caring so beautifully for Sophie. After dinner, Dia always did the washing-up for Niang while Li and I had some special time with Sophie.

Li would regularly give his parents money to spend around town. They would do massage and pressure point acupuncture for each other to ease their aches and pains. They were both in their sixties after an extremely hard life, so no doubt had quite a few aches and pains – especially carrying Sophie all day. She rarely went in the stroller!

~

Li and I had been invited by Garry Trinder, the director of Hong Kong Ballet, to guest-perform *The Nutcracker* with Hong Kong Ballet in December. I was to dance the Sugar Plum Fairy to Li's Prince. I only had five months after Sophie's birth to get back into shape. It was hard to leave her for work, and I felt incredibly guilty, but Li's parents treated Sophie as the daughter they'd never had.

After four months of exercising, Pilates, swimming and doing class every day, I started to rehearse. My comeback was proving to be much harder than I'd anticipated. I felt I was about a month behind schedule but was very motivated to make the performance in Hong Kong.

How would we manage it? We couldn't leave Sophie with Niang and Dia – not with the language barrier, in case they needed something urgently and couldn't get help. Hong Kong was still a British territory at that time and getting them visas would be tricky. It all seemed too much, but then I had an idea and excitedly called Mum.

'Mum, I wonder if you and Dad would consider coming to help us with Sophie in Hong Kong? I think it's only a nine-hour flight from Brisbane, isn't it?' I asked hopefully. 'Maybe that's not too long a flight for Dad? I'd love him to see Sophie. And we really need someone to look after her.'

Coralie was excited now. 'Sounds like a wonderful idea, darling. Let me talk with Dad.'

Soon Mum delighted me with the news that not only would both of them come, but Brig would come too. I hadn't seen Dad since before Li and I were married. I knew that taking this flight was a big effort for him. So Hong Kong would be an extra-special time with my parents, Brig, and Niang and Dia too, as Li had managed to get their visas after all. It would be the first time our parents had met. Li really wanted to take his parents as he wanted them to experience Hong Kong. This economic powerhouse held enormous fascination for many Chinese people. Everyone on the mainland wanted to go there.

We all booked into the same hotel. As soon as Dad walked in, I kissed him and handed Sophie over. He gazed at her. 'Hello, Sophie,' he said in his soft, caring way. 'My precious pearl.' And that's what he called her from then on.

Then Li introduced my parents to his. It was a little emotional to see my dad finally shake hands with Dia. *Both such strong but gentle men*, I thought, my heart melting.

My parents and Li's parents spoke in their own languages for the whole visit. Sophie was the conduit. They worked together looking after her while not understanding a word the other couple said. They treated each other with such respect. There was a lot of gesticulation going on – pointing to mouths for food and bottoms for nappy changes. Somehow they managed.

Brig was good with babies too, so yet again there was no shortage of loving arms for Sophie. My brother Mick had produced the first McKendry grandchild the year before: Jessica. They shared stories about her – how fair she was, how strong and how clever. The family was happy to see Li again as well. Dad chatted with him about what was happening in both US and Chinese politics – heaven for Dad.

And then it was our opening night. The Grand Theatre on the harbour in Kowloon was quite a modern theatre. I hadn't been on stage for a whole year. I was nervous but, knowing Li would be beside me, I was able to stay calm. Li was extra careful with me. As soon as the music started, I was focused. There's no time for anything but focus as your whole world becomes the music and the story. My parents and Brig were there and Li's parents stayed back to look after Sophie. When it was over, I felt relieved and looked forward to the next show, hoping to get stronger. The season went well and reviews were good, but I knew physically I wasn't up to my usual standard yet, and I was frustrated with myself. I just needed more time and to work harder.

It was quite cold in Hong Kong but full of Christmas atmosphere. Sophie was sitting up now, propped against cushions, holding on to her rattle or a banana by herself, and so responsive with her cute smiles, laughter and babbling. I was sad to be saying goodbye to my family, but keen to be out of the hotel room and back in our own home with the baby.

~

Life in Houston was pretty wonderful and the early months of 1990 flew by. Sophie was very strong and had been walking around holding on to the furniture, when at nine months she started walking all by herself – amazing, since she was rarely out of her grandparents' arms. My Mad Mothers group came to every ballet, and loved it – we had opened their eyes to a whole new world. Niang and Dia came to our performances often as well. They had never seen ballet before they came to the West. Niang always made her tongue-clicking noise in awe at the skills of her son and the other dancers.

Sophie's first year was gone in a flash. We decided to have a first birthday party. It started small: it was just to be the Mad Mothers, their babies and a few others, including John, Megan, baby Austin, Charles, Lily and little Zachary, as well as both lots of Chinese grandparents. But then we couldn't leave out Sophie's godparents, Ben and Ava Jean. That meant we had to invite the rest of our friendship group, including Preston and Peggy, and the list just grew and grew to include dancers and other ballet friends. Thank God for Niang and Dia. They cooked a feast for the multitudes – dumplings, Niang's steamed bread, and lots of delicious traditional northern Chinese dishes. Dame Margot sent Sophie a copy of her children's picture book of *Swan Lake* with a personal inscription. How thoughtful! Ben arrived with a plastic rocking horse that Sophie could ride and push along with her feet. She was the centre of attention as she scooted around the guests. With all those people, it was really quite a raucous party. When she got tired, we put her in a cot out on the verandah, not far from everyone, where she fell sound asleep despite all the merry laughter and loud noise. 'What a wonderful baby. So easy! You're so lucky!' people commented. It was true. Whenever Sophie was tired, she put her thumb in her mouth, cuddled her 'silkie' and just went to sleep, no matter the noise.

Around that time Ben bought Sophie a beautiful red velvet dress from Italy, so when we had a family photo taken, it had to be in that dress. I remember seeing the photo and Sophie's wide eyes and thinking that the flash had given her a real surprise. For some reason this concerned me. When we took her for her first-year check-up with the paediatrician, Li took the opportunity to mention something he'd noticed. 'Doctor, sometimes she doesn't turn when we call her name.'

The doctor looked at us inquisitively, and turned Sophie away from him and clapped his hands, then clapped again. Sophie turned around at the doctor's second clap. He looked at Li with an expression that said, 'See, what's all the fuss?'

'She's fine,' the doctor said definitely. 'Children growing up in a bilingual household are processing a lot more language before making sense of it, so they often speak later.'

That sounded reasonable, so we left feeling reassured.

~

I was now fully back in shape. Ben even commented at a dinner one night: 'Mary is dancing stronger and better after having Sophie.'

Honestly, I did feel that I was dancing better now, with an extra maturity. But the reality of returning to work full-time was sinking in. I had to leave Sophie five days a week and some evenings for performances. It was a wrench, even though she was so nicely cared for and the commute was short. I could even dash home if I had a break between rehearsal and performance.

Yet the dancing was so exciting – it was amazing! We performed *Romeo and Juliet*, still a ballet I absolutely loved. Although it's a three-act ballet, it isn't as technically demanding as *Swan Lake*, so it was perfect for me at that time. In September, we were invited by Christopher Bruce to go to Denmark for the filming of *Ghost Dances*. We decided to leave Sophie with her *nana* and *yeye* this time.

'Ask them if she's babbling more or forming any words, Li,' I whispered to him when he rang home one day.

'Not yet,' he replied, once he'd hung up.

Sophie had been happily babbling 'Gaa gaa gaa', 'Maa maa maa' and 'Baa baa baa', but we were waiting for more. I was anxious to get home.

We were working in a film studio and I was one of the three Indian girls in the ballet and Li was one of the ghosts. As part of the filming, we had to repeat the dance sequences over and over on the five-day shoot to give the filmmakers what they wanted, so there was a lot of standing around between takes. Christopher was a perfectionist and in the end it was a very good film. It is still frequently used in dance education classes around the world. But I was relieved to get back to Sophie.

~

One evening, out of the blue, the phone rang. It was the Australian Ballet's general manager, Noel Pelly.

'Mary, how are you?' he said. 'How's life after the baby? I hear you're dancing as well as ever.'

He was such a charming man. I have to admit it was a joy to hear his Australian accent, but I was more interested in why he was ringing. 'I'm loving being back on stage,' I replied.

'I'm glad to hear it, Mary. We are planning an all-Australian gala at the Sydney Opera House in November. Maina and I would really like you to take part. It would be so wonderful for the Australian audiences to see your beautiful dancing.' Maina Gielgud was the Australian Ballet's artistic director.

My heart skipped a beat. Who would I dance with? What about Sophie? Brisbane was easy with all my family there, but Sydney? All kinds of thoughts were running through my head.

'Thank you, Noel.' I was overjoyed. 'Can I bring my husband, Li, as my partner? He's a very good dancer.'

'Maina wants to make this an all-Australian gala,' Noel replied.

'Well, Li is married to me and that makes him half-Australian,' I said, half-jokingly.

He laughed, and then said, 'Ross Stretton has already agreed to come. We would love it if you and he could dance together, especially since both of you are living in the States, which will make it easier for you to rehearse. How do you feel about that?'

'Okay, Noel. I would love to, but I need to get permission from Ben first. Can I confirm at the end of the week?' He agreed.

Niang and Dia could tell I was excited about something. I was clapping my hands with joy and Sophie, toddling around, started clapping her little hands too.

'Well done, darling. You must do it,' Li said.

Over the previous few years I had been invited by Maina Gielgud to guest with the Australian Ballet, but I could never make it. The first time I was pregnant, and the next time I wasn't available due to other performance commitments. I was always so flattered to be asked, and disappointed I couldn't make it happen. I was longing to perform again in my home country. Ben gave his permission. I could hardly believe it was happening!

This was going to be such a special experience for me, in the iconic Sydney Opera House, in my home country. It was what I longed for – to perform at home at the height of my career. Soon after, much to my delight, I was invited by the Queensland Ballet to dance at their thirtieth-anniversary gala performance in Brisbane after the Sydney performances. They'd heard I was coming to dance with the Australian Ballet. Finally, the timing was just right.

But I couldn't run off and do it just like that. Sophie was my prime responsibility now. Should I leave her in Houston with Li, Niang and Dia? I knew Li would say, 'Don't worry about Sophie. She will be fine with us.' But I didn't want to leave either of them behind. Sophie would be sixteen months old by the time of the trip and I wanted my Australian family to meet her. Could we bring Niang and Dia? They'd always wanted to see Australia and they could meet my brothers and sisters too.

I'd heard that Ross Stretton was a wonderful dancer and partner.

He was an Australian and a principal dancer at the American Ballet Theater. I was all set to fly to New York to rehearse with him, but he called a week before my flight. 'Mary, I'm so sorry. I've injured my back and won't be able to make the gala,' he said apologetically.

I was so disappointed for Ross – what a blow! I wondered if there was a chance the Australian Ballet might now allow Li to dance with me, as there wasn't much time left to prepare. I really wanted the Australian audiences to see him dance too. We both knew that audiences always liked the fact we were a husband-and-wife team. People found it so romantic. I called Noel, and suggested that with Ross injured and time running out, I would like to come with Li as my partner.

By this time Noel had already heard from Ross. 'All right. You can bring Li, but we won't be able to pay him,' he said.

'That's fine, Noel. I'm sure he would be fine with this,' I replied. Li knew how much it would mean for me to perform in front of my family and in Australia. He'd be happy to come and support me. Whether he got paid or not, and he would never want me to lose this opportunity. To have him as my partner would make it even more wonderful.

Now we had to ask Ben for permission for both of us to go. We weren't sure how he would react, but the timing was good. He was happy to let us go and agreed for us to dance his *La Esmeralda pas de deux*. It is simply divine, and would be a fabulous showcase for our particular talents. It requires virtuoso technique as well as being very sexy and fun. *La Esmeralda* would have me in a luscious green-velvet tutu with a bright-orange flower in my hair, and a tambourine – a gypsy girl, both fiery and innocent. I knew this *pas de deux* was going to be a huge hit with the Australian audience and Li would be the added bonus. Now I knew for sure that with him as my partner for both performances, the experience would be all the more special for me.

I couldn't wait to tell Sophie, and as soon as I was home that afternoon I scooped up my daughter and lifted her high in the air.

'Sophie, Sophie! You're coming to Australia. You're going to meet all your uncles and aunties. They're going to love you so much! You're going to see Sydney Harbour and you're going to see the famous Opera House, and you're going to see cockatoos and kangaroos and have Vegemite on toast!'

She laughed and laughed and I held her close until we settled down to dinner. I rang Mum and Dad, too, so that the family could make arrangements. They were over the moon. 'Now I can show off our precious pearl to everyone,' said Dad, with his usual enthusiasm.

I couldn't wait to see my family and show them my daughter, and I swore I would dance the dance of my life.

~

Finally we were there: Li, Sophie and me with Niang and Dia in a three-bedroom high-rise apartment right on Sydney Harbour. The view from our window blew me away just as it had done when I was a child when our parents took us on our 'cultural' holidays – that vast blue sky, the sparkling water, the shining boats and magnificent bridge.

There is a quality of light in Australia, a clarity, like nowhere else in the world. I always loved the distinctive smell of eucalyptus trees, and the sounds of familiar raucous birds always told me I was home. I was going to dance at the iconic Sydney Opera House, which some say is the eighth wonder of the world.

This was Li's first time visiting and performing in Australia. 'I can't believe how beautiful Sydney is, Mary,' he told me. 'But so quiet. Where are all the people?' After China and the busy freeways of Houston, harbourside Sydney certainly was sleepy. *If you think this is sleepy, wait until you see Brisbane*, I quietly laughed to myself.

'See you later, darling,' I called to Sophie as Li and I headed off. She waved and did her cute little blow-kisses. And we left her with her grandparents to wander around.

As Li and I walked I watched him as he took in the magnificence of Sydney Harbour. It was a warm and clear day, with a light breeze. And there was the magnificent Opera House perched at the very edge of the water, glistening in the brilliant sunlight. The elegant tiled sails that make up its unique roof line looked stunning against the blue, blue of the Aussie sky.

We walked up the wide front stairs and met with Noel and Maina. We got our schedule for the week and appointment times for some publicity shots. It was wonderful to meet the other dancers and to be among all those familiar Australian accents. It was also nice to put faces to the names of some of the dancers I had only heard of. We were shown to our dressing rooms. I was sharing with Lisa Pavane, Miranda Coney and Lisa Bolte.

We started rehearsals the following day and were a little surprised when we saw the size of the stage. It was really small – much smaller than we had anticipated. Li is a very big mover and *La Esmeralda* requires a big stage to do the choreography justice. Li had to do a huge *manège* (split *jeté* leaps around the stage in a circle). We could see straightaway that the stage would be quite inhibiting for both of us.

We bumped into Jack Lanchbery, a world-renowned conductor and fellow Australian whom Li knew well as he had conducted at Houston Ballet. Knowing he was going to conduct for us had given us confidence. He had intimate knowledge of the dance steps and we trusted that he would bring out the best in us. It makes such a big difference when you have a conductor of that calibre.

Jet lag was catching up with us by the end of that day and we returned to the apartment exhausted. Soon after dinner, I crashed out and felt that I had slept for a long time when Sophie's cries woke me up at midnight. Poor Sophie was wide awake and ready to play. Li and I had to take turns with her, so one of us could get some sleep.

Mum and Dad flew in to Sydney the next day. Our parents greeted each other like old friends.

We told Mum and Dad about the small stage. 'It's all because Jørn Utzon's design was compromised,' Neil George told us. 'His sails were revolutionary and his design was very courageous, but it scared people. His original design was for only two walls and to have it open to the harbour, but the government insisted on four walls, so that meant the stages had to be downsized. What a great shame.'

Sophie had a Western-style breakfast first with us and Mum and Dad, then Chinese food for lunch with her *nana* and *yeye*. We would come home in the late afternoon and all have dinner together. Niang and Dia were nervous to walk too far without Li, but Coralie and Neil George did take them to visit a few nearby sights, including the Chinese Garden of Friendship at Darling Harbour, which was built in 1988 to symbolise the friendship between Sydney and the city of Guangzhou in Guangdong province.

Before we knew it, it was opening night. As I sat in front of the dressing-room mirror putting on my make-up, I realised I was nervous. I felt I was dancing well since having Sophie. Once you have a baby, that baby is the most important thing in the world, and afterwards I had just become more courageous and danced with a new maturity. I wanted to give my home audience the best performance I could, and I knew I was safe in Li's hands.

I put on my green tutu with its velvet bodice striped with glittering silver and the bright tangerine flower in my hair, and took my place in the wings with Li. We were on at the end of the first half. I knew Mum and Dad were sitting in the middle of row E, the best seats in the house, and I just knew in my bones that this would be the best performance I'd ever done for them. We noticed there were a lot of the company dancers standing in the wings eagerly waiting to watch us, which added even more pressure.

'Take a deep breath, relax and enjoy,' Li said, as he squeezed my hand. I took a deep breath and simply nodded. The orchestra started and after a few bars we charged on stage together. Li took my hand and I stood *en pointe*, lifting my leg to attitude and balancing for a few seconds. The audience burst into applause immediately. This opening is a dramatic way to start, and gives the audience a taste of what is to come. And Ben's *pas de deux* delivers from the beginning to the end. In the final steps I walk towards Li, my hand in his, and lift my leg up to a split *en pointe*, and on the last beat of the music, pop my head against his. The applause was rapturous! Then it was Li's turn to perform his solo with all those stunning double turns in the air to the right, to the left and to the right again. His solo was technically brilliant, with high leaps and dazzling *pirouettes* that he delivered with such charm and ease. Then I did my solo with the tambourine, a solo full of challenging steps that was a little cheeky and lots of fun. By this point we were already spent, but we had two codas to go and they were complete show stoppers. The music really takes off and we did turn after turn – for me, thirty-two *fouettés*, hitting my tambourine with each one. Then I had to do a circle of high *jeté* jumps, banging my tambourine above my head at the precise moment my legs reached full split. Finally, we flew towards each other on centre stage. Li spun me around furiously for multiple *pirouettes* and I finished with another dramatic whack of the tambourine. The cheers and thunderous applause were instant. The audience loved it!

I remember feeling so elated, especially knowing that my parents and friends were there in the audience. And I knew we had performed well. I was overcome with emotion.

'Thank you,' I said to Li in the usual understated way that dancers show their appreciation to their partners.

'That was good, Mary!' he said.

My eyes shone with happiness. Li hugged me tight. He knew how much this performance meant to me. *Yes, it was good!* I thought.

Later, at the opening-night reception, Noel, Maina and others associated with the company were all effusive in their praise. How wonderful to receive such a response at home. And, of course, Li was a huge hit. 'The height of those leaps!', 'The speed of those double ensembles!', 'That ease and confidence!' they exclaimed.

It was so wonderful to see Mum and Dad at the stage door.

'Splendid!' Neil George exclaimed.

'You danced beautifully,' Coralie added, with a kiss. She was always just a bit nervous for me.

How many Scotches did she have to calm herself down this time? I wondered. She knew what a perfectionist I was, and I was happy and relieved when it was all over. Brisbane was yet to come. We all walked back to the apartment together, happy.

It had been a smart move to include Li in the gala: the audiences were so taken by how stunning he was as a dancer. At the end of the fourth and last performance in Sydney, Noel actually paid him, even though he had told me a fee wasn't possible because of the budget. I think the Australian Ballet was quite embarrassed in the end because Li brought the house down. We thought this was quite funny and laughed about that for days. What a bonus!

~

Once the season was finished in Sydney, we took the short flight to Brisbane – sunny capital of Queensland, the north-eastern state of Australia – to perform once more, guesting at Queensland Ballet's thirtieth-anniversary gala this time.

Mum and Dad had been living in Brisbane for several years now, as had most of my brothers and sisters. My parents had invited us to stay in their apartment. It was a relief that we didn't have to stay in a hotel as it wouldn't be as relaxed, and it'd be nice for Niang and Dia to meet the rest of my big family. All the children had left home now, so Mum and Dad had moved to a three-bedroom apartment high on a hill in Wooloowin, which had glorious views from almost every room, including vast views of the city.

Niang and Dia just fitted in as if they'd always belonged, despite the language difficulties. Maybe having the shared experience of many children made it easy for everyone to relate to each other. It was such a fun time for all of us to catch up, and Sophie wasn't at all fazed about meeting that many people, all of whom wanted a piece of her, hugging and kissing and swinging her around. It was wonderful to see Sophie that happy and that adaptable. At sixteen months she was still the most easy, delightful child.

Brig had us to a barbecue at her home. She had married and was pregnant with her first baby. Mick and his wife, Robyn, were there with their two children, Jessica and baby brother Tim. Ger and his wife, Marlene, were there with baby Kate, who was not yet 100 days old, much to Niang's distress, as it was the Chinese custom that both mother and baby not be out and about for the first hundred days. Pat and Dom were there too, but Jo was living in New York doing some freelance contemporary dance. Matt and his wife, Annie, weren't there either. They both worked at the Queensland Performing Arts Centre, where we'd be performing. Matt was staging manager and Annie was a stage manager. As usual, everyone talked at once and was able to take part in multiple conversations at the same time. Li was feeling right at home. This was like being with his own large family in China.

There was only one performance, and this time my brothers and sisters were all coming to watch us perform, as were some of my old friends from school. Unfortunately, Miss Hansen was not well enough to come to the performance, so I arranged with the artistic director, Harold Collins, for her to come to that afternoon's dress rehearsal instead. At least she saw us practising *La Esmeralda* on the stage. Although we weren't performing fully, as we had to save energy for our performance that night, she was thrilled with us. We spoke briefly and I noticed she looked quite frail but was still immaculately dressed and beautifully poised.

'I so enjoyed that, Mary!' she told me. 'You are dancing beautifully. Your husband is a good dancer too. I'm so sorry that I can't be there for you tonight. Good luck with the performance.' It meant the world to me that she was there, and I treasured her words.

My family had booked a lot of seats in Brisbane's 2000-seat Lyric Theatre. It was a far cry from the old Festival Hall where Grandma Bridie had brought me to see my first ballet. Now here I was back in Brisbane in this beautiful theatre about to perform myself. Grandma Bridie would have been so proud of me.

Many Rocky friends came, as well as students from Miss Hansen's ballet school. Normally I could control my nerves, but this time the combination of nerves and excitement made it worse. What would my family and friends think about my dancing? For years they had supported me in my ballet lessons in Rocky, and from afar when I moved to London. Now I was a principal dancer with one of America's premier ballet companies, who had been invited to Australia especially. This performance meant the world to me – I did so want them to be impressed.

As soon as we stepped onto the stage we were in that other place, with room only for the music and the movement and each other. Li partnered me beautifully once again. Then it was all over and I swear I could hear my brothers whistling as I saw my whole family standing and clapping above their heads, calling, 'Encore! Bravo! Encore!' Li took my hand and we stepped off stage, then returned again and again to more applause. The feeling was indescribable. My whole family had got to see me dance at the top of my career for the first time. And, in front of my family, I really did feel like a star.

Backstage, Li hugged me tight. 'Darling, you were wonderful. It was such special performance. I'm so proud of you!'

'We did it, Li! We did it together. I love you.' I kissed him. I knew that his dancing had blown the Brisbane audience away, just as it had in Sydney and all over the world.

After we changed, we found that Matt had shepherded the whole family into the backstage bar, where we were showered with hugs and drowned in bouquets of flowers.

'Just stunning, Mare,' said Ger.

'It was a triumph, darling,' said Mum.

It was delicious to have them all with me, even for so short a time. The whole lot of us went to a Chinese restaurant in Chinatown in Brisbane's Fortitude Valley afterwards. As always with my big family, we had to work out how many cars to take and who would go in which. The restaurant was very overdone in Chinese decor, with dragons on the wall and wallpapered with Chinese prints. The food was Australianised Chinese, Li commented – sweet and sour pork, honey prawns, chow mein, fried rice with chunks of Windsor sausage – but my family liked it.

Luckily Niang and Dia weren't with us as they wouldn't have approved. In fact, they had offered to cook for the whole family, which they did for Sunday lunch. They chopped and cooked all morning – steamed vegetables, succulent pork ribs falling off the bone, tender stewed chickens and pork stir-fry. There were chopsticks for the pros, forks for the rest. It was a real feast – well, they *were* cooking for about twenty-five people. The whole McKendry clan descended and we just ate and ate. Everyone loved Niang's feast, and they still remember it. Niang was shocked and kept saying to Li, 'If only I'd known how much they can eat, I would have cooked more dishes.' In the Chinese tradition, the host would rather have too much than not enough food.

The next day, Li, Sophie and some of the others went to a park. I was in the flat helping Niang prepare the food for dinner. She was preparing the minced pork for Li's favourite dumplings, while I was cutting pastry into circles, rolling it out thinly, and putting in the pork filling. Dia was keeping an eye on the rice. A couple of hours later, Li and the others arrived back. Sophie was hanging onto a string with a burst red balloon at the end of it. Everyone bustled around and started to ooh and aah at the lovely smells emanating from the kitchen and the hundreds of dumplings Niang had made.

Li took me to one side, clearly agitated. I asked, 'What? What's the matter, Li?'

'Mary,' he said with a worried look on his face, 'we passed birthday party on way back. Balloons everywhere and Sophie got hold of one. I was following her up stairs and balloon popped with loud bang.'

'Yes, yes, I saw that. I hope she put it in the bin,' I said, and turned back to the pastry.

But Li said, 'I think something going on with Sophie. She right in front of me coming up stairs. When balloon popped, other children all startled but not Sophie. She didn't move.'

'So what?'

'Mary, you're not listening,' he persisted. 'The balloon popped. It was very loud and Sophie just stood there. All other children startled.'

'What do you mean, Li?'

'She didn't move.'

'Don't worry,' I said. 'She's fine.'

I completely dismissed what Li was trying to say at that moment – Sophie was fine. She was meeting all the baby stages according to the books, and although she was a bit late talking, she was definitely making sounds, babbling and pointing, just like any other baby her age. And as Dr Boyd had said, she was living in a two-language household. In any case, I couldn't think about it right then. We had a meal to cook and family to entertain. It was a gathering that couldn't be put to one side, a rare occasion to be enjoyed to the fullest. Nevertheless, the thought of Sophie not responding to a loud balloon pop played in the back of my mind.

We were at Mick and Robyn's house the next day with the clan for yet another barbecue. Ger was downstairs holding baby Kate, watching the kids run in the garden. Sophie was playing with her cousins in the backyard when she got bitten by an ant and started to scream. I raced over and took her in my arms. All eyes were on her, and with Li's words clearly in my head, I went with Mick to get some ice for the bite to help ease the pain. Once the commotion died down, I asked Mick, 'Do you think everything's okay with Sophie?'

'It's just an ant bite, Mare. She'll be fine.'

'No, I mean generally,' I said. 'Li said she didn't react to a burst balloon the other day.'

'If you're worried, why not have her checked?' he said.

I couldn't imagine anything being wrong with Sophie. She was such a perfect child, didn't hide behind my skirt and just had a wonderfully calm personality. Nevertheless, I knew that Li – ever the doting father – was worried. So when he said, 'Let's go and see the doctor when we get back,' I agreed. But I was still not overly worried.

The next morning, exhausted but energised – still euphoric – I scooped up my beautiful girl. 'Come to Mama, Sophie. Listen to this!' She smiled her sweet smile as I jiggled her on my knee. 'We're going to the park today. You're going to see all of your Australian family one more time before we go home. Niang and Dia are coming, and lots of other people too. Let's go.'

To be honest, I couldn't wait to show her off to my relatives. My uncle Jock – Neil George's older brother – had organised a McKendry family reunion for our last day in Australia. We were to have a real Aussie family barbecue in Kalinga Park in inner Brisbane, and I was so looking forward to it. It's a large park along a creek, lined with huge eucalyptus trees.

It was a nice sunny day, not yet too hot, and we all brought food, drinks, folding chairs and picnic rugs. It was wonderful to see Dad's sister Auntie Carmel, her husband, David, and their girls, Shauna and Megan, as well as Uncle Jock's wife, Auntie Marg, and my cousins Cathy, Jenny, Terry and Libby. I remember how proud Jock was to have us all there together. I was happy to have Li and my little girl with me. Sophie wore tiny black Clarks shoes, pink shorts and a pink T-shirt. She looked so cute, running around happily with all the other children. Li was charming and chatted to everyone easily. He was translating for Niang and Dia, who looked like they were in their element – another large, noisy family get-together. And babies were a universal language.

We hadn't been together like that since we were kids. It was so special to spend rare time with the family, especially when introducing Li and his parents to everyone else. It made me happy and proud to be able to introduce them and Sophie to a happy Aussie family gathering.

Our ten-day visit to Australia was over rather quickly. We'd said our goodbyes to the clan at the park. Everyone was grinning stupidly but choked up at the same time.

I didn't know when I would see my dad again. Though he'd given up smoking by now, he wheezed a lot and of course he still had his big beer belly. It concerned me that he seemed to tire more easily these days. He shook hands with Li. 'Look after your girls, Li,' he said. 'I love them more than the world.'

Mum stood to one side, calm and elegant as ever, but sad, too. Then both sets of parents offered each other a handshake and I noticed the way Neil George and Dia gently clasped each other with both hands as if sealing the friendship. Such a lovely moment! I held Sophie up as we got into the taxi, saying, 'Wave goodbye, Sophie! Bye-bye, Grandma, bye-bye, Grandpa. Love you!'

And, watching all the hands waving, Sophie did her cute wave and blow-kiss back, and we were gone.

～

As soon as we landed in Houston, we were back to rehearsals for the Christmas season of *The Nutcracker*. I was to dance the role of the Sugar Plum Fairy with Li as my Prince. We were totally exhausted, as Sophie again was experiencing some dreadful jet lag and wouldn't go to sleep. In desperation we took turns to drive her around the neighbourhood at 3 a.m. in the hope of getting her to sleep. It was brutal for the first few days just getting back into swing of things.

My concern at Sophie not reacting to the balloon was getting stronger. I did watch her more closely, but I still refused to believe anything was really wrong. Nevertheless, I made an appointment to see our paediatrician on our first company-free day.

Our worries were only increased a few days later, when Annie was visiting with baby Nina. The children were playing together on a blanket on the floor when Li came in the front door and the screen door slammed loudly behind him. We all jumped – except Sophie. Little Nina was about to burst into tears, but Sophie didn't even flinch.

'She didn't react to that noise. I'm going to do it again,' Li said worriedly. Sophie was sitting with her back to the door as, once again, Li let it slam loudly. No reaction.

When we went to our appointment, Li told the doctor what had happened. The doctor didn't seem worried. 'Are we back to that again?' he exclaimed. 'As I said to you before, Sophie is being brought up in a bilingual family, so her language acquisition is bound to be a bit slow. I think an auditory brainstem response test would be a waste of time and money.'

Again I felt reassured, but Li continued to insist on a proper hearing test – an ABR test. In the end, the doctor begrudgingly wrote the referral. We booked the first available appointment, which was six weeks later. In the meantime, we began testing her hearing. 'Sophie! Sophie!' we'd call. Sometimes she'd turn and sometimes she wouldn't, so we still weren't sure.

I was more positive than Li. 'See, she turned this time. I think she's fine,' I'd say.

I told my Mad Mothers group that I was going to have her tested. 'Why?' they all asked, because Sophie seemed just the same as their children of around the same age.

Before we knew it, Christmas was upon us. Ben arrived on the doorstep on Christmas Eve. He couldn't wait one more night: he'd bought Sophie a pink battery-powered Barbie car. I'd never seen anything like it. 'Ben, you're outrageous!' I told him. He was delighted when Sophie drove the car around the verandah with the biggest smile on her face.

We went to Ben's for Christmas lunch the next day, as had become our annual tradition, but Li and I had a performance of *The Nutcracker* the following day so we tried not to eat and drink too much. There was a big Christmas tree and presents for everyone – a fun day with Ben playing Santa Claus.

Then the six weeks had passed and it was time to take Sophie for her hearing test. 'I still think we are being overzealous about Sophie. This is totally a waste of time and money,' I said to Li as I strapped Sophie into her car seat.

'I hope you're right, Mary, but we need to know for sure,' he replied.

When we arrived at the hospital, we were chatting away in the waiting room and having fun with Sophie. She looked so beautiful in her little red shoes and cute denim skirt embroidered with flowers and matching jacket – yet another outfit that Ben had bought her in Italy. How could there possibly be anything wrong with her? I was her mother. I would know.

The specialist arrived and explained that Sophie would be given an anaesthetic. She was to be put to sleep before the sensors were placed on her head for the ABR test. These sensors would send sounds over 100 decibels to her brain. Normal conversation is about 30 decibels so this was pretty loud – like a motorbike or a jackhammer. It was all quite alarming.

'Won't that wake her up, doctor?' asked Li, looking more than usually worried by now.

'No, no. She won't hear anything,' said the specialist, 'but we'll be able to record any reactions from her brain sending nerve signals to register the sounds emitted.'

It sounded awful – poor Sophie! – but I was confident the results would give us peace of mind.

Li went in with her and laid her gently on the little bed. She seemed incredibly calm and he stroked her head while the specialist put a mask over her face and a needle in her arm. Then the round glass cover that was part of the ABR testing equipment was lowered over the bed, with her inside it. Poor darling. I was glad she was asleep.

We were guided into a little room with a glass window so we could see Sophie, lying there peacefully. 'She's a sleeping beauty,' I whispered to Li.

Li didn't respond. He wore a worried face. 'She'll be fine,' I added, squeezing my husband's hand. 'Just you wait and see.'

No one came to talk to us, but I was not particularly anxious. A little anxious about missing rehearsal, but not about Sophie.

The test took about an hour, and though Sophie would need another two hours to fully come out of the anaesthetic, the doctor returned to us at the end of the testing. We both stood up straightaway, waiting to hear the good news. 'How is she, doctor?' asked Li anxiously.

Without any preamble, the specialist said, 'Your daughter is profoundly deaf.'

Just like that, he delivered his verdict.

We were dumbfounded. We kept staring at this stranger in the white coat and then at our child, thinking this could not be true. Li tried to speak, but nothing came out. I was speechless too. We were in total shock. We felt our perfect world had fallen apart. A bomb had exploded in my head. I couldn't comprehend what had just happened, or what it all meant.

Eventually Li said, 'Can we fix this?' His voice sounded so hopeful and yet so hollow.

How? I thought. I knew nothing could fix it. I had seen the movie about Helen Keller. I knew what this meant.

The doctor left the room after advising us to go to the nearest deaf school and have Sophie fitted for hearing aids. He was so matter-of-fact and unemotional. There were no brochures given, just a few little words and facts exchanged. He spent less than five minutes with us. We were completely blindsided. Soon I would learn that appointments involving the hearing booth would always cause me great agony.

'Stunned' is not a strong enough word. I couldn't speak. The blood drained from my face. I felt like I was going to faint. Li took hold of my arm but I couldn't look at him, I was in too much shock. My mind went into a spin. So many thoughts and questions flooded in. I couldn't think fast enough or clearly enough. In an instant, I could see some of the scary reality of what lay ahead. For a heartbeat I had flashing thoughts of rewinding and going back to my life of no responsibility in London. Then I was struck by all the things Sophie would never hear.

In that moment, the world that I knew collapsed.

AFTER

PART FOUR

Houston
1991–95

Our mother–daughter relationship was completely changed.
The mother I thought I was and the daughter I thought
I had were taken away from me.

8

We had walked into that hospital with our little girl and a very special life, but Li and I knew everything had changed in that instant. That was it. There was no way for us to communicate with Sophie.

We drove home in silence, dumbfounded. My mind was a jumbled mess. Sophie was in her car seat but we both kept looking behind at her. I knew from her expression that she felt something was going on – she was quite intuitive in that sense. *How could someone so beautiful and responsive have no hearing!* I thought.

Li carried Sophie from the car, and then we laboured up to the front porch with the heaviest of hearts. As we went through the door, Sophie darted towards her *nana* and *yeye*. They were having tea in the sunny front room. Their faces lit up when they saw her. Sophie ran into their arms, giggling, while tears began to well in my eyes and I couldn't stop them. I watched Li deliver the most devastating news to his parents in their Qingdao dialect. I could see their happy expressions turn to shock, then disbelief and incredible sadness.

'*Wu de tian na!*' Oh my God! said Niang, holding Sophie close. Dia shook his head incredulously and stared from Sophie to Li and back again. They were completely stunned. It broke my heart to see their distress. I couldn't speak, and just sobbed. Niang continued to murmur in Chinese as tears welled up in her eyes, too. Sophie could sense the new sadness in our home and walked innocently from one to

the next staring at our faces, completely lost. She knew something was wrong, but didn't realise that she was the reason.

Sophie had never heard their voices, or anything, ever. She'd never heard us say 'I love you'. Would we ever hear her say 'Mum' or 'Dad', 'Yeye' or 'Nana'? The only way she had read the world was from our faces. Niang and Dia were distraught for us and for her. Like us, they had been waiting to talk to Sophie – to have another Chinese speaker in the family.

Li's parents heated up some leftovers for lunch, but nobody had any appetite except Sophie. Afterwards, I took her for her nap, feeling so hollow, so helpless. I tried hard to stop my tears in front of her, but as soon as her eyes closed, I went to my own bed and curled into a ball, unable to hold back. Li came in to try to comfort me.

'Leave me alone!' I blurted. Poor Li. I knew he was also in pain. But I couldn't help it. All I wanted to do at that moment was to have my own space. My own space to cry and try to cope with my extreme distress.

Li went back to work that afternoon. He didn't know what else to do. He told Ben the news about his goddaughter, then word spread quickly throughout the company. Everyone was stunned.

Next I had no choice but to share the news with our friends. I walked mindlessly to Maria's house. The Mad Mothers group had arranged for our children to play there that afternoon. As we watched the children play, I turned to the mothers. 'Sophie's profoundly deaf' was all I managed to say. They looked at me, speechless.

As I watched, I noticed for the first time that the other children were saying occasional words: 'Mine!' 'Mama!' My ear tuned immediately to their toddler language. As I walked the few blocks home, an incredible sorrow overwhelmed me. In the space of one morning our perfect world had turned into utter devastation. Now we were trying to imagine a completely different future for ourselves. A musical world with dancing and laughter was no more.

When Li returned from work that evening, I was still numb and didn't know what to do next. 'Mary, *chi fan ba.*' Mary, let's eat, Niang said, peeking her head into our bedroom. I took one look at her red eyes and knew then that she was suffering a great deal, too. She had cooked a delicious dinner, but I still had no appetite. For the first time in my life, I felt sorry for myself. 'Mary, *guo le!*' Enough! Niang said sternly as she gently slapped her hand on my shoulder. 'What's the use of crying? Get up and get on with your life. Help your daughter.' There were no tears in her eyes now.

I sat up, wiped my eyes and followed her to the dining table. Niang's words shook me to the core and my initial response was to reject her. At the same time, deep down I knew that she was right. I had to somehow shake off my self-pity and sorrow. *Yes, this is my lot to deal with*, I said to myself. *Sophie is my daughter. I'm her mother. I have to help her. There's no other way.*

Niang and Dia continued to be an amazing source of strength and courage. They just got on with it. Food kept coming, the washing was done, the house cleaned, the vegetable patch tended, while Li and I walked around dazed, trying not to think about the future, going into rehearsals as usual. Each night, we all tried to keep up appearances for Sophie – playing and laughing with her as we'd always done. Li was much better at pretending than I was. A few days later he went to see Charles Foster to share the news and cried on his shoulder. He admitted it was the first time he'd broken down about Sophie's diagnosis.

I couldn't face calling my parents. Giving them the news and knowing how upset they would be just added to the burden of grief I was already feeling. I knew we had to get Sophie fitted with hearing aids as soon as possible, as her diagnosis was very late. I had to stop my weeping if I was to ring the Houston School for Deaf Children. So I did. We were invited to come in for a meeting with Sophie on Monday.

Li met us outside the school. 'I think I'm going to throw up,' I told him. He just held me tightly while I pulled myself together and in we went – our first steps into the deaf world. We met with the head of the school, an audiologist and two speech therapists, all sitting in a circle on the floor with Sophie on my lap. I could hardly take in what anyone was saying, and didn't have a clue what the professionals were talking about when they spoke of what 'profoundly deaf' meant in terms of development and language. All I knew was that Sophie was eighteen months old and couldn't hear.

When it was our turn to speak, Li said, 'My name is Li, this is Mary and Sophie. Mary and I are dancers at Houston Ballet. We're just hoping you can tell us what's the best thing for our daughter.'

'Are you both planning on continuing to dance?' the older speech therapist asked.

'We would like to . . .' I replied.

'Do you want your child to speak?' she asked calmly, looking at me.

'Of course!' I replied. And she looked at me quite doubtfully.

'If you both want to continue your careers, then she probably won't learn to speak,' she said bluntly.

The full realisation hit me. Li's eyes met mine and he understood, too. Diagnosis was one thing, but its implications were profound and everlasting. Sophie had not heard anything in her entire life. Her life had been completely visual. Suddenly I could feel the world moving forward but we were at a standstill. As devastating as the therapist's words were, I knew she had spoken the truth and I admired her for this. Here, just when I needed her, was someone with knowledge and experience of this unfamiliar world.

The discussion moved on to language options for Sophie – sign, cued speech or oral method. For me signing was the last option. How could we keep working and both learn to sign? Even if I learned to sign, she would only be able to communicate with me and not with the rest of our family and friends. And she would never understand Chinese. I couldn't see how signing would translate to the written words. How could she live without reading?

Cued speech was another option but was not very common. Like signing, it was a visual, phonic-based system, with small hand shapes near the lips representing consonants and vowels, and mouth movements supplementing these. But it was not verbal language.

'I want to hear her voice,' I said simply. This was my greatest desire.

After the meeting, we walked past a classroom and looked through the window to see a teacher with a microphone clipped to her shirt. There were eight children aged three to four, each with what resembled a thick plastic necklace connected to a box strapped around their waist. This was their FM wireless system, we were told. It assisted their hearing aids by transmitting only the teacher's voice through her microphone, even in the noisy classroom environment. I could hear the children making loud noises, and the class looked like mayhem. It was quite distressing. *Is this Sophie's future?* I feared.

A couple of days later I took Sophie to an audiologist to be tested for her hearing aids. Carol Cascio was a lovely woman who couldn't have been more different to the specialist who had delivered the diagnosis like a guillotine! She was warm and friendly, and very good at dealing with parents' grief.

A test would provide a clearer picture of Sophie's hearing loss. I sat with her on my lap in a soundproof booth. She played with toys while the audiologist relayed sounds through speakers on each side of the room. If Sophie turned towards the sound, the audiologist would mark it as a response and a clown puppet would appear as a reward. As the test went on, I could hear every sound. I resisted the urge to turn her head towards the sound. If only Sophie would look up! The sounds got louder and louder but still she did not respond. My agony grew as I observed her, seeing her utterly oblivious! The testing dragged on for what seemed like hours of torture as I watched my unresponsive girl. Finally, she turned. She must have heard something! My heart leapt in hope.

Eventually, the gruelling process finished and Carol came into the booth. Sophie gave Carol her usual big smile. Carol didn't say anything, so I had a sinking feeling, yet I clung to a small thread of hope. Maybe her hearing wasn't as bad as first thought.

Carol began to explain that Sophie had detected some low-frequency sounds, but that she was profoundly deaf.

'What do you mean by that?' I asked desperately. 'What exactly did she hear?'

'In one ear we had a small response at 60 to 100 decibels – that's about the same as a jumbo jet flying overhead, but barely registers for her. In the other ear, it was 60 to 107 decibels, like a very loud rock concert. You and I would go home with our ears ringing, but to Sophie, it's just a slight reverberation.'

Carol handed me a graph. It indicated, in what was called a 'speech banana', the points within the 30 to 50 decibel range at which Sophie had detected sounds and where speech was detected. Sophie had no high-frequency hearing, which is where most of the useful speech sounds are located. My heart sank even more as I realised that even with hearing aids, Sophie would only ever hear the 'O' in her name. This final diagnosis hardened my resolve. 'Right.' I swallowed. 'Okay, what happens next?'

'We will make moulds to fit Sophie's ears while we wait for the hearing aids to arrive,' Carol said. 'The hearing aids won't enable her to hear, of course, but they will act as amplifiers to enable her to detect sound. That's the first step.'

As Carol was preparing the moulds, I realised I had to somehow explain to my daughter what was happening. I pointed to my own ear and smiled while Carol pushed a jelly-like substance into Sophie's ear. Sophie was so good about it all, which saddened me even more.

As we drove home, I started to prepare myself to tell Mum. I knew she would be devastated for both Sophie and me. That night I dialled the familiar Australian number and after the initial greeting, I just came out with it. 'Mum. We just found out Sophie's deaf,' I blurted.

'Mary, what?' I could hear the disbelief in her voice.

'I took her for a test, Mum. An ABR test. An auditory brainstem response test. It shows her response to sounds by looking at her brain activity.' I took a deep breath. 'Sophie is profoundly deaf, Mum.'

'I'm so sorry, darling!' she said, then asked, 'What can I do?'

'Nothing,' I said, through tears. I told her about getting the hearing aids and trying to learn how we could communicate with Sophie. Immediately, Mum got it. I could tell she understood everything.

'Oh, sweetheart. So much for you to take in. But I know you and Li will make the best decisions for Sophie,' she said.

~

It would take a couple of weeks for the hearing aids to be ready. For Sophie's sake, we tried to live life as normally as possible until then. I was also soon to go on a ten-day tour to Canada with Li and Houston Ballet. Cancelling at the last minute wasn't possible. It was excruciating to leave Sophie now, but she would be fine with Nana and Yeye. There was nothing else I could do.

I realised that the hearing world was changing for me. I began listening more closely to nearby conversations, realising, 'Sophie can't hear this!' Even the Mad Mothers group became hard for me to enjoy. Though they were supportive, and sensitive to my feelings, their delight in sharing their child's latest development was something I could no longer bear. I went less and less frequently.

Too soon, Li and I headed off to Canada with heavy hearts.

'I really want to see if we can fix this,' Li said as we departed for the airport. 'I think we need to leave no stone unturned. I want us to try everything, Mary.'

'Of course, Li,' I agreed, but deep down, I believed there was no fixing it. The fact of Sophie's deafness was now very real to me. I knew that Li was thinking of Chinese medicine. I understood that in this extreme circumstance he needed to turn to his roots. He had a lot of faith in Chinese treatments, and acupuncture in particular. This was his way of dealing with the grief. He was Sophie's father and felt he should take some sort of action to fix things.

While I missed Sophie, I appreciated the time away as it gave us space to talk about what had happened and what our future would be. As we continued to tour in Ottawa and Toronto, Sophie and her diagnosis were constantly in the back of my mind. We were performing *Ghost Dances*, where the end of the piece has the mother leading the whole village, rocking forwards and backwards in unison. This repetitive sequence evokes a powerful feeling of oneness. In this moment, a thought occurred to me that gripped my heart like ice. *Oh my God, Sophie will never hear this sound, this hauntingly beautiful Chilean music or any music – ever.*

I rushed to the dressing room afterwards and sobbed. It was then I knew I couldn't leave Sophie again. I *wouldn't* leave Sophie again. Not ever. This would be my last dance. When we got back to the hotel, I told Li: 'I have to stop. I just have to be with Sophie. We have to think about how we're going to feel in ten years' time if I don't stop now to help her and give her every possible opportunity available. We've lost so much time already. She is already eighteen months old!'

Li stared at me. 'Oh, Mary, you think that's best?'

'I really do. It'll be the best for all of us.'

This decision ripped through my soul and I sobbed even harder as Li held me. He felt so sad for me. He was also going to lose his ballet partner, but there was no question: our daughter was more important. I had known that one day I would have to stop dancing. But I hadn't known when that day would come until I walked off that stage and into the freezing Canadian night.

I was exhausted from all the worrying and thinking and decisions. When we returned to Houston, Li and I went to see Ben. I told him in a rush, 'I'm so sorry, Ben, but I have to stop dancing. I have to be with Sophie. I have to teach her to speak. I don't know what it's going to take, but I have to give it a try.'

Ben leaned forward and said, 'Mary, I understand. You need to do what you need to do for Sophie. I'm just so very sad for all of you. The door will always be open for you to come back. Don't ever forget that.'

'Thank you so much,' I managed through tears.

I felt such a sense of relief. No longer would I have that rending pull between the ballet and Sophie, and with this decision I felt I regained some control of our lives. I had also taken the first step to hearing Sophie's voice and the possibility, at some point, I hoped, of having a conversation with my daughter.

∼

The hearing aids were finally ready, so we returned to the Houston School for Deaf Children (HSDC) for Sophie to be fitted. As I drove, I knew this would become a journey I would make many, many times. And it was just going to be Sophie and me. Although Li would always be by my side, he couldn't always be there physically. He had to work to support our family, and that meant long hours and some-times days and weeks away from us. Before Sophie, I had dedicated my life to ballet. From this moment on, I was going to dedicate it to my daughter.

Now I was grieving for two things: my darling daughter and my dancing career. Since Sophie's diagnosis, our mother–daughter relationship was completely changed. The mother I thought I was and the daughter I thought I had were taken away from me. We now had to start building a new kind of relationship, one with no verbal language, with me being a different kind of mother and Sophie being a different kind of daughter. It was daunting to think about this because every time I learned more about deafness, the journey ahead appeared more difficult. Having a conversation with my daughter now felt like an impossible dream.

Li saw my pain and even offered to give up his own career to teach Sophie instead. His generosity meant so much to me but I knew it had to be me, as he was still learning English. His pronunciation was still all over the place. In any case, it was no use grieving for my career as there was nothing else I could do about it. My only goal in life was for Sophie to have her own voice.

~

Due to her profound level of deafness, Sophie's hearing aids were huge. I was shocked by the size of them. They were as big as her ears. Carol fitted a little piece of plastic tubing to hook the hearing aids around Sophie's ears so they wouldn't fall off every time she moved her head.

I also learned the hearing aids had to be pushed in quite aggressively to fit flush into Sophie's ears. If the placement wasn't airtight, the devices would whistle and not function properly. As I practised putting them on, I kept smiling and acting as if it was a fun game. Sophie was so good about it, she didn't even throw them off. We sat alone in the same sound booth as before. I could hear the beeps and, once again, willed her to react to the sounds. This was not even hearing – this was just detecting the difference between sound and silence. Listening and language were things she would have to learn.

After what seemed the longest hour of testing, it was finally over. The results, with the amplification of hearing aids, now showed Sophie could detect some low-frequency sounds. After eighteen months of silence, the beeps were Sophie's first sounds. The audiogram also revealed that she still couldn't detect high-frequency sounds, such as *ssss* and *shhhh*.

If I had any hope before this day, it was finally quashed. I finally, fully comprehended the words that the specialist had uttered on that fateful day: Sophie was profoundly deaf. I had never felt a deeper sadness.

Putting on the hearing aids was the first step, but she also had to be okay with wearing them. 'Sophie!' I said loudly, slightly exaggerating my lips. 'How lucky are you! These are your hearing aids!'

As one of eight children, I grew up surrounded by babies. Here I am holding Paddy, baby number seven, in the yard of Little Kellow Street, Rockhampton, aged seven.
McKendry family collection

My parents Neil George and Coralie McKendry with all the children, and one more on the way. Clockwise, Neil George, Coralie, Gerry, me, Matt, Paddy, Brig, Mick, and Jo sitting on Coralie's lap.
McKendry family collection

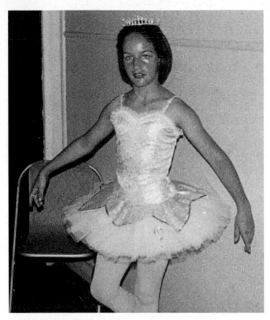

Modelling the first tutu
I ever wore for a ballet
competition, at age twelve.
Courtesy of Marise McConaghy

Preparing for my ballet concert in Rocky at the age of fourteen. In the mirror's
reflection from left to right is me, Debra Parker and Nina Veretennikova.
McKendry family collection

This is the audition photograph I sent to the Royal Ballet School as part of my application in 1974. My acceptance to RBS changed the course of my life.
McKendry family collection

In rehearsal with
Nigel Burgoine
at London
Festival Ballet,
1980.
McKendry family
collection

Together with
Mum and Dad
on one of their
visits to me in
London, just
before they
boarded the
Orient Express.
McKendry family
collection

Performing the Black Swan in 1982 was one of my most challenging but rewarding roles at London Festival Ballet.
Photograph by Anthony Crickmay

The fur coat my parents bought me kept me feeling snug – and glamorous – while on tour with London Festival Ballet. *McKendry family collection*

A highlight of touring Australia in 1979 with London Festival Ballet was seeing my family. *McKendry family collection*

Performing *Giselle* with Houston Ballet in 1986.   Photographer unknown

Giselle will always be a special ballet for Li and me – the ballet during which we fell in love.   Photographer unknown

After partnering each other on stage for some time, our relationship developed off-stage – and made quite a splash in ballet circles.
Photograph by Phyllis Hand

Li and I married in October 1987, in Houston. We held a modest reception at our new home in Euclid St – it was such a happy day.
Photograph by Wu Dazhen

Li's beloved Niang and Dia lived with us in Houston soon after Sophie's birth.
We feel so blessed to have had that special time with them.
Photograph by Wu Dazhen

Family has always been at the heart of who we are. We have made many visits to
Li's family in China over the years. Here I am holding Sophie in the Li commune
in 1990.

I returned to professional dancing six months after having Sophie, and we would often bring her in to the studio.   Photograph by Ira Strickstein

In 1990 I was invited by the Australian Ballet to dance in the Australian Gala at the Sydney Opera House. Li stepped in as my partner, and won the hearts of Australian audiences.   Photograph by Branco Gaica

My last performance for Houston Ballet was *The Nutcracker* in 1991, dancing with Li.

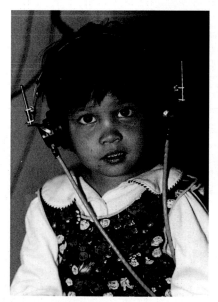

Sophie's journey has included endless hearing tests and speech therapy.

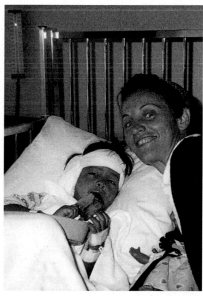

In 1993 Sophie underwent her first cochlear implant operation, in Houston.

We became a family of four when Tom was born in 1992. This Christmas portrait was taken on the verandah in Euclid Street.
Li family collection

Sophie and me in our backyard in Houston.

Photograph by Leticia London

Li dancing with
Sophie, here aged six.
Li family collection

We moved to Australia in 1995, when Li accepted the position of principal artist
with the Australian Ballet. Bridie was born in 1997, and Melbourne became our
home for seventeen years.

Photograph by Simon Schluter / *The Age*

Deafness has never prevented Sophie from following her heart. At fifteen she was cheerleading at St John's School, Houston.

Li family collection

The premiere of *Mao's Last Dancer* in Melbourne, 2009, was such a special night for us all. We were all so proud of Li.

Li family collection

Teaching ballet has been a wonderful way to channel my passion following the end of my performing career, and is a way of giving back to the art form that's brought me so much joy.
Photograph by Tamara Hanton, courtesy of Queensland Ballet

Living in the Sunshine State once again, I feel I have come full circle. Together Li and I have made Queensland Ballet our cultural home. Here we are after Li was made Officer of the Order of Australia in 2019.
Photograph by Mark Cranitch / Newspix

With my happy family in 2020: Bridie, me, Li, Sophie holding Nala, and Tom.
Li family collection

I will always have Sophie to
thank for helping me write
the story of my life.
Li family collection

Once they were turned on, I made sure Sophie's eyes were fixed on me when I was speaking. This ensured that I never wasted a sentence.

I was then keen to get started with speech therapy. I don't think HSDC had ever come across anyone who wanted to move as fast as I did. There was a little white house at the back, separate from the main building, where the speech therapy was held for toddlers. We immediately started going there twice a week. Other parents dropped off their kids, but I stayed with Sophie to be part of these classes. I wanted to learn so I could repeat the lessons again at home.

The teacher started with pictures of animals. She pointed to a dog and said loudly, 'Woof woof!' The next step was to repeat the sounds and ask the children to point to the correct picture. More pictures followed: cow – 'moo moo'; duck – 'quack quack'. Mimicking these three sounds was the focus for the entire hour.

Sophie was an angel, sitting down patiently the entire time even though she was not yet two. As the lesson went on, Sophie still could not repeat the words or the sounds and she soon grew tired. When we left to go home I looked at her adorable tired little face, remembering her quizzical expression when new sensations reached her ears.

Despite her struggle with the lesson, I determined there and then to never let a moment go by when I wasn't with her, building on what she had learned, teaching her to recognise sounds even if it would take me a lifetime. She was my daughter and I was her mother. I owed her nothing less.

~

As if the hearing aids weren't already bulky enough, two months into our new routine, full of speech therapy lessons, we were given a big FM system consisting of a microphone for me to wear and a receiver to connect to Sophie's hearing aids. The FM system was to help Sophie better hear me if she was more than a metre away. Like a trouper, Sophie took this new equipment in her stride. The system came with two specially designed bumbags, one for me to wear around my waist and one for Sophie to carry her FM receiver. Niang took one look at them and shook her head, then made a little pink silk purse to go around Sophie's neck to hold her receiver. Sophie broke into a huge smile. It looked much better! She was happy with her new purse with her FM goodies.

Niang always made a loud clucky sound with her tongue when she was amazed at something. One day, I clicked my tongue like Niang and to my surprise, Sophie turned to me. I couldn't believe it! I turned my head away to try again and Sophie again responded. 'Sophie! You heard me!' I was so delighted that I danced around and hugged her and kept on clicking. What a breakthrough! I now knew she could detect some sounds with her big powerful hearing aids.

My focus on Sophie did not waver. I set up her cot next to our bed so that I could put on the hearing aids and the FM equipment the minute she woke up, and then started talking. 'Good morning, my beautiful girl! Let's change your nappy. Nappy time! Nappy time!' And I talked loudly all day, every day.

Funnily enough, Sophie rarely tried to take out the clunky hearing aids. She could read my face very early on, so perhaps she knew leaving them on made me happy. I quietly savoured this small achievement.

Though Sophie and I combined lessons and play, it was often to the point of exhaustion. At times like this, I would remind myself of the story of Helen Keller and her devoted teacher Annie Sullivan. Their one-on-one struggle to find a way for Helen to comprehend and to communicate gave me strength. Could I do what Annie did? I would certainly try.

Niang and Dia continued to work in the garden and cook our favourite meals, while Li, when not at rehearsals or performing, was still determined to look for a cure. He spoke to a good friend who was passionate about *qi gong*, a healing, spiritual exercise with flowing movements and deep breathing. The friend believed *qi gong* could help Sophie with her deafness. Late one night I woke up and thought I heard a strange, low humming voice: 'Hmmmmmm . . . Hmmmmm . . .'

I turned in bed and noticed Li wasn't there, and rising quietly, I followed the voice. There he was, sitting on the edge of Sophie's bed, cross-legged like Buddha, and he was humming. His hands were in prayer position in front of his chest and his eyes were closed.

'What are you doing, Li?' I asked in hushed tones, startling him.

'Oh! San Huang told me that this exercise will heal Sophie's hearing loss,' he replied earnestly.

'You are mad, Li! Come to bed now! It's not going to work,' I said, annoyed.

'Well, how do you know? It's worth a try!' Li insisted, closing his eyes and continuing his 'Hmmmmmm . . . Hmmmmm . . .'

He also began asking around in the Chinese community for the best acupuncturist. Eventually, he found one in Washington, DC and we flew there a couple of months later and met a small, middle-aged Chinese woman who spoke very good English. She peered into Sophie's ears. 'She's not going to see anything like that!' I thought.

At the end of the examination, the acupuncturist said, 'Yes, I think acupuncture could return some hearing, but I think you need some very special expertise.'

I cringed at the thought of having to hold Sophie down for all those needles to go into her head and ears. I was sceptical, but Li visibly perked up at the referral to an acupuncturist in Beijing – the best in the world! There was a lot to discuss when we returned to Houston.

In the meantime, I continued Sophie's speech therapy sessions. I would tell her out loud exactly what we were doing and repeat it again and again. Our life was filled with my voice. At the park I would say, 'Up, up we go! Up we go!' as I pushed her on the swing. Always at the back of my mind, I was trying to imagine her life without sound.

Over the next six months, I watched the language capabilities of young children the same age as Sophie explode, yet she continued to have no language. It was a cruel thing to see. In fact, the 'Ba ba ba' and

'Ma ma ma' she had once babbled had stopped. I would later learn that this was common for deaf children.

I also learned that most babies start developing an auditory memory bank from the sounds they hear in utero. Humans need this bank of sounds to form a language. Deaf children don't have an auditory memory, so Sophie had none of that memory. I began to realise the enormous complexity of the English language, and that we were fighting against time.

Our new way of life became very challenging at home. Up until Sophie's diagnosis, our lives had been all about music and the two languages. Now, we packed away music and other noises from the house – stereo, radio and television – to create a quiet environment to best enable Sophie to hear. I became very aware of background noise at all times. And I kept thinking, *How could anyone have a life without music?* We still had Niang and Dia with us, but it wasn't the same as before. How could it be, when such a pall of sadness hung over us all?

It came to a turning point when the speech therapist advised me not to confuse Sophie by having two languages spoken at home. Oh, God, how would we manage this?

'Li,' I said, swallowing hard, 'the therapist told me two languages will confuse Sophie. It might delay or even stop her totally from learning English.'

'So we shouldn't speak Chinese in front of her?' he asked, the hurt visible in his eyes.

'Yes, and you need to speak English,' I replied, feeling incredibly sad for him.

I could tell Niang and Dia didn't really understand but they respected our decision. No longer did we see their smiling faces and hear their endless chatter at the dinner table. We now ate in silence. It was bewildering for Sophie, too. I started to worry for Niang and Dia and their relationship with their granddaughter. They couldn't speak English and we were not to speak Chinese, yet they had come to look after Sophie and help her become bilingual. That's when I knew the current situation was not going to work.

'How was Sophie today?' Li asked me one day when I took Sophie's hearing aids off and put her to bed. My joy in any small achievements was also his joy.

'I don't know, Li. I can't tell. I'm so distracted. I am really worried about your parents.'

Li remained silent. He was thinking.

'Niang feels helpless. It's obvious,' I continued. 'And it's awful to see Dia so quiet and withdrawn. Sophie can see there's something different about them. What are we going to do?'

Li spoke quietly and I had never seen him look so forlorn.

'Mary, I think they will have to go back to China. It will be best for Sophie. I'll talk to them now. They will understand.'

This broke my heart. Poor Li. He had been separated from his parents from such a young age, and the time spent with them since Sophie's birth had been the happiest of his life. The thought of them being separated again was gut-wrenching.

Over the next few days and nights I saw Li and his parents in deep conversation. I could only guess what they were talking about. Sometimes Niang would come and take my hands and look into my eyes, and Dia would sit with his head in his hands, despairing yet resigned. It was agony for all of us. But all too soon, and in another way not soon enough, Niang and Dia made the difficult decision to return to China.

Later, it was agreed we would all go to China together. Li wanted to take Sophie to the acupuncturist in Beijing, so it was the perfect opportunity to visit Li's family too. The timing was good because Houston Ballet would soon close for the summer break. Li also wanted to take Sophie to see a famous Chinese healer up in the Laoshan Mountains in Qingdao. His brothers had told him about the healer. I was sceptical, but understood it was important to Li.

It was a hot day in August when we flew to Beijing. Niang and Dia had a lot to pack – all the gifts they had bought for the extended family – but soon we were ready to go.

'Sophie! In the car! In the car! We're going to China! China! With Nana! With Yeye! It will be such fun! Fun, Sophie!'

I strapped Sophie into her car seat, dressed in her little Italian-made sun frock, her hearing aids sticking out and her FM receiver in Niang's silk bag hanging around her neck. How could I communicate to her that this would be the last time she would spend time with her grandparents and they were not coming back? I fought hard to hold back my tears.

We landed in Beijing and, just like the last time, the Bandit was there to meet us. He greeted Li with a huge smile, then grabbed Sophie and hugged her, talking at a hundred miles an hour. He collected us in a twenty-seater bus with no seatbelts, which was the only thing left from his recently failed plastics business that Li had helped establish. The bus ended up being a godsend as we had a great deal of luggage. I tried not to look out at the overwhelming chaos on the roads as China still had no discernible road rules in the 1990s.

We stayed again at the Front Gate Hotel and Li arranged an appointment with the acupuncturist. We went to the hospital the next day and ended up in a room with three Chinese doctors, none of whom spoke English. I silently handed Sophie over to the most respected acupuncturist in the world, and he peered into her ears. All communication was in Chinese, so I had no idea what they were saying. Sophie was blissfully unaware of what was going on.

Finally, Li translated what the specialist had said after the examination: 'I could lead you on and give you false hope that acupuncture could help, but your daughter's deafness can't be fixed by acupuncture or Chinese medicine. I'm sorry.'

I was very grateful for his honest assessment, as I didn't think I could have allowed them to put needles into our daughter's ears!

We went back to the hotel to relay the news to Niang and Dia. They saw this as a small setback and told Li they were confident in the Chinese healer in the mountains in Qingdao. '*Ta zhi haole ren, ta shige shenyi.*' He has cured many people. He is a miracle man, they said.

The next day the Bandit and Fengtian drove us to the Beijing train station. The station was a chaotic zoo, full of people crowded shoulder to shoulder. The only way to get through was to push and shuffle through the gaps. We had many suitcases full of Niang and Dia's gifts, which included second-hand suits for all the brothers, jewellery, make-up and, of course, alcohol. Dia loved the occasional Scotch whisky. And there were many cartons of Western cigarettes. We struggled against the bustling crowd with our mountainous luggage. I held Sophie tightly as the Bandit and Fengtian carved a path for us and eventually shoved us onto the crowded train to Qingdao. Despite our cabin being first class, we barely slept as people smoked, coughed and spat throughout the night.

The following morning, we arrived at the Qingdao station and were greeted by all the family members. Everyone was delighted to see Niang and Dia again. Two babies had joined our family: fifth brother's daughter, Yan Yan, and seventh brother's daughter, Rong Rong. They had been born just months before Sophie, so she now had two little playmates. There was nothing much I could do about the Chinese language being spoken, so instead I forced myself to relax and enjoy the time with Li's family. The Qingdao local dialect, Shandong Hua, is a very guttural Mandarin dialect that I learned to love. It sounded like a language filled with passion.

Discussions went on about getting a meeting with the 'miracle healer' up in the Laoshan Mountains. Oldest brother, Cuncia, and second brother, Cunyuan, told us what to expect the next day when we went there. As it was a two-hour trip, the brothers needed to find a van first, then an experienced driver who knew the way – there were no paved roads and the brothers didn't know exactly where the healer lived. Before I heard of their plan I was already sceptical, and now

I was apprehensive about getting lost or having an accident in the middle of nowhere. Li said I didn't need to go with them. As if I was going to let Sophie go without me! I didn't believe in the healer, but Li did. There was no stopping him. It was something he had pinned so much hope on, so I just had to go along with it.

The day was going to be scorching hot so we started early. We sat at the small table outside for breakfast, next to the wok. I picked up Niang's steamed white bread, dipped it into the salty sauce and ate it with a fried egg. Sophie loved Niang's food and ate heartily. I was reminded how she would miss her cooking when we returned home. Meanwhile, the conversations continued about what to eat for dinner. While it seemed that food was mostly what the family would talk about, quietly I was grateful for the feeling of normalcy, no matter how small.

The driver arrived and beckoned us to follow him through the narrow laneways lined with smelly sewage gutters. Cuncia carried Sophie, along with her FM receiver in the pink silk bag, and Li and I followed with second brother Cunyuan and the gifts we had brought for the healer.

The van was more like a bus. It reminded me of Neil George's fourteen-seater people mover back in Rocky. 'Look, Sophie!' I said loudly to reassure her, but perhaps more to reassure myself. 'We're going on a bus! With Daddy! And with your uncles!' She looked excited, mirroring my expression, and I kept my fingers crossed that we weren't heading into a nightmare.

We drove through the narrow dirt streets to the outskirts of Qingdao and soon started our ascent. Every part of the mountain was cultivated with row upon row of different crops, and the make-shift roads between the fields were riddled with deep potholes. I sat in terror as the old bus creaked on, threatening to break down at any moment and leave us stranded forever. The bus had no seatbelts or air-conditioning and there were still no mobile telephones in case anything happened to us. It didn't help that Li's brothers had given the driver cigarettes – he smoked like there was no tomorrow.

I was thankful when we got out of the bus two hours later. We found ourselves in front of a concrete-box-like shack, much worse-looking than Niang and Dia's place back in the commune, with chickens, ducks, pigs and dogs roaming freely in the front courtyard. At least it was cooler here in the mountains. I looked around and saw the amazing view across the landscape, but I was in no mood to enjoy it.

An elderly woman hobbled across the crumbling threshold and beckoned us inside. There were only two rooms, with a kitchen on one side of the wall and a small mud bed, a *kang*, on the other side, on which the healer sat cross-legged. He had a long grey beard and a lot of missing teeth. The healer and his wife smoked so heavily that we were choking on the smoke. They invited us to sit on the *kang*.

Li and I somehow fitted on the *kang* with Sophie on my lap. We laid out our gifts of wine and cigarettes. The fact it all came from the West was very important. Western cigarettes were treated as a valuable commodity.

The healer and Li began to talk. I did not speak once, and Li did not translate much. The healer looked across to Sophie to assess her deafness with a thoughtful and serious expression. He occasionally stroked his long sparse beard while he continued to smoke heavily his pipe. Li and his brothers nodded gratefully while he spoke. After a while, I became impatient and asked, 'Li, what did he say?'

'He said he can fix Sophie's hearing,' Li simply replied.

Thirty minutes later, we left the healer with a couple of gallons of Laoshan mountain spring water, a dozen mountain-hen eggs and some smelly, black-looking Chinese herbs. We were ushered into the bus and started the rough journey back to the village. Li began to tell me more about what the healer had said and his confidence that Sophie could be healed. He had given us his ancient and secret family recipes to treat her. But we had to do it back at home in Houston.

I was sceptical, to say the least. 'How are you going to take all this through customs back to America?' I asked.

'Don't worry, Mary.' Li smiled.

I tried so hard not to roll my eyes! However, I knew that he would never be able to accept our daughter's reality until he'd tried absolutely everything.

I was so relieved to return to the Li commune, out of the scorching heat and out of that deathtrap of a bus. Some of Sophie's cousins were there: Yan Yan, Rong Rong, Li's fourth brother's daughter, Feng Feng, and his second brother's adopted daughter, Jie Jie. Sophie squealed with delight. 'Go and play, Sophie!' I said loudly in English and gestured. All the children ran to play in the courtyard.

Li and his brothers were sharing the day's adventure with Dia and Niang. I just wanted to lie down with a cup of Chinese tea. The trip to the mountains had exhausted me.

Soon it was time to go home to America, along with the healer's ingredients and Li's hopes in them packed in our suitcases. I was emotional as we waved goodbye to dear Niang and Dia – we all were, except for Sophie, who gave her happy smile and blow-kisses. She didn't know, of course, that her grandparents wouldn't be there in the granny flat back in Euclid Street.

9

When we got home, the place felt empty and silent. Li and I had no words. We could hardly bear to go into the granny flat. It was bare and silent now without Niang and Dia, who had been such a huge part of our household for so long. Sophie pointed to their place and wanted to visit. I was heartbroken for her.

For Li, to lose his Niang and Dia, the Chinese language and culture from our home was an additional deep sadness. His dream of Sophie speaking Chinese and being a conduit to his family was no longer to be. How would he ever be able to bear this, after everything he had gone through in his life?

To my relief, Li somehow managed to smuggle in the Chinese herbs, mountain water and hen eggs. He followed the instructions to make the special brew with the eggs. Soon our entire house stank. I had never smelt anything so foul in my entire life. Sophie just pinched her nose and ran as far away as she could. How would Li ever get her to eat those eggs? I felt like telling him to chuck them out, but I held back. After all, he and his family had made such an effort for this cure and all their hopes were riding on it.

Finally, after several hours of cooking, the eggs were ready. Li called Sophie and peeled the blackened shell off one egg. 'Sophie, this is delicious! It is from your *nana*! Let's eat it,' Li lied cheerfully, opening his mouth in the hope Sophie would mimic him and open hers too. Instead, she took one look at the black and smelly egg, made a disgusted face, moved her face away and shook her little head.

'Come on, Sophie. It taste good!' Li chided as he broke a small piece and ate it himself, in front of her. I could detect a fleeting shudder from him and then he was all smiles. Sophie then reluctantly took a small piece and put it in her mouth. Immediately, she spat it out and made another disgusted face.

Poor Li! All that effort had come to this, I thought.

~

It was late summer in Houston and there was nothing for it but to get on with our new life as best we could. Our days were now very full. Li was back in the studio and Sophie and I continued with our twice-weekly speech sessions, which we then repeated at home. Patience is not one of my virtues, and I had to be doing something. The discipline I'd brought to dancing was essential in keeping up the intensity and consistency needed to teach Sophie to listen and then, hopefully, to speak. Every night I lay in bed thinking, *Have I done enough today?* The answer was always no. *I have to do more tomorrow*, I told myself.

I wanted the speech therapy to move faster. Sophie was two years old and falling further behind. I felt the constant pressure of time running away from us. I yearned for the day when Sophie would utter just one word to me, but I didn't know if she would *ever* speak or gain language. The red light of her receiver blinked as I spoke to her. I so hoped she could hear me, but I knew she was profoundly deaf. Of course she couldn't hear me! This realisation always made me feel sad and lonely. I deeply missed Li and being at the studio, but I would push this to the back of my mind as it was not to be.

Over time, I learned that I had to say a word over a thousand times for it to sit in Sophie's auditory memory. I would focus on the high-frequency sounds while we were playing with dolls. 'The baby's crying, shhhhh!' I put my finger to my lips as I shushed. 'The baby's sleeping, shhhhh!'

One day I called out her name: 'Sophie! Sophie!' She turned. Like the day when I mimicked Niang's clicking noise, it happened again! Delighted, I rushed over and scooped Sophie up and danced around the room. 'Sophie, you heard me! You clever girl!' She laughed. For me this was huge. It was the next breakthrough I'd been working towards.

Slowly, everything we did at home became a language lesson. 'Have a drink,' I'd say loudly, keeping to very short sentences. There are many words around this situation: 'glass', 'water', 'drink', 'sip', 'pour'. Drama seemed to work with Sophie. I had to be quite animated or she would lose interest. If I spilt milk, I would lift my hands and say, 'Uh-oh!' Then one day, she said it! 'Uh-ooo,' and raised her little arms, head to the side – soooo cute! I was beyond excited. After that, I'd deliberately make things happen, even falling over myself sometimes to hear her little voice say, 'Uh-oh!' Clearly, some of the things we worked on were clicking for her. I just didn't know how much. The irony was not lost on me – I was performing all day long, for Sophie!

'Weet-Bix!' I'd say. 'Let's eat Weet-Bix.' Then I'd pour the milk. 'Pour the milk! It's cold,' I'd say, and hold her little hands around the bottle. 'Pour the milk. Where is the spoon? Eat the Weet-Bix! Yum!'

I did this all day, every day. And every day I waited for her to say the words back. This was how the rest of that year passed. I hardly had time to be aware of what was going on for Li with Houston Ballet. I was just so focused, bordering on obsessed. Every situation was a learning opportunity for Sophie, and I was not going to let a minute go to waste.

~

Some nights, unable to sleep, my little girl breathing quietly beside me, I would imagine myself on stage again, free as a bird. Then I began to berate myself. As if dancing should matter when Sophie had no hearing and could not be part of our world. I should have realised something was wrong.

'How did I not see it, Li?' I asked him one morning. 'It's all my fault! We could have found out about Sophie's deafness much earlier. I blamed the doctor, but really, I am her mother. How could I have missed it!'

'Mary,' he replied, taking my hands in his. 'We accepted doctor's advice, like any parent would. For God's sake, don't blame yourself! Blame me instead! And Mary, remember I read *The Good Earth* by Pearl Buck?'

'I remember that. What about it?'

'I never told you before, but I remember my heart murmured when I read the daughter was deaf, then I prayed this wouldn't happen to our children. Looking back now I feel some kind premonition. I should taken more notice when Sophie wasn't turning for her name.' He said in his imperfect English.

'Oh, Li. Do you think we were too preoccupied with our careers and left too much to Niang and Dia?' I despaired.

'Mary, we didn't know. We are doing all what we can. You are marvellous mother to Sophie. I am sure soon you be able to have conversation with our daughter.' He looked at me earnestly. 'I'm sure of it.' He nodded, so definite.

'How can you be so sure, Li?'

'There only one person in world I know who can make this happen – that's you!'

I was touched by his belief and trust in me, but I still couldn't stop thinking about all the time wasted. After that brutal diagnosis I switched doctors. I never spoke to that particular doctor again. I don't think I ever forgave him for being so negligent and careless.

The challenges ahead for Sophie just kept getting tougher. To be honest, it was so overwhelming sometimes that I just wanted to close my world. How I wished that we were just everyday people, as opposed to theatre people, with my mum living around the corner.

I decided I needed answers. Why did we have a deaf child when there was no deafness in either of our families? Sophie was tested for cytomegalovirus (CMV), a virus that can affect hearing development when the infection is passed across the placenta from a mother to her developing baby. She tested negative. That, too, was hard to take. When you are given a reason for something, you can understand and hopefully come to accept it more easily and move on. But not knowing anything at all left both of us feeling isolated and bewildered.

I felt I was in the tumble-dryer of life. Nothing was making sense. And my body, so attuned to constant movement, didn't feel like my body. I felt disembodied. When I needed an escape from reality, I occasionally brought Sophie with me to the studio, where I would take my place at the *barre* and do some stretching. But it wasn't enough. Sometimes, I thought I would go mad without ballet. A two-year-old toddler is a challenge at the best of times, but a profoundly deaf toddler is something else altogether. Mostly Sophie went along with the intensity of our days, but occasionally she would end up banging her head in silent frustration, and then go into her own dark space. When she was in that space, she could stay there for a long time. I often wondered whether the process we were going through was worth it. By the time Sophie was asleep, her equipment put aside for the night, I would be flat out in despair.

Li could see how exhausted I was and how exhausted Sophie was, too. He would try to take over when he got home to give me a break. Whenever he could, he would take her with him for his massage sessions. One day, he came rushing through the door from a session with Mad Charles. 'Mary, Sophie said "elbow"! Charles heard her too!' he said excitedly.

'What?' I said in disbelief. 'Get her to say it again.'

Li pointed to his elbow. 'Say "elbow", Sophie. Say "elbow",' he pleaded, willing her to form the word.

I ached for her to speak, but she wandered off to play with her toys instead. Li was definite that he had heard her. Any new word Sophie uttered made us ecstatic.

~

Ava Jean, Sophie's godmother, became an angel in this time of need. One day, she offered to take Sophie every Saturday morning. I began to look forward to having a morning off so Sophie and I could both have a break.

Sophie absolutely loved going to Ava Jean's house. As soon as we pulled into the gravel driveway with its avenue of leafy trees looking like a secret tunnel, her eyes would light up. 'Ava Jean! Hi, Ava Jean!' I would say in a singsong voice, and Sophie would run off into Ava Jean's arms. She had learned to say 'Bye-bye' by now and I was thrilled to hear her little voice say it to me.

'Buh-buh!' she called, waving.

'Bye-bye, Sophie!' I replied, waving right back.

Ava Jean's house was perfect for small children. It was always a little messy, with papers, ornaments, paintings and sculptures on every surface. To Sophie's eyes, the house was full of treasures, and bright colours. They also had a gentle old red-setter dog that Sophie adored.

Oh, it was such a relief to get away for these few hours! Sometimes I would just go for a quiet coffee by myself or for a long walk; at other times I would call in at the studio and spend some time with Li. Before Sophie's diagnosis, my life had always been overflowing with people and I wasn't used to being on my own, yet I found these long walks crucial for my sanity now.

One Saturday, coming home I returned to Ava Jean's to collect Sophie and Ava Jean beckoned me into the kitchen. 'Mary, I've been thinking,' she said in her Texan drawl, 'and I've been chatting with your friends from the ballet.'

I wondered where she was going with this.

'We want to see you dance again, Mary.'

'Well, that's not going to happen, Ava Jean. Sophie is my life now.'

'I know, Mary, I know. But we want to celebrate you and your marvellous career. Just one more dance. You haven't danced since you walked off the stage that last time in Toronto.'

'That was my farewell, Ava Jean! That was my last dance!' I couldn't see how it would be possible.

'Of course, Mary. But it was your farewell to Canada. You need to have a farewell here in Houston, for those who know you and love you like I do.'

Ava Jean, bless her, had touched a nerve. My body was like a tightly wound spring and it needed to dance. It needed to get back in shape. I felt it. And Ava Jean knew it.

'Mary, I'm begging you. We all want this to happen.'

And with that, the seed was planted in my mind. I went home with Sophie feeling strangely elated. Could I do this? It had been nine months since I had walked off the stage in Toronto. I decided to talk to Li about it that night.

'We need to think about this, Mary,' he said in his measured way. 'It will be a lot of work, but I think you can do it. We'll just have to get someone to look after Sophie while you return to the studio.'

'You will have to be my partner, Li. I don't want to do it with anyone else,' I told him.

'Of course, I would love to! It'll be wonderful for you to get back on the stage one more time,' he said, echoing my own thoughts as he always seemed to. He understood how important it was for me to have closure to my dance career.

Thankfully, Ben was also supportive. 'That would be great, Mary!' he said. 'And maybe you can come back for more performances occasionally, if you want to.' What a generous man!

Maria from the Mad Mothers group mentioned Pat, her mother-in-law, would be happy to babysit Sophie at home each morning while I was working in the studio. Luckily, Sophie was quite easy with new people, so that was a relief. I needed to do this, and our relationship would benefit from the break in the relentless days of speech therapy.

'Hey, Mum,' I said a couple of nights later. 'I've decided to dance one more time with Houston Ballet. I will be dancing with Li, and I would love for you and Dad to be here.'

'Oh, darling, that's wonderful news! I wouldn't miss it for the world. And I can help you with Sophie, too.' It felt wonderful to hear Mum's reassuring voice.

'That would be amazing, Mum. Thank you! What about Dad?' I asked.

'Oh, I don't know, Mary. His fear of flying has got a lot worse recently, and his doctor doesn't like him flying because of his emphysema. But let me talk to him.'

Then a couple of weeks later, Mum called back. 'Darling, he's been having hypnosis, of all things!' she said, chuckling. 'He seems confident he can fly, and his doctor is okay with it, so it looks like we'll both be there. We can't wait, Mary!'

They arrived a few weeks before the performance. I was so happy to see them again. The hypnosis seemed to have worked and I walked into my loving father's arms, not believing *both* parents were here! 'Hi, Dad! So good of you to come! How was the flight?'

'Shitty, but we're here now,' he replied with a twinkle in his eye, then, turning to tickle Sophie, 'Hello, my precious pearl!'

'You look wonderful, darling,' Mum said to me. 'And how's our beautiful baby girl?'

Straightaway I shared everything with them, explaining the progress Sophie was making, the things I was learning about deafness and our changing relationship since the diagnosis.

'Thank God for your energy, Mary. If anyone can do this, you can,' Mum said, encouraging me as always.

'What can we do?' Dad asked.

'Just love her and take care of her like you normally would. And talk a lot,' I added.

Incredibly, there seemed to be an instant connection between my parents and Sophie. Dad would walk her around the neighbour-hood in the pram, chatting about the houses on the street. He would hold her little hands tight as she jumped on the trampoline. 'You're a champion jumper, Sophie! Champion!' he'd tell her, laughing. And he and Coralie would sit on the porch with Sophie in the swing and chat as they waited for me to get home.

Having Mum and Dad there was a respite for Li, too. He and Dad both read the *Wall Street Journal* and discussed what was happening at the big end of town. It was an education for Li to be talking to Dad. He and Mum were so like Li's own parents in many ways. In the end, it was all about the family and the next meal.

I had eight weeks to prepare for *The Nutcracker*. The plan was for me to do four performances as the Sugar Plum Fairy, and I was warmly welcomed back into the studio by the whole company. 'They look so young!' I thought, as it seemed a lot had changed in the company while I was away. Upon reflection perhaps I had matured with what had happened with Sophie. It felt glorious to be back to the studio and the familiar rhythms of a ballet class. However, I knew I had a lot of work in front of me and I had to stay focused. The mirrors all around the studio didn't lie. I was facing a body that was out of condition. My muscles were soft, my body stiff. My feet ached and my Achilles tendons were tight, and I hadn't even put on pointe shoes yet. But as I listened to the music, I felt it lifting my soul. It was nice to sense my body naturally responding, and thankfully, my muscle memory was still there.

Li was tough on me. 'Do it again,' he'd say for the hundredth time, and yet I wouldn't have had it any other way. He knew I wanted to be the best I could be for my true last dance, and he knew what was needed when the lights went up. 'You have to push through it, Mary,' he said, knowing that I had been hobbling in pain since day one of rehearsals.

The weeks became a blur and the day was suddenly upon us. As we put on our make-up for the first performance, nerves were high. Li admitted later that he thought he was more nervous than I was.

The orchestra upstairs began, and I made my way up to the wings. Soon it was our turn. This was it! My heart thumped loudly as I took my first step onto the stage with Li. I had done many Sugar Plums in my life and still loved this *pas de deux*. The orchestra started to build up as our outstretched hands finally touched. Immediately, I felt electricity and nerves ignite. I looked into Li's reassuring eyes, and then I knew I would be fine. The performance was electric with our wonderful partnership. Suddenly, the first performance was over – I had made it through! The audience applauded loudly.

With each performance, my strength and stamina improved immensely. *Maybe I can continue dancing. Maybe I can still dance occasionally.* I entertained the thought as I continued to enjoy each performance more than the last. But then I reminded myself that the physical reality of getting my body ready for *The Nutcracker* over the previous eight weeks proved that I couldn't dance part-time. You have to do it all day, every day, and do nothing else but ballet. I knew deep in my heart that if there was any possibility of having a conversation with Sophie one day, I had no choice but to give up my lifelong love of dance. She was always on my mind.

The thought that this would be my last dance kept repeating in my head. There would be no more comeback after this. Everything felt surreal. All the years of passion, love, dedication and hard work towards perfection would end here. The make-up, my pointe shoes, my costumes – had me choking with emotion. How I wished it was just a bad dream.

Then it was time for my very final performance. Pat babysat for us that night so Mum and Dad could see me dance. My heart was bursting with joy as I walked onto the Wortham stage and I knew Li was feeling the same. As the Sugar Plum *pas de deux* music sounded, I blocked all thoughts and just let the music flow through my body. With Li by my side I was able to let my emotions fly, as all I wanted to do was to savour this last performance. I felt emotionally transported, I felt totally free – soaring above the score one last time.

It was almost over, just a few more steps to go. I sprang forward for Li to lift me high into the air before promenading me around, turning me in fast *pirouettes* and finishing with a show-stopping *arabesque*. The audience burst into applause, thinking it was the end of our *pas de deux*. I then jumped forward in a catlike step for the audience to clap again in delight. The music intensified as I reached out for Li's outstretched hand to suspend me in a striking high *arabesque*, then catch me darting to the side in a breathtaking finish just when the music reached its last crescendo. I had done it.

The audience erupted in thunderous applause and a standing ovation. They roared *brava* as we took our curtain call. Flowers were flying onto the stage. I was elated and my body was completely spent. Li gazed at me, smiling with love, as he took my hand and walked me to the front of the stage for the curtain call. I looked at him, our eyes locked, and I knew he understood me completely. The audience faded to a blur and only he and I shared this special moment together. We had experienced many highs and lows in our lives – this was such a high and it was wonderful to be in that moment together with just him. After several more curtain calls and bouquets of beautiful flowers bestowed upon me, the curtain finally came down on my dancing career.

~

Soon after *The Nutcracker*, it was time to think seriously about our future. Li and I started to talk about having another baby. He had always wanted many children – five, in fact, but I was the driver now. There were a couple of reasons why it made sense. Li and I both came from large families, so the idea of having an only child was not something either of us could contemplate. 'Another child would give both you and Sophie a bit of space,' he said to me. It was a subtle way of saying I was too obsessed with Sophie and her deafness. Another child would change the family dynamic, taking the pressure off the two of us being together all the time. Perhaps this would be healthier for our family as a whole. I also knew deep down that Sophie needed a sibling.

Mum and Dad continued to be a big help to us in the weeks after the performances. Mum felt that Houston was great for us. She was positive about my support network and could see how admired and loved Li was in the city. 'He's a superstar here,' she noted.

Li took the opportunity to talk with Neil George about doing an accounting course. He had always been interested in finance and knew that one day his own dance career would come to an end, too. Li also felt he had to step up and start preparing for the future. With Sophie's ongoing medical costs and me not working, things could become difficult for us financially. Our medical insurance with the Houston Ballet was quite generous and allowed us to cover the cost of Sophie's deafness. However, if we left the ballet, she would no longer be covered. I could sense that Li was feeling apprehensive about our future and wanted to ensure that we were financially secure.

It was time to get on with teaching Sophie to speak, but the feeling of isolation became worse. Sometimes it was more than I could bear. Li saw this and suggested that I return to the studio occasionally to coach him. It would provide some brief respite between speech therapy lessons. I thought it was a good idea – I had always been interested in teaching ballet since Miss Hansen took me on to help teach the younger classes in Rocky. But Li and I knew that there was another reason: to keep my sadness at bay.

'Mary, can you have a look at this solo I'm doing?' he'd ask. I would then watch his solo in the studio and discuss what he needed to do. I began advising him on footwork, lines and elevation. 'Point those feet faster and longer . . . Don't worry about landing,' I'd say. Eventually, I became his private coach, and he continued to allow me to be his teacher for many more years. It was a very generous and brave thing for him to do. He understood I needed it, and in a way he did, too.

At the end of each day he would offer to take care of Sophie, seeing how tired I was. I was grateful and would ignore his terrible accent as he'd sing, 'Rain, rain, go away' and 'Incy Wincy spider'. With Sophie he also endlessly watched videos of a popular Australian children's TV program called *Play School* that Mum had sent from Australia. Over this period, Li became very mindful of his accent and pronunciation and syntax. He paid more attention to me as I was teaching Sophie, and his English improved enormously.

~

I fell pregnant quite quickly. I was excited, but nervous about this baby also being deaf. Once you have a deaf child, there is a one in four chance of having another. But we were willing to take the risk.

I was also anxious to know what sex the baby was. For some reason I felt that having another girl so close to Sophie could be difficult for her as girls usually attain language early. So, a baby girl would surpass Sophie like a bullet. I worried that the comparison could become a disaster for their relationship. Boys usually acquire language slower than girls and I was so relieved to learn we were having a boy.

A little brother for our girl! A boy for Li to rough-and-tumble with! Apart from the worry about his hearing, we were both deliriously happy and excited.

Sophie and I worked harder, making the most of the time we had left as a twosome. By this time, her vocabulary had not expanded to more than fifty receptive words – words she could comprehend and respond to. A two-year-old hearing child would not only have vastly more than fifty receptive words but also could *express* those words. With her third birthday not far away, I became more aware of Sophie's lack of language and concepts. I paid special attention to other little children and analysed what they were doing. Many had started asking 'Why?'. I learned that hearing children's language snowballs after the age of three. Progress with speech therapy was painfully slow and Sophie could only recognise my voice in a quiet, close environment, so how would I ever teach her this concept?

As if that wasn't enough, we decided to move house. With our growing family we needed more room – including an extra bedroom for the baby. We enjoyed living close to the ballet studio and theatre so that Li could dash home quickly. I looked around our neighbourhood and found one house for sale just up the street. Perfect! It was in an ideal location. We bought 423 Euclid Street, a nicely renovated double-storey house with a wraparound porch at the front and a small yard at the back. There were lots of trees and a trampoline. The kitchen was new and flowed out onto the backyard. The carpeted bedrooms upstairs were quiet and there was also a cute little library nook great for reading.

Moving was an undertaking. Li had so much stuff. We hired a van and Li's good friend John Grensback and some other company dancers came to help. I desperately wanted to get rid of some things, but Li just wouldn't throw anything out. There were old papers, diaries and letters from right back to his days at the Beijing Dance Academy. There were also programs, posters, photos and videos in the thousands from just about every ballet he had danced, and artefacts like the Buddha heads he'd bought in Bali. On top of this, there was a garage full of hardware: nails, old chairs and even windows and doors. These were from Niang and Dia trawling garage sales. Li was very suspicious if I tried to throw anything out. If something couldn't be found, I'd be blamed. Luckily, we also had a garage at the new house. But the cars wouldn't live there, just all Li's junk.

Eventually we settled into the new house. We were glad to move into a bigger space. The thought of two children running around the yard as they grew up filled me with happiness. I couldn't wait to see my little girl and boy bouncing together on the trampoline and climbing the old trees in the backyard. It brought back wonderful memories of my own carefree childhood.

But moving house was difficult for Sophie, as I wasn't able to explain it to her – everything had to be lived through for her to understand it. She didn't know what was happening and she was stubborn.

I'd also been having a lot of trouble toilet-training her. How could I ever explain what the toilet was for if she didn't have the language yet? Because her life was so visual, whenever we moved or changed anything, any little thing, the only way she could control the situation was through her bowels, and that's what she did when we moved. She wouldn't go for a whole week!

Another big thing was to get her into her own bed. She had been sleeping with us for about a year, but now it was time to make way for the new baby. We set up the little room next door to our bedroom. It was a lovely room with her favourite toys and a window that looked out to the leafy neighbourhood. However, Sophie was having none of it. She loved being in her room, but not to sleep alone. Often she would get up and follow me to our bed.

I was very conscious of how difficult it was for Sophie to understand new situations. A birthday party would be unfathomable to her, with all the new language it required. So, I decided we wouldn't celebrate Sophie's third birthday. Then my friend Virginia Trier called. I had met 'Ginya' just before Sophie's diagnosis. She was a good friend of Ava Jean's, with a six-year-old daughter and a three-year-old son of her own. She was surprised to learn that I was not celebrating Sophie's birthday. 'Mary, I'd love to organise a party for her. Let me do that,' she offered. I could hardly refuse and was deeply touched by her generosity.

It turned out to be a beautiful Sunday afternoon at Ginya's place. She bought a pretty cake, decorated the house with balloons and streamers and invited all the Monday Mad Mothers and their children over to swim and have cake. The husbands came too. Li and some other dads swam with the children in the pool and he quickly developed a good friendship with Ginya's husband, Clayton, a CEO of a successful company. I had to take out Sophie's hearing aids for her to go in the pool, which gave me an afternoon of no teaching stress and instead I relaxed with the Mad Mothers. Unfortunately, though, Sophie developed a stomach-ache and was holding her tummy all afternoon.

Sophie's birthday parties were very confronting for me. For other children, these milestones represented the passing of time, but for me each birthday highlighted that Sophie was falling further behind.

~

A couple of months later, on 14 September 1992, a week after my thirty-fourth birthday, I went into labour and Thomas Charles was born. We named him after Sir Thomas More, who had written the seminal work *Utopia* in 1516 – the treasured gift I had received from Betty Anderton when I left London. The search for utopia, More said, was not a healthy attitude: the grass was not really greener on the other side of the fence; your life was what you could make it. The second name, Charles, was after Li's best friend, Charles Foster.

Our gorgeous boy took only hours to arrive. Li was very excited. 'Niang and Dia will be so happy! The Li family name is continued,' he said proudly. A second grandson was cause for celebration. Li called them as soon as he could but they didn't want to believe he was a boy.

Niang said, '*Bie pian ren, ni shuo zhi xiang rang women gaoxing.*' Don't fool us. You are just trying to make us happy. We had to send them a photo of our naked baby to prove their wishes had come true.

During that first day, I watched Tom intensely – could he hear? Thankfully the answer came quite quickly. A nurse was moving around in the adjoining bathroom and the toilet seat fell with a loud bang. I was looking at Tom in his crib next to me and saw him startle. This baby could hear! I hugged his tiny body with relief and kissed the top of his head. 'He can hear! He can hear!' I told Li excitedly, beaming with happiness and relief. The official hearing test was done the next day and, of course, he could hear.

Sophie had stayed with our good friend Marcia Nichols overnight. When Marcia brought her in the next morning, she was wearing an adorable white tutu and no shoes, with her hearing aids on and a big smile. She bounced onto the bed and gave me a hug. 'Sophie, here's our baby. Here's your baby brother,' I told her. She looked at him and smiled. I could see that she thought he was a beautiful doll. He only weighed 6 pounds 11 ounces, and could fit in my cupped hands.

I called Mum from the hospital as soon as I could. 'How wonderful, Mary!' she said. 'Do look after yourself. Don't forget to drink lots of water for your milk. And try to rest when you can. We'll be thinking of you. Much love, darling!' I knew she would be spending the next hour calling all my siblings with the news.

When we took Tom home, he and I got settled in the downstairs bedroom. Li would sleep upstairs with Sophie as I didn't want her to wake up alone and scared because she couldn't see anyone nearby. It would also give me a break to focus on Tom. I'd feed him at night and put him down, then go up to Sophie's room. However, Li could see the toll these early weeks were taking on me, so in his half-asleep state, he would also get up to bring the hungry baby to me to be fed in bed. These arrangements continued until Tom was old enough to share the room with Sophie. She was finally happy to sleep in her room as she had company. And when Tom cried to be fed in the night, it didn't disturb her, of course.

Sophie loved her baby brother instantly. I suppose she was relieved that there was someone else to occupy my attention, as well as being a playmate. And there we were, the four of us. It was beautiful and it was exhausting.

It was also challenging just feeding Tom with the FM wires wrapping around my chest and the microphone on the collar of my shirt. I had to wrangle the wires around my breast so I could properly position him for feeding and still speak to Sophie. Sometimes, taking them both with all their paraphernalia to the speech pathologist on top of the feeding was more than I could handle.

Sophie started kindergarten the month before Tom was born. I had chosen a nice small mainstream school. I wanted her around children who were talking, rather than with deaf children who were just making random sounds or none at all. The teacher kindly agreed to wear the FM. However, over the semester I soon saw that the background noise from the FM was confusing to Sophie when the teacher was teaching class. Although I desperately wanted her to be with hearing children and to speak, it was obvious that one-on-one was still the best option for her. Eventually I pulled her out of that school and returned to the deaf school. That night, I broke down in tears.

'Are you okay, darling?' Li said when he came home from work. 'What's wrong?'

'No, I'm not okay,' I blurted. 'Sophie's school isn't working, so I pulled her out today. She will go back to the deaf school for half a day and then I will spend the rest of the time one-on-one with her. Honestly, I don't know what else to do. I'm exhausted and there's no dinner . . .'

'I will cook dinner,' he said.

'Li, I don't even want to eat! Let me just sleep. Please. You can feed Tom at his next feed. I've expressed some milk and it's in the fridge.' I was totally exhausted. I mean totally!

'Okay, okay, darling. Do what you need to do. I can see that you need a break. I've been thinking about it lately . . .'

'Whatever, Li,' I snapped. 'Thinking is not doing, is it?' I was at the end of my wits.

'I know you're exhausted,' he said. 'Listen, here's what I've been thinking. You know I've got a break for a couple of weeks at the end of October.'

'How does that help me? Are you going to take over talking to Sophie all day?'

'Well, yes, actually. I was thinking we should take Sophie to China to see Niang and Dia, and you'll get some rest as we'd have lots of help from the family,' Li suggested. 'Also, my family is desperate to meet Tom.'

I knew the one-child policy was still in place in China, so the birth of Tom was a very significant and precious moment for Li's family.

And Niang and Dia really longed to see Sophie, too. I admitted it wasn't a bad idea, but I just couldn't see how it would really work. Tom was barely six weeks old, and knowing the lack of a bathroom at the commune, a hole-in-the-ground toilet and no running water, I was fearful that he would get sick. Plus dealing with Sophie and her hearing aids, her FM and my breasts entangled with the microphone wires, and no electricity to charge the equipment. I laid out all the reasons that made his idea impossible.

'I understand, Mary, but I hate to disappoint them. Maybe I could just take Sophie. They are missing her. This would give you a break and time alone with Tom.'

'Won't they be disappointed not seeing Tom?' I asked.

'Yes, but they will understand. I could take plenty of photos of him.'

'I think that would be fine,' I said, the question of how well Li would deal with Sophie's equipment still buzzing around in my head. But I just had to go with it, for all of our sakes.

Then I had an idea. Maybe my sister Jo in New York could come down and stay while Li was away. I called her, but she was dancing, she explained.

'Maybe I could come to you? Tom's a very easy baby. Would we fit?' I asked, knowing that she lived in a small apartment.

'Oh, yes! Please come, Mare. Please come!' Jo said, delighted at the suggestion.

Li and Sophie soon left for Qingdao. I missed her terribly. It felt like I had a limb missing, but I knew I really needed time with our son, and to attend to my own health, get some sleep and recharge. I headed to the airport with Tom strapped to my chest and we flew to New York. We cabbed to Jo's apartment in Manhattan, where she fell in love with Tom immediately.

For once, Sophie was not the centre of my universe. Jo and I both focused on Tom. He was such a sweet baby and so good with his feeding. It was nice to just relax and enjoy him. It was starting to get cold towards the end of October. Jo would go off to dance for a few hours each day, then join me on a walk through Central Park, rugged up with Tom strapped to one of our chests. She wasn't making much money in contemporary dance so I was really happy to treat her to a meal occasionally. This was such a special time to have with my little sister. We had not spent much time together as adults but now we were reconnecting. Jo was very relaxed, a delightful person. She didn't ask too many questions as she knew I needed a break from it all. 'You'll go back to Sophie refreshed,' she said reassuringly. I could see a glimpse of our gentle mother in my sister, and we planned for her and her Australian boyfriend, Bruce, to come to visit us in Houston for Christmas.

It was so restorative being with Jo for those couple of weeks, reliving our childhood memories. I looked back at my younger self – the wild girl who could never keep still, running all over town to anyone who would have her; how I channelled that energy into my dancing and the purpose and discipline I'd brought to bear on my career. And what for?

For a moment I felt the weight of where I was now – going back to Houston where there was nothing but constant therapy with Sophie, my baby son having to fit into our isolated, hyper-scheduled existence. But truth be told, I was overflowing with love for my children and didn't really want to be anywhere else but home right now.

I was overjoyed to see Li and Sophie walk through the door. They'd had a wonderful time in China. Sophie was very excited to see us and still so tender with her baby brother. When I saw her little face gazing up at me in such concentration when her FM was switched on and I was drilling new words and phrases into her, well, I could see she really wanted to learn, and that gave me renewed strength. She could speak about sixty words by now, but still could only hear the low-frequency sounds, so 'Sophie' sounded like 'oooeee', which seemed miraculous. But would she ever form a sentence, or ask a question?

10

As 1993 unfolded, I had to juggle more balls than I could ever imagine, and then some.

I was concerned that I was neglecting Tom. Although I was completely besotted with our son, a lot of my focus was still with Sophie. She was not going to be relegated to the periphery of our family just because we had a new baby. Li would have to step in with Tom, to do all the things I wouldn't have time for. And before long, that's just what he was doing. The minute he got home from work, he was on board with Tom. That became our new routine. Like all the Chinese people I'd met so far, Li was fabulous with babies – relaxed and hands-on. However, he was often dancing on Friday and Saturday nights, so on weekends I would get up and take the children out early. I'd go to friends who also had children, to the park or the bakery. I knew Li needed his sleep to dance well. Sometimes, later in the day, we'd meet with Charles and Lily Foster or Ginya and Clayton Trier and their children. Through our children, we started developing close friendships.

Tom seemed to have a very easygoing temperament. I felt blessed. Indeed, he was every bit as beautiful as Sophie and in every way the son we had wished for. But for Sophie, I always felt guilty when the dreaded annual speech and hearing test came around and there was no change in her results. She was three-and-a-half now and still there were no signs of improvement. I would go home in despair, and the sense of overwhelming helplessness would descend again – that heavy, dark cloud. In the beginning, I had hoped her hearing would improve over time with all the hard work. It took a while for the penny to drop and for me to face the fact that her hearing would never improve. Her language might, but her ability to hear would not.

In May, Li was on a break, so we decided to take the children to China again. Of course he was desperate to take Tom this time, but he also needed to take a business trip. He was often thinking about business ideas and how to help his brothers as well as the Bandit. I knew Li's strong desire was to help them no matter what, so I just went with the flow.

The Bandit picked us up from Beijing Airport and took us back to his apartment. It was wonderful to see Marji again, too. While the men discussed their new venture – a factory to make toys for the Chinese market – we discussed the children. Their son was such a sweet and clever little boy. Everyone made a big fuss of Sophie and particularly Tom – a second baby, and a boy at that! 'You are so blessed!' they kept telling us.

Both the Bandit and Fengtian, warned us that children, especially boys, were being abducted all over China because many Chinese people were desperate to have sons. The one-child policy meant that boys were very precious. 'Watch your children. Don't let them out of your sight,' they warned us.

A few days later, we went to Beijing station to take the train to Qingdao. As we made our way through the chaos with Li holding Sophie's hand and me pushing Tom in his stroller, I thought of how it must have been for Li when he saw Beijing for the first time as an eleven-year-old, leaving his family and all he knew to be taught as a ballet dancer under Madame Mao's cultural regime. I recalled him telling me how he became separated from the rest of his group at the station when he first arrived there, alone and terrified and so far from home. I thought of what the Bandit and Fengtian had just told us about the one-child policy and I shuddered. I looked down at Sophie, wondering how it must be for her: so many people, all that confusion, the distortions she'd be hearing through those big hearing aids. I just wanted to hold her close.

As always, it was wonderful to be with Li's parents in Qingdao. They were devoted to Sophie and embraced baby Tom as their own, too. '*Hao haizi! Hao haizi!*' Good boy! Good boy! Niang kept saying, and she couldn't stop tickling his little penis. Dia just smiled and smiled. 'The Li family name and the family bloodline is made stronger with Tom's birth,' Li explained.

Sophie was happy to be running wild again with all the cousins. Sometimes, she would put her little hand over my mouth to stop me talking when we were doing speech therapy. I decided to let her enjoy her time with her relatives. Sophie would run with her cousins from one household to another, the care of the little ones simply shifting from one adult set of eyes to the next. And there was a constant flow of people and food. Even though they were poor, there was always food!

Our journey home began with a train back to Beijing. We disembarked into a swirling mass of people and began navigating our way through. Sophie pointed at the toilet sign further down the platform and Li volunteered to take her. After a while I began to worry. They had been gone for ages. I started looking around but it was impossible to pick out any individual in that mad place and Tom was starting to grizzle. Suddenly Sophie was there beside me, holding on to my legs. I knelt down and held her close. But where was Li? Why wasn't he with her? 'Where's Daddy? Daddy?' I kept saying to Sophie, looking intently at her and speaking directly into my microphone. She glanced around but whether that was in response to my question, I didn't know.

About five minutes later Li rushed back, completely ashen-faced and trembling. He seemed to be in utter panic. He saw us: me, Tom, and then Sophie. 'Thank God, Mary. I thought I'd lost her!'

'What do you mean?'

'She was there with me and then gone. I ran out as fast as I could, and couldn't see her anywhere!' Li grabbed Sophie, startling her.

It hit me, what he was saying. 'Oh, Christ, Li! She could have been kidnapped!'

'I know! I was in agony! How was I going to tell you?' He turned to Sophie. 'Sophie, never run away like that again! Sophie, you hear me? Don't do that!'

And then Sophie burst into tears. How could she know what was going on? All she'd wanted to do was come back to me, and clearly, with her incredible visual sense, she knew exactly how to find me.

What a terrifying end to our journey. These instances just reiterated the need for language when Sophie could not communicate in scary situations. I don't think either of us got over that near-tragedy for a very long time. I was never so glad to get home, and I suspected Li felt the same.

~

One afternoon, I set Sophie up in the TV room to watch *Mary Poppins*, thinking it might work like a speech lesson, as Julie Andrews' diction was so clear, and I could spend a bit of time with Tom. At one point, I went back to the room to check on her. Her eyes were glued to the screen. I discreetly turned the sound off to see if she would notice. She didn't even turn her head, just laughed and smiled in the same way. She was reacting to the sight of Dick Van Dyke dancing with the chimney sweeps but hearing no music or dialogue at all. I fled from the room, unable to stop sobbing. What did it matter? She couldn't hear music. She couldn't hear me. She couldn't hear anything!

Two years of hard work and she didn't recognise the difference between sound and silence. She'd had no response. I could hardly believe it. Through all this time, since that brutal diagnosis two years earlier, I had been getting up early every day, talking all day and all night, seven days a week, full-on, and I'd genuinely believed that

Sophie was hearing something. It was like a death blow to see in front of my eyes that she couldn't hear a thing.

Li was shocked as well but tried to comfort me. 'We can't expect too much, darling. You know the microphone doesn't work with the TV.' But he understood the realisation I had come to. Despite how much I'd worked with Sophie, she wasn't getting information from anywhere else but me.

I had to keep going, and I spent time researching what the next best thing was to do for Sophie. Should we keep going with speech therapy, or would it be better to accept that she would never be a part of the hearing world and teach her to sign? What sort of schooling would be right for her, isolated from the hearing world and from us? What about the recently invented cochlear implant, which was still experimental? My mind was in a whirl with all the decisions Li and I would have to make about our daughter's life. It was as exhausting as it was mind-numbing.

All the while my hands were full with two children, I went on a massive quest to find the best solution for Sophie. Without the benefit of the internet, in those days I relied on word-of-mouth to become informed. I spoke to anyone who had information – parents of deaf children and experts. I researched all the different therapies and looked into sign language. I didn't know how widely used sign language was in Houston at the time and never saw a single deaf person signing. There were no successful deaf adults around me to talk to about the options as right up to the 1970s, most deaf children in the USA had been institutionalised away from their families. Deep down, I was still determined Sophie would be part of our hearing world, and that she and I would not become strangers. So I decided that we couldn't contemplate sign language. Not yet, anyway. Part of me still clung to the hope of that moment when we would converse with each other.

Someone had told me about a speech therapist named Linda Daniels who practised the auditory-verbal therapy (AVT) method. She was apparently a passionate trailblazer in her field and quite

brilliant – a real dynamo. However, Linda's approach was criticised by many experts. They thought her methods were too radical
and risky, that profound deafness and AVT didn't mix. But I was
intrigued. It made perfect sense to me. While it was all still very new
back then, I felt it would be right for Sophie and besides, we had
nothing to lose.

I vowed to go and meet Linda. The only problem was that she was
based in Dallas, over 385 kilometres away. 'Darling, if you feel this is
something you want to explore, fly to Dallas and see her,' Li encouraged me. I called Linda and arranged travel to Dallas the following
week for two sessions over two days.

~

I saw straightaway that Linda had a huge personality. She was a tall,
dark-haired woman, energetic and forceful, and spoke with a strong,
clear Southern drawl. She was confident and believed in her own
teaching experience of the AVT approach.

'I'm so worried that Sophie will never be independent, no matter
how hard we try every minute of the day,' I said to Linda as we got to
know each other a bit more. 'Given her reliance on the FM system,
she can't hear anyone but me.'

'Don't worry too much about that for now, Mary. How often do
you think you can come to Dallas?' Linda was getting her diary out.

'I'll come as often as it takes. I'll make it work.'

'That's good, Mary. How about we try every three weeks to start
with? You can sit in on our sessions, I'll give you notes and you can
continue with the program at home. In fact, you can video the sessions
to watch later.'

'Great, Linda! Thank you!' I was grateful for her suggestions and
I trusted her straightaway.

At one of our first sessions, I apologised for Sophie being lazy
because she didn't pronounce the ends of any of her words.

Linda paused and turned to me. 'Mary, don't you think that might be because Sophie can't hear those frequencies?'

Of course! It clicked for me that Sophie was not in fact lazy. What had I been thinking? How ignorant was I! After all this time, I was still not getting it. I must have appeared crestfallen, because Linda looked at me and said, 'Mary, Sophie will always be a deaf child in a hearing world. Her hearing is not going to improve. She just has to learn how to navigate the world with this disability.'

This was another 'light bulb' moment and it really hit home. I could now conjure a picture of Sophie in a classroom of children, still struggling. That was never going to change. Linda was right about that. I could have felt this was a brutal delivery but coming from Linda it was different. She was on my side and she was teaching me the way forward.

The more Linda told me, the more I understood how difficult it was to teach the English language to a deaf child. She never promised what progress we would make, but she gave me hope. Her knowledge, attitude and obvious skill inspired me. Over time, Linda showed me that Sophie needed to really learn to listen. This was a revelation to me and hopefully would progress her language more quickly.

For the first time since the *Mary Poppins* incident, I felt I had found the next level of support for Sophie. Never mind the naysayers. Instinctively I felt that Linda was going to be my guiding light.

Dallas became a regular trip for Sophie and me. Eventually a few other families in Houston came on board, which meant Linda could fly to Houston instead. This made her trip worthwhile. The sessions were held in a hotel room.

Often Sophie was exhausted after the kindergarten classes and lessons. She was not yet four and naturally only wanted to play. Sometimes, she would have what I called her 'dark moments'. She would sit very still, not speaking or making any sound, just looking with those big brown eyes, quite crossly, and refusing to eat or do anything asked of her. Therapy sessions with Linda were no different. At times, Sophie would just sit and glare at Linda with her eyes. And I knew Sophie could glare like that for hours! As I watched her stubborn little face, I'd be thinking, *Well, there's the $120 therapy session gone down the drain . . . as well as the flights to Dallas!*

Amazingly, Linda could manage to pull Sophie out of her dark moods most of the time. 'Does she have these mood swings very often?' she asked.

'Not really,' I replied, brushing it away. But when I thought about it, I could see Sophie's dark moments were occurring more and more frequently.

At our next therapy session in Houston, Linda took out a picture storybook, *Goldilocks and the Three Bears*. Sophie began looking at the pictures. Linda said in her strong clear voice, 'There are three bears!'

Sophie lip-read and repeated, 'Eee ber.'

'Mama Bear, Papa Bear, Baby Bear!' Linda continued with an enticing expression while pointing at the characters in the storybook. Then she asked me to repeat for Sophie, 'Mama Bear, Papa Bear, Baby Bear!' This was so Sophie could understand the game by copying Linda and me.

Sophie repeated: 'Ma-ma, Ba-ba, ber.'

Linda then continued to speak in a singsong tone: 'Mama has a pretty dress!' I jumped in to repeat, 'Mama has a pretty dress!'

Sophie just nodded and started pointing again: 'Ma-ma, Ba-ba, ber.' At this point she decided to pick her nose and grab the sleeve of my navy shirt to wipe off her snot. I ignored it. What else was I going to do?

Linda bent over with laughter at my embarrassment, then continued. 'Mama has a pretty dress.'

'Mama has a pretty dress!' I said, mimicking Linda's rhythm, pointing to the picture.

Sophie looked at the picture, then to Linda and then to me. She slowly put her head down, almost seeming to be stuck, and mumbled with a confused expression, 'Hamamem . . .'

'Mama has a pretty dress,' I said again, pointing with each syllable. Sophie looked at the book and then looked at me. 'Can't you say that, Sophie?' I was starting to feel that panic and frustration when things weren't progressing as fast as I'd like.

'The bear's house,' Linda read on, turning to another picture. Sophie just nodded.

'Goldilocks,' Linda said. Sophie repeated, 'Goo'oo.' She was catching on!

'Little girl,' said Linda, pointing.

'Liee irr,' Sophie repeated.

'The bears went outside!' Linda read with excitement. Sophie nodded, but didn't say it back.

'The bears went outside,' Linda repeated.

'Ber ooi'e,' Sophie finally responded.

'Good, Sophie!' Linda encouraged her.

Linda was an incredible teacher. She was inspirational and dynamic. I was amazed at how she could get Sophie to sit there for an hour paying attention to the lesson. And after six months, I thought I could see progress.

~

I really felt that something was happening for Sophie, and it made me think harder about her schooling. While it was crucial that Sophie keep up her therapy, she also needed to socialise. Schooling was a good opportunity for her to learn to do that. One day as I was walking Sophie to her morning kindergarten class, I looked through the window at the eight deaf children, several of whom had additional disabilities as well. None of them could speak. All were just making random sounds. This was the oral method that focused on lip-reading, not training the auditory memory. My instinct was that this wasn't going to be the right environment for Sophie in the longer term, as how was that going to help her develop language? Suddenly everything became clear. *Sophie is not going to be one of those children,* I said to myself determinedly. *You are going to be a successful deaf child who speaks, even if it kills me.*

I knew in my gut what had to happen next. 'Li, Sophie's been at the kinder for six months now, and I can see it's not right for her,' I said.

'Why is that, darling? I thought she was going well.'

'She needs to be socialising in the hearing world, don't you see? How will she ever progress if she's only with other deaf children? I want to switch kinder.'

'Won't that be confusing for her though, Mary?'

'Well, the alternative is that she lives an institutionalised life, and we don't want that for her.'

'No, of course not. You know I trust you on everything when it comes to Sophie. You're her mother and there's no one who knows her better.'

Regardless of any differences we may have, Li and I always end up on the same page eventually and come to a decision together. Although HSDC was a caring environment for Sophie, it was time for her to move to a mainstream kindergarten. I took Sophie with her bulky hearing aids to an interview at the new kindergarten. She smiled at Sophie. 'Hello, Sophie. It's nice to meet you. When is your birthday?' she asked straightaway.

Sophie just sat in her chair, then she looked at me, lost. My heart sank. She had no idea what the principal had said. She couldn't possibly have answered that one simple question. That's when I knew immediately that this woman didn't understand and was not going to be able to support Sophie and her needs. I couldn't bear to see Sophie being so vulnerable. I'd walked in with high hopes only to walk out crying. Sophie grabbed my hand and gave it a squeeze, looking up into my face with a confused and worried expression. She was very perceptive, particularly about me, but life was so often unexplainable to her.

However, I was still determined. I approached the next school on my list, one that prided itself on developing leadership skills and high academic results. I had contacted them and explained Sophie's deafness and they were happy to take her into their kindergarten program. I believed it would work well for our daughter. Unfortunately, this school didn't work out either. Sophie was often miserable when I picked her up and this made me unhappy. Her teacher wasn't communicative and I realised the difference between a speech therapist and a classroom teacher.

The fact of the matter was that Sophie couldn't go to school without me. So back to half-days at HSDC she went, while I contemplated the next move.

~

I lay in bed that night reflecting on all that had been happening in the past year. The idea of the cochlear implant had popped up now and then and had me thinking. This new invention was highly controversial in the deaf community and with experts alike. But I refused to dismiss it completely. What if it could work for Sophie? I learned that it was an Australian invention made by Professor Graeme Clark. It was an electronic device with a curled metal rod that was inserted into the cochlear, in the inner ear. Unlike hearing aids, which amplify natural sounds, the metal rod would connect via a magnet externally, sending electrical signals directly onto the auditory nerve, which are then processed in the brain as artificial sound. I couldn't find any published research, but I heard that specialists were just starting to implant children as well as adults in the US. It would only take place if the deafness was so profound that hearing aids didn't help, and they would only implant one ear.

I decided to ask Linda about it, as I trusted her to be honest. 'Linda, what are your thoughts on Sophie having a cochlear implant?' I asked her at our next session. 'Do you think it would help her?'

She stopped what she was doing with Sophie and looked up at me. 'Mary, personally I think the cochlear implant is a revolutionary device,' she replied. 'But as you know, it's very new. It's something you and Li are going to have to decide for yourselves, regardless of what I think.'

'I know. It's risky. All the speech therapists and audiologists I've met are completely against it.'

'Yes, they have only just started implanting children in the States. But a boy I work with received the implant in 1991 when he was two. Now, at four, he can hear, Mary. I can tell you that much.'

This was both terrifying and exciting news. These were the first children to receive the implant, so there hadn't been enough time to gauge the outcomes. It would take years for the recipients' language to develop, if at all. Some people even claimed the cochlear implant didn't work.

'I can't bear the thought of a surgeon opening up Sophie's skull and implanting a foreign object into it. But what if it could help her hear better? Oh, I don't know!' I was torn with the indecision.

'I think you need to meet with the experts on this. We can then talk after that.' Linda paused. 'I do believe the implant is the most amazing invention ever. It's going to turn deaf people's lives around. But you need to understand the risks involved and hear all the points of view.'

'Can I talk to a couple of parents whose children have had implants?' I asked. 'The ones you know?'

'Sure,' she replied.

Later that night I discussed it with Li at home. 'I don't think what we're doing is enough, Li. I think we should think seriously about getting the implant for Sophie.'

Li took a deep breath and sighed. 'But it's so risky, Mary. What if something goes wrong? Maybe we could look at it when she's older,' he said, anxious about the idea as well.

'It's best if it's done at a young age,' I told him. 'They're starting to fit children with implants from the age of two, when their brains are more receptive to language, and Sophie is almost four. I don't think we should wait. We have to do *something*. If we don't try this, we *will* have to resort to signing and Sophie will *always* be a deaf child in a hearing world, and she will *never* be able to communicate with Nana and Yeye.' I felt bad throwing Li's parents into it, but I was getting desperate.

Li seemed troubled and sat quietly. I knew that look – he wanted time to think. I pushed on: 'Linda said the implant works, and I think Sophie should have it.'

'Let's sleep on it. And you . . . you should call your family and see what they can find out about it in Australia.'

I agreed and called Mum later that night. 'Mum, you know about the cochlear implant that's invented in Australia?' I asked her.

'Yes, darling. Your dad was wondering if you'd heard about it,' Mum replied.

'I'm looking into it for Sophie. Could you ask Uncle Alan what he thinks about it?'

'Of course, Mary,' she replied.

Dad rang me back a couple of days later with feedback from Dr Alan Agnew. 'Hello, beautiful,' he greeted me. Oh, I loved to hear my father's voice! 'Alan says the usual thing – any surgery has risks. But it's not a really complicated surgery. Remember his daughter Julie? She's an ear, nose and throat surgeon now. She said they were getting children to hear after the surgery. It's not a miracle cure, but they are responding to sound.'

Mum and Dad wanted to believe the implant could work and Sophie would come through the surgery fine, but they couldn't help me make the decision. 'Remember that Mum and I always trust you. Whatever you do decide, we will back you. Take care, darling girl.'

This piece of news from Dad gave me more hope and comfort than I'd had in a long time. Li and I both went to see the ear, nose and throat specialist Dr Herman Jenkins. Dr Jenkins was in his fifties with greyish hair, glasses and an imposing physique. He appeared very gentlemanly and self-assured. I liked his quiet demeanour. He explained that recipients had to fit certain criteria to be considered for an implant. 'To be a candidate, Sophie will need to have profound hearing loss with little benefit from hearing aids. She will require an assessment to determine that,' he said. There would be a lot of stitches and a couple of months of rehabilitation.

'Every recipient's response to the implant is different,' Dr Jenkins said. He couldn't give us an absolute guarantee that the implant would work for Sophie, but he was confident about the procedure. 'A successful implant involves many steps, from hearing screening through to post-operative rehabilitation. This is crucial.'

'I see. Dr Jenkins, the Houston School for Deaf Children is against it. Would you be willing to meet with them and explain everything? They might understand you better?' I begged him.

We walked out of the meeting feeling we had made some progress. Dr Jenkins agreed to meet representatives from HSDC, who were acting as the advisory panel for the consideration of Sophie's cochlear implant. He also gave us permission to make an appointment for Sophie to be tested. I had mixed feelings – both worry and excitement. Even though I felt sick at the prospect of the surgery, I believed it was the right thing for Sophie. There were costs to worry about, too, but I left that to Li.

When I told Linda that I was still conflicted on whether to go ahead with the process for Sophie's operation, she listened intently before leaning forward to ask, 'What if you could buy the cochlear implant without the surgery?'

I suddenly knew my answer: 'I would mortgage our house to get it.'

Linda had helped pinpoint my doubt, which was the surgery itself, not the cochlear implant. And actually, it wasn't that I knew whether the cochlear implant would work or not. It was the fact that we had nothing to lose.

We were fortunate that Li was on his summer break during this time. Every day we debated and argued. We went for long walks while Sophie was at kinder, pushing Tom in the stroller, and talked and talked. For Li, the negatives seemed overwhelming and the pros mostly based on my faith in Linda's opinion of the cochlear implant. 'Mary, I feel very uneasy about this,' he said to me gravely. 'Shouldn't we wait to hear the expert panel's opinion?'

'No one on that panel has a deaf child and they have no idea what we are going through with Sophie. Li, what are you really worried about?'

Li was silent. Finally, he said, 'I'm scared, Mary. What if something goes dreadfully wrong in the operation? We could lose our daughter. I don't want to take that risk.'

'Li, this is not a high-risk operation,' I batted back.

'You think you know everything!' he almost shouted at me in frustration. Christ, the stress of this decision was simply unbearable.

After many arguments we finally agreed to talk to Dr Jenkins again. He assured us that the risks from the surgery weren't high. The major risk was that the device wouldn't work for Sophie and would have to be removed. I continued my research by talking to parents of children who had implants and reached out to Dimity Dornan, the founder of the Hear and Say Centre in Brisbane. She was a speech therapist and a supporter of cochlear implants and was so reassuring.

Soon, the all-important meeting between Dr Jenkins and representatives of HSDC was held at the hospital where the implants were being done in Houston. The advisory panel included the principal of HSDC, two speech therapists, and an audiologist. Dr Jenkins arrived soon after Li and I got there, and then the discussions began. The experts against the cochlear implant argued that Sophie was doing well as a deaf child. But she wasn't doing well when I compared her to hearing children. 'Compared to what?' I wanted to challenge them. The hearing world was always going to be the world she would be part of. Li squeezed my hand, knowing how hard it was for me to hold back. I had to bite my tongue.

At one point in the meeting, amid all the opposing views, Dr Jenkins looked me straight in the eye and said very calmly and simply, 'I can give her hearing.' My heart skipped. In those simple words I saw hope and a better future for our daughter. I completely understood what he was saying. If he believed he could give her hearing, then I would be able to teach her language.

Despite our countless arguments and indecisions over the past weeks, Li and I walked out of that meeting in agreement. With one exchanged look, I knew instantly that he'd come to share my view that indeed we had nothing to lose, and maybe, just maybe, everything to gain. We were finally going to ask Dr Jenkins to go ahead with an implant for Sophie.

It would take a few weeks for testing and the final assessment. In the meantime, Li started checking our medical insurance to see whether the procedure and the implant device might be covered.

The Methodist Hospital was responsible for making the final decision on cases that were difficult to determine. Sophie's case was one of them, and I went to see the hospital's in-house audiologist, Louise Loiselle, to see what the problem was. 'The guidelines are that if there is any residual hearing that is responding to amplification with hearing aids, doctors won't operate,' she informed me.

I was furious as I felt this policy was unfair.

The test was simply to decipher syllables, and I knew Sophie would do well. All she had to do was pick up the difference between shorter and longer sounds. Through repetitive training with Linda and me, her ability to determine the difference between sound and silence had improved. But it was *not* language and it had taken two years to get her to this point.

I was like a dog with a bone. I refused to let a black-and-white interpretation of the guidelines block the opportunity of surgery. 'Regardless of what the tests say, I'm not going to stop here,' I told

Louise firmly. 'If I have to, I will fly Sophie to Los Angeles or even Australia to have the operation.'

We went to as many people as we knew who could help us argue our case. Eventually, to our surprise, the hospital relented and approved Sophie's case. We never really found out exactly why. Maybe there was an element of fear – of the negative publicity if we went elsewhere for the operation. With Li's high profile in the city, there was sure to be publicity.

However, the operation would only proceed if we signed an indemnity stating we understood the risks, giving us no legal recourse against the hospital if the operation wasn't successful. We had considered the risks and signed it.

Then Li got word from our medical insurer that the $40 000 operation was not covered by our policy. We were doing it outside of the eligibility criteria of the hospital, so we ended up mortgaging our house to pay the cost.

~

Finally in October 1993, with all the pieces in place, we just had to wait for the big day. From the time the surgery was scheduled, I made myself stay calm. Sophie was so intuitive about my feelings and would pick it up the second I showed any anxiety.

A month beforehand we had another meeting with Dr Jenkins to discuss the operation procedure. Li and I both went along with Sophie. Dr Jenkins showed us the implant and demonstrated how he would cut into her scalp around the ear to insert it.

'She will need her head shaved in that area, and there'll be quite a lot of stitches,' he said. Then we would have to wait three weeks after the surgery for the implant to be mapped to see if it worked. 'There is always a risk with surgery, but the main risk you need to know about is infection. You can avoid this through good care of the wound,' Dr Jenkins told us.

I could sense Li's unease at this point, so I reached out and held his hand. Dr Jenkins then went on. 'There are other risks, such as she may react to the anaesthetic or the electrode is not placed in exactly the right spot. There is also a small chance of problems with the nerves in the face and some dizziness. But this is rare. Looking at Sophie's X-rays, I'm fairly confident the operation will all go to plan.'

I could hear Li taking a deep breath as Dr Jenkins talked about the possible nerve problems in her face, but we had been through the nauseating decision-making process many times and it was now time to act.

The operation would take three hours. Li drove Sophie and me to the hospital once Pat had arrived that morning to look after Tom. We had decided there was no point in Li staying and worrying. Work would help take his mind off Sophie's surgery, at least a little. 'Mary, should I stay?' he asked. I could see that he was reluctant to go.

I urged him to leave. 'Just go, darling. You'll be late for class. I'll see you later with Tom.' The plan was for him to collect Tom and come to the hospital in the afternoon. I was trying to keep everything normal for Sophie, as though this was just another appointment.

Ava Jean was already at the hospital to meet us. We walked into the admission room and met a nurse who had a small gift for Sophie. It was a special doll. Sophie smiled and was very pleased with her gift. The doll had a bandage around its head and under the bandage was an implant. Sophie kept trying to take the bandage and implant off, but the nurse was insistent and took the doll away every time she did this and put the implant back on its head. Sophie soon got the idea that in order to keep the doll, she needed to leave the implant and bandage on. The nurse started gesturing to the doll and then to Sophie, trying to help her understand that she was going to have an implant like the doll. Sophie started looking very worried as it began to dawn on her. Luckily, it wasn't long before she got her sedative, and soon after that she was wheeled away.

11

Waiting for Sophie to come out of surgery felt like an eternity. The operation took over three hours, and then there was a further one-hour recovery time. Ava Jean stayed with me the whole time. She was an enormous comfort as we either sat or walked the corridors or drank coffee.

'Darling, we'll be praying for the surgery to go well. Call us when it's all done,' Mum said when I rang her. I could hear the apprehension in her voice.

I had never felt so anxious in my life. This was a different kind of anxiety to pre-performance nerves – Sophie's future lay in the surgeon's hands, and so did mine and our family's. What if Li had been right about the risks? How would I ever live with myself if anything went wrong?

Finally, Dr Jenkins came out of the operating theatre. 'Hi, Mary. The surgery went well. Everything was straightforward,' he confirmed.

'Thank you. Thank you, Dr Jenkins!' I was so relieved.

He led me into the recovery room, and there she was, lying against the pillows. Half of her head was covered in white bandages. She looked so fragile and vulnerable. I rushed to her side and stroked her face, smiling as best I could as I looked into her eyes. Slowly she tried to open them. 'It's all right, darling,' I said, even though I knew she couldn't hear me. 'I love you so much, you brave girl!'

I sat down, and held her hand and showed her the doll with its own bandaged head. I put it next to her, and then she drifted off back to sleep. I felt emotional and elated. 'I must ring Li and my parents.' I told Ava Jean. Of course, each of them was just as relieved as I was that Sophie had made it through surgery.

With all the bandaging, Sophie couldn't wear her hearing aid, so she could only read my face. In her half-dazed state she noticed the drip in her arm and was quite troubled by it. 'It's okay, darling,' I said, nodding and smiling. Thank God for the doll! It became the centre of attention. I kept showing it to her and saying what a good doll it was to keep the bandage on.

Finally, Li was there, with little Tom. Li looked at Sophie and I felt his heart clench. 'You have to hold it together for her, Li,' I told him.

'Hello, sweetheart!' He gave her a very gentle kiss on the forehead, being careful to avoid her heavily bandaged head. She smiled and showed him her doll. Li then started to spoon-feed her homemade fried rice he had brought from home. I hugged Tom tightly. I felt overwhelmed with emotion, but I had to hold it together, too.

The day after the surgery, the room started filling up with teddy bears, balloons and flowers from our friends. The next afternoon, Ginya and Clayton came with their children, Kelley and John. Sophie stayed in hospital for two more nights and I was with her the whole time. Tom was looked after by Pat during the day. I was lucky to have her to help us.

A few days later, we went back to Dr Jenkins for him to remove the bandage. I was not prepared to see half of Sophie's beautiful jet-black hair shaved off. Big ugly stitches stretched from behind her ear in an arc across the side of her head. It was horrific to see, but I kept my happy face on. For Sophie.

'It looks good,' Dr Jenkins declared upon inspection. 'We won't be covering that with another bandage. It will heal very quickly. The main thing is not to get it wet or bump it. Keep her quiet for a few days and maybe just give her a sponge bath, no shower or bath. Come back in ten days to have the stitches out. And we'll set up the appointment with the audiologist to switch her on.'

I nodded. It was a lot to process, but I was so grateful for Dr Jenkins' honesty and professionalism through all this. Sophie could see I was happy, so she smiled too. I carefully brushed back the remaining hair on the left side of her head, scooped it up into a lopsided ponytail and tied it with a large red bow. That would keep the hair away from the stitches for now. Then we were off home with the cochlear doll in her hand.

~

For the next ten days, I tried to keep Sophie quiet and happy. We looked at picture books, I let her watch television and play in the cubbyhouse. Luckily, she seemed to recover remarkably quickly. When we returned for the removal of the stitches, she sat on my lap like an angel as Dr Jenkins snipped the seventy-five stitches from her head. Just amazing! I was relieved that it looked much better when the stitches were out. Now we had to wait for her hair to grow back to cover the large scar. An appointment was made with the hospital audiologist, Rose, for Sophie's new implant to be switched on in three weeks time.

The day finally arrived. I was beyond excited. This could change Sophie's life, and ours, if it worked. Butterflies filled my stomach as I drove with Sophie to the hospital.

Rose was setting things up and gave Sophie some toys to play with. She then put a magnet with a cord attached onto Sophie's head, connecting to the internal magnet that had been surgically implanted. She was extra gentle with Sophie, which made her feel at ease, as her scar was still tender. The cord led to a little box the size of a cigarette packet sitting on the table, which Rose said was Sophie's new speech processor. Then it was connected to a computer with all sorts of cords and other various testing devices. Rose explained cochlear implants have twenty-two electrodes inside the metal rod to transmit electrical impulses that trick the brain into thinking it is sound. The computer program would 'map' the electrodes to give Sophie some simulation of sound. *Incredible, really*, I thought.

Rose told me that she was going to send soft beeps to Sophie's implant. Progressively, she would increase the sounds to louder beeps until they got to an uncomfortable level. She left me with the instruction to read Sophie's expressions. 'I need you to let me know as soon as you think she is hearing anything, any reaction at all. That way we will get the most accurate map for her,' Rose said, while clicking away on the computer screen filled with what looked like mostly vertical lines with lots of dots. 'At the upper levels, the sound can get too loud, which could startle Sophie, so let me know when she starts to look uncomfortable.'

Rose began to slowly click her computer mouse. I tapped Sophie's shoulder to get her attention, pointing to my ear to indicate that she needed to listen. Rose clicked again and I saw Sophie move her head. I inhaled sharply. Her eyes seemed to say that she'd heard something. I told Rose this. She smiled and nodded at me and we continued on. Click. Click. Rose had warned me that getting a full map could take over an hour, so I had brought snacks and a drink to keep Sophie happy. I was playing gently with Sophie but watching her intently for any subtle response. She looked up occasionally from the toys. Click. And sometimes she blinked a bit, showing slight discomfort.

'Please, God, let Sophie hear,' I prayed. 'Let her get a good map!'

After an hour, Rose told me it was done. She unplugged the processor from the computer and gently fitted Sophie with her new device. There was a harness that would hold the external processor and sit at the front of Sophie's chest. It had a wire connected to what looked like a hearing aid but was part of the implant. Rose then connected the wired magnet behind Sophie's ear.

Sophie didn't seem to mind all this equipment. Rather she was curious about what was happening to her. I marvelled at her patience and tolerance. I suspected she knew that this was about her hearing. It was now the moment of truth: the implant was switched on. I held my breath.

~

From that time on, I never stopped talking. I knew I had to put the sound in there for Sophie to develop language. Every waking moment was full-steam ahead with speech therapy. Li was overjoyed. 'So she can hear from the implant?' he asked, not quite believing.

'Yes, I think so! But that's just beeps. Let's not get ahead of ourselves. This is not language. This is only the beginning.' I also tried to contain my excitement. It was too early to be sure.

'It's fantastic that she can hear sound,' he insisted.

'But the real work starts now, Li,' I said, knowing what was ahead of us.

Over the next few weeks, I would test whether she could hear me. When she turned away, I would click-click with my tongue like Niang used to do. Sophie would turn every time. Next, I would try calling her name and she would turn. She was hearing my voice like never before! I celebrated every one of these small victories.

The first thing I did every morning was to put on Sophie's harness with the implant turned on. Then I would look down and test the little red dot was lighting up as I said, 'Ba ba ba'. Each time the red dot lit up, a sound signal was transmitted into her brain. That's when I knew it was on and working. While she was wearing the implant, I watched her constantly. If I felt she wasn't hearing well, I would say 'Ba ba ba' and check to see if the little red light on the implant box was flashing. Sometimes it did break, and I had to figure out if it was the magnet, the wire attached to the magnet, or the wire attached to the box or the rechargeable batteries. I always had spare batteries on hand.

The FM had four AA batteries and the implant had one. The hearing aid for the left ear also needed to be checked every night. If something was wrong and it wasn't the batteries, then it must be the wires or connectors. In that case, it would require a trip to the hospital to have it looked at. It was quite an ordeal sometimes, dealing with all this first thing in the morning while feeding Tom and changing nappies. It was a steep learning curve.

Then one day, a real breakthrough came when I was sitting on the couch and she was standing a few metres away playing.

Let's see how this goes, I thought to myself, and then started singing, 'Rain, rain, go away . . .'

Sophie didn't turn, but I heard a little voice sing, 'Ome ain o'er ay.'

I could hardly believe my ears. An utter miracle! It was the miracle I'd been praying for!

My heart swelled and I felt such happiness. Now, for certain, I knew she could hear sound! But I didn't grab her or cry or jump up and down, I just kept singing. I wanted to hear more and more of her sweet voice. I had to learn patience.

~

By the end of the following month, Sophie had returned to half-days at HSDC. It was the best place for her right now because I was free to spend time there with her whenever I wanted. Speech therapy was included, and her teachers, speech therapist and I could monitor her progress with the implant. We were all learning about it together.

I constantly sought different ways to teach Sophie language. This was the first year of her implant, so she was auditorily the same as a one-year-old child. I had learned that a hearing person has tens of thousands of tiny hairs within the cochlear that vibrate and transmit sound to the brain, while Sophie's implant only had twenty-two electrodes to work with. The progress was still slow, but all new discoveries and breakthroughs were triumphs, no matter how small. I tried not to think about the future, just focused on one day at a time.

Within six months, as if a switch had been flipped, Sophie started babbling like crazy – because she was actually hearing things. It occurred to me that she was mimicking conversation just like a toddler would. She was even using rising and falling intonations. I loved it! This kept me going with extra vigour. It was down to me and Sophie's therapists to turn the sound she was now receiving into language. She had to be taught to understand what she was hearing. We still had a big mountain to climb, but what a huge milestone for Sophie!

'Ooe eee ba?' she said one day, with her sweet voice lifting at the end like she was asking me a question. I was so delighted to hear this and followed her around the room. She walked over and put the dolly in its bath.

'Oh, dolly needs a bath?' I repeated, very excited. This was a major moment. 'Clever girl, Sophie! Let's bath dolly!' I talked loudly and clearly. For the first time I held a small but firm hope that she could grasp language. It felt like a miracle, a true miracle! I could see light at the end of the tunnel.

It helped that Tom was still such an easy baby. If we wanted him to go to sleep, all we had to do was to give him a 'silkie' – a piece of silk cut from my old nightdress, and just like that, he was fast asleep. The silkie was his comfort, and my saviour.

Surprisingly, Tom had also gained a lot from observing and listening to our unusual family dynamic and routine. I could see he was developing in leaps and bounds. No sooner did he say 'Mama' and 'Dada' than he came out with 'Mummy, I want my milk. Now!' At only sixteen months old. It's funny, because I never remember him cooing or babbling. I was always too busy with Sophie to listen out for it. Now he had a huge vocabulary and very advanced language skills for his age.

'Tom's really flying,' I said to Li one Sunday when we were at the park together while Tom was attempting to climb up the slide. 'At this rate he'll be overtaking Sophie before we know it.'

'He's a clever boy, Mary,' Li said, seeing Tom gently interact with Sophie. 'He will be such a lovely brother for Sophie as they grow up.'

We were touched to see Tom being so tender with his big sister. It was as if he knew there was something different about her. I took great comfort from that. 'I think so, too, Li. And his language. It's incredible. We have our own extra speech therapist in him,' I joked.

'It's because he hears your endless speech lessons with Sophie,' Li laughed.

At around the six-month mark since Sophie's operation, I realised her voice was starting to sound better, showing more clarity, but it was all still such a struggle. Occasionally, I would let her watch TV in the afternoons. It was a necessary break for both of us. Poor Sophie. She did look tired and fed up with me a lot of the time. Her tantrums continued to be silent performances. She would rock in the corner or simply glare at me and refuse to do anything. I was guessing this was her way of showing her frustration.

Over time, I learned not to sweat the small stuff. If Sophie wanted to go out wearing the bright yellow frilly dress from China with her red Texan cowboy boots, I didn't care. As long as she wore the harness and implant, she was allowed to wear or do whatever she wanted. Miraculously, she never once complained or tried to remove the harness, even though she looked different to other children. I also noticed that she adored the freedom she had when the implant was off and she could perhaps escape from my constant nagging voice singing all the time. She played beautifully with the Mad Mothers' children. She would watch the others closely and go along with the game quite happily. But I made sure we didn't have long play dates, as we still had to work on her therapy without background noise.

With Sophie's newfound progress, Li and I felt that she needed to move to a mainstream school. We chose Duchesne Academy of the Sacred Heart, which was considered one of the best private schools in Houston. Duchesne was relatively small and it was also an all-girls' school. I felt that having boys in class would be too noisy.

Social and emotional development were part of the school's ethos. Most importantly, the principal was happy for Sophie to do just a half-day of school each day. I could then take her home at lunchtime for a nap as she was so exhausted from processing new sounds. Then we would do our own therapy lessons in the afternoons following videos of Linda Daniels.

Duchesne turned out to be wonderful for Sophie. She picked up on some social behaviour – maybe not language, but this skill was important to learn too. Soon she was five and was settled into a new routine. The teachers were kind and the children accepted her – bulky equipment and all. Luckily her hair had grown over and you could hardly see the implant.

Sophie's teacher asked me to perform a dance for the preschoolers for one of their weekly Show and Tell sessions. What a good idea. I sweetly convinced Li to join me. We decided to perform the famous *pas de deux* from *Le Corsaire*, the classical ballet based on Lord Byron's epic romantic poem. This is one of the most performed in the world and requires virtuosic dancers – well, Li was certainly that! I knew the children would adore the costumes, Li as the swashbuckling pirate and me a beautiful maiden in tutu and full pointe shoes. Almost like a prince and princess in a Disney tale, perfect for five-year-old girls. I really wanted to make it memorable for the other children as well as Sophie.

On the day, we were all up early. We left Tom with Pat and set off with our dance paraphernalia – costumes, make-up and the tape recorder. Sophie saw the costumes and knew something was going to happen. She was excited. I still had to keep my language simple, but she could now just about understand some whole sentences. 'Sophie, we are going to school now,' I said to her. 'Daddy and Mummy are going to dance!' I did a little twirl and curtsey to act out what I was saying. She smiled happily. That cute smile!

'Scoo . . .' said Sophie.

'That's right, Sophie, your school,' Li said, joining the excitement. 'Let's go to dance in your school.'

We put on our costumes and make-up in the gym change room. Li looked dashing with his satin harem pants and bare chest, and I had managed to squeeze into a frothy midnight-blue tutu and wore a glittery tiara. There were little gasps of excitement as we made our entrance. 'Quiet, please, girls,' said the teacher. All the little girls gazed at us in wonderment while Sophie looked very proud – sitting up tall and grinning from ear to ear. I showed the children my pointe shoes and they touched the tutu.

Li led me to the centre of the space to Adolphe Adam's romantic score, and we began. The carpeted floor felt different for me *en pointe*, but then the music and movement took over and it was all fun. It felt good to be dancing again. I was happy to be doing this for Sophie and her classmates. The music came to a climax and we took our last turns, then Li lifted me high above his head, finishing in an *arabesque* position to loud gasps from the enraptured audience.

The children and teachers jumped to their feet, clapping with delight. We stood there hand in hand and both looked at Sophie. She was positively beaming. The teacher turned to us. 'Mr and Mrs Li, it has been a great honour to have you here for our girls today. It's very generous of you to give up your time with Houston Ballet to be here, Mr Li.'

'It was a pleasure,' said Li, squeezing my hand. 'I hope the children enjoyed it.'

'I'm sure they did. And it's lovely for Sophie. Look how proud she is.'

It was exactly the outcome I'd wanted – a connection of some kind, an understanding of her and us.

~

The new routine of school, therapy and play continued for the next year. By now, I knew it was useless to hope that Sophie would pick up language from her surroundings. I had to be the one to put the language in our lessons. We were getting through more things in therapy, beginning to touch on concepts like 'How', 'What', 'Where' and 'Why'.

To get the concept 'Why' could take a long, long time. But her vocabulary was picking up, so her auditory memory was beginning to develop. By the time she was approaching her sixth birthday, her language was slowly beginning to form. She still didn't make much sense, but I could understand what she was saying. Sophie and Tom began to talk with each other, too. She would babble at him and he would take up the conversation when she paused. At two, he was speaking really well.

'Let's go to the park!' I'd say. 'Why won't the door open?' I'd say, looking at her with a puzzled expression. 'Oh, look, Sophie! The door is locked.' When she'd had enough of my constant talking, she'd reach up to try to put her hand over my mouth and plead, 'Sto Mummy, pleeeee!'

The big test of her progress was the annual language proficiency test done in the auditory booth. Although it showed she was improving, she had the auditory memory of a one-year-old, and she was five.

Saturday mornings with Ava Jean continued to be an oasis in the week for us all. Sophie and I were usually so exhausted with each other by then. I often felt there was no time for me just to be her mother. I longed for Saturdays. As soon as I turned into the long leafy driveway that led to Ava Jean's bungalow, Tom and Sophie would start jumping up and down in their car seats. Then, there she was, our very own Mary Poppins! The children absolutely adored her. She let them run wild, free to play, grow and explore.

'Ava Jean, Ava Jean,' Tom sang.

'Yes, Tom,' Ava Jean would reply.

'Ava Jean, Ava Jean,' Tom would call out again.

'Yes, Tom,' Ava Jean giggled at Tom's calls.

'You are soooo fun!' Tom would giggle back and run off to play.

Ava Jean was not only a friend, she was family too.

~

The McKendry clan back in Queensland was growing. Everyone had moved from Rocky to Brisbane. Ger, Mick and Matt had two or three children apiece, and Brig was having her second baby. Paddy and Dom were both working, Paddy as an industrial relations advocate and Dom in insurance. Jo was still footloose in New York and Dad was retired and slowing down with Mum. His heart wasn't too good.

I yearned to be back with my family in Australia. You couldn't take away that crazy childhood we had shared – we had formed such a strong bond, always there for one another. I wanted to be an aunty to the growing number of nieces and nephews. I wanted Sophie and Tom to know their cousins, uncles, aunties and grandparents. I wanted a simpler life.

I also knew that Li's career was nearing its end. 'I'd like to retire while I'm at the top, Mary,' he told me one day. But I knew that even at thirty-three, he was at the peak of his career and had more to give to ballet. Maybe it was because I had stopped mine prematurely, but I felt quite strongly that he really needed to stay with it for as long as he could.

'I know your back is not perfect, but I think you will still be able to dance at this level for a few more years. I mean, what else would you do?' I asked him earnestly.

'I could do real estate. I've bought, renovated and sold a few times now, and I know the local market well. I could also do business in China,' he said.

Even though Li did buy, renovate and sell houses successfully and had established two joint ventures in China with his brothers and the Bandit, this all sounded precarious to me. Working at Houston Ballet was stable and we would lose our medical cover through the ballet if he left. How would we pay for Sophie's medical costs?

'Maybe you just need a change,' I said. 'After all, you have been with Houston Ballet for fifteen years.'

Li began considering the possibility of moving to New York City to join American Ballet Theatre. It was considered the crème de la crème of international ballet, with a massive repertoire, and it performed in one of the best theatres in the world. However, the company only offered nine-month contracts for dancers, which would have meant Li finding a second job to sustain our family for the rest of the year. Besides, I didn't think New York City was right for bringing up our children, even if Jo was there. Li also considered the Royal Ballet, but he wasn't convinced that living in London would be good for the family either.

Then we heard on the grapevine that the Australian Ballet was in need of experienced dancers. Two of their top principal dancers, Greg Horsman and Lisa Pavane, had accepted principal artist positions at my former company in London, now called the English National Ballet. The Australian Ballet's artistic director, Maina Gielgud, had once said to Li, 'If you're ever interested in joining the company, I would be most delighted.' Li called her to see if her offer still stood. Without hesitation, she offered him a principal artist position.

The company was very well regarded internationally, but few people in Australia would know who Li was. He would have to start all over again, make new friends, gain respect for his artistry, learn a different repertoire and fit in to the rhythm of a new company. He would be dancing alongside Lisa Bolte and Miranda Coney, as well as Steven Heathcote, David McAllister and other principal artists.

I was so excited when he got off the phone. Melbourne, the Australian Ballet's home city, was where the cochlear implant had been invented. I also knew the Australian medical and education systems were among the world's best. And of course my family was there. It was home.

There was a lot of work to do to get us back to Australia with two children. How was I going to explain this to Sophie? I couldn't yet. With some help from the Australian Ballet, we started arranging a shipping container for our belongings. I was very excited for the move. I had come to America for the ballet, for my career, but hadn't expected to bring up my family here. I had only stayed because

I had fallen in love with Li. While Houston was kind to me and I dearly loved our friends, I realised how deep-seated my desire was to go home.

On the other hand, I was concerned about Li leaving Ben, his mentor and father figure of nearly sixteen years; leaving Houston Ballet, the company that had made him a beloved ballet star; and leaving America, the country that had welcomed him and given him his freedom. America had also welcomed Li's parents and allowed them to live there with us. Would they even be allowed into Australia? And then there were his incredibly successful career, his close friends, and the properties he had worked so hard to purchase and renovate. He would be leaving his life behind.

Telling Ben was extremely difficult for Li. Understandably, Ben was totally shocked, but admitted he had known this would happen one day. I felt so sad for both of these men who had journeyed such a long road together, almost like father and son.

~

Online real estate websites weren't yet a thing at that time, but Dad leapt in to help, studying Melbourne's maps, transport routes and the architecture of each suburb. It turned out there wasn't much to rent there, but there were plenty of nice houses and apartments for sale. The real-estate market was severely depressed, and Neil George suggested we buy something instead.

'If we're buying, you should fly to Melbourne,' Li said. 'I'd feel more comfortable if you go.'

Mum agreed to meet me in Melbourne. I went on a Friday and was back in Houston by the following week. Before I left, I heard from Dom, who was living in Melbourne in a crappy little one-bedroom unit in St Kilda East. 'I'm on my own,' he said, 'and it would be great to have company. Would I be able to move in with you and your family if you get a big enough place? It would help me save money to buy something of my own. And I could help you out with the kids when Li's on tour.' Fantastic! Now I was getting really excited.

It was autumn in Melbourne. Mum and I stayed in a hotel near the Botanic Gardens, not far from the Victorian Arts Centre, where the Australian Ballet performed. People were out walking, jogging or cycling, or sitting at pavement cafes with their newspapers, drinking Melbourne's famous coffee as trams rattled by. So that's what we did too, walking around this green leafy area on the fringe of the CBD and having coffee at South Yarra's famous cafes, scanning the real-estate pages in the weekend paper.

We mainly focused on the historic inner-city suburbs with old Edwardian houses and Victorian workers' cottages, all near Port Phillip Bay yet still in close proximity to the city and the Australian Ballet Centre in Southbank. I liked the feel of the place very much, and despite Melbourne still being a long way from Brisbane, at least it was in the same country. Finally, after twenty years, I would be closer to my family.

My favourite property was a newly renovated townhouse in South Melbourne with three upstairs bedrooms and two bathrooms. It would be perfect for us and to accommodate Dom. *Li won't be tempted to renovate. Yes!* I thought. Dom liked it too. It was in Park Street, close to the South Melbourne Market, a big farmers' market. It was also on the tram line, so Li could get to work easily. Just down the road was the charming Albert Park Village and St Vincent Gardens, with a children's playground and a tennis court. All were within walking distance.

We moved quickly to secure the house, and it was done. Melbourne, Australia, here we come! Dom would move in a week before we arrived.

Our home in Houston sold very quickly, too, as it was such a nice area for families. Li's junk in the garage was more of a problem. It was still full of Niang and Dia's garage-sale bargains. It all had to go. Li tried to sneak out some things he wanted to keep, such as his

two Balinese Buddha heads. 'How many Buddha heads do we need?'
I exclaimed. Large Buddha heads and children didn't go that well
together, in my opinion. I didn't have time to reflect on the fact that
we were shedding so much of our American life. We had ordered a
12-metre shipping container, so I was focused on what we could fit
inside it. To Li's horror, I managed to get rid of a lot of stuff.

Li also had to rehearse for *Romeo and Juliet*, which he was to dance
in Beijing and Shanghai before we would make the move to Australia.
Performing in China had always been a dream of his. He was so
excited about this chance to dance at long last, in front of his family,
teachers, friends and countrymen.

The Mad Mothers and other friends were devastated by our
decision to leave, especially Ava Jean. However, they all understood
and were supportive of us. We were deeply touched by how many
people wanted to host farewell parties in our honour. After all, Li and
I had established our reputations, developed lifelong friendships and
made our lives here in Houston. Li did a farewell-to-Houston performance of *Peer Gynt*, and many of our friends and his fans came. *Peer
Gynt* was one of Ben's best creations, with the story centred around the
lead male dancer. The performance was emotional and electric. Li had
been making such an impact in Houston for almost sixteen years.
He was their adopted son who'd risen to international stardom and
brought them pride and joy. The public wanted to see him dancing
for the final time and to show their appreciation for the happiness
he had brought during his time there. The bittersweet feeling in the
audience was palpable that night.

I went into Li's dressing-room at intermission and saw him sitting
in front of his mirror. 'It's going well, darling,' I said to him.

He looked at me through the mirror, then said, 'I can't believe this
will be my last performance in America.' I could only imagine what
was going through his mind and how emotional it must be for him.

I really felt for him. 'Oh, I know, Li. But for now, just focus on
your performance. You can think about other things afterwards.'

I didn't know what else I could say. I gave him a gentle kiss on the cheek and left him to concentrate on the remainder of the ballet.

At the end of the show, the curtain went up and Li was standing centre stage, alone. He had performed so beautifully. The audience spontaneously stood up, cheering and applauding, and flowers flew onto the stage. One by one, each of the seven female lead dancers in the performance presented Li with a red rose. It was very touching. All the dancers cried on stage, and many in the audience shared the same sentiment, overwhelmed at the thought of losing him. It was deeply emotional, but I knew instinctively that the move was the best thing for our family.

The night before we left, Li was very ambivalent. 'Have we made the right decision, Mary?' he asked. I understood how he was feeling. Thank God he had his performances in China to look forward to. This made it just that bit easier for him to close the door to our Houston home for the last time. 'Yes, I think so, darling,' I told him, stuffing Tom's precious silkie into my handbag.

I suddenly remembered something and looked back at Li and said, 'Remember what your mother said when you left for Beijing?'

'Don't look back!' we said together. With a smile, I knew we were going to be okay, no matter what happened next, as long as we had each other.

~

Besides leaving our life behind, there was another great sadness for Li. 'Mary, my brothers' dreams of coming to America are shattered now.' He swallowed hard. Now that we were leaving, he felt he had failed them. I understood. He was making an incredible sacrifice for his young family, for us. We had often talked about sponsoring his brothers in the early days, but it never worked out. And there was not just one brother, but six! However, Li had been helping them all these years, including helping to finance a small theme park in Qingdao that had failed.

Then I had an idea. 'Darling, I would happily help educate your brothers' children in Australia,' I said. 'I think that might be better, actually. All of them are young enough to take advantage of the Western language and culture, and this would give them a better future.'

Li nodded. But I knew his guilt persisted.

While we were preparing for our descent into Beijing Airport, most of Li's family were on the long overnight train trip from Qingdao to see him perform the lead in *Romeo and Juliet*, in the place where everything had started for him. His parents, his brothers and their wives, other relatives, and some villagers, not to mention the Bandit, Fengtian, Teacher Xiao and other former teachers and classmates, were coming to see him dance. As we disembarked, I felt a rush of emotion, thinking about all that was happening for us.

For Li to perform in Beijing meant so much to him. Now here he was, in his home country – the country that had for so many years refused to ever let him return. He was about to dance in front of his own people, to show them all that he had achieved in the West in the sixteen years since he'd left China. It was overwhelming.

'Li, it's fate, isn't it?' I said. 'We didn't see it at the time, but it's fate that Houston Ballet has been invited to tour China at this moment in time.'

'Well, maybe. I just know I am so lucky. *Romeo* will be my first performance as a professional dancer in front of my own country and my last with Houston Ballet.'

'What a full circle for you, Li!' I said.

And then we saw the Bandit and Fengtian waving at us from the crowd.

~

Once the Li family had arrived, it was chaos. They exclaimed and doted over Tom, making a huge fuss of our little boy. Sophie was beside herself to see Nana and Yeye, who couldn't hug her enough. We'd booked them hotel rooms and gave the Bandit and Fengtian the responsibility of showing them around Beijing.

The dance of Li's life, this opening night, was to be broadcast live in prime time by China's Central TV to more than 500 million people across the country. Even I couldn't get my head around that.

A convoy of taxis took us to the theatre. Sophie and Tom were safely at the hotel being looked after by Marji. I glanced at Dia and Li's brothers, so handsome in their suits, and Niang and the sisters-in-law, who looked elegant in their silk blouses and pants. For all of them, with the exception of Niang and Dia, this was the first time they would experience ballet and theatre. I could see the awed expressions on their faces as they spoke excitedly. We patiently lined up and took our seats with the thousands of other people in the audience. Being China, there was none of the glitz and glamour of a gala performance in America. It was all rather low-key.

Regardless, it would be one of the most important moments to Li and his family. He was finally able to come home and be recognised as an international star. I was looking forward to seeing him dance in one of my favourite ballets. I had to suppress thoughts that I would not dance the role of Juliet ever again. Then, the lights went out, the noise died down, the orchestra started the familiar music and the curtain rose. There was Li on stage. 'My Romeo,' I smiled, feeling so proud of him.

Li danced magnificently that night. If I had any nerves for him, they disappeared as soon as he started to move. In the part where he was sword-fighting with Tybalt, I turned and watched the faces of his family and friends. They were mesmerised. I swelled further with pride at the famous balcony *pas de deux* at the end of Act One. Li and his partner, Janie Parker, had the audience entranced.

In fact, the audience was sitting on the edge of their seats through-out the ballet. When Li took his curtain call, I could see he was fighting very hard to hold back tears. His family screamed and clapped wildly. The Bandit and Fengtian led the standing ovation among Li's former teachers and classmates, and the entire audience was on its feet. There were many emotional people that night. I noticed Li's family and Teacher Xiao's eyes were full of tears. They were tears of pride and joy. How special it was for Li to be welcomed back this way!

~

Two days later, Li had to go to Shanghai with the company for two more performances. He would be away for a few days. The rest of us would return to Qingdao on the overnight train with our eight suitcases, and the children and I would wait for Li there.

Suddenly everything seemed too hard. The kids were fractious. Tom was now a two-year-old pocket rocket I couldn't let out of my sight, and at the same time I was worried about Sophie. The entire Li family were constantly gabbling in a language I couldn't follow, and Beijing station – well, it was Beijing station! Even buying the tickets was an ordeal. Children's tickets were charged according to the child's height. A heated fight broke out between Li's brothers and the officials because Sophie was tall for her age and they demanded that we pay a higher fare accordingly. Of course, Li's brothers would have none of that. Finally it was sorted, and we were allowed to board the train.

It was wonderful to walk into Niang and Dia's new apartment, which we had bought for them. It had two bedrooms, a living room and a small galley kitchen. Best of all, there was a little shower room, a sink and even a toilet! They kept the apartment spotlessly clean and the beds were comfortable and warm. Dia's small fold-out stools were squeezed around any available tables for all the brothers and sisters-in-law to make hundreds of dumplings. Then there was planning for who would help with the next meal, and the next. It was still only about food and family.

When all the little Chinese cousins came to visit, Sophie and Tom would run off with them or play on the *kang*. Rong Rong (seventh brother's daughter) and Yan Yan (fifth brother's daughter) were Sophie's age. Lulu (third brother's daughter) was a few years older, as were Jin Jin and Feng Feng (fourth brother's daughters). Second brother had two older daughters, Liu Liu and Li Li, as well as their little Jie Jie. The eldest brother had a son, Jiang Jiang, about nine years old. And Tom, the only other boy in the Li family, was treated as treasure. While at times I worried about Sophie's language with all the Chinese being spoken I decided love and family beat all. She was gaining much more in other ways.

I was relieved when Li safely returned from Shanghai. While it was wonderful to spend time with them, I couldn't wait to get us back to Australia and settled in to our Melbourne home. I suddenly felt the weight of all we had done in the past few months, only to then have to pick up our lives again in a new place. It would take enormous energy to set up a new life for our family, including finding therapists and a school for Sophie. I felt anxious and suddenly needed to hear Coralie's voice. I called her as soon as we got to the airport. As always, her encouraging words calmed me down.

'Mary, I raised eight children in Rocky and your father wasn't always there. You're strong, I know you can do this.'

I took a deep breath. *You can do it!* I told myself.

PART FIVE

Melbourne
1995–2012

*I just kept going, day by day, with sheer
determination and focus and one goal in mind:
I wanted a conversation with my daughter.*

12

We landed in Melbourne with our eight suitcases piled into a maxi taxi and drove off to our new home in Park St, South Melbourne. It was now winter and it was freezing. Driving from Tullamarine Airport, the landscape was flat and dull, and as we came into the city, it looked more like a country town to us.

Dom was waiting on the doorstep to welcome us. My once baby brother was now a tall, handsome 27-year-old man working in insurance. I had always wondered what it must have felt like for him to be the baby of the family, and here he was now, all grown up. I was so proud of him, and it seemed that none of the years that had separated us had made any difference to our relationship at all.

The children raced in and I looked anxiously at Li as he walked in the door. This was the first time he'd seen the house. 'It's a bit small' was all he said. I knew he was thinking of our spacious house with the wraparound porch in Houston. I liked the new townhouse. We now owned a bit more than half of what was originally a grand double-storey Victorian terrace house. It was painted beige with green and rusty-red trim on the traditional iron lacework around the balcony on the second floor. A brick path led through a small garden to the red front door. It was newly renovated and we could still smell the fresh paint inside.

I tried to shrug it off. 'It will feel more like home when the furniture arrives,' I assured him. Our belongings would not come for another six weeks. The only really important things were Sophie's cochlear implant – batteries, coils, magnets, FM and rechargers – and, of course, Li's ballet gear, and we had these with us.

Li's attention soon turned to food. Luckily, Dom had bought us a little shopping trolley and directed us to the nearby South Melbourne Market. It became an exciting discovery as Li found the market had several Asian grocers. A trip to the market was going to become a weekly outing for the family.

Then it was our first night in our new home. I pulled out some quilts from the suitcases and attempted to set up makeshift beds on the floor. By the time we were fed and had put the children to bed, Li and I both collapsed onto our patchwork quilts on the floor. As I lay there, I wondered how our lives would pan out from here. Little Tom would be fine. At nearly three he was developing so well and he was ready for kinder. But Sophie. What lay ahead for her? What lay ahead for us together? And how would Li settle in Australia after being in America for sixteen years?

We only had a few days to get things together before Li started at the Australian Ballet. I worried he would look back on his old life and think our move to Melbourne was a step backwards. He couldn't even find anywhere that sold the *Wall Street Journal*! Li was a household name in America so I was also nervous about him having to start again professionally in a new country. This was difficult at the beginning of your career but even harder near the end. He would be turning thirty-five in January.

~

I was thrilled when Li came through the door on the evening of his first day, beaming. 'You'll never guess who's working at the company, Mary!'

'Who, darling?'

'Jiahong Wang! One of my old teachers from the Beijing Dance

Academy. He's the company ballet master. I didn't even know he was in Australia. His class was amazing! And his wife, Shuyuen, is a teacher at the Australian Ballet School. I can't believe it.'

'That's fantastic, Li!'

'And Emma Lippa is still there playing music for the company,' Li added. Emma was the brilliant former principal pianist of the Bolshoi Ballet, who Li had enjoyed working with in the past.

How marvellous for Li to have Jiahong there as his new teacher at this point in his career. He befriended Kenneth Watkins, who was relatively new to the company as well, working in development. I could hardly wait to get to the Australian Ballet to see for myself what it was like there. But first, I had to get the kids settled.

I called Brig for advice about Sophie's schooling. Brig was a passionate schoolteacher who by now had two young children. Grace was four and Mary Rose was seven months old.

'I'm going to take my time looking around for the best school for Sophie,' I told her. 'I don't think I want to start her until the beginning of the year.'

'Don't wait, Mary. There are good Catholic schools in every neighbourhood. Put Sophie in one as soon as possible or you'll go mad,' Brig advised.

The nearest local school was Galilee Primary School. I met the head teacher, who explained that through government funding they could provide a speech therapist for an hour a week. Great! I enrolled Sophie in Grade 1 for the last half of the year. The school was very sweet and the children were really kind to her.

Sophie befriended an older girl called Ksenya Masendycz, who looked after her. I was so pleased that Sophie was making new friendships. It was a good step forwards. I met Ksenya's mother, Liza, too, and started to learn about the situation in Australia for young families. It was wonderful to be able to talk with them to find out what was going on at school, as Sophie could not tell me. I could already see we were living in a neighbourly community. We could walk to lots of places – parks, schools and other activities. No more having to get in the car for every outing.

I soon discovered that Sophie had been put in a Grade 1/2 composite class. This worried me as she was not yet reading or communicating at Grade 1 level. She had quite a few words but was still babbling, unable to put them into sentences. Li, Tom and I were the only ones who could really understand her. I also started looking at what hearing services were available for Sophie. I called Australian Hearing, delighted to learn that they were able to supply batteries and help service Sophie's left hearing aid.

Next I contacted the Cochlear Implant Clinic, the birthplace of the very first cochlear implant. It was located at the Royal Victorian Eye and Ear Hospital in East Melbourne. There we met Shani Dettman, a brilliant audiologist and speech therapist who was in tune with what was happening in the world of cochlear implants.

Shani was straightforward in her approach and honest. It seemed that she was very good at what she did, so we began visiting her once a week for therapy. I went to every session, sometimes filming them for future reference. Tom was stuck with me in those early months. Once the lesson finished, we would go home to start all over again – the same routine every week, just as we had done in Houston.

Soon we formed another close community at the Australian Ballet including Jiahong, Emma, Kenneth, Steven Heathcote and his wife, Kathy, and their children, Sam and Mia. Sam often played backstage with Tom as we waited for Li and Steven to finish. I found that Kathy and I shared the same challenges and difficulties with our partners being principal artists touring for nearly half the year.

We both enrolled our boys at the same kinder for two days a week. It was around the corner in Albert Park, not far from the bayside beaches. Tom was in his element, settling in quickly, and making a few good mates.

I had learned early on in my marriage that with Li's ambitions, dreams and endless projects, he couldn't always be there for me. Not only was he the breadwinner and very conscious of how important that was for his family, but he always had a huge work ethic as well. I was on a different trajectory, raising our children, which I believed to be just as important. I also strongly believed in the importance of friendships, grateful of support we'd received no matter where we were in the world. Soon, through Tom's kinder, we met some other parents who became my closest friends in Melbourne, such as Bronwyn Morrison and Nadine Hibbert.

Over the next month, I researched schools that had deaf units. Methodist Ladies' College had already reached its quota that year and was unable to accept another deaf student. The Victorian School for Deaf Children only offered signing, and we had already made our decision against taking that path. Yarra Valley Grammar School also had a deaf unit but was located too far away from where we lived. I was frustrated at the lack of options available.

~

The rest of the year unfolded. Li was finding Melbourne difficult – it was too quiet. After the glitz and glamour of America and the bustle of Beijing, it felt like a small country town to him. The speed of life was much slower and people were also more laid-back. We were both accustomed to moving fast and making things happen. I did just that, walking into the Victorian College of the Arts and accepting a part-time job on the spot to teach teenage ballet students.

While Dom babysat the kids for the night, I went to see Li's first performance as Vronsky in *Anna Karenina*. What a night! I was thrilled and relieved that Australian audiences embraced him from the start, and I was confident that in time Li would come to like Australia.

Soon it was November and I was dreading the Sydney season when Li would be gone for two whole months. Thankfully, I had Dom for company. By early December, the Christmas school holidays had commenced and I was driving to Sydney – over 800 kilometres – on my own with the two small children. We stayed for a few weeks in an apartment in Manly while Li performed at the Opera House. Sometimes the children would play in the Opera House canteen while I peeked into the nearby studio to watch Li rehearse. An extra bonus was having the Heathcotes in Sydney as well. They stayed at Bronte, not too far away from the Opera House. The children and I often met with Kathy, Sam and baby Mia for outings to the beach.

After the Sydney season finished, we drove up to Brisbane to catch up with the McKendrys. This was my first Christmas with my family in Australia since I was sixteen. I had longed for this moment for so many years, and took great delight in seeing all the children and the cousins play together in the hot summer sun.

~

In the end, Shelford Girls' Grammar School in the nearby suburb of Caulfield was the best choice for Sophie. I felt I'd hit gold in finding this school with its small classes – only eleven students in each, and there were no noisy boys. Not that I minded noisy boys – it was just that they would interfere with Sophie's hearing.

Sophie's behaviour, including her dark moods, continued to worry me terribly. I sensed they stemmed mainly from frustration. However, I gave Sophie's new teacher permission to remove her from the classroom if she descended into one of her moods, explaining that she was not to put up with Sophie sulking in the corner. Sophie had to learn the consequences of her own behaviour. Thankfully it worked. Her dark spells were gradually dissipating by the end of the year. I felt so relieved and only hoped things would stay that way.

As Linda Daniels had helped me understand the difference between hearing and language, I wanted to find someone in Melbourne who was also trained in her method of AVT. To my dismay, I found that many were still trained under the old oral method relying on lip-reading. And yet Shelford somehow found a very special teacher of the deaf who shared Linda's philosophy. Louise Paatsch had a lovely personality and was highly qualified. She seemed to understand the potential of a child with a cochlear implant, as well as her pushy mother! I was going to learn a lot from her.

I asked how Sophie's first session went, and she said, 'The lesson went fine, Mary. Sophie gets frustrated easily, doesn't she? I can see that she knows what's expected of her, but it's very difficult for her. Today, she put her head down and her hands over her ears, and refused to listen or speak.'

'Oh, I'm so sorry, Louise!'

'It's natural, Mary,' she said. 'The important thing to remember is this: the first rule of developing children's language is to take the child's lead.'

'What do you mean?' I asked. This was new to me.

'Well, when Sophie slunk to the floor and sat under the table, quite elegantly, I must admit,' she laughed, 'I simply got under there with her and we worked on her speech and language there. It's so Sophie could see I was on her side and she felt in control for once. Then we actually developed a very creative narrative together.'

What Louise said was an inspiration. I started to adopt the same approach at home. I was still a 'tiger mum', but if Sophie would be more receptive when we worked on her terms, then I was all for it.

One session a week with Louise wasn't enough, so I asked if she could come to our home and teach Sophie one night a week, too. She agreed and brought learning materials that were appropriate for Sophie's actual age – six – rather than her auditory age, which had now reached two. Soon Louise became a good friend and part of the family.

As Sophie was attending a mainstream school, in order to progress towards her actual year level in understanding, she had to do the work as well as her therapy sessions. School assignments in particular were a nightmare, as she wasn't reading yet. I would panic! Thank God we had Louise to guide her through it.

While I watched Louise work with Sophie, Li would take care of Tom. Li was brilliant with him. Sometimes they would read books together for hours on end. Other times he would take him to the park to play. There was no TV during Sophie's therapy time. No music or radio. Nothing that could interfere with her ability to hear and comprehend.

Although Sophie was still not reading, she and Tom loved Li's Chinese fables, particularly 'The Monkey King' and 'The Frog in the Well'. Sophie had started to say sentences, and could answer simple questions like, 'Which cake do you want, Sophie?' She would point, 'Tha one!' But the most charming thing she was now doing was saying 'Coose me' for 'Excuse me' when she wanted to speak. We loved it!

~

Beginning ballet lessons for Sophie was my next project. Ballet lessons were structured and students were to face the teacher. This set-up was almost like one-on-one teaching and I thought it would be something Sophie could manage. She started a Saturday class at the National Theatre Ballet School, close to where we lived. I explained her situation to the teacher, who promised to keep an extra eye on her.

'Sophie, you're going to a ballet class today, to learn how to dance!' I told her excitedly on her first day. She smiled and was eager to get into her leotard. I took her in. Her implant in its harness stuck out under her leotard. I gave her a little wave as I left. All seemed to go well that first session, and thus began our new Saturday routine.

I inquired whether they needed any part-time teachers and I was hired immediately to teach on Thursday mornings for advanced students, while Tom was at kinder and Sophie at school. It didn't matter to me that they didn't pay much. It was an opportunity to further my teaching knowledge and to stay connected to ballet.

Now, I had to learn how to plan and deliver structured classes, and to teach specific movements to the music. It felt wonderful to be back in the studio!

'You are the best coach, Mary. You do have the gift. I have no doubt everyone will love you,' Li encouraged me. Life was still frantic, but at least now I had something to call my own.

Then one day I bumped into Anna Veretennikova, the sister of my old Rocky friend Nina. It turned out that she also lived close to us and was running a small ballet school, Dance Partners, in an old chapel just down the road. Incredible! I was so pleased I'd bumped into her. Anna and I had both been trained by Miss Hansen, and I knew Anna would be a good teacher. We went for coffee to catch up, reminiscing about our childhood and sharing stories of our lives since. When she learned that Sophie was at the National Theatre Ballet School, she suggested that she attend Dance Partners instead. I agreed that it was a good idea.

Anna was thrilled. 'Mary, don't worry,' she said. 'I've taught other children with disabilities, and there's a girl from Galilee Primary School who comes here. Perhaps Sophie knows her. She has an unusual name – Ksenya.'

Finding Anna was another chink of daylight for me. At first, I was a little tentative about how Sophie would go with Miss Anna, knowing how strict Miss Hansen had been with us, but I soon realised Anna was a very different teacher. With her strong voice, the words she used to describe movements and her sharp eye, she had just the right combination of skills to work with Sophie. She was making it her mission to ensure that Sophie understood her.

Anna would clap her hands and call 'Sophie!' before any instructions were given. And best of all, the exercises and movements were taught first without the music. Just the teacher's voice. 'Turn around.' 'Jump up and down.' 'Arms up.' 'Smile.'

Not only was Sophie learning to dance, but she was also learning to hear the music and understand the French terminology. I soon realised that the ballet class was actually just as much a speech therapy lesson for Sophie.

Sophie was getting a lot out of her training with Miss Anna. Ballet boosted her self-esteem, because she was physically capable and quite talented, whereas at school she struggled to hear the teachers to just keep up with her class.

Later, I would confide in Anna about Sophie's general progress and she would assure me. 'She will get there in her own time, just a bit slower than others.' It was a relief to have someone alongside me who understood.

Come midyear, it was time for Sophie's first ballet exam. Luckily, her visual skills meant she could follow the other students. Miss Anna always placed her in the middle of the group to take advantage of that. It was good for Sophie and a relief for me as she was finally the same as everyone else. In her first exam, surprisingly, she received higher marks for her musicality than some other girls in her class, coming out with a distinction. The look of pride on her little face was something to behold. I was filled with joy and hope like never before.

~

I started to dread Sophie's upcoming seventh birthday because these occasions always made me incredibly sad. Nevertheless, it was something to celebrate.

'Sophie, it's your birthday. We're going to have a party. Who would you like to invite?' I asked her.

She gave me the names of three children in her class, but I decided we couldn't leave anyone out. We invited all eleven girls, plus Ksenya from her old school. Ksenya's mum, Liza, came along to help.

The party was at home and I hired a fairy performer as a surprise. As we didn't have a suitable outside area, they were all inside and chatting noisily. Once again it was difficult to watch. Sophie was totally lost. All the noise meant she couldn't hear anything clearly. Conversations were too quick. I was annoyed at myself for putting her through this agony again. Birthday parties were not for her – or me.

Then, it was as if all the stars aligned. Li was to perform *Don Quixote* with the Australian Ballet in Brisbane the very week that Paddy was getting married. Finally, I'd be able to attend a family wedding. Jo was coming home from New York and suddenly I realised that for the first time in over twenty years my big family would be together in one place.

My brother Paddy was marrying a beautiful Rocky girl. Sharon was a demure lady like Coralie, gentle and kind. They were married in St Stephen's Cathedral in the city. The speeches at the reception were full of funny anecdotes about Paddy and life in the McKendry clan. These were met with hysterical laughter from all of us. I could see the joy on our parents' faces as they watched their children together once more.

Not long after we returned to Melbourne, Li badly sprained his ankle. The injury meant he was going to be out of action for a few weeks. As neither of us can cope with inactivity, he decided to ask for work experience at the stockbroking division of ANZ bank, which was a major sponsor of the Australian Ballet. Bryan Madden, the managing director of ANZ Securities, had agreed that Li could come in for a couple of weeks while he was recovering.

I pictured Li with his crutches, hobbling on one leg, working alongside the high-flying stockbrokers. What a contrast! ANZ Securities started him in the back office, filing paperwork. Bryan then moved him to observe and help some experienced brokers. This gave him a real taste of what the inside of a stockbroking operation was like. He'd had some success with share investments in America and had always been fascinated with the financial world.

Li limped in one evening and said, 'Mary, I think I can do this!'

'Do what, darling?' I asked.

'Stockbroking,' Li replied. He was elated.

'Really? Fantastic!' I said.

For Li to study for a degree was out of the question. We just couldn't afford for him not to earn a salary. He needed to have a proper paying job and stockbroking just might be it. And the sprained ankle was a warning that he was just an injury away from ending his ballet career.

Li learned so much during his time at ANZ Securities, but little did we know then where that journey would lead us.

~

Sophie was learning and Li was learning, too. On the last day of his work experience at ANZ Securities, Bryan offered him a job on the spot. He said to Li that he recognised the passion, dedication, discipline and strong work ethic that had enabled him to get to the top of his profession as a dancer. So he was confident Li would be successful if he applied the same attributes to stockbroking. What an opportunity! We were very excited. This was the 'proper job' we both knew Li would need when he retired from ballet, and he immediately accepted, agreeing to start early the following year, 1997.

During Li's rehab, the Australian Ballet had announced a replacement for Maina Gielgud, who had finished her tenure and was returning to the United Kingdom. The new artistic director was Ross Stretton from the American Ballet Theatre. He was the principal dancer who should have partnered me at the gala in Sydney in 1991. When Li's contract had come up for renewal, Li told Ross that he had decided to retire. Ross was stunned by Li's decision and challenged him, asking if he could do both ballet and stockbroking as he did not want to lose him.

'Do you think I could do both, Mary?' Li asked me when he got home.

'If there's one person who can do it, it's you!' I replied, as he was still dancing so well.

'I'm not sure if ANZ will allow it.'

'Why don't you ask Bryan what he thinks?' I suggested.

The next day, Li rushed home to tell me that Bryan thought it was a good idea too, as it would take a while for Li to build up his stock-broking clientele.

'That's fantastic, Li!' I was very excited for him, and for us as a family. But how was he going to manage two full-time jobs?

Soon the reality set in. He would get up at 5 a.m. to do a class at home using the staircase banister as a *barre*, then shower and have breakfast, get into his business suit and be in the ANZ Securities office by 8 a.m. At midday, he would go to the Australian Ballet to start rehearsal and often perform at night as well. His days were long and tiring, but he was motivated and inspired. Both Bryan and Ross were very accommodating and understanding.

And that is how our second year in Melbourne continued to unfold. By September, Tom turned four, and at that stage was into Pokémon, Power Rangers and dinosaurs. Li came up with the crazy idea of taking Tom to Qingdao. The Australian Ballet was planning a tour to China and Japan, and his idea was to leave Tom with his parents for two weeks while he performed in Beijing, Shanghai and Tokyo. He desperately wanted Tom to spend time with his family.

I was aghast. 'No, Li!' I said. 'Tom is way too little for you to leave him with your parents for two weeks!'

As usual, Li saw a bigger picture. 'Don't be silly, Mary. My whole family will love him and he'll be the centre of attention. They'll spoil him. It will take him no time to settle in with his uncles and cousins.'

'But he won't understand the language,' I argued.

'That's precisely why he should come with me, Mary. He'll pick up some Chinese.'

Li was adamant. Despite my fears I eventually relented, because it was hopeless trying to change Li's mind when he was so determined about something. And deep down I knew how important this was to him.

Before long they left for China and I tried to tell myself that Tom would be all right with Li's family, but then I got the news that Li's perfect plan had gone horribly wrong. 'Mary, I can't leave Tom in Qingdao. He won't leave my side,' he told me over the phone.

'Bloody hell, Li. What did you think was going to happen? Didn't I tell you this wasn't a good idea?'

'Darling, not to worry. It's all arranged. I'll take him with me to Beijing. The Bandit will help out. I will figure out the rest.'

With that, I hung up. I was so mad at Li, and so concerned for Tom. And there was more to come. On his first night in Beijing, Li was expected at a welcome banquet hosted by the Chinese Ministry of Culture. The plan was for him to drop Tom at the Bandit's place beforehand. However, the plane was very delayed and, in desperation, Li ended up taking Tom with him to the banquet, walking into the grand reception room with Tom asleep in his arms.

Luckily, the host was none other than Ding Wei, the Chinese consul who had attended our wedding in Houston. Crisis averted! But after that, Li got sick and lost his voice. I wasn't surprised, given what he'd had to deal with on that tour. I was anxious to have Tom back with me and we discussed the possibility of me flying to China to bring him home, but Li said, 'No, you can't leave Sophie. Don't worry, I will manage.'

In the end, things worked out. Nicole Rhodes, one of the dancers on that tour, sustained a back injury and was being sent home to Melbourne. She said she'd be delighted to bring Tom with her. I was beyond grateful.

~

Soon we had Sophie's first ballet concert to look forward to. Li came back early from a Sydney tour to see it. We both thought it was very important for all of us to be there. We did Sophie's stage make-up at home and off we went.

The end-of-year concert was at a charming little theatre in nearby South Yarra. Everyone was there with their families – just as Coralie and Neil George had been at my first ballet concert a lifetime ago in Rocky. Tom was sitting on Li's lap as we watched the preschoolers perform their dances. It felt like an eternity waiting for the seven- and eight-year-olds to come on. Finally Sophie appeared, looking divine in her tiny pink tutu and gazing happily out into the audience. We held our breath.

The music began and there she was, front and centre on the stage – like she was the star! I panicked and grabbed Li's hand. 'She won't be able to watch anyone from there, Li,' I whispered. But my God, she was right on the music. The toe-taps, jumps and quicksteps looked very sweet. She wasn't only doing the steps, I could see that she had Li's natural stage presence. I looked at Li and his teary eyes said it all. We were utterly blown away. The consistent repetition that was just part of ballet class had worked, together with Miss Anna's kindness and patience.

After the performance, we went to congratulate Sophie back-stage. 'You were fantastic!' Li told her, scooping her up into his arms. 'Sophie, you were so good. Beautiful dancing!' I added.

We were beaming – and so was she! All around us, other parents were happy and proud of their children too, but our shared pride was something else altogether. Moments like these kept us going. And this was a huge milestone.

It may sound odd that we wanted to put our deaf child into ballet, into the world of music and dance, but we felt it would give her a sense of control over her life, and with us both being dancers she had inherited our physical abilities. Of course, it was more challenging for her than a hearing child, but visually she was so strong that she was able to copy the movements demonstrated by the teacher. Even though the piano music would be massively distorted, the beat of feet on the floor would be like timpani to her. It was through ballet that we truly understood that Sophie was smart. We just had to find a way to release that intelligence so she could participate in our hearing world. Now her language had to catch up.

What a frantic eighteen months! So much had happened in our lives. What I didn't know was that life was about to get even more hectic.

13

The new year brought fresh challenges. Although I was overwhelmed with Sophie and Tom, Li really wanted another child. I promised him that we'd think about it when he got a proper job. Once he became a stockbroker we decided the time was right. I was thirty-eight and knew it might not happen as easily. We yet again had to come to terms with the possibility of having another deaf child. The thought of putting in the effort I had put into Sophie all over again was truly daunting. I was also still hoping against hope that I could get back into the workforce at some point. Just like I'd been at the age of three, I was still uncontainable.

I fell pregnant rather quickly. Then I found I was extraordinarily happy about it and decided to put all my worries aside until after the baby was born. Li was over the moon, naturally, and Dom was thrilled for us, too. 'I'll be an uncle for the eleventh time, Mary!'

The kids were back at school in February, Melbourne's hottest month. Getting them out the door was an ordeal. My first focus was always to make sure that Sophie's hearing aids and FM were charged and ready to go. I would get Sophie up first and let Tom sleep a little longer. I came up with the idea of putting him to bed in his sports uniform, to save time in the morning.

They did look cute heading off on those sunny mornings. I just hoped it wouldn't get too hot for them. I always worried that sweat would lead to ear infections for Sophie. My fears weren't crazy – she did develop a really bad infection in her hearing-aid ear. The whole side of her face blew up and she couldn't open her jaw. It was very scary. We had to leave the aid out for a while. In fact, I realised she was getting no benefit from it, so once she recovered, I didn't make her put it back in.

It wasn't long before various sports were added to the children's out-of-school activities. Sophie joined Tom at tennis lessons. For her, learning to follow the rules was another therapy lesson – a whole new vocabulary – and learning to work as part of a group was crucial in her development. Swimming lessons early on Saturday mornings also became part of our routine. Tom had an emotional maturity beyond his years. He seemed to understand his sister and the difficulty she was going through with her deafness. It was wonderful to see how much they loved each other. They rarely fought over anything.

Sophie's progress was being well documented at the Bionic Ear Institute. She became part of the research into children with a single implant in those early days and was doing incredibly well for a child who had not been implanted until she was four.

We met the inventor of the cochlear implant, Professor Graeme Clark, and his wife, Margaret, at some events. Margaret was gentle, clever and devoted to her husband. They were straightforward, friendly people, always happy to engage. Graeme was very interested in Sophie's progress. I remember him asking me about her doing ballet and whether the music induced an emotional response. 'No, I don't think so, but perhaps she gets more from the physical feeling of dancing,' I told him. He seemed fascinated. I felt so beholden to him. He was our shining light. Our life would have been very different without his groundbreaking invention.

We continued to take Sophie to the Eye and Ear Hospital for therapy with Shani once a week. Surprisingly, Sophie spoke without that flat tone that many deaf people have, which comes from not hearing properly. She sounded a bit like me, developing a nice intonation.

I think it was because I sang the phrases to her. Now, she could clearly say things like "Ello', "Ow are you?', 'May I pease 'ave a drink?' And she could answer familiar questions, like 'How are you, Sophie?'

Now that she was starting to hear and comprehend, Sophie was more confident to engage with people. I was overjoyed to see this. When she wanted someone's attention she would gently touch them on the shoulder, just as people did so often to her. Then she would tilt her head into their field of vision (also as she was used to people doing for her) and say, 'Coose me . . .', and then tell them something. She did it with such gentleness and charm. She was developing much more quickly with the implant than she had with her hearing aids, and her dark moods were becoming even less frequent.

All through that year we lived at this crazy pace, and by late in my pregnancy I was finding all the running around, my teaching and the endless talking with Sophie quite exhausting. Dom was at work most days, and Li was busy with stockbroking and the new ballet season. Mum and Dad came to help, my saviours as they had been many times before. They took over just about everything. We had found out the baby's gender some months back and now I was able to get some rest and think about our new daughter. Li and I were beyond excited to meet her.

Mum and I would sometimes walk to Albert Park village for lunch, and Dad would often collect Tom from kinder and the two of them would walk together to the local pub so Dad could have a beer while his grandson had a fizzy lemonade and a packet of chips. In the evenings it was a relief to relax and let them do all the talking for a change. Around this time, my sister Jo had moved to Boston, where her husband, Bruce, was a Harvard University professor. Most of my siblings were working on producing grandchildren, and to Mum and Dad's great joy, they just kept on coming. Our little girl would be next. And Matt and Annie were also expecting their third.

Li had suffered knee pain on and off for years. Around this time, he felt he had put up with it long enough and decided to have the surgery a specialist had recommended. The specialist had told him that he may have another two to three years of dancing, but only if he was very disciplined about his rehab. Li's discipline and tenacity were never in doubt. We decided that the best time for the surgery was before the company's Christmas break, when Li would miss a minimal amount of work. But the operation would clash with the baby's birth, and there was nothing we could do to avoid it.

Luckily, Bridie Rose arrived two weeks late, on 12 November 1997. She looked like a beautiful Asian princess, with porcelain skin and a huge tuft of jet-black hair sticking straight upwards. She was so petite and stunning, we fell in love with her immediately. We were delighted that she could hear. We called her Li's little present, as he was insistent on having a third child. A true gift!

~

Life thereafter was manic. How we managed while Li was juggling two jobs and continuing to do rehab after his surgery was completely insane. What were we thinking? Our days now were quite different. Li was working harder than ever. He was surviving on minimal sleep, often waking at the first sound of Bridie's cries at night. I would tell him to go to another bedroom and leave the crying baby with me so he could get a decent night's sleep. The catchphrase in our home was 'Exhaustion won't kill you' – but to be honest, the exhaustion nearly killed us both.

I decided that I definitely needed help and remembered how Coralie had always encouraged me to have help in those early years so I could focus on the children. The cleaner was a godsend. She certainly knew more about housekeeping than I did!

I always looked forward to Louise's sessions with Sophie. They gave me insight into Sophie's progress. While she was working with Sophie at the table, the other children played and I got the dinner ready, keeping one ear on the lesson at the same time. The family chaos didn't deter Louise from pushing Sophie to listen and describe what she heard, and help her learn to predict. 'Is somebody at the door? Who could it be?' Louise would ask. I learned so much from observing these sessions.

There were times that Sophie gave us a good laugh when she would simply copy people talking, mostly by copying me.

'Okay, kids, hurrr up, we nee t'go dow tennis. Shoes on ev'one!' It was hilarious; we'd laugh and hurry up to encourage her.

Around this time, she also said, 'Shit!' I was thrilled. I knew I hadn't taught her that one so she had overheard and picked it up. 'Fantastic!' Li said when I told him.

'We must be the only parents in the world to celebrate the first swear word out of their child's mouth,' I chuckled.

How we got by with all this mayhem, I have no idea. It was no wonder Dom moved out to his own place quick smart after Bridie was born!

I shouldn't have been surprised that Bridie was so physically active, given my own background, but once she began to move around, I had to be watching her at all times. She crawled incredibly fast and was soon pulling herself up on the furniture and scrambling. Whenever she saw me pick up my handbag, she would bolt in a lightning-fast crawl for the front door, determined not to miss out.

Sophie was very protective of Bridie, like a little mother. Tom continued to pick up on anything Sophie missed, misheard or didn't comprehend. He explained gently and allowed things to flow on. He was extremely empathetic and attuned to social situations and how people were feeling, especially me. 'Thanks, Tom, for being so kind,' I'd tell him. And he'd always say, 'That's okay, Mum.'

~

By now, Sophie was nine years old. It had been five years since her implant. But the annual tests revealed she still only had the receptive language of a three-year-old and the auditory age of a five-year-old. Receptive words are not the same as concepts such as 'How' and 'Why'.

Sophie had no idea what she was missing, so she had no ability to ask questions. Hearing people learn to question very naturally through being in a hearing environment, but that's not the case with oral-deaf children. I had to feed her the language and then teach her how to deconstruct it. When I had to teach her the concept 'Why', I nearly gave up. *When, if ever, would her language snowball?*

I continued to listen to her every word, correcting her pronunciation and syntax and making her repeat things correctly. It was difficult to read to her as she was still developing her language – the baby books were actually more her reading level, but she was not interested in those. Her auditory ability did not suit her age. I wondered if she would ever learn to read.

Then a miracle happened when a mysterious parcel arrived addressed to Sophie. It was from Li's former masseur, Mad Charles, in Houston.

'Sophie, you got a present!' I told her.

Sophie tore off the paper, looking at me with wide eyes, wondering. Inside was a complete set of *The Adventures of Tintin* comic books. Sure, they were all pictures, but Tintin wasn't a child and the stories that unfolded frame by frame were sophisticated.

I would never have thought to try comics, but I could see that the images with the speech bubbles fascinated her. In fact, she took the books to her room and shut the door. She stayed there for hours, and we soon realised that she had been engrossed for all that time. She absolutely loved the Tintin books. From time to time, we could hear her laughing out loud reading them, and as the pictures told the story, she eventually guessed the words in the speech bubbles. She read them avidly for over a year. It was another milestone and we were beyond happy. She eventually moved on to the *Asterix and Obelix* series as well.

With Li back in Sydney for the July season, we were both wondering how many more seasons he could manage combined with working in the financial world. Every day I continued to ask myself if I had done enough for Sophie. Every day the answer was still *No, there's more to be done.* There were many times when I wished we were an ordinary family without two languages and two cultures, just simple challenges and a husband home every evening. But I knew I had to stop wishing for things that weren't realistic. I just kept going, day by day, with sheer determination and focus and one goal in mind: *I wanted a conversation with my daughter one day.* I didn't want Sophie to be locked into a smaller world. I wanted her to be able to move in both worlds. But I knew that we were racing against her impending puberty.

For now, all I could do was keep on doing what I was doing and wonder what would happen when Li did finally retire. Using my ballet brain again was my saviour. I was now teaching the pre-professional program at Dance World. This was much more to my liking than teaching younger students. Also, three mornings a week and on Monday nights I taught the senior girls at Miss Anna's Dance Partners studio.

One night, Dom came to babysit and Li and I went out to dinner on the St Kilda foreshore. A rare treat! The days were getting longer and it was such a joy to look out over the bay as the sun went down over a calm and glassy sea. Li poured the wine and said excitedly, 'Darling, you know what an interesting time it is right now in ANZ Securities history, as well as the stock market.'

I just smiled, waiting for him to go on.

'ANZ Securities is going through an expansion phase and there's so much going on.'

'That's exciting, Li,' I said.

'I don't think it's time for me to give up dancing yet, but Mary, can you promise me that you will let me know when it's time to retire?'

'Yes, of course.'

The waiter brought our meals to the table. Li continued: 'I'm starting to meet with some ANZ branch managers who are referring me to customers with investment needs, so my client base is starting to grow quickly. It's very exciting. I'm learning a lot. It means that when I do retire from ballet, as hard as that will be, we will be okay financially.'

I had to admit, the future did start to feel less scary when I heard him say that. I raised a glass to my brilliant, hardworking husband. 'It sounds incredible, darling. You can't continue with dancing and stockbroking forever, though. You know that, don't you?'

'Yes,' Li replied. 'My injuries are lingering longer now. We'll know when the time is right.'

~

For Christmas that year, we stayed with Mum and Dad in their unit on the hill in Brisbane. Neil George was in his element, playing grandad to the now thirteen grandchildren. He and Mum were still devoted to each other. Coralie had always been so caring and attentive to all of us children, and now Dad with his oxygen tank by his chair was the beneficiary of that care. Just as he had poured a Scotch for Mum in Rocky as she sat in her chair after our dinner, now she brought him his beer as he sat in *his* favourite chair. He loved watching the passing parade of the McKendry children and grandchildren. At any time of the day, Mum would say, 'Here's someone!' and footsteps could be heard coming up the stairs.

Mum had made the apartment beautiful, as she did with everything, with antiques and fine art. Her exquisite taste never left her. Neil George was always preparing for the times ahead, and had his eye on the apartment next door, with a view to someone in the family living in it sometime down the track. I sensed he was anxious about what would happen to Mum when his time was up. We all were. It was truly awful watching him struggle to breathe and speak. *Soon he will be in a wheelchair*, I thought, and my heart broke for him.

14

For Chinese New Year that year, we decided to visit the Li family and introduce Bridie to them. It would be the first Chinese New Year Li would celebrate in China with his own children.

Li's family all thought Bridie was the most adorable baby with her porcelain-like skin, which they valued highly. Once again it was a typical visit with so much love, so many gatherings, so much food. And, of course, so many spectacular fireworks, now that they could afford them. It was as though Li wanted to make up for the lack of money in his childhood by ensuring his own children and his brothers' children enjoyed the festivities. Everybody was caught up in the frenzied noise and excitement, including Sophie. And all the children loved the traditional red money bags.

As always, any concern we had that Chinese might confuse and disrupt Sophie's language development and progress was superseded by how important we felt it was for her to know her extended Chinese family. As long as she was experiencing the vast and different things the world had to offer, she was also experiencing language visually. This would inevitably broaden her comprehension and expression. Well, that is what I hoped – only time would tell.

Back at school in February it was clear just how far behind everyone else Sophie really was. She still wasn't comprehending everything and often misunderstood conversations. She couldn't complete the homework for her year level and the grades were moving on too fast for her. I felt strongly that she needed to repeat Grade 4, as I knew she couldn't possibly cope with Grade 5. Shelford advised us against it, making me contemplate a move to another school closer to home. After much research we settled on Melbourne Girls Grammar School, which also offered Chinese. Li and I wanted her to have the opportunity to learn his native language. Tom was already learning Mandarin at Melbourne Grammar's junior school, Grimwade House. I also felt this school would have more resources to help Sophie in her secondary education.

Louise had moved with her family to Geelong, outside Melbourne, but she remained a good friend and continued to provide us with advice when needed. Sophie's new therapist, Sharon Klieve, would work with her at school and also came to our home for extra therapy sessions.

I tried to keep things positive for Sophie by making a fuss over how beautiful she looked in her new school uniform. The first thing was just to get her settled. Her teacher, Mr Prideaux, was young and gentle, and quick off the mark. He was comfortable with the FM microphone that Sophie still needed in order to hear him in the classroom.

On the afternoon of her first day I walked to the classroom door and anxiously waited with Bridie on my hip. Sophie came out looking exhausted and a bit confused. 'She's a very good girl, Mary,' Mr Prideaux told me. 'But it's going to take a bit of extra time for her to settle in.'

As we walked to the car, I asked Sophie, 'How did you go today?'

'Okay,' she replied simply, but she looked overwhelmed. I felt bad that I couldn't explain the reasons behind our decision to move schools when she just didn't have enough language to understand.

I knew that the first few months would be hard, and I felt sick in the stomach that Sophie couldn't really tell me how it was going. She made one nice friend quite quickly, but soon the friend's family moved interstate and Sophie was heartbroken. She cried and cried.

She only needed one person who understood her and could translate what was going on for her and support her.

She started Chinese lessons, first just numbers and days of the week. Li would go over them with her, '*Yī, Èr, Sān, Sì, Wǔ,*' as they drove to school. Sophie seemed to enjoy these lessons, especially the writing, because the characters are visual, like individual pictures. Li loved the thought that his children might speak Chinese one day.

~

The weeks leading up to the March opening season in Melbourne were intense. In addition to his work at ANZ Securities, Li was preparing for his big role in *Don Quixote*. Rudolf Nureyev's acclaimed version was a wonderful ballet – a showcase of Spanish knights and maidens, gypsies and fortune tellers, windmills and donkeys. Li would dance Basilio again, with upcoming talent Nicole Rhodes as Kitri.

The role of Basilio requires immense technical brilliance and Li was worried about how his body would hold up. *Don Quixote* is even more challenging if you are near the end of your career and juggling two jobs. It was a big ask, and every spare minute was given over to practising. Here's where my coaching skills came in handy. Some of Rudolf's intricate steps weren't Li's forte, so I'd work with him and Nicole.

One day, I could see something was bothering Li. 'It still doesn't feel quite right, Mary,' he said.

'What do you mean?' I asked.

'Well, to be honest, I never felt I conquered this role – and maybe it's too late,' he said.

Li was quiet. He then confessed, 'When I dance this role, I always have the images of Baryshnikov and Nureyev in my mind, and I never feel that I measure up to them.'

He had never shared these feelings with me before. 'Darling,' I said, 'technically you're not any less than Baryshnikov or Nureyev.

But they danced with their own individuality and created their own unique characters. That's what you have to do. Forget them. Forget what they did. Invent your own character.'

I could see he understood me. From that moment onwards, our rehearsals took a different approach. We solely focused on the character and what felt natural for him.

On opening night, Li was incredible. He was alive. He was flying. He *was* Basilio. He drew the audience into his world. His energy, wit and technical brilliance are something I will never forget – and the audience adored the performance. It was just stunning. As always, Li partnered Nicole with such care and assurance. He danced the performance of his life that night. Even though I had seen some pretty spectacular ballet from him before, this night was electric.

I let Li sleep in the next morning, but when he woke, he came hobbling down the stairs. I could see he was hurting. 'God, I'm sore,' he said.

'But you were amazing last night! Everything worked.'

He looked at me, and said, 'Mary, I'm not sure I can make it through the year.'

I was shocked, even though I knew this moment had to come. Then he asked, 'Tell me honestly. Is it time?'

'Li, you have danced pretty much all the major ballets you ever dreamed of dancing; you have had a wonderful career. I know you always wanted to finish on top. If you feel you want to stop now, you should. You have nothing more to prove.'

'Mary, I feel it's time,' he said. 'Last night's performance was special. I'm happy to end my career on that one. I can't keep going. I think I should finish my career in Sydney when we complete this season.'

I could see that his mind was made up. It wasn't unexpected, but I was sad. I knew what this realisation felt like. For different reasons, I had made the same decision in Canada. This was Li's fourth season with the Australian Ballet and he had built up a strong following with

Australian audiences, who had discovered just how magical he was. And now he would be gone. But I would have him home.

I could see he was feeling emotional. I had to be strong for him. 'You never thought you'd dance this long anyway, Li,' I said. 'Especially in big classical roles. You've been incredible, really pushed the boundaries. You can move into stockbroking with no regrets.'

It was announced that Li would officially retire from ballet in the autumn. His farewell was a big deal for the company and a huge deal for Li. Dancing had been his life. For his swansong he would again perform the role of Basilio that he had so successfully made his own. His final performance would be on 2 March 1999 at the Sydney Opera House, but before that he would say goodbye to Melbourne.

We were so excited on that special night. I explained to Sophie what was happening, and we put on our best frocks and Tom actually changed out of his tennis gear for once. He was now almost seven and had seen Li in a few performances. It was extra-important that Sophie and Tom see their dad perform one more time. Dom – bless him – stayed home to mind Bridie. We all knew this night would be one to cherish and remember.

The audience was filled with our friends and Li's adoring fans, who wanted to witness his final performance in their city. The applause for his leaps and the *pas de deux* was so enthusiastic – 'Bravo, bravo!' They farewelled him with a standing ovation. I rushed backstage with our kids and friends to Li's dressing room. Tom flew into his arms and Li hugged him tight. There was hardly room to breathe with everyone laughing and congratulating him.

Two weeks later, we flew to Sydney to see Li's very final curtain call. What made it extra special was that Ben Stevenson surprised us by arriving from America. It was short notice, and we were deeply touched that he had come.

When Li appeared onstage, he had such presence with his expressive face that communicated so much. Then he started to dance, and his body moved with incredible grace and confidence. He had such impressive physicality with his long arms and legs. He flew high in the air and his *pirouettes* were a blur. His maturity was on show, and of course his love for the ballet. Li took over the stage, and everyone else was swept along with him. It was a brilliant, emotional performance. And then his illustrious career was over, to another marvellous standing ovation.

I went backstage with Sophie. 'That was wonderful, darling. A spectacular show!' I said.

Li simply smiled.

'You have to be happy with that, Li!' I told him.

As he sat in front of the mirror, I noticed he wasn't moving. 'How are you feeling?' I asked.

He took a breath. 'You know, Mary, I've just realised that this is the last time I'll be taking my make-up off.'

I could see he was overcome. I had to be strong so I started to help pack up his gear. 'Li, I hate to tell you, but Ben and everybody are waiting for you,' I said. I didn't like to rush him. I knew this was an especially sentimental moment in his career.

While I waited for him to finish his shower, I couldn't help but feel a sense of sorrow, both for him and for me. Ever since we had become partners in Houston, we had built up an incredible trust both in the studio and on stage. I constantly marvelled at how honest and truthful he was about his shortcomings, how humble he was in taking up my and other people's corrections, how much passion he had demonstrated in every performance. It surprised me that he had mastered his footwork towards the end of his career. Most dancers would have stopped listening and improving, or even stopped dancing before thirty-five. But here he was dancing beautifully until the end. Who could ask for anything more?

An afterparty was held in the foyer of the Sydney Opera House. It was quite a celebration, including dancers, company staff members, friends and family. But it was very sad. The dancers gathered around Li and told him how much they would miss him. Li spoke from the heart – he has a gift for it – and on this emotional night, he had everyone in tears as he thanked the people who had helped him over the years. Many people had supported him on his journey from peasant to prince of the stage. He paid special tribute to Ben and I could see Ben was touched. He was beaming proudly. It meant so much for Li to have him there. Ben had been the single most important mentor in his career. I knew Li felt forever indebted to him.

You never know what the end is going to be. *He was so lucky to have the opportunity to get a final performance*, I thought, as I watched Li hug his way around the room. He was exhausted physically and mentally, but could always find more energy for the people he loved.

Tom and Bridie were being looked after by a babysitter. I turned to find Sophie. It was important for her to share this milestone with her father – and there she was. She had fallen asleep on the carpeted stairs, her bottom on one step and resting her head and hands on the next.

Once we said our last goodbyes and headed to our apartment, Li turned to me and said, 'God, Mary. I can't believe my career as a dancer is officially over. I'm so relieved. I did it.'

I hugged him, and was relieved for him too. It had been enormously hard – not only getting ready and then doing his last-ever performances, but the extra demands on his time over the last three years. He had just started with a new firm, Johnson Taylor, one of the oldest Melbourne-based stockbroking firms, to set up the first dedicated Asian desk in stockbroking in Australia. To get through it all and live up to his own and others' expectations was an incredible achievement. And the reviews of his final performance were some of the best he'd ever had.

In a long, arduous and extraordinary journey, Li had conquered two continents and danced around the world with some of the best companies. He had defied amazing odds. A true rags-to-riches story. What are the chances of a Rocky girl meeting a Chinese peasant prince from China?

Li convinced his parents to come and visit. It was their first time in Melbourne. How wonderful it was to have them back with us again. We were treated to Niang's delicious Chinese feasts, and Dia happily walked Tom to the park. Li was in his element and Sophie adored having her *nana* and *yeye* back with us.

But Niang hadn't been well, and we were conscious this might be the last time she would be able to make the trip. She arrived very sick, coughing constantly, and was visibly older and more frail. She was worried that she would be a burden on us and was anxious to go home. We suspected that she had a bad pneumonia. Li wanted to take her to the hospital but she adamantly refused. A week later, with our persistence, she finally agreed to see a doctor – but a Chinese one, she insisted. The one thing I'd learned early on about the Lis was that they could be very stubborn. It was a family trait and there was no use trying to change her mind.

Niang and Dia were besotted with sixteen-month-old Bridie, but Niang was disapproving that I was still breastfeeding her. I was desperate to stop breastfeeding, but didn't have the strength until Niang told me to go away for a weekend and they would sort it out. I always loved her honesty and wise advice – and her plan worked.

By the time Li's parents' visit was over Niang was feeling better, but the illness had taken a lot out of her. She was in her late seventies and had lived a very hard life. We tried to convince them to stay longer, but they were determined to go home.

～

It was the beginning of another phase of our life. The excitement of Li's last performance abated, but there was no time to rest. His full-time stockbroking career would start the following Monday. The process of adjusting to our new and different 'normal' life began. Li had walked out of his ballet shoes into a suit and his only job now was a nine-to-five one. He could focus on that one job and spend more time with us.

We were not a family who stood on ceremony; everything was pretty casual, and we had a lot of laughs. Black jazz pants, a T-shirt and bare feet were the order of the day for me. Li looked good however he was dressed, suit and tie for work or casual slacks at home – the way clothes sat on his body, well, he could have been a model! But always at night and in the morning, it was his beloved pyjama pants, handmade by Niang years before. He just would not part with them. He was too sentimental, especially with anything to do with his dear Niang. The kids liked to tease him about them, especially once the drawstring collapsed and he took to holding them up with his hands. 'Dad, they are so tatty! Get some new ones!' they would say, poking at the holes.

Li's reply was always the same: 'Never! Why?'

'They don't look good on you any more!'

Li would turn to me and ask, 'Mary, how do I look?'

'Darling, you look just marvellous,' I would laugh with him.

The kids would shriek delightedly and we'd all end up rolling around on the bed in fits of laughter. They just adored their dad and were always all over him.

Bridie was getting more physically active. She was one of those babies who wanted to go out all the time. 'Like mother, like daughter,' Coralie said to me when I complained.

Tom, on the other hand, was always independent and self-contained. Ever since I had dropped him off to his first tennis lesson, he'd been obsessed with the sport. At home he took the paintings off one wall and volleyed against it for hours at a time. It wasn't long before he was playing in competitions across Melbourne. He had a very good ballet physique and was a natural mover, but he didn't want to go near a dance studio. He did try jazz and tap, but the classes didn't last long despite the inducement of his favourite lollies. Dance just wasn't for him, and there was no point forcing him. Now he had more time for tennis. He was happier.

Sophie was ten years old when she was asked, along with two other children, to make commemorative presentations to the president of China, Jiang Zemin, when he visited the Bionic Ear Institute. Li was thrilled for her. The Nucleus 24 bionic ear had by then been implanted in around 25 000 people in fifty countries, including China, where more than a million people with profound hearing loss had been helped by the device. It would be such a fantastic opportunity for Sophie to speak in public. A speech was prepared and she practised it over and over.

On the day, Professor Graeme Clark spoke first, about the history of the bionic ear, his 33-year involvement and the many technical and scientific challenges that had been overcome. President Jiang Zemin then told the gathering, 'Your work has brought so much joy and happiness to so many profoundly deaf people around the world.'

When it was Sophie's turn, she delivered her speech beautifully, as clearly as I'd ever heard her speak: 'Mr Presiden, welcome to Austraia. I would like to presen you with this gif – a bionic ear, jus like the one inside my hea.' And she presented the president with her gift, a replica of the cochlear implant. I was bursting with pride. There was my deaf daughter, speaking on behalf of the Bionic Ear Institute and meeting the president of China. It was one of those very special moments for us. Only we knew how far she had come and all the work involved to get her to this point.

Once the rhythm of our new way of life began to settle, I started teaching more classes at Dance World. As my reputation as a teacher grew, some of the dancers from the Australian Ballet asked me to coach them privately. This was what I'd hoped for. Working hard to refine my own body and technique in my career had certainly helped me to be analytical and inquisitive. I constantly thought about how I could help the dancers discover their potential. I was home, doing what I was born to do.

Li, on the other hand, fully embraced his new life as a stockbroker. As with everything else, he committed himself totally to his work, and stockbroking soon became his passion. He loved learning, loved a challenge, and always strove to be the best. He was a visionary, big-picture person – *like Neil George*, I often thought. He was also in the right place at the right time. It was during these first couple of years that the technology side of the market became hot, and somehow Li managed to tap into a network of tech-savvy people. It was an exciting time. It was his first bull market and he was riding it. But Li, always with an eye to the future, knew this once-in-a-lifetime technology boom wouldn't last.

'Mary, make sure you remind me to get our investments out of the stock market before May next year,' he urged me time and again. 'Don't let me get carried away. The bubble has to burst sometime and we want to be out before that happens.'

~

Sophie's reading was improving. She graduated from her beloved Tintin and Asterix books straight to Harry Potter, and reading soon became her passion. This was a breakthrough. I was relieved to see she was starting to comprehend much more about daily life. But there were other issues.

We were about halfway into the school year when I received a troubling call from Mr Prideaux. 'Mary,' he said, 'I am really concerned about Sophie.'

My stomach flipped like it always did when something wasn't going well for Sophie. I took a deep breath. 'What's wrong?' I asked.

'She is doing well, but she isn't mixing with the other fourth-graders. She is still playing with the Grade 2s.'

'I see,' I said, instantly deflated, and then told him, 'Although she's eleven, her speech and language skills are still like a seven-year-old's. She can't possibly keep up with the speed of language in her peer group. I appreciate you letting me know, though. Let me think about this.'

I had always thought we would get to a certain point and she'd just take off. After seven years with her implant I had been imagining that her language acquisition would get easier. During these prepubescent years, it was very challenging for Sophie, me and Li. If I thought too much about it, it would make me cry. I questioned myself after a setback like this. 'I've put her on this track of mainstreaming and there are no other options. What have I done? How will she ever be independent?'

But, as always with my crises of confidence, Li would remind me, 'Mary, her deafness won't go away. But just look how far she's come.' There was nothing else to do but move forward.

I asked Sophie why she was playing with the girls in Grade 2. She told me it was easier to join in younger children's ball games than catching the conversations of her classmates, and then she said, 'I don' 'ave any frien' in my clas'.

Times like this were like a dagger to my heart. How I wished that life would just get easier for her, but every time I thought she had made a breakthrough, inching closer to her peers, I'd be reminded again that they had raced on and left Sophie further behind.

Tom was now eight and was instinctively wise about Sophie and her needs. 'Tom,' I asked him, 'do other eleven-year-olds play with the Grade 2s? Is that normal?'

'No. Girls in Grade 4 don't play much. They sit around and chat together,' he explained. 'That would be too hard for Sophie. She wouldn't fit into a group like that.'

This gave me new worries. How on earth could I help?

I was always looking for ways to expand Sophie's vocabulary through new experiences, and thought it was the right time for her to learn an instrument. This would give us a new topic to talk about, and she might make new friends her own age. With music lessons she would learn new language as well as musical terms, and further broaden her vocabulary and comprehension. I didn't mind which instrument – perhaps something small, I thought, but she insisted on cello.

We never knew the quality of sounds she actually heard from the cello. We understood that the implant produced mechanical sounds and that recipients drew meaning from those sounds. Each person would interpret them differently, depending on the benefit they got from their implant. We assumed that Sophie enjoyed the sounds she made with the cello, and were just delighted that she liked practising it. Amazingly, right from the start, her playing was beautiful.

~

All this coincided with another change. For a few months, we had been considering buying a new house for our growing family. Li cashed in some of his share-market profits so we could put a deposit on a new house, 74 Park Street, St Kilda West. St Kilda is a dynamic area, once a popular tourist mecca, just one block from the iconic beach. It was an excellent location that happily suited our needs. The house was quite a bit larger and nicer than our townhouse, and many of our friends were living in the area. Our new address was still close to the ballet school and everything else we needed. We had four good-sized bedrooms, a proper sitting room at the front, steps down into a family room with a fireplace and a big courtyard, and a 1500-bottle wine cellar under the kitchen floor. There was a tram line out the front and we were next to a small park, with a little coffee shop nearby.

We were sponsoring one of Li's nieces, his third brother's daughter Lulu, to come to Melbourne to do a TAFE diploma, and we would have room for her to stay in the new house. This made Li extremely happy. Li's family, my family, they were simply the most important thing to us. If you know that and feel that, then you are always happy to go the extra mile.

Lulu was twenty-one when she came to live with us, Sophie eleven, Tom eight, Bridie nearly three. We moved Bridie and Sophie into one room so Lulu could have her own room. She was a confident girl with a sweet nature and would often help me in the kitchen or babysit Bridie.

Lulu didn't speak a word of English when she arrived. She started an intensive English course immediately and soon got a job at the local supermarket, which really dropped her in the deep end. Adding another person with English-language difficulties to our already frantic family was extra-challenging. Every time I got frustrated, I kept reminding myself that Li had always dreamed of being able to help his family. How could I deny his generous wish? I had to make it work.

We soon grew to fill the space of our new home. The children, especially Tom, loved the garden. He could now practise his ball-hitting outside, 24/7 if he wanted to. We had a dining area for socialising and a rather big kitchen, perfect for when Li made his mother's dumplings. He would stand for hours rolling the dough into long tubes, then slicing and rolling them into thin circles. He was just happy to see everyone having a good time while he waited on our guests. What a joy that was, especially for me. I think my years of toasting ten loaves of bread and peeling forty potatoes for the McKendry clan really did spoil cooking for me.

One day, Sophie came home from school and handed me a note. 'We 'ave conert, Mum,' she said.

I read the note. A music concert. And my heart lifted. She was to be part of the school's end-of-year concert. 'Oh, Sophie. That will be such fun!' I told her.

The one thing we had always carried heavy in our hearts was that Sophie would never know the beauty of music – the sound that filled our lives. So when she played the cello, it was a joyous thing for us. We never would have dared to hope for more than that. She was actually getting enjoyment from it! 'Sophie, it sounds beautiful,' Li would tell her when she practised.

We went along to the school hall to watch Sophie play. I was amazed that she was rather calm. The music began: the magnificent 'Ode to Joy' by Beethoven. Because she was part of the orchestra, we watched like hawks to see if she was in time with the other cellists. We marvelled that she absolutely was. We didn't really care about the sound. Instead we were simply thrilled that her bold, confident movements were in step with the other players. Li and I looked at each other in amazement. Although we had experienced some very special performances in our careers, watching Sophie perform like that, so confident and poised, was more satisfying than anything we had achieved.

Christmas soon followed and, as was now our tradition, we spent the holiday season in Brisbane and then at Rainbow Bay on the Gold Coast. But there was a massive sadness casting its shadow over us this year. Neil George's emphysema was taking its toll. Our beloved father was really struggling to breathe, even with his oxygen tank in tow. He had very little energy and very little to say. Well, it was too hard for him to speak. Because of this, neither Mum nor Dad would join us at the beach this year.

Mum managed to look calm as usual, but we could see the situation was taking a toll on her, too. We rallied around to help when we could, but it was really devastating. The grandchildren would sit and play at Neil George's feet. He'd giggle at them and they at him. He was always even-tempered and never a grumpy grandad. The thought that this might be our last Christmas together was something not one of the family could contemplate.

～

Life never stands still, and soon it was time for Bridie to start three-year-old kinder. Where had the time gone? The last of our three children was now out in the world. Bridie was as lively as ever. Kindergarten provided necessary structure for her while at the same time freedom to explore on the playground equipment. She didn't socialise much but played a lot, mostly upside down on the monkey bars.

I felt guilty as Li and I were so incredibly busy and didn't involve ourselves that much in Bridie's kindergarten life. I tentatively told Li that she wanted us to help with her Show and Tell, and I suggested that he should make dumplings for her kindergarten class for Chinese New Year. 'We *have* to do this for her,' I said. I knew I could trust him to make this happen. The children would enjoy watching him roll out the pastry circles, stuff them with tasty fillings and then cook them in a boiling pot. It would be very special, I thought.

Bridie's teacher, Ken, agreed. Li had to take along everything: flour to make the dough; Chinese cabbage, pork, ginger, green onions, oil and soy sauce for the filling; a rolling pin for making the pancakes; and a knife and wok. He showed the children how to make the dumplings and each of the twenty-five children made their own. But when they were boiled in water – disaster! Many of them fell apart. Luckily, Li had made some at home that he was able to cook instead.

He also told the children stories about Chinese New Year and the history of dumplings. He was a big hit. But the thing that he treasured most was seeing the pride on Bridie's face to have her dad as the star at kinder that day. Ken said to Li afterwards, 'Promise me you'll come back next year.'

~

Around this time, we learned that Ross Stretton was to leave Australia to take up the artistic directorship at the Royal Ballet in London. The Australian Ballet needed a replacement, and Li was encouraged to apply. He had turned down a previous offer to run a ballet company overseas, but the Australian Ballet was a different proposition. Deep down, I'd always felt it was a great shame that he was no longer part of the art form that he was so incredibly passionate about. He still had so much to give. Despite never saying so, I knew he really missed the dance world. I believed he could be an excellent director. Stockbroking had added to his knowledge of business, which would only be an advantage.

We were both very excited about this new opportunity. We discussed the pros and cons and Li decided to go for it. He got into the last round of selection and spoke to me very seriously about the challenges he would face if he got the job, and the challenges I would face raising three children often on my own. 'Mary, the touring commitment is huge. The sheer amount of performances would be overwhelming. Do you think we can manage? I will be away a lot.'

'I know, but I think I can manage,' I said. In my heart I knew that Li would be a wonderful leader, the kind who had vision, integrity, honesty and empathy. Once he put his mind to something, nothing could stop him.

Li was excited about the possibility of directing the Australian Ballet, and thought his final interview had gone well. A couple of hours before the official announcement, he received a call from the headhunter to discuss salary, his choice of assistant artistic director, and his referees. Right after that conversation, he phoned me. 'Mary, it sounds like they may offer me the job. Are you sure you're ready for this?'

'Oh God.' I took a deep breath and said, 'Yes, I'm sure!'

But then, on the ABC radio news bulletin at noon, it was announced that they had chosen the then principal artist David McAllister as the new artistic director. It was a shock, to say the least. Of course we were happy for David, but to have come so far and to hear the news this way was devastating. We couldn't believe it. It was too much to take in. Above all, I was terribly disappointed for Li and for what he could have done for the company. He would have been such an inspiration.

Poor Li was stunned, and subsequently fell into a slump. He was clearly going through some soul-searching. I had never seen him like this. The next weekend, he went to the garage to start building birdcages. Birdcages! Out of bamboo, Chinese style. I thought to myself, *If a psychologist knew Li's story, they'd have a field day.*

Li was actually depressed. 'Darling, are you all right?' I asked him. He didn't reply, just nodded. He has always been a doer and was looking for something to help him get over his disappointment. 'But why birdcages?' I said.

'I always liked birds, ever since I was a child,' he replied. 'I want to make some nice cages and buy some beautiful birds, so they can live in comfortable homes. I'm sure we will get so much joy out of them.'

What on earth? I thought.

Thankfully, three things happened after this. First, and luckily for me, David McAllister offered me a job to teach and coach the company dancers. He asked if I could teach every day and take some rehearsals. I was elated. To have the chance to work with professional dancers of such calibre was beyond my wildest dreams. And Li was happy for me, too, despite his own sadness. At last, I had the opportunity to reconnect with ballet on a professional level.

Not long after, the second thing happened. Li was asked to join the board of the Australian Ballet as the dancers' representative. This gave us the opportunity to share our ballet passion together and to make contributions to the art form, though in a different way than Li had originally envisioned. It is so true in life that when one door closes, another opens.

The third thing happened on a weekend getaway with friends to Erskine House at Lorne, a seaside town on the Great Ocean Road a couple of hours from Melbourne. Being a typical Melbourne winter, it rained most of the weekend. The heavy downpour made the tin roof echo. We were cosy inside enjoying the lively conversation with an interesting group of people: doctors, lawyers, teachers, a marketing executive, an interior designer, a stockbroker, an author and an artist. During dinner we agreed that each of us would share our life story. When it came to our turn, we decided we would dance a little. Li lifted me in the air in the *Giselle présage*. Everybody cheered – we were all quite tipsy by then.

Whenever Li talked about his life, the audience would be in the palm of his hand, and that's what happened this time. It was Graeme Base, the celebrated children's author and illustrator, who said Li should write his story.

What a great idea, I thought. *I won't have to keep listening to it wherever we go!* After all, I really did know it inside out by now.

Li initially said no, telling Graeme he didn't see a compelling reason to share his private life with the public, and he couldn't possibly write it himself. Graeme suggested Li write a short summary, which he would take to his publisher.

'I think it'd be rather self-indulgent to write my own story,' Li protested.

'Li, don't look at it as though writing your story is just for you,' Graeme said. 'Your story is full of hope and courage. There aren't enough inspirational stories in the world.'

'But I can't write. My English is too poor,' Li said.

'If you don't want to write it yourself, they can find a good writer to help you,' Graeme told him.

Over breakfast the next morning, I asked, 'Li, what do you think about what Graeme said last night?'

'I'm not sure,' he replied.

I didn't mince my words. 'Li, quite frankly, I am sick and tired of you telling and retelling your story at dinner parties. You should just get on and write the damn book, so when people start asking questions about your life, we can tell them to just read the book instead.'

Li laughed, but I was dead serious. Over the years, he had been offered numerous movie and book deals but had declined them all. I hoped that Graeme could change his mind this time.

We arrived home from the weekend happy and exhausted, but the fire was lit for Li. The following Friday night, when he came home from work, he said to me, 'Darling, I'm going to the office tomorrow morning to write a couple of pages for Graeme.'

By Sunday he had sent Graeme an eight-page synopsis with bullet points about his life. Now he was focused again, but little did we know that Li's story would become his therapy. Throughout his life he had been busy pursuing his next goal and never had time to reflect on the life he'd lived. Writing his story gave him this opportunity.

Li had always been a good storyteller. From time to time he would tell me snippets from his childhood, and I'd always wanted more.

This was the evolution of Li as a writer and storyteller. As soon as he started to write, I thought to myself, *Here we go*. I hoped it would stop him making those bloody birdcages! Although writing in English was a struggle for him and sometimes he wondered what he'd started, he eventually came to enjoy it.

As a relatively young man, Li had experienced so much upheaval. His devastating poverty-stricken childhood in China, the lonely years at the Beijing Dance Academy, his marriage breakdown, his defection and subsequent separation from his beloved family, making a home in three different countries, Sophie's deafness, and his agonising career change. He had always remembered his mother's words: 'Never look back.' Her wisdom had helped him through the most unbearable difficulties. But now it was as though years of his memories and experiences needed to come out. And through this process of reflection, he began to come to terms with a lot of things about his life.

Graeme sent Li's summary to the then publishing director of Penguin Australia, Robert Sessions. Li was then invited to lunch by Penguin's executive publisher of young adult and children's books, Julie Watts. He came home that evening and told me, 'Mary, I had lunch with a publisher from Penguin today. She seems to be very genuine and nice. I like her. I think she will be sensitive to my story.'

'Really? That's wonderful. Is it going to be a children's book?' I asked.

'She told me not to worry about this right now, just concentrate on writing. She also said that I have my own distinctive way of writing, which is my own voice. She seems to think that I can write.'

I could detect a hint of doubt in his eyes.

'I think you can do it,' I told him. 'Nobody could write your story without having lived it.'

From then on, Li wrote in every spare moment he had. He just wrote and wrote. He wrote on the weekends, and deep into the night after reading the children their bedtime stories. After he had written 40 000 words, we went to a meeting with Bob and Julie. We didn't know what to expect, but in the middle of the discussions about the potential of Li's book, I made an outrageous comment: 'Li has a universal story. His book will be a bestseller and it will sell millions,' I blurted out.

To this day, I still don't have the faintest idea why I made such a claim. Li looked at me aghast, hoping I would shut up. Bob burst into laughter and said, 'Mary, I don't want to appear rude, but every writer in the world thinks their book will sell millions. Do you know how many sold copies of a book constitute a bestseller in Australia?'

I shook my head.

'Between five and seven thousand copies,' he said.

I was thoroughly embarrassed. Millions of copies? What was I thinking? But I liked Bob more for his honesty.

Julie was incredibly nurturing and skilful with Li. She was all positivity and encouragement. Her questions would lead to more writing from him, and over the ensuing months the pages from the printer piled up on the desk and then the floor, so much was pouring out of him.

~

Neil George was excited for Li. He would always ask how he was going with the book. Sometimes Dad sounded very tired and breathless, and I'd ask Mum to tell me how he really was. The news was never good. One day soon our family would be altered forever.

Dad did live to see another Christmas, but with what else was going on in the world – the September 11 attack on New York's Twin Towers rocked us all – I just wanted to keep my young family close. We decided to have Christmas at home, so we stayed in Melbourne. Our dear friends from Houston, Ginya and Clayton, came with their children, Kelley and John. We had a rare and fun Christmas Day at home. Bridie was excited by the preparations, such as buying the tree and decorating it, and couldn't wait to open all the presents. We had so often travelled to our extended families at this time of year. This year she loved having us all to herself.

Ginya and Clayton were amazed at how Sophie's communication skills had developed, and were drawn to her sweet personality. Then one day, Ginya said, 'We'd love for Sophie to stay with us and go to St John's School. It's one of the best schools in America.'

'That sounds nice, Ginya,' was my polite reply, but it actually sounded ridiculous to me. Sophie was only twelve and there was no way I was going to let her go. Li had heard of the school and was really taken with the idea. He was excited, but I was sure nothing would come of it.

Occasionally Li went away for a weekend to write, or stayed at work late to focus on his book. But mostly he was at home with us, with Sophie's therapy lessons happening in the background, Bridie rollerblading down the stairs and Tom kicking or hitting balls around. I was enjoying teaching professional dancers and the children were doing well; even Sophie was calm and accepting despite her struggles. We had good friends nearby. Australia felt far away from international ructions, warm and safe. Sometimes I marvelled at how lucky we were.

But things were looking dire for Neil George. Five years on oxygen was enough, and to see the shadow of my once energetic father having to use a wheelchair was painful. He was a different person, almost unrecognisable. His face was pale, his limbs were thinner, but he would never lose his beer belly. He was determined not to have to go to hospital or a nursing home. Under Coralie's loving care, we didn't think he'd have to. I hoped Mum could keep going.

The early weeks of 2002 went by in a blur. With three children at school, I couldn't get up to Brisbane often and was on the phone regularly to Mum and Dad. Even speaking seemed to take his breath away, but he always managed those dear words from my childhood that I knew so well: 'Hello, beautiful!'

Stoic to the end, he didn't spend one night in hospital until 9 April 2002. Coralie had to call an ambulance because his breathing worsened. His first night in a hospital would be the last night of his life. I got the call from Mick at 2 a.m. to say he was gone. Coralie was with him at the end, which was what he wanted. He died with his rosary beads in his hand.

Paddy spoke beautifully at Neil George's funeral and mentioned how the moment Neil George married Coralie he knew he had struck gold. And we all knew it, too. Li and my brothers carried the coffin out of the church after the service, with such care and heavy hearts. We wept at the funeral service and again when his coffin was lowered into the grave.

Even though I had mentally prepared for this day, at that moment I still couldn't quite come to terms with the idea that Neil George – that kind, interesting and brilliant man, the centre of our universe – would never make us laugh again. The giant figure in our lives was gone forever. He had shown such kindness and generosity and instilled those qualities in all of us that would continue to guide us through our lives.

I'll forever miss you, Dad.

15

Enrolling four-year-old Bridie in gymnastics was the best thing. Her body was made for it – lean, agile, strong and small. She soon became obsessed, to the exclusion of all else. It was astonishing to watch her perform the manoeuvres. The movements were so different to ballet, and yet the power and beauty of the body on display was just the same. It was a relief to see all that energy contained at last! She was put into the intensive stream and just lapped it up.

Sophie, on the other hand, seemed to be coming apart in new and unexpected ways, though perhaps we should have been prepared. After all, she was nearly thirteen, dealing with all the hormonal activity that happens at puberty. I was surprised when the school counsellor called me and said Sophie had come to her very upset. She told me Sophie didn't want to do ballet any more.

'Really? That's news to me,' I said to her. I was annoyed. She was ignorant of Sophie's situation and the benefits we had seen emerge from ballet.

When I picked Sophie up from school that day, she spoke to me as soon as she got into the car. 'Mum, I don' wan' to go ballet any more.'

'Why?' I asked. 'Where is this coming from?' I wondered. But when I thought about it, I could guess why. At that stage, ballet gets really hard. There's a huge change in the skills required when it's time to learn jumps and turns. Sophie was attending four classes a week – a big commitment – as well as fitting in homework, music practice and friends.

'I jus don' like any more. Too much ballet,' she said firmly.

What Li and I knew for sure by now, and Sophie probably didn't realise, was how much she gained from her ballet training with Miss Anna. Through ballet, she learned that she should work to her best capacity, be on her best behaviour and dance the best she could. She was good at it so it boosted her self-esteem. Ballet is learned in a controlled social and disciplined environment. This meant Sophie could follow the exercises, feel the music, and pick up visually what the corrections were. And ballet had revealed how naturally expressive Sophie was – and that's something that can't be taught easily.

I knew she was entering that stubborn teenager stage. I was firm with her. She would have to continue ballet until the end of the year, I told her. She had to work hard every day and in everything: in speech therapy, in ballet and at school. I knew she just had to do it if she wanted to get ahead. And she had started learning the piano instead of the cello.

Outside of ballet things were becoming harder for her, too. Children of around thirteen don't play, they talk. All talk and no play was impossible for Sophie. *How must it be*, I thought to myself, *to be nearly thirteen but still in Grade 6, in a world where your classmates are already talking about boys, movies and music, but you simply can't catch what is being said?* No one her age was going to wait around while Sophie tried to work out what was being said and then wait for their turn to speak.

For this reason I often thought about signing. I understood that in this form of communication there was a protocol for waiting for the other person to finish what they wanted to say before responding – unlike the speaking world, where people often talk over each other, particularly young girls. Girls can be so hurtful sometimes, even without meaning to be, and it distressed me just thinking about it.

The possibility that we may have set Sophie on the wrong path from the beginning often niggled at the back of my mind.

Sophie's struggles became clear to me when we celebrated her becoming a teenager. We decided on a sleepover at home, just three girls. We played it safe there, or so I thought. She and the girls were very excited. During the whole excruciating night, Sophie pretended to be having a good time but I could see it wasn't working. I watched the other girls and they were having fun, but they didn't understand that with a deaf person, everyone has to take their turn talking. In their excitement, they didn't even realise that Sophie was being totally excluded. And at her own birthday party!

The next day, the girls couldn't get out of bed as they'd been up all night. But Sophie had taken her implant out and slept – isolated once again. I couldn't wait for them to leave. I was angry and berated myself for not realising that a sleepover would end in disaster. I never seemed to get Sophie's birthday right!

Sometimes I felt I was the worst kind of mother, pushing and pushing, never letting up, especially when I could see that it was all too much for her, and then I'd be filled with remorse and think about whether she could ever really catch up. In less than six months we'd finish climbing the mountain that was primary school, only to face the taller peak that was secondary school.

At this age, Sophie was mostly happy to come home from school and answer basic questions, but other times she refused to listen or talk. 'Sophie, don't shut me out,' I'd say. 'I'm just trying to help you.'

'Mummm, I'm jus' tire'. I don' wan' talk any more.' She would take off her implant and retreat to her bedroom.

Conversely, there were times when I thought Sophie was the wisest one in our family – especially the time I really let myself down as a mother. Tom was about to go on school camp to Tasmania and Li was away at a friend's country property for the weekend to concentrate on his writing, hoping to finish the first draft of his manuscript by the end of the year. Sometimes I thought he was never going to finish it – he'd already done 500 000 words, which was four times more than Penguin actually needed. It seemed that once he'd started opening up, he just couldn't stop.

This particular morning I had to get Tom to the airport very early. I decided I'd quietly sneak away with him. I'd be gone an hour, max. Sophie would be there to look after her not yet five-year-old sister. Bridie would be safe with her when they both woke up. Well, I should have known better. I was on my way home when I received a call from a very angry Sophie.

'What?' I yelled into the car phone. 'Calm down, Sophie. I can't understand you!'

'Bridie ran 'way, Mum! Police here!' she screamed.

God, I nearly crashed the car then, and had to pull over while Sophie did her best to explain to me what had happened. Apparently, Bridie had heard the door close as I left. She got up and somehow managed to reach up to open the door and run out of the house, hoping to catch us in the car. She continued on a couple of blocks all the way up to Fitzroy Street – well known for sex workers, drug addicts and homeless people – where she got picked up by two patrolling police officers.

'Police in my bedroom, Mum! Bridie crying! It's scary. Don' dare do that again!'

'I'm on my way home and we'll sort it out,' I said. 'Is Bridie okay?'

'Yes! Where were you? What you thinking?!'

'Sophie . . .'

'Stop! You're crazy, Mum!' She cut me off and slammed the phone down.

When I got home, the girls were curled up on the sofa together. Bridie looked worn out, her face all puffy, and Sophie just glared at me before recounting the rest of the episode. A distraught Bridie had led the two police officers back to our house and woken Sophie, which scared her as she had no idea why they were in her bedroom. After she'd connected her implant, she was able to take control of the situation. She relayed her name and age and assured the police that all was fine. The worst bit was that they told her in no uncertain terms that if Sophie had been under thirteen, they would have had to take both girls into custody immediately as they were considered too young to be left alone.

So there we had it. A near miss for Bridie and a wake-up call for me. It left me pretty shaken. Bridie was terrified afterwards so we didn't scold her too much. She stayed glued to me for the rest of the year.

At least Li had almost finished writing his bloody book, thank God – he'd produced 680 000 words! 'Julie told me it's enough, Mary,' he said towards the end of the year. 'She said we can make a beautiful book out of what I've written.'

He sounded relieved and excited. I felt the same. *He'll be the family man once again, I thought.*

~

I was dreading Sophie's transition to high school, as I knew secondary schools didn't like parents being too involved, and I would have to educate a teacher for each subject instead of just one classroom teacher. Would they be on board with Sophie's needs? It would be so hard to monitor. It made me feel tired just thinking about it.

Then something delightful happened to end Sophie's primary school years on a high. 'Mum, the school wan' me to stan' up and speak at church,' she told me one afternoon. She looked really happy.

'Darling, fantastic!' said Li. 'Show me your speech.'

For the next couple of weeks, Sophie practised and practised her phrasing, pronunciation and intonation. 'Don't be afraid to look up at the audience from time to time to make a connection,' Li said. 'And take a deep breath before you start.'

Li and I took Sophie to St Paul's Cathedral in Melbourne's CBD. We sat with her near the front. She seemed both excited and a bit tense. Then the service began. As we sat nervously in the front pew, we were in awe of Sophie as she walked up to the podium to speak in front of hundreds of people. Her face was calm and she read with great clarity. She looked up a couple of times and paused in the right places, and her voice was beautiful with lovely intonation. The whole audience was captivated.

After dinner that night, Li and I were still on a high. 'Li, did you ever imagine that Sophie would be able to do this?' I asked him.

'No.' He shook his head. We were over the moon with what Sophie had done that day and how she was doing now. We knew too well how long and hard this journey had been for her, for me and for us as a family. It was a small but important breakthrough, one of those special moments that made all the hard work worth it for everyone, especially Sophie.

Moving up into senior school in February meant a massive adjustment for Sophie and me. It soon became clear that she didn't like the academic side of life, not at all, and who could blame her? Her vocabulary had increased but she had a lot of syntax errors in her speech and therefore the quality of her writing was weak. The teachers were fabulous, but keeping up with the chatter of her peers was now even harder for her. 'Sorry, what you say?' Sophie would ask. Mostly girls replied with, 'Don't worry. It wasn't important.' But it was. Because she could only pick up part of a sentence, she couldn't find her way into the conversations. This was never going to be easy.

At least she still had her dancing. Miss Anna suggested she add tap and jazz, which expanded her friendship group and became the highlight of her week. She became a very good jazz and tap dancer, but she got so busy with the extra dancing that something had to give and she told me, 'Mum, I'm too busy. No more piano.'

~

I continued to wonder if we'd made a mistake in not allowing Sophie to learn Australian Sign Language, called Auslan. Now that she was a teenager, I had developed a new fear for her. Like all teenagers, she would no doubt become more concerned about her looks, and refuse to wear the bulky implant processor in its chest harness. Realistically, this was a high probability. Then we would have no way to communicate at all. And if I couldn't communicate with my daughter, never have that conversation that I'd yearned for all these years, this would break me.

Then we heard there was an upgrade to the implant technology. Sophie was given a behind-the-ear processor for the first time, so she wouldn't have to wear the harness ever again. She was overjoyed. She could now hide the processor under her hair, and for the first time there was no lumpy device under her shirt or leotard.

Around the middle of the year, Louise called and told me that there was going to be a trial for a new generation of deaf children to be implanted in the second ear. This piqued my interest. Louise was working at the Bionic Ear Institute and had heard about a research project with a second implant that should help directionality. Louise believed it would be beneficial for Sophie. What an opportunity! Two implants would be better than one, I felt sure.

Unfortunately, Sophie had just turned fourteen and the trial was restricted to children under the age of ten. Were we too late already? Well, I was never going to accept that. My friend Dr Amanda Nutting knew and spoke highly of one of the surgeons doing the implants, Dr Rob Briggs, so I made an appointment to see him. He told me he could definitely implant Sophie on one condition: if she was part of the trial. How could we make this happen?

I also got the name of a surgeon in Western Australia who said he would be willing to do the surgery outside of the trial. I then made contact with the researcher, Karyn Galvin, and asked if Sophie could be included in the trial. I argued that her maturity and language capabilities would give them more information about the second implant.

Karyn wasn't convinced, but she probably hadn't come across anyone with my determination before. We called everybody we knew who could possibly help us with this. 'I just know that two implants are going to be better than one,' I said to Li. 'Just like two ears are better than one.'

'I agree. Mary, I trust you, but we need to talk to Sophie.'

Sophie wasn't so sure. 'You have to trust me, Sophie. It's got to be better than no hearing in the left ear,' I told her.

Li tried to convince her, too. 'Sophie, there is so much you could gain if it works, and you would have lost nothing if it doesn't work.'

After quite a few days of discussion, Sophie was reluctant and scared, but eventually agreed. 'It better work, Mum,' she told me.

To our relief, Karyn finally agreed for Sophie to be included in the trial and have the operation in Melbourne with Dr Briggs. Due to advances in cochlear surgery, the operation would be less invasive this time and the incision would be a small opening just above the ear. Only a small portion of her head needed to be shaved and bandaging would be minimal. She would stay in the hospital overnight and be out the following morning.

Surgery was scheduled for 27 November 2003. The thought of a three-month wait seemed interminable, but thankfully those months were full and exciting with end of the school year activities so time passed quickly.

~

It was nearly two years since Li had started to write his story. It had been a labour of love, and he'd enjoyed the process, learning so much from his highly skilled editor, Suzanne Wilson. Finally, fresh from the printer, his outpouring of words was reduced to a proper book length and we had an advance copy in our hands. *Mao's Last Dancer* it was called, with the strapline: 'From bitter poverty to the stardom of the

West – this is the extraordinary true story of one boy's great courage and determination'. Well, that got it in one!

It was such a thrill to see the cover with Li's young eleven-year-old face set against the backdrop of his commune village – it moved me to tears. I was very proud of him. He'd worked so hard, stockbroker by day, writer by night, two jobs at once as always, and here was the result.

Publication was scheduled for October 2003 and a launch was held at the Australian Ballet Centre in Melbourne. What an occasion it was! Li was relieved that the book was finally published and I was relieved that now we would have him back. Little did we know that his life and ours were about to be catapulted into a whole new crazy literary world.

Well over 500 people attended the launch. Champagne flowed, and there was such positivity in the room. 'What a lucky journey it has been for me. Ballet has given me a life,' Li said simply to the audience. He went on to briefly mention the highlights of his journey, with loving mention of his family. 'My life changed profoundly the minute Mary entered my life. She was the one who led me to the world of Western literature. Because of her I started reading and really working on my language skills. I'm a lucky man to have three beautiful children and a wonderful wife.'

Hundreds of books were sold that day and I remember Li being thrilled to sign many copies. To our surprise, that number would just grow and grow.

Then it was Sophie's turn to shine, and she was able to end the year on a real high. We were particularly keen to see how she would go in her first tap and jazz concert. We didn't know what to expect. She looked especially upbeat as we packed her Irish folk costume and tap shoes into the car. We arrived at the theatre and took our seats while Sophie went off backstage.

Suddenly there she was – our daughter, bursting onto the stage. Li and I gripped each other's hands and I whispered, 'Li, she's at the front!' I watched open-mouthed and captivated. Tap was different to ballet. She could really listen to the taps – her own and those of all the other dancers – and she could feel the rhythm. We held our breath as Sophie continued to weave in and out of the group. She was magnificent.

'What a miracle! Who would have thought,' I whispered to Li.

'Wow, Tom! Wasn't she amazing,' I said after the applause died down.

'Mum, sometimes you don't give Sophie enough credit,' said clever Tom.

That gave me pause for thought. I really needed to relax and enjoy these moments when Sophie showed how far she had come.

~

And then it was time for her surgery. Sophie was dreading it, so I had to be positive even though I was nervous about the outcome. We didn't know if there would be any benefit at all. What if something went wrong?

The operation loomed large in Sophie's mind; after all, she was fourteen now and very aware of the procedure. While she had agreed, she was still hesitant the night before her operation. I took her hands and looked into her eyes. 'Darling, remember, hearing with two implants will hopefully give you better sound. Maybe even better direction. Noisy classrooms might not be as difficult for you . . .'

'You don' know tha', Mum,' she said.

She went in overnight at the Eye and Ear Hospital. She looked so vulnerable when she came out of surgery, with half of her face swollen. 'We have to be strong for her, Mary,' Li said, as he held my hand tight. Dr Briggs told us that everything had gone really well and she would be fine to go home in the morning. I stayed with her that night.

We took it slowly over the next two weeks then returned to the hospital two weeks later for Sophie's new implant to be mapped and switched on. The result was not an instant moment of hearing, but she did hear soft beeps. My heart rejoiced. Surely things could only improve from here.

She had to take the first implant off for a while so the sounds to the new implant could be recognised. 'It's the same theory as the lazy-eye syndrome,' the audiologist explained. Sophie needed sounds in that ear to stimulate the use of the new implant.

'I canno' hear!' she would shout in frustration.

'Remember, it could take three to six months. You just need to persevere, darling,' I said to her.

She wasn't happy, but I kept pushing. Sometimes she would push right back.

When she put the new cochlear implant on, she received an annoying faint sound. 'It' awful, Mum,' she would say.

'Just listen with it for five minutes and I'll give you five dollars,' I'd say cheekily.

She would mostly give in, although not for the money. She would close the door to her bedroom and put it on, saying she needed a quiet space as the onset of unclear sounds was quite overwhelming. She would leave it on while reading a book, to help her get used to it. 'If I like it, I keep on,' she told me.

Soon afterwards, we flew to the Gold Coast for Christmas with the family. Sophie was still grumbling at having to take the first implant off to practise hearing with her new one and was uptight and stressed. No wonder. She'd been relying on sound from her first implant for ten years – ten years of sheer hard work that right now seemed like it was all in front of her again.

Sophie's dislike of her new implant continued. She kept begging me to put her first bionic ear back on and not use the new one at all. 'It' shit, Mum. It' a waste of time,' she told me repeatedly.

'Sophie, just keep going. You just have to be patient,' I told her.

'I don' like it! You wear if you like it,' she said stubbornly.

We persisted all through the summer of 2004 and eventually Sophie started to hear more sounds, albeit still unpleasant ones, robotic and unnatural. But she found it hard to decipher words. I prayed we would get there one day, but how successful this implant could become, only time would tell.

Sophie was still participating in the bilateral implant trial. She responded well in the testing after her surgery and had been able to give the researchers valuable feedback. Although the new implant wasn't giving her the direction of sound, it did help her guess where the sound was coming from. Now if I called her in the house to come help me – something I had never been able to do before – she would yell, 'Where are you?' She was getting some level of surround sound. Noisy situations remained difficult, and she still required subtitles for TV, which were rarely available then.

She couldn't understand everything at the movies but sometimes went with friends anyway. She had retained a few friends from Grade 6 and was occasionally invited to parties. They weren't the popular group, but they were kind to Sophie. I decided that she might benefit from having some deaf friends, so I started to explore opportunities for her to meet deaf kids her age. At Sophie's weekly therapy appointments, I often chatted to other parents and made the occasional playdate for Sophie and their young teenage children.

~

As for Li, well, he was on yet another career trajectory. Within weeks of its publication, *Mao's Last Dancer* hit number one on the bestseller lists, and there it stayed and stayed. My instincts had been right all along. It was wonderful to see people reading his book in public, to overhear others raving about it. It had quickly become one of those books whose success is achieved as much by word-of-mouth as official publicity. Perhaps even more so.

Before we knew it, Li was combining stockbroking with travel around the world to speak at company, charity and industry events. He wore his heart on his sleeve when he spoke. Audiences would gasp, laugh and cry. His years of performing on stage had made him comfortable in front of an audience, and gave him the ability to relate and get his message across. He had the same charisma as a speaker as he'd had as a dancer. And international film directors and producers were after him as well. Who would have thought our life would take this turn.

I missed him terribly when he was away and was always so grateful when he returned as he would always ask, 'How can I help, darling?'

I would say 'Cook, please cook!' and he would head off to the kitchen and whip up something delicious. However, his car-pooling duties were not as good – sometimes he'd get lost dropping the children to their activities – but it was bliss to have the shopping done and dinner cooked. He never once criticised me for an unmade bed or a messy home. Sometimes I had the home immaculate, but other times it couldn't be helped. I would be completely exhausted, and he understood.

Li's book had been published in partnership with Penguin in the US. There was a lot of media interest. At Easter time, we decided to take all the children to the launch in Houston, where we reconnected with Ben, Ava Jean, Charles and Lily, Clayton and Ginya, the Mad Mothers and many ballet mates and friends. It was wonderful to be back in the city where our careers had flourished, and sharing this part of our lives with the children. Li loved being back in his old hometown, where he'd first known a life of freedom. Houston would always hold a special place in his heart. The response to his book showed that his popularity had hardly waned after more than nine years of absence.

The family felt at home staying with Ginya and Clayton. Li would thank them by preparing a Chinese feast. During dinner, Ginya brought up the topic that had been shelved since they visited us in Melbourne in 2001.

'Mary, Li, have you thought any more about Sophie coming to live with us and going to St John's School?' she asked. My stomach sank a little.

'Yes, Ginya, but Mary is concerned about all the logistical challenges with her deafness,' Li replied.

'Sophie has come on marvellously. Just look at her now,' Clayton said.

'Mary, we understand it's a huge thing for any child to do something like this, but Sophie would benefit from St John's. And we really want to do something for her,' Ginya said.

'Ginya,' I replied, 'we love you guys, but Sophie isn't ready. Her challenges are so different to hearing kids' and it's not easy to handle. I'm not sure whether she would cope without me . . .'

'Of course it'll be hard, Mary, but we're prepared to do everything we can to make this a special experience for her,' Ginya said. 'You know our offer is open, but younger is always better with learning. Why don't you sleep on it?'

Li was bringing a whole steamed fish to the table at that point. 'Mary, don't close the door on this before we've thought it through,' he said. 'Think what Sophie would gain and how she would mature. The more she's exposed to the world, the sooner she will be more independent.'

I really wanted to steer the conversation away. But Sophie's eyes lit up and she said, 'Mum, can I go see school?'

I felt I was losing the argument. 'Let's not talk any more about this now,' I said. 'Let's eat.'

Back in our room Li was very persuasive, saying St John's was not only one of the top academic schools in the USA, it was renowned for its outstanding teachers. 'Darling, teachers are a key ingredient in any child's life. Look at those who made all the difference in ours. It's time, Mary. We should have some faith in Sophie.'

As I lay there fretting, I knew Sophie would be well cared for but I was full of misgivings. I would miss her terribly. Without Sophie, there would be a huge hole in my life, I just knew it.

The next day we all went to visit the school, with its elegant stone buildings set in manicured parkland. The affable and smiling headmaster impressed us all no end, especially Sophie. Instead of getting cold feet, she was in love with the promise of an adventure. As we walked out of the school, she turned to me and said, 'I want go here, Mum.'

I said we would talk about it when we got home, hoping that everyone would see some common sense once we'd left Houston behind – though I feared I was outnumbered and didn't stand a chance.

Back in Melbourne, Sophie wouldn't let up and neither would Li. I sometimes wondered if Sophie just wanted to get away from the girls with their quick conversations that excluded her, or from me with all my relentless pushing and insistence. Li often told me I needed to lighten up and give her some space. Was I doing too much for her? I only ever wanted the best for my daughter. It was curious, then, that I didn't share Li's views that a stint away was for the best. I was concerned that the progress we'd made with Sophie's speech would come to a standstill. I had never taken my foot off the pedal, but without me that would happen. These thoughts nagged at me, and I talked a lot with Mum and Brig. Neither of them thought it was a good idea.

Li's belief in Sophie's independence was very strong, and I couldn't argue with that. He was her father and had to have a say. He was already teaching her his recipes for four basic Chinese meals so she could cook for the Triers from time to time.

Before I knew it, just about everything had been taken out of my hands. It was decided. Sophie would return to Houston in a few months and start eighth grade at St John's in August. Melbourne Girls Grammar School had granted her the permission. She would attend the school on a full scholarship, which we suspected had something to do with the Triers making a special donation to St John's to enable this.

Her flight was booked, her cases packed, and she was beside herself with excitement. I still hadn't changed my mind and tried very hard to convince Sophie to stay, right up until her final night at home. I felt sick in the stomach and I recalled how Coralie told me she had a stomach-ache when I first left for London.

Li put his foot down. 'Mary, stop it! If it doesn't work out, I'll go and get her. All she has to do is call and I will be there to bring her home.' This eased my mind only a little.

The next morning, there I was with the rest of the family at Melbourne airport. I still felt sick but put on a happy face. It would be the first time Sophie had been away from me for more than a week, and now she was jetting off on a US adventure for six months at the age of just fifteen.

Back home I was bereft with sadness and fears. I lay on Sophie's bed thinking of her, missing her terribly. Some days I could barely function. I marked off the days, counting down on the calendar the day she'd come home. It was a long way off. It was agony. I felt ill, like one of my arms had been cut off, without Sophie by my side. I worried about her constantly and couldn't concentrate on anything else. I was hardly talking to Li, given he had put me through this.

The only place I found I could escape was in ballet class. God, how I loved that studio at the Australian Ballet, helping talented dancers perfect their art. After class I always felt satisfied and a littler calmer.

The weeks continued to drag and I longed for Sophie's weekly calls. She told us how fun it was being with the Triers, but mostly she would talk about school, adjusting to working with boys for the first time and struggling with the sheer amount of homework. It seemed the school was more challenging than she'd imagined. 'Sophie, we don't care if you are deaf or not,' one of her teachers had said to her. 'If you don't put in the work, then don't even bother coming to school.' Sophie soon realised she had two options: stay and work harder, or pack up and go home. So, she decided to put in the extra effort. I was proud of her.

Life with the Triers was good. They looked after Sophie as one of their own, taking her to ballet classes and picking her up from cheer-leading where she was a bit of a star due to her dancing ability. I knew she felt safe and loved, and that was really all that mattered to me. And she had the opportunity to reconnect with Ava Jean.

But the most fantastic thing was that Sophie was making friends. Her classmates were inviting her to places, and she was going to pizza nights and sleepovers. Despite one intense pang of homesickness when she phoned missing us terribly, she was having an incredible time.

I planned to visit her in November, near the end of her stay. Li reassured me that he could juggle work and home life while I was gone. I hoped I'd feel more at peace with it all once I saw her.

As soon as I arrived, I could immediately see that the experience was marvellous for her. I couldn't decide whether she'd gained confidence in living with another family or by establishing herself in a new school environment where she was accepted for who she was. Probably it was both.

I loved being there, just her and me. Ginya and Clayton loaned me one of their cars and I dropped Sophie and John at school in the mornings and picked them up in the afternoons. It was such a full week of activities and I felt emotional when it was time to say goodbye. Ginya and Clayton would soon be taking Sophie skiing in Utah for Thanksgiving, and after all, it was only six more weeks until she'd be home.

She finally arrived two days before Christmas. It was just heaven. I was ecstatic. We were all waiting at the arrivals gate with big hugs, so relieved to have her back. It was my best Christmas present ever, and over the next few weeks we learned more and more about her time in America.

'You were so brave, darling,' I said. 'Dad and I are so proud of all you've achieved.'

'I wasn't brave, Mum. I had to escape. Escape from *you*.' She winked at me, and we all laughed.

That was something else she'd gained. Sophie had started to make jokes. In the past she had asked me to teach her how to be funny, and

I didn't know where to begin. Now she had a new self-belief in what she could do and achieve, especially academically. 'Mum, Houston made me realise that I'm *actually* smart. I jus' missed things, but I can catch up. I know I can do it now.'

And she was proving it – she even started to offer me book recommendations. One of them was the coming-of-age novel *The Secret Life of Bees* and it was great.

This was a first! The important realisation for me was that other people had been able to teach her, so I knew she had become an independent learner. I had to admit the trip to America ended up being life-changing for Sophie.

'Lucky it turned out okay,' I told Li with a wry grin.

~

It was obvious straightaway that Sophie's oral skills had also improved in her time away. She continued to use the new implant even though it was still not working as well as we had hoped. I wondered if it would ever deliver. But on the other hand, her language development was finally starting to snowball. There were less and less syntax errors, but she still struggled with complex words. It was what we had been waiting eleven years for! She was beginning to be more motivated to take on that responsibility herself. Li and I agreed that our daughter was becoming even more amazing.

It was a joy to be able to have simple exchanges such as:

'What' for breakfast, Mum?'

'Would you like scrambled eggs?'

'Can I 'ave pancake' with lemon and sugar? Bridie likes those too.'

'Of course you can. Why don't you cook it?' And she would! I couldn't do pancakes anyway.

Originally, I had desperately wanted my daughter to say one word. Then I'd wished for a paragraph, then whole conversations. My dream was slowly becoming a reality. Sophie was now able to tell us more and be much more expressive. I hung on to every word and provided quiet places to allow this to happen. She began to share more.

'Thank you for sending me America. It was bes' time of my life. But Mum, food in the US is awful – a lot of hamburgers and fries, and heavy meals,' she said, pulling a face. 'I missed Dad's Chinese, especially the veggie dishes.'

The change in the dynamic between us was wonderful. We actually started being able to have meaningful conversations. I found that Sophie had returned almost more mature than a lot of other teenagers.

Li was ecstatic that he too was now able to have conversations with his daughter. 'Mary, the whole environment has pushed and challenged her, and she coped with it all by herself.'

16

For now, I was in a whole new space, happy at home and at work. I felt we were really coming out of the woods at last. Bridie at seven was unstoppable with her gymnastics; Tom was at secondary school at Melbourne Grammar, still playing tennis and also singing in Chapel Choir; and Sophie was navigating her way in the world with such strength and determination. What an amazing girl, so poised now, and the spitting image of her father – kind, generous and with the same strong work ethic. I couldn't have been happier as she headed into Year 10.

But our life was never plain sailing. With the success of Li's book and the platform it had provided for him to become a celebrity speaker on the international circuit, he was travelling more than ever. At the same time he was still managing the Asia desk at the stockbroking firm, now called Bell Potter Securities, where he had started after leaving the Australian Ballet. His client base had grown considerably.

Li's seventh brother, Cungui, called to ask if his daughter, Rong Rong, could stay with us as she had been accepted into a school in Melbourne the following year. Lulu had stayed with us for three years and was now making her own way, enjoying life in Melbourne with her Mauritius-born fiancé, Yannick. With our kids growing up, though, sharing bedrooms was no longer really an option, and fitting Rong Rong in was going to be a bit of a problem. A bigger house in our local area wasn't really in the budget, but neither were proposed extensions to our current house – not to mention the financial stress on top of heavy school fees and the extras for Sophie.

One day that autumn at one of Tom's tennis matches, I noticed people walking into an open-house inspection across the street. It was a grand Federation-style home that which I had admired before. The location was perfect, in the most desirable part of South Yarra, right opposite Fawkner Park and five minutes' walk from the Royal Botanic Gardens. Out of curiosity, I followed a few prospective buyers inside. I was totally sold on it just walking through the door. It had been built in 1923 and was a well-known boutique hotel called the Tilba. It had soaring high ceilings, generously proportioned rooms, and was well kept with some lovely original features, including a castle-like turret. But best of all, it had six bedrooms and six ensuites – five for us and another for Coralie when she visited.

I rang Li immediately and said, 'Li, I've found us a house and we can all fit, including Rong Rong. It's grand and beautiful, exactly what we need.'

'Mary, don't be silly. We're not buying a new house – we're going to renovate our own,' Li replied, annoyed.

Although we'd had renovation plans drawn up, I still thought the house wouldn't be big enough for us all. There'd be no room for extras, and we always seemed to have those!

'I know, darling. But this one is perfect,' I argued. 'We don't have to go through all the agony of a renovation. Please, at least go and see it.'

We made an appointment for Li to inspect the house the following day. I even brought the children with me. As soon as they saw it, the whole family gave it their tick of approval. It was also close enough to our old home that they wouldn't face any disruptions.

'Can you tell me if anyone has made an offer?' Li asked the agent as we were leaving.

'No, not yet,' she replied.

'Would the sellers consider a good offer before the auction?' Li asked.

For the next two days, we were on tenterhooks as Li negotiated with the agent. The day before the auction, we received the news: the house was ours! I couldn't believe we had bought this magnificent historic home in one of Melbourne's best suburbs. We were thrilled. There was space to entertain, and everyone would have their own bedroom and bathroom. And I didn't think we would ever have to pack up and move again.

~

When Rong Rong arrived from China later that year, she couldn't speak any English and I was reminded once again of the challenges we all faced in our Australian-Chinese family. Though having Rong Rong speaking Chinese in the house was good practice for Sophie and Tom, the only person she could converse with properly was Li. Rong Rong, who was the same age as Sophie, was dreadfully homesick and looked lost when Li wasn't there. We had been through this with Lulu not long before, and I knew it would just take time.

We worked hard on Rong Rong's English during our summer holiday in Coolangatta, and to our delight she passed the English proficiency test and got into Year 10 at Melbourne Girls Grammar. We were thrilled that she would be going to the same school as Sophie, and they became close mates. Rong Rong came everywhere with us. She slotted into our family and became one of our own. She had a good sense of humour and reminded me of her mother, whose wedding we'd attended in the commune back in 1988.

~

One day I was humming to myself and doing some *barre* work in the foyer at home when Li burst through the front door.

'Mary, darling!' he said. 'I had a call from Jan Sardi today.'

'Who is she?'

'*He* is the person who wrote the screenplay for the film *Shine*, about the pianist David Helfgott.'

'I love that movie!' I said excitedly.

'So do I, and I told him so, too. He said he's interested in my story.'

'What, to write a screenplay?' I asked.

'Well, I guess so . . .'

Over the years, Li had received numerous offers for the rights to his story, even met with some people in Hollywood, but had declined them all. In his mind, he could never allow it unless the right people came along, people with integrity and honesty who would have the respect to make a movie that was truthful and authentic. If any movie were to be made about *Mao's Last Dancer*, it would have to be one that Li and our children and grandchildren could live with. He'd recently had discussions with London-based producers.

'I think it can't hurt to meet him,' Li continued. 'What do you think?'

'Your story would make the best movie, Li. It would be interesting to hear what he has to say,' I replied.

The next afternoon, Jan arrived at Li's office with a tattered-looking copy of *Mao's Last Dancer* covered in sticky yellow notes. Clearly, he had come prepared.

'I was impressed by Jan's passion and intellect,' Li told me that night. 'I do feel good about him. And guess who his proposed business partner is?'

'Who?'

'Jane Scott, the producer of *Shine*!'

'Wow! Well, don't get too excited, Li. You know these things often go nowhere,' I said. And we both remained circumspect until after he had met with Jane and learned that Bruce Beresford, the Australian director of *Driving Miss Daisy*, *Breaker Morant* and other famous movies, was among the directors they were considering. We couldn't believe it. Imagine having Bruce Beresford tell the story of Li's life! It was then we felt that this movie would be made with the kind of integrity that Li could accept.

As part of the agreement, he was to work with Jan on the screenplay. And so began another chapter in Li's life as a writer. Several jobs at once now – stockbroker, speaker, assisting Jan on the screenplay, plus serving on the Australian Ballet and Bionic Ear Institute boards. As if I should have expected anything less from him! It was so exciting and I couldn't wait to hear who the actors would be. I'd have to be patient about that, though. The process of making a movie was even longer than producing a book.

In the meantime, Penguin had published a young readers' edition of *Mao's Last Dancer* and Li was now working on a picture-book version, illustrated by award-winning children's book illustrator Anne Spudvilas. This edition had the fairytale-sounding title of *The Peasant Prince*, which summed up my husband's life perfectly.

~

It was two years since Sophie's new implant. It had been two very frustrating, long years for her, years that had severely tested her and my patience. She seriously doubted if the new implant would ever work, and to be honest, I started to doubt it myself as the days, weeks and months rolled on. *Had we made a wrong choice?* I questioned myself often during this time.

Then, one day when Sophie and I were driving home from a visit to friends, something truly amazing happened. 'Mum, Mum! I can hear you with my left implan'!' Sophie exclaimed.

I immediately pulled the car over. 'What? Sophie! Tell me you're not kidding!'

She shook her head emphatically, looking at me with a huge smile. 'I can, Mum. The battery just died on my right implan', but I can still understan' what you saying with my new implan'. I can't believe it!'

What an important moment it was. It was the breakthrough we had been hoping for. I was over the moon with happiness. It had all been worth it! This improved Sophie's attitude to the new implant and it would be the beginning of better-quality sound for her. I was relieved, because if the first implant broke down, she would have a backup.

It seemed there was never a dull moment in the Li household. Tom was doing well at school, forming strong friendships and very active in all the school sports. Then it was time for all of us to feel another absence in the family because it was his turn to accept the Triers' invitation to go to St John's for six months. I didn't want to send him, either, but Li insisted again, saying, 'Mary, I was eleven when I left home – Tom is three years older.' And of course he was right again.

The time away in Houston proved just as beneficial for Tom as it had been for Sophie. Like her, he came back full of confidence and maturity.

Bridie, now nine years old, was attending gym sessions almost every day. It was an intensive and incredibly demanding schedule for one so young, but she was talented enough that her coaches wanted her for the elite state team. Li and I were concerned that she was doing so much gymnastics that her overall education was suffering. I don't think she picked up a pen at school all through those years. She was really struggling due to exhaustion, even falling asleep in class.

'Where are all these somersaults going to end, Mary?' Li asked. 'She needs a good education, because there isn't much of a career in gymnastics.'

Not long after, I received a call from the gymnastics coach telling me Bridie had fallen off a high beam. I rushed to the gym and there was Bridie, cradling her arm and trying to be brave. When she saw me, tears started rolling down her cheeks. We hurried to emergency and the X-ray showed clean breaks in both bones in her right forearm.

She had to be operated on and was put in plaster for eight weeks. It was clear to us that she had spent too many hours away from us. Our family was more important than gymnastics, and so was Bridie's education. We told her simply that she wasn't going back. She didn't take the news well initially, so Li and I made a secret pact. We would see how it went for a few weeks or so. If she was still longing to return by then, we'd allow her to continue with it.

Being without gymnastics left Bridie a bit off kilter, but before the six weeks were out, her sadness was gone. She had moved on and taken up tennis. She even confessed later that she was relieved she wasn't going back to gymnastics but couldn't bear making the decision herself.

Before long, we found ourselves back in Houston for a special occasion. The Houston School for Deaf Children, now known as the Center for Hearing and Speech, had asked Li and Sophie to be guest speakers at their annual black-tie fundraising event. The event was held at the Houstonian, a five-star hotel. Sophie wore a lovely strapless black dress and looked stunning and grown-up with her hair up.

First Li spoke, sharing some of his life experiences with the audience. He then introduced Sophie. 'Ladies and gentleman, my wife Mary and I could never have imagined that our daughter Sophie, a former student at this school, a profoundly deaf child, could be where she is today. We would have been so happy if she could just have basic language and be able to read, and to have a simple conversation with us. We never dreamed how much Sophie could achieve. And without further ado, I'd like to introduce Sophie Li.'

You could sense the surprise when Sophie walked directly to the piano. She sat down calmly and started playing a piece from her Grade 5 syllabus. The audience went crazy with applause. I turned to our friends who had joined us – the Mad Mothers, Ava Jean, Ginya and Clayton, Charles and Lily, Marcia and Mike Nichols, Kate Crady and even some of Sophie's St John's friends. They were teary-eyed listening to her play.

After the applause, Sophie stepped up to the podium. As soon as she began to speak about her journey as a deaf child coping in a hearing world, I could feel the whole room was in awe. It was full of people who understood how difficult it was for a profoundly deaf child to speak, let alone play the piano and get up before 500-plus people to speak with such poise, intonation and clarity – and such insight into her subject. Finally, she thanked the school for helping to change her life. Li and I were lost for words. Mainly they were parents of deaf children, and they approached me later to say what an inspiration Sophie was.

Afterwards, Sophie told me, 'You know, Mum, it was really you who changed my life.'

This meant the world to me. How I loved her. This had been a huge journey for both of us. Did I ever, ever imagine that she would be able to do this with such confidence? No, it would have been an outcome too impossible for me to even dream.

Back home, Sophie still struggled with friendships at school. She was more serious about schoolwork than her peers, who were more focused on boys and parties. She had one deaf friend, Pip Russell, but they didn't go to the same school and didn't see each other often. Luckily, Sophie and Rong Rong were becoming closer and closer. Socialising outside of the family wasn't a big part of Sophie's life.

At home, though, she was increasingly moody, because it was exhausting to work hard academically, listen and socialise. It was so upsetting when she'd lock herself away in her room, take her implants off and withdraw inside herself. I could feel her sadness. 'Why am I deaf? Why am I the only one in my family who's deaf? Why is my life so hard?' These were the kinds of questions she would throw at me, and I'm sure they constantly plagued her. 'I'm sick of trying so hard to get past my deafness and make friends! It's too hard! How am I ever going to have any friends?'

'Am I being punished for something I did in a past life?' was something else she truly seemed to believe. Poor Sophie!

These regular meltdowns were inevitable, I knew that. But God, they were hard to take, and often I would end up in tears of despair myself. How I wished that I could give her a magical answer that would make her happy instantly. But I knew deep down that the only thing we could give her to help was encouragement.

Li would tell her, 'Others might be lucky enough to be born without any disabilities, but they will still have other challenges to deal with. Sometimes the worst experience in life brings out the best in a person. Sophie, this is your challenge to overcome.'

But we really had no answers for her.

~

On Sophie's sixteenth birthday in 2005, we didn't have a party – we just had an afternoon tea at home with a small group of her friends, including her blind friend, Marina. Marina was at Melbourne Girls Grammar too, in a different year level. I used to tear up when I saw them together. It was so touching. Marina always wanted Sophie to go shopping with her to help choose pretty clothes, and Sophie always wanted Marina to teach her to sing. Marina had an angelic voice.

It wasn't a normal party. History had shown us they didn't work. So Sophie just had birthday cake and some savouries with her few friends. They stayed for an hour or so and then went home.

After one more of Sophie's meltdowns, I rented the only two movies I knew of about deaf people: *The Miracle Worker* and *Children of a Lesser God*. 'These might help give you some answers,' I said to Sophie when my own answers weren't helping her. But as she watched them I saw only more frustration and sadness.

'Mum, Helen Keller was deaf *and* blind, so that's hardly the same as me. And Marlee Matlin is a signing deaf person, and I don't sign!'

Which was true. Sophie was oral, but it was tough. She knew no others like her. None of us did. She was constantly struggling. If only there was someone who was going through something similar.

'Mum, why don't you get it? No matter how hard I try or how many times I ask, it's always the same! When I speak up to ask friends to repeat jokes or comments that I miss, they just brush me aside and move on, saying, "Oh, it's nothing, Sophie."'

It broke my heart to hear her despair.

I was excited to learn of a new research program that was seeking deaf adolescents and adults to explore voice coaching in a drama setting. The project was run by the Head of Voice at the Victorian College of the Arts, with one of her acting students who happened to be deaf. Both women were inspirational and Sophie looked forward to the sessions every Saturday for ten weeks. The project taught breathing skills to increase voice quality, and it was very beneficial for her.

Sophie always went into these things hopeful and couldn't wait to make friends with the other participants, to share in conversations with them. Others taking part in the project could speak and some were proficient in Auslan. They were very patient and understanding with one another. What a great opportunity. I was now sure that the time had come for her to broaden her social life and be part of the deaf world as well as our hearing one.

After the ten weeks, the participants appeared in a short play, with all of them speaking. Everyone in the audience was crying by the end, and the actors were elated with the response.

Another niece, Yan Yan, Li's fifth brother, Cunfar's, daughter, who was a few months older than Sophie, was coming to Melbourne to study, too. But I just couldn't take on a fifth child, even though she was a young adult. I felt guilty about it. Instead, I checked nearby homestays and visited several schools to find the best one for her to do Year 10.

Sophie told us that she wanted to complete one of her Year 12 subjects ahead of time, which would mean she had one less subject to worry about in her final year. She had decided to include dance for her Victorian Certificate of Education, so throughout Year 10 and Year 11 she became really focused on her choreography and dancing skills.

We thought it was wonderful, because she was talented and we could both help her.

For the dance subject, Sophie had group assignments in Year 10 but solos in Year 11. She worked very hard on her major assignment. She had to choreograph and dance two very different solos and for months locked herself away in her room, marking out lines on the floor and going over and over her creations, practising her movements, finding music and working hard. I would often find myself comparing her life to her peers who were out partying or playing sport, and wishing she could have more freedom, but then I'd remember how both Li and I, at the same age, were applying all we had in us to become the best we could be in our chosen field.

Eventually Sophie was ready to show us and invite feedback. I kind of knew it would be good, but truly we were amazed. For her technical piece she used a Chinese calligraphy concept and made it a dance, mimicking the movement as if the space were the paper for her expression. It was beautiful, delicate and flowing. I found myself transfixed. I glanced at Li to see what he was thinking and he was quietly smiling and nodding. 'Wow, Sophie! That was great!' we said in unison as she looked to us for feedback.

For her contemporary piece, she had choreographed a dance about being locked in a cell, longing for freedom. It demonstrated all the despair, longing, hope and remembrance of a lost romance and, most importantly, the desired freedom. What she had achieved here was so moving, so expressive, so accomplished. What impressed us most was her ability to inject meaning through movement, developing the layers and weaving emotions with the music.

Although both pieces were only in their early stages, we believed that with further practice and refining she would do well in her exam. But we wouldn't know her results until the end of Year 12 nearly twelve months away. I was so happy when she asked for my help in this; we agreed to put in the time on Saturday mornings when I'd finished teaching.

I hadn't expected our first session to go pear-shaped quite so quickly, though. Sophie took exception to my corrections and stormed towards the door, looking thunderous. 'Sophie, if you want my help, it's now or never!' I called out.

She stopped, looked at me with her stubborn stare, and finally said, 'Okay, Mum.'

'Let's start again,' I said. We then continued, more calmly.

Sophie had evidently decided she had nothing to lose by taking on what I had to say, and from that moment on she opened up and became an amazing student.

~

A year after Sophie's speech at the Houston Center for Hearing and Speech, she took her desire to speak Mandarin to a whole new level. I was amazed when she decided to continue Mandarin in Years 11 and 12. 'Mum, Dad. *Wo xiang tigao wo de zhongwen shuiping. Wo ye xiang qa Zhong guo liu xue.*'

'What?' I said, my jaw dropping somewhat. I looked at Li. His eyes were shining.

'She said, "I want to improve my Chinese, and I also want to do an exchange in China,"' he told me.

Sophie gave me a radiant smile. 'The best way to improve my Chinese is to go there. I saw how much Tom improved from his exchange. I really want to do well. Can I go, please?' she asked.

Tom had gone on a six-week school exchange to Tianjin the previous year. It was an intensive Chinese course especially designed for foreign students. Not only had his Chinese improved immeasurably, he had also gained an understanding and appreciation of Chinese history and the Chinese people. It was a brilliant trip for him. However, we'd never thought about it for Sophie because there was no such exchange program on offer through her school.

'What about through Tom's school?' she suggested. 'I can join theirs.'

Li was just as keen as she was, so he asked Tom's Chinese tutor if there was any way that Sophie could enrol in the same program. The tutor contacted a host family in Tianjin and soon everything was in place. It was nearly three years since Sophie had gone to Houston by herself, and she was more mature now, I could hardly object this time. It would mean so much to Li. So in early December 2007, at the end of Year 11, Sophie and two students from Tom's school headed off to Tianjin, a city about one hour north of Beijing. *She's not on her own and it's only for five weeks*, I told myself.

Sophie sent emails and called regularly. It was clear she was having a ball, enjoying her host family and their daughter, Sophia, who was the same age as her. They attended the same school, though Sophie was in the special class for foreign students learning Mandarin as a second language. 'It's freezing here, Mum,' she told me, 'but everyone talks to me slowly so I can understand. I'm happy with how my Chinese is going. The tonal language is very challenging, but I think I'm getting it.' Amazing!

One day Li got off the phone with Sophie, stunned. 'Mary, we just had a conversation in Chinese!' he told me, really excited. 'I can't believe our deaf daughter is conversing with me in Chinese.' After that, whenever she called, she would talk with Li in Mandarin. I had never seen him so proud and happy.

Then a week later Sophie called and told Li she had dreamed in Chinese. He was over the moon. 'When you start dreaming in a different language,' he explained to me, 'it means you are thinking in that language as well.'

We were both thrilled. It was still unsettling to be without her, and it would be the first time she'd missed Christmas with us. In China they don't celebrate Christmas and it was school six days a week.

Back home we were having Christmas with our Chinese relatives. Rong Rong's parents came to visit, and Lulu and Yan Yan joined us for Christmas Day lunch. It was Cungui and his wife, Xiao Zhu's, first Christmas experience. They were fascinated by the traditions and tasted turkey and lamb for the first time. And they loved it.

Sophie called her *nana* and *yeye* during her exchange, speaking in Chinese. They were speechless. The last thing they'd ever thought to hear was their beloved deaf granddaughter speaking to them in Chinese.

When Sophie returned home, her interest in learning Mandarin didn't wane. I've never seen anyone put in more effort than her with Chinese. Her commitment was just relentless. After dinner, as part of her homework, she would write short essays and stories in Chinese. She worked extremely hard just trying to get the four intonations right, then there were the accents and pronunciation. She was quite frustrated with the limited lessons at school so she continued to rely on Li to help her, even waiting up late for him to come home so they could work on her Chinese together.

'If anyone else with normal hearing and average intelligence was as industrious as Sophie, their Chinese would be impeccable,' he told me.

~

Li continued working with Jan Sardi on the screenplay and now, a year and many edits later, they finally had one he was happy with. At one stage, he mentioned to Jane Scott that if she ever needed any help to finance the film, he had some leads. Ultimately Bell Potter came on board to back the project by offering the opportunity to their sophis-ticated investors. In the end, Bell Potter and Li raised the majority of the total film budget.

Bruce Beresford spent two days sitting at our dining-room table talking with Li. He wanted to make sure that the screenplay was a true representation of Li's story. Bruce had a great sense of humour. He told Li that the biggest challenge would be finding a dancer of the same calibre who could speak Chinese and English and who was also handsome. They both laughed. Li assured Bruce that he knew a couple of very good Chinese dancers, but he didn't know if they could act. Bruce responded confidently, 'Unless they are totally stupid, I think I can teach them how to act.'

Li eventually suggested Chi Cao, a principal dancer with Birmingham Royal Ballet, and Chengwu Guo, a very good young dancer with the Australian Ballet. They were both engaged to play Li at different stages of his life. After Bruce's visit, we gained more confidence in the project. We felt he was a man with integrity, experience and talent. We also discovered his love of music and were thrilled to hear that he wanted Christopher Gordon, a well-known Australian composer, for the film score.

While all this was going on, Sophie started her final year of schooling. It was 2008 and we were all thinking about what might lie ahead for her, whether she would get into university to study architecture as she wished. Architecture was a surprise. Perhaps Neil George had had more of an influence than we realised! But first she had to get through Year 12.

Academically Sophie was doing extremely well, and she hoped that Year 12 would bring a change socially. She had put her hand up for school captain for her final year. Although she didn't get it, it was amazing that she had the confidence to go for it. She was still working hard on her dance subject. It was a relief for her not to have to sit down to study like in her other subjects, which included maths, chemistry, accounting and English as well as Chinese. Her VCE dance teacher told me she'd never received as many emails with questions from a student as she had from Sophie during Year 12. That reassured me. Sophie was motivated to do well.

Meanwhile, Tom was flying at school. He was playing inter-school tennis, Australian Rules football and basketball. He never seemed to do much homework, but his teachers told us that he was doing well in his academic subjects anyway. He was such an easy and happy boy.

Bridie had developed a big friendship group through tennis. Two days a week, the whole team would come across the road from the Fawkner Park courts after morning practice and I'd give them a snack, then drop them off to school. Bridie was always busy. Saturdays and Sundays included ballet and netball. She just loved being with her friends. She was a social butterfly bouncing in and out of the house. Like Tom, she didn't do much homework.

What took our minds off exam pressure at this time was a speech that Sophie was invited to give in October as part of the inaugural Graeme Clark Oration held at Melbourne University. The oration had been established to honour Graeme's achievements. In his own address he talked about his research and how it had led to his invention. Then there she was, up on the podium talking to hundreds of people about how bilateral cochlear implants had changed her life. Sophie spoke beautifully and people were clearly moved by her personal story and amazed at how far she had come. Our daughter had once again represented the hope that stories like hers could be replicated in the growing number of people, now more than 100 000, around the world who had received a bionic ear.

Sophie was then right back into exam mode for her dance subject. Her written subjects were still to come, but it was the performance component of the exam that mattered most right now. It would count for 50 per cent of her total mark. She was nervous but excited as was I. On the morning she headed off, her hair in a bun, her leotard, pointe shoes and audiotapes in her bag. I couldn't wait for her to get home and tell me how it went. As I knew all too well, anything could happen in a live performance.

When I picked her up, she was devastated. She wouldn't tell me what was wrong without a lot of coaxing. Eventually I discovered that in the middle of the second solo, during multiple *pirouettes*, both of her implants had flown off. This never happened before. Oh God. I had helped her put them on so carefully, but they hadn't held! Naturally this had affected her focus, but she'd kept going. She felt she'd done well up to that point, but we were concerned about her results.

It would be a long wait and I felt so worried for her. I could see Sophie was struggling. Eventually her spirits were lifted by the results of her hard work. She received an excellent mark for Chinese, but was even more thrilled with her dance results. She was awarded one of the highest scores in the state, which led to her receiving a Premier's Award for Dance.

And then before we knew it, Sophie's secondary schooling was over. The end of any year always rushes up to meet you, but this one seemed to come at us even faster than usual because so much had happened in those last twelve months. I looked back and wondered how on earth we'd done it all.

Sophie just had to wait to see if her application to Melbourne University to study architecture was successful. She also talked about going back to China for a gap year. This idea terrified me. Deep down I felt that at the age of nineteen she had not yet found a sense of belonging. It was something that kept me grounded even though I was away from Australia for twenty-one years. I wanted this connection for Sophie. I knew that having a home in her heart would allow her to spread her wings further.

17

It was time we visited Li's family again, and this trip was actually becoming more urgent. Niang had been in and out of hospital over the last couple of years after a stroke. Dia was coming up to his eighty-fourth birthday and was in poor health too, due to his own stroke four years earlier. He had been left unable to speak but had been living at home with Niang. Now she'd had a second stroke and been hospitalised again.

All of Li's family would be together for the first time in ages and we were looking forward to it immensely. Sophie and Tom could practise their Chinese and Bridie could get to know her father's side of the family better. Li could also update his family about the movie, and I just wanted to see Niang and Dia again.

I had just started to pack when our plans came crashing down. Li's mobile rang and I saw the colour drain from his face. 'What's wrong?' I asked when he got off the phone, fearing the worst.

'It's Dia. He's in intensive care,' he told me. 'They want me to get there immediately. My brothers think he may not make it.'

'Oh my God. What happened?'

'My fifth brother didn't say, but I just need to get there,' Li said, upset. 'They haven't told Niang yet. They're worried it'll be too much of a shock for her while she is still in the hospital recovering.'

'Oh no, Li. You need to tell her,' I said.

So it was decided that Li would go alone, and as quickly as possible. He caught the first flight he could get. I was beside myself with worry and waited anxiously for his call. Finally, it came.

'Mary, Dia is still unconscious, but it's only the medications keeping him breathing.'

'What about Niang? Did you decide to tell her?' I asked.

'Yes, we did. She just closed her eyes. She sobbed, Mary. I have never seen her like this before. It's heartbreaking.'

'Oh, darling. And have you found out what caused Dia's illness?'

'Dia had a bowel blockage that caused severe pain in his stomach, but with everyone's attention focused on Niang in the hospital, he didn't tell anyone until it was too late. He is too far gone, and we have to let him go.' Li's voice was choked with emotion.

'Oh, Li. I'm *so* sorry! I wish I could be there with you.'

Niang was being cared for in the same hospital, so they wheeled her to Dia's bedside to say a final goodbye.

'She called his name and looked at him tenderly for such a long time. She told him to go and wait for her, and then cried and cried,' Li told me.

'I'm so sorry, Li!' I didn't know what else to say.

A day later, Dia passed away. The brothers were devastated. Dia had been so special to all of us. Sophie felt the loss acutely, as she had a special connection with Li's parents. They had such strength, perseverance and love for each other and their family. Even though I was sad, I also felt very blessed to have known and loved them. I knew I would have this feeling in my heart for them always, just as I did when I thought of my own father.

Li would stay for the funeral, an event that lasts for three days in China. Dia always said that he would go before Niang, but Niang insisted that he was as strong as an ox and he'd outlive her. She had put huge love and care into making their burial clothes in a meticulous way according to Chinese tradition.

Dia's body was kept in the cooling room at the hospital, which was different to the old times, when the body of a loved one would be laid in an open coffin in the family's living room for three days of grieving, kowtowing and weeping. But the law no longer allowed dead bodies to be openly displayed; instead, Li and his brothers placed a photo of Dia on a table in the living room at Li's parents' apartment. Dia's name and birthdate were written in big black characters on a white card, and candles and incense holders were placed on either side of it. This would be Dia's spirit's temporary resting place until the cremation. The Lis' relatives and the whole village would come to pay their respects. I was very relieved to hear that Li's blood brother, the Bandit, was by his side during this time.

Two burial plots side by side had been purchased by the family. Li told me that the setting was 'surrounded by hills with a small lake and an alley, and it has a pagoda, a shrine of the god of mercy and good feng shui'. I could just imagine it being a beautiful resting place for Dia.

Li would not be home for three weeks. He was helping to manage Niang's discharge from hospital and transition to home. She was mainly confined to a wheelchair, couldn't feed herself, and would need a full-time carer. Li stayed with her, sleeping in the same bed, feeding her and helping her with toileting. I was desperate for him to come home, but knew this was something he needed to do.

When he finally returned, he was still devastated and struggling to come to terms with the loss of his beloved Dia.

～

Li's movie was finally ready, and it became something to distract us from Dia's passing. We were invited to a private screening. I was really nervous. This was Li's story – what had they done with it? I hadn't seen any footage, not even photographs. I reassured myself that Bruce Beresford had never made a bad movie, and prayed for the best.

On the night of the screening, Li was running late getting home from work. Thank goodness Mum had flown down for the screening, too. We waited with the children at the Gold Class theatre in Chapel Street, not far from home. Jan Sardi and Jane Scott were there to greet us. As we waited for Li to arrive, I got more and more agitated. I'm quite a private person and was deeply anxious about seeing our lives up on the big screen. How could he be late for his own movie? By the time he finally arrived, I was fuming.

Watching the film of *Mao's Last Dancer* for the first time with Li and the children that night was an incredibly intense experience. We couldn't take our eyes off the screen. Niang and Dia were portrayed beautifully by famous Chinese actors. That was very important to both of us, particularly after Dia's death. We shed tears seeing them together again on the screen.

Before we knew it, the film was over. There was so much to love about the adaptation, which was a huge relief. All the actors were well cast. Joan Chen as Niang gave a tear-jerking performance, and Shuangbao Wang portrayed Dia with great humility and authenticity. The three actors playing Li at different ages did him proud, especially the Birmingham Royal Ballet principal dancer Chi Cao as the adult Li. He was brilliant. I couldn't believe that Bruce had made him and other ballet dancers good actors, as he had promised. And for him to get into China and shoot some of the sensitive scenes was nothing short of a miracle.

I never thought I'd experience anything like it in my lifetime. Seeing our lives unfold on screen wasn't something I would have wished for. But this was Li's life story, and I was so happy for him. I'm not someone who believes in fate, but after the screening I got the feeling that the film was always meant to be. Li's extraordinary story was one that had to be told, and Niang and Dia had to live on. They were too special not to.

I turned to Li and he was in tears, emotional and relieved. I kissed him and said, 'It was great, Li. It's an incredible film.' He just nodded.

I looked at Coralie, keen for her opinion. 'What did you think, Mum?'

'Oh, it's wonderful, darling!'

Bridie kissed us both. Sophie and Tom gave us the thumbs-up and said, 'It's really good, Dad!'

'Do you think so?' I turned to Tom. He would always tell me straight.

He nodded, with a huge smile. 'Yes, really good!'

We could only hope that the film would go on to please the public just as much when it was released in September.

~

Then, another milestone. Sophie had been accepted into Melbourne University – long considered one of the best in the country. She was to study a Bachelor of Environments, a new course, majoring in architecture. The academic opportunity would be incredible, but I was more interested in her first foray into living independently, as she had also been accepted into a residential college. Sophie didn't want to go to the same college as her classmates from Melbourne Girls Grammar, so she had picked one that would give her a fresh start. She would still be fairly close to home.

Newman College is an L-shaped, two-storey sandstone building framing a beautiful lawned courtyard, and I thought it had a nice feel. I helped Sophie set up her room on the Saturday before university started. It was a tiny shoebox with one little window, a sink, a mirror and a wardrobe, with a shared bathroom down the hall. 'Oh, it's great!' I said, doing my best to appear upbeat. We bought a few new things: sheets and towels, a pretty quilt cover. Sophie was a neat person, so it looked homely in the end.

I was going to miss her terribly. 'She'll be fine,' Li reassured me, but Sophie wasn't the same as other students: she had a disability. There were things like fire alarms, which she could not hear. She had already been using a vibrating alarm clock under her pillow but occasionally the battery would die.

At college on that first February morning, the clock battery did die and she missed her orientation breakfast. She called me, very upset. 'Mum, I can't believe I missed the first breakfast!'

'Sophie, this is a good lesson. You need to have someone next door to check on you,' I suggested. 'You're going to need that if there's an emergency.'

I knew that I wouldn't always be there for Sophie, and this was an important life experience for her.

Sophie didn't like having to ask us for money and wanted to become financially independent. Soon, she got a weekend job selling handbags at David Jones department store. Although I was immensely proud of her, I initially wanted her to work less and get involved in the social activities in college.

I continued to love teaching at the Australian Ballet. This year, the company was doing some classics I adored: *The Sleeping Beauty*, *Swan Lake* and *The Nutcracker*. Even better, Li and I got to spend time together at the opening night of each ballet. They were dates I always looked forward to.

Sophie was gradually finding her way into uni life, learning to get over her sensitivity about missing out on some conversations in a noisy social setting. But she couldn't miss out on lectures. This was the first time she'd had to seek assistance on her own. Luckily someone recommended Nola Birch, a caring and dedicated woman in the university's Special Needs Unit who took her step by step through the process. She became Sophie's lifeline over the next three years. Sophie asked for a note taker – a person who would sit beside her and take notes for her during lectures. She also had to sit up close to the lecturer so she could hear as well as lip-read. It was agreed that she would get pre-reading notes ahead of the lectures.

By the second semester she had such a workload that she gave up her weekend job to devote more time to study. Still working hard at becoming independent, Sophie then surprised us by getting a job at a small architectural firm in Port Melbourne. However, she soon realised that sitting in front of a computer was a big part of it and she didn't want that. Architecture, it turned out, was not for her. What she really wanted, she said, was to get out into the workforce as soon as possible. But I felt that emotionally she still had a way to go to reach social maturity.

For me, Friday-night drinks with my friends became a regular event. Parents we'd met through Tom's kinder introduced us to Amanda Nutting, Tammy Hall and Mandy De Steiger. While some of our children had now gone their separate ways, our own friendships continued to grow. We laughed a lot and I started to feel that I was coming out the other side at last.

~

The official world premiere of Li's film was at the Toronto International Film Festival in September 2009. We knew it had attracted strong Australian and international distribution interest, but the Global Financial Crisis was in full swing, and finance in the movie industry became extremely difficult. Unfortunately, many distribution companies went out of business overnight.

We were rather bemused when we weren't officially invited to the world premiere, or to be part of the official red-carpet party. It was a bit strange. However, we weren't going to miss it for the world, and neither were my sister or our close friends. So Jo, Charles and Lily, Ken and Annie, and Clayton and Ginya made the trip to be there with us. After all, the film was about Li's life and he had also helped to source a large part of the finance for it. In the end, he was included as part of the VIP group to walk the red carpet.

We were overwhelmed when the audience jumped to their feet and gave the film a standing ovation. Afterwards there was a glamorous rooftop party with all the stars and the movie executives, including Bruce Beresford, Chi Cao and Kyle MacLachlan. We were never going to exclude our friends from this special event, and Li somehow managed to wrangle them past security. Toronto by night was so gorgeous that we didn't want the evening to finish. Li, of course always thinking of food, suggested we go to Chinatown. We filled three tables in a Chinese restaurant with our friends, including the actors and Bruce. Li ordered for everyone. What a night to remember! Li was thrilled when the film was selected as runner-up for the festival's People's Choice Award.

We left Canada on a high and felt that the film's success there augured well for its release back at home. Jane Scott had agreed to Li's suggestion to make the Australian premieres in the major capital cities fundraising events to benefit the Australian Ballet and the Bionics Institute. The premiere in Melbourne was a black-tie event at the Regent Theatre. Li's seventh brother and his wife joined us, as well as our children and some of our nieces. Walking the red carpet with the children by our side was quite an experience, cameras flashing and Li pausing to talk to the media.

The Regent is a grand old theatre rather than a cinema. As we walked down the aisle to our seats, our friends greeted us from every side, wishing us well. The 2000-plus audience spontaneously applauded as we sat down, and we felt the happiness and support in the house. Then the lights went down and the movie began. I held Li's hand and whispered, 'This is surreal.'

He just nodded, and we watched our life play out on the big screen once again. I was very concerned about how Li's family would react to the movie after Dia's death. Cungui and Xiao Zhu had no English. They had come from China especially to be at this special occasion, with Rong Rong no doubt quietly interpreting. When the film finished, I looked straight at them and could see they were drying their eyes with handkerchiefs, completely overcome with emotion. Everyone in the theatre stood up, turned towards Li and applauded! We walked up Collins Street to the Sofitel hotel for the fundraiser. The organising committee led by Kenneth Watkins and Robin Campbell had created a sumptuous red-velvet Chinese theme.

There were also premiere galas in Sydney, Brisbane and Adelaide. Li went from one interview to the next. He was constantly away during this time. In Brisbane, it was special to finally be able to share the movie with my family. Of course, they all loved it. I was pretty exhausted at that point and didn't know how Li was even standing upright.

As if the movie release wasn't enough excitement, Sophie was still on the up and up academically. Before the year was out, we learned that she had been awarded a Graeme Clark Scholarship. The scholarship had been set up to financially support implant recipients who achieved high academic results, and to nurture those with a demonstrated commitment to the ideals of leadership and humanity. We were very proud of Sophie and beyond grateful to Graeme Clark for his invention. He was the reason that our daughter was able to flourish and live her own life, even though the journey hadn't been easy.

Sophie also decided to study Spanish. We couldn't believe it – English, Chinese and now Spanish. When she spoke at a Bionics Institute event that year, she put her goals eloquently. 'By mastering the three major languages, I hope to have access to communication on a global scale,' she said. 'I believe that communication is essential to making positive contributions to mankind.'

My God! Now my daughter was not only able to have conversations with me, she wanted to communicate with the whole world!

~

The next two years sped by. Tom completed secondary school and also decided to go to Melbourne University, to undertake a Bachelor of Arts majoring in Chinese and Spanish. He took up residence at Trinity College and began to truly blossom. He auditioned and was accepted into Trinity's chapel choir, singing several nights a week and every Sunday at church. Tom has a beautiful voice. He later joined a young male vocal group called the Trinity Tiger Tones, who became quite popular around Melbourne singing at weddings and other functions, even performing on TV on *Australia's Got Talent* and making it to the semifinals. He won Trinity's Arts prize for his contributions and was keen to take advantage of everything else the college had to offer. Our son was growing into a very fine young man – respectful and loving, and completely independent.

Bridie, our social butterfly, had settled in well to secondary school at Melbourne Girls Grammar, and Sophie was pushing on at uni as best she could. I was still teaching at the Australian Ballet. I visited Coralie in Brisbane more often now that she was getting older and a little frailer, as well as my brother Matt, who had been unwell.

When Li was away travelling, Coralie would often come and stay with us in Melbourne. We'd go to lunch or visit the wool shop in Albert Park so she could knit scarves for the grandchildren. Coralie was always great company. Li and I had both lost our fathers and Niang was ill, so I just wanted to be with Mum whenever I could.

Since moving to our new home the McKendry clan would descend on Melbourne to spend Christmas with us. We now had the space to entertain. It was heartwarming to have our home full of family and friends, and the house was perfect for this. Li would take everyone to a restaurant in Melbourne's Chinatown on Christmas Eve, and then on Christmas Day he and Coralie took over the kitchen, roasting the turkey and ham. These festive holidays became unforgettable for all of us – although one time I forgot to lock in one of the legs of the foldable table, and as our niece Lucy placed the last dish, the table buckled at one end and the entire Christmas lunch slid onto the floor! I had never seen Li so mad, he simply returned to the kitchen until we had managed to salvage most of the food. Coralie just poured herself another glass of Scotch.

Lulu and her husband, Yannick, now had a baby girl, Yanelle. Rong Rong had moved out in mid-2010 after she started uni, but often came to visit as well. Life – especially when Li was away, which was often – was pretty quiet compared to when the children were all at home and there were seven for dinner.

Sophie was keen to travel overseas and decided to join a Contiki tour. To celebrate her twenty-first birthday in July, I was to meet her in Paris. I asked Ginya if she would join us and she agreed. Soon we were in Paris on Bastille Day, sitting in the gorgeous Cristal Room restaurant with its stunning old-world baroque-style decor, looking out at the Eiffel Tower bathed in its special light show. It was a truly memorable time together. After Paris, we went on to London. We visited the Victoria and Albert Museum, where Sophie began explaining the architectural characteristics of ancient cultures she'd been studying at uni. Who would have thought that my daughter would be teaching me more about the world!

Back home, though, she was coming to terms with the fact that studying was not going to fundamentally change her situation. Her ongoing struggles with university study were compounding and her frustration was showing no signs of abating. One day in her second year she came home sobbing: the architecture professor was no longer providing her with notes before each lecture.

'He doesn't think I need them, Mum. I can't believe it!' she said.

'Maybe you should switch unis, Sophie,' I suggested, not knowing what the answer was. 'Melbourne Uni is so big.' *She was getting lost, despite her effort*, I thought.

Fighting for my daughter was as natural to me as breathing, but I wondered sometimes if it would ever end. Failure would be devastating for her. She'd never failed at anything she'd really put her mind to. I knew if she just had the information she needed, she'd be fine.

I called my friend Louise Paatsch to discuss the situation. 'Mary, you've always been Sophie's champion and you won't stop now,' she said. 'Transition to high school, transition to uni – it's always going to be difficult for Sophie, because she has to explain her situation to everyone, and not everyone will understand her needs.'

'Her lecturer won't give her the notes ahead of time and she's convinced she's going to fail,' I said. 'Louise, would you consider going with Li to see the lecturer to explain just how challenging it is for her? You're a language professor and he'll take it better from you, rather than me as her interfering mother.'

'Sure, Mary. I can do that,' Louise said, without a moment's hesitation.

We never told Sophie that we were stepping in on her behalf – she wanted to fight her own battles. The professor reluctantly agreed to do better with providing her his notes, but he didn't end up delivering on that promise. Ultimately, Sophie decided to swap her major to property for her third year. It was a relief for us all, and we hoped her final year would go more smoothly in every respect. Property seemed a sensible choice, too, as there might be more chances of employment for a hearing-impaired person in that field. She also decided to move back home. She'd had enough of college.

~

Sophie was delighted to graduate at the end of 2011 with a Bachelor of Environments and could not wait to find work after the Christmas holidays. We went to Coolangatta, where Ger's and Brig's families joined us. It was a joy to see the children bodysurfing with Li in the sea or swimming all day in the pool. Dinner was often together at one of the apartments, then all the children would gather to play some very competitive card games. Mum stayed with us for a few days. Sitting back with a Scotch, she'd listen to the noisy conversations bouncing around the room and smile gently at seeing us together.

When we got back to Melbourne it was almost time for Li's fiftieth birthday. We had decided to hold it at home as the flowing spaces of the house would allow people to mingle easily. I had cooked up a secret plan that involved our grand staircase and Tom's singing teacher, Dermot Tutty. I wanted it to be a night to remember for my husband, who had become an Australian citizen ten years earlier and whose birthday quite serendipitously fell on Australia Day. What an opportunity also to toast the year ahead, the decade ahead! What lay in store for us remained to be seen, but one thing was certain: life with Li was never going to be dull.

Li was loved by so many people that in the end I made it an open-house party with over 150 people invited. I wanted the whole family to enjoy the night, so I decided to hire some serving help and catering, including a chocolate fountain – the kids' idea.

In the middle of the party, I pulled Li up the stairs to the first landing. He was puzzled, and asked, 'What are you doing, darling?'

'Just wait and see,' I replied.

As I gathered our family and friends at the foot of the stairs I gave a short speech with Sophie and Bridie by my side and told Li that we had a surprise present for him – a performance created by Tom and Dermot. Li had no idea about any of it. Dermot started playing the piano while Tom and his choir friends walked down the staircase and started to sing. Then, suddenly, an exquisite voice floated from above.

'Do you recognise this?' I whispered in Li's ear. He looked at me questioningly.

The magical voice belonged to Siobhan Stagg – a beautiful country girl with blonde hair and the voice of an angel who would soon go on to international fame. That night, at the top of our staircase, she was a star!

Very quickly Li recognised the song and turned to me with a big smile and damp eyes, and kissed me. It was 'Solveig's Song' from *Peer Gynt*, the first dance Li and I had performed together in Houston, the very ballet we'd fallen in love over. We had danced to the music with a full orchestra but had never heard the lyrics to the song. We watched and listened as Siobhan made her way down the staircase. It was a very special moment.

~

The memories of that perfect night stayed with us throughout the year. Then in September, I got a call from Brig to say that Matt was in hospital and in a very bad way. I had visited him just weeks before, fearing the worst, and the whole Brisbane family was by his bedside. Anxiety and depression had eventually led to major health issues for him, and he was taken from us far too soon.

We were bereft. Even though he had been unwell for some time, we were still stunned. One of the eight was gone! How could it be?

~

I knew I wouldn't get over the loss of Matt for a long time, if ever, and so I wanted to be closer to the McKendry clan. Then, even though I don't believe in fate, something happened next that you could say was meant to be. A woman from a recruitment firm contacted me, completely out of the blue, wanting to pick my brains about Queensland Ballet's search for a new artistic director. I laughed and told her, 'Quite frankly, I don't know anyone who could direct a ballet company except for my husband.'

I truly believed that. Li would be exceptional. I knew it in my heart as I knew his vision and ability.

'Would Li be interested in the job?' she asked.

'No, I don't think so,' I replied. Ever since the disappointment of the Australian Ballet position, Li had buried this lifelong dream. In fact, he had declined several approaches from ballet companies around the world since then.

During dinner that evening, he said, 'Darling, I had a call today about Queensland Ballet. The recruiter asked for my thoughts on the attributes and experience they should be looking for in an artistic director.'

'*And?*'

'And what?' Li shot back.

'What else?' I pressed.

Li shrugged his shoulders. 'I told him what I thought, and at the end he asked if I would be interested in the job. I told him no.'

'I don't think you should just dismiss it, Li. You would be a wonderful director.'

'Mary, I never want to go through that process again.'

'But Li . . .'

'No, Mary, stop it. I don't want to talk about this any more.'

Faced with Li's stern expression I dropped the discussion, but I waited eagerly for him to come home the following night to talk further about it.

'Darling, have you thought any more about the Queensland Ballet job?' I asked him once he'd changed out of his suit.

'Yes,' Li replied.

'And?'

'I don't think so. We've got too much to lose,' he said.

'What do you mean?'

'We have a great life now, Mary,' Li replied. 'I've built up a successful stockbroking business and a good speaking career, and I'm considering new book ideas with Penguin. You have a teaching job at the Australian Ballet that you love, and our family and close friends are here . . .'

'But Li, everything happens for a reason. You didn't get the Australian Ballet job and then the opportunity came up to write your book. That was the greatest thing that's ever happened to you. Your story reached the whole world. And you have been home with the children more than you would have been if you were touring with the ballet. So it's all worked out. But now here's another opportunity.'

Later that night, I saw him at our dining-room table writing something down. I quietly leaned over and saw a list of pros and cons for the Queensland Ballet job. I smiled inside.

'What are you doing, darling?' I asked cheekily.

'I'm making a list,' Li replied.

'What do you think?'

'Well, more minuses than pluses,' he said. I could clearly see that the negative column was much longer than the positive column.

I singled out 'passion' on his list for discussion. I knew that he still had a passion for ballet. By the end of the night, I had got him to admit that if he had to choose one dream job in life, it would be to return to the ballet world. And I believed that this was where he could make the greatest impact.

'Wouldn't it be nice to give something back to the art form that has given us so much in our lives?' I asked him before we went to bed.

I'd always hoped that Li would be in the ballet world forever, but we both understood that opportunities for a job like a ballet director-ship didn't grow on trees. There were only three professional ballet companies in Australia, and he had assumed he may not ever get the opportunity to work in any of them. But deep down I had never let go of that dream for him. I wasn't assuming anything would happen now, but God, my heart started beating that little bit faster!

I knew that Li had much to offer the new generation of dancers and to the art form itself. Ballet needed the talent and experience of someone like him.

'Li, think about it. You've done well in the business world for the past fifteen years, but you need to think about what you would really enjoy doing for the *next* fifteen years.' I challenged him: 'Nothing will be lost if you throw your hat in the ring.'

'It doesn't matter, applications are closed,' he said.

'Just tell them you're interested and see what happens,' I urged.

Sure enough, Queensland Ballet extended the deadline for Li and he hastily put in an application. The wheels in his brain had started turning. We just had to wait until the interview early the following year. I could hardly bear it.

~

In the new year, Sophie became deadly serious about finding work. She thought she might look for work in the real-estate industry. It was going to be a big step towards independence and, more than anything, Sophie wanted to prove she could do it.

'Good luck, darling,' I said as she set off down Toorak Road towards the cafe where she was to have a job interview. She just waved happily at me as if there was nothing to worry about.

When I saw her later that afternoon, she was elated. However, the interview hadn't gone well, she told me: the interviewer had been uninterested and left after a short while. That was the news I'd been dreading, so why did she look so upbeat?

'Mum, a man and a woman were sitting next to us. They saw how that guy treated me and they were appalled.'

The couple turned out to be from a local real-estate company that handled prestigious properties in Melbourne.

'So the guy leaned over and said if I'm ever interested in a job, I should give him a call!'

'Really, darling?' I said as my heart lifted. 'That's marvellous!'

Sophie did call him, and she was determined to take her chance without any help from us. With no real prior experience to speak of, she started working for the agency a week later in an administrative role. No gap year for this girl! But my God, it was tough. Although they knew about her hearing loss and were to be commended for taking on an inexperienced graduate, their office wasn't suitably equipped for someone with Sophie's disability. As the days went on, she became more and more disenchanted.

'The phone goes all day, Mum, and it's impossible. The phone connector to the implant isn't automatic – there's a long delay to connect and sometimes the wait is so long that I miss the call. It's so frustrating!'

Sophie was coming home depressed and exhausted. Over the ensuing weeks we saw her new-found confidence plummet completely. It was devastating. How could I go to Queensland, if it came to it, if this was how challenging life was going to be for her?

What our resourceful girl did, however, was join Hear For You, a volunteer organisation that had been founded and was run by deaf people specifically to support deaf teenagers. She volunteered to help at a Sunday workshop, mentoring students from years 7 and 8, and loved it.

'Mum, if I can support and inspire these young hearing-impaired teenagers to be the best they can be, I'll be so happy,' she told me.

Maybe this would be a better, more rewarding option for her in the future.

One day Sophie came home looking very excited. 'Mum, I've been offered a paid job at Hear For You, running the program for Victoria!'

'How fabulous! Will you take it?' I asked.

'Yes, I think so,' she replied. 'I really love this program.'

I thought it was fantastic, exchanging a stressful job in the hearing world for one where she was discovering another, happier way to navigate her life. Finally! Maybe this would be her niche – bridging the divide between the deaf and hearing communities. *Wouldn't that be wonderful!* I said to myself.

~

After our January holiday, Li heard from the recruiter that he was shortlisted for the position at Queensland Ballet. His interview a few weeks earlier must have gone well. In preparation for the final interview, he pored over Queensland Ballet's annual reports, reviews, articles and anything else he could get his hands on.

'Mary, the company has a very small budget, their financial position isn't strong. Whoever gets the job has a huge amount of work to do to take this company to the next level,' Li told me with a serious expression. 'Without funding, none of my vision and dreams will be possible.'

One thing I knew was that Li wouldn't shy away from a challenge, and sure enough he started to draw up one-year, three-year and five-year plans for the company. He became obsessed. He was flown

to Brisbane to have his crucial interview with the selection committee. Incredibly well prepared, he presented an exciting vision to make
Queensland Ballet a global-standard company and an Asia-Pacific
powerhouse in dance.

'How did it go?' I asked him when he called afterwards.

'I think it went okay,' he replied. 'But you never know. I'm fully
prepared not to get it.'

'Are you sure you won't be building birdcages again?' I asked,
half-jokingly.

He laughed. 'No, no. Never.'

I was relieved.

A few weeks later, Li was offered the job. My dreams for him were
coming true. In my heart I believed that there were very few people
in the world who could do what he could do, both business-wise
and artistically. He would improve the company's fortunes and put
Queensland Ballet on the world stage. His mind was swirling with
ideas, and he was champing at the bit to get started.

My mind was in a spin too. Brisbane! Even without the lure of the
ballet, my McKendry clan were there. The children were thrilled for
their father especially. They were unanimous: 'Dad, you have to do
this. And Mum needs to be with you.' They knew it was important for
the next stage of our lives.

Tom would stay in Melbourne and finish his degree. Bridie was
nervous about moving schools, but she would be going to the same
school as Matt and Brig's girls so she wouldn't be alone. She should, in
fact, have been going off to St John's School in Houston, but now the
timing was wrong.

While we weren't that worried about leaving Tom behind, as he
had always been independent, we were particularly ambivalent about
leaving Sophie. When she sensed our concerns, she had nothing but
reassurance for us: 'Mum and Dad, don't worry about me – it's time
for me to live my life in my own way. I need to see what I can do for
myself. We can always Skype, right?'

'Yes, we can do it every day, sweetheart,' said Li.

'Don't worry about us,' Tom said. 'We'll be fine. Sophie and I will look after each other.'

I knew he would be a caring brother for Sophie but Li could see I was still unconvinced.

'Mary, we have never said no to opportunities,' he said. 'Instead, we have always said, "See what you can do with that opportunity." Haven't we?'

And that's when I knew this had to happen. It was true – we'd always been quite firm in making big decisions. Suddenly it seemed mad to have any doubts. I looked at Li, who was once again on the brink of something wonderful, and felt the great excitement.

Once the decision had been made, Li resigned from Bell Potter Securities and gave his business to his long-time assistant. He then went on a tour of Asia, Europe, Cuba and North America to renew his ballet connections. He came back full of motivation and ideas, even though he wasn't officially commencing at Queensland Ballet until January the following year. He couldn't help himself; he was so eager to get started.

Eventually, it was decided it would be best for Li to move up to Brisbane in May to get to know the company and start planning future programs. Bridie and I had planned to move there at the end of the year, but we decided to go earlier too, so Bridie could settle into her school before the new year started, and I could give Li a hand.

Queensland Ballet thought there was no chance Li would be able to get his own season ready for 2013 that quickly, but they didn't know my husband. Less than five months after he was offered the job, it was coming together. When he told me he was going to open the 2013 season with Ben Stevenson's *Cinderella*, one of the most beautiful but most difficult classic ballets, I just laughed.

'Mary, I'm going to get new costumes and sets as well,' he enthused.

Li had to find the money to finance everything. Thankfully his amazing contacts proved invaluable. One of his entrepreneur friends from Melbourne, Gerry Ryan, pledged five-year support, all paid up-front, which enabled Li to mount his first brand-new production for Queensland Ballet. It was the most expensive show in the company's 52-year history.

Once that was settled, Li turned to me and said, 'Darling, I will need someone to coach the dancers. I need someone with your experience. I want you to do it.'

I had loved dancing Ben's *Cinderella*, so to work on this production would be a joy. I felt very comfortable with the choreography and coaching the leading roles as I knew this was my area of expertise. A good ballet mistress is vital in any company, to make sure the dancers perform to their best. There was no budget for me to work full-time, but I wasn't in it for the money and needed to be available for Bridie starting her new school anyway.

The Queensland Ballet studios were located at West End on Brisbane's south side, but we started looking for a place to live on the north side, near Mum. A few weeks later, Li spotted a classic Queenslander that he liked. It was out of our price range, but he took Brig along to have a look at it anyway, and decided there and then that he wanted it. He made an offer and to his amazement the vendors accepted. I had never even seen it!

After Li signed the contract, I flew up for a viewing and liked the house straightaway. It took me right back to my childhood, to that leafy street in Rocky where stilt houses with shady verandahs opened louvres for the breeze. Our new home was situated in a leafy street, on an elevated block with lush greenery and fragrant tropical flowers. Bougainvillea grew through the ornate fretwork. It was smaller than our Melbourne home, but there were fewer of us now, so that didn't matter to me. The whole property was beautifully landscaped, and it had a swimming pool in the backyard.

Back in Melbourne, life was manic. I was trying to pack up the home we'd lived in for seventeen years. With sadness I resigned from my position after a decade at the Australian Ballet. Above all, making arrangements for Sophie was a priority. Separation was going to be another big step for each of us. We found a nice apartment for her not far from home, and with our cast-off pots, pans, towels and bed linen, her own bed and other favourite things, she soon had it how she wanted it. It was lovely spending that time together helping her set up home, just as my mother had done for me in London. I felt strongly that Sophie needed to share the apartment with someone who could support her, especially in case of emergencies such as fire, and eventually she found a couple of nice flatmates.

I knew I would miss Sophie and Tom, but told myself this was a much-needed step in their development. I soon found myself in an aeroplane moving to my new stage of life, this time with fourteen-year-old Bridie beside me, looking through the tiny window at Melbourne receding below. I had never lived anywhere for as long as I'd lived there. Melbourne was where we'd raised our three children, forged some of our dearest friendships, welcomed our extended family from China, created marvellous new opportunities, and taught our beloved hearing-impaired daughter to speak. There was so much to say goodbye to – but also so much to look forward to.

PART SIX

Brisbane
2012–18

Family was what it was all about for us.
It always was and it always will be.

18

The flight to my new life this time was quite different to any flight I'd taken before. In the past, I'd always embraced the future with a sense of anticipation and excitement. This time the pangs at departing were acute, for I was leaving behind the daughter I'd lived side by side with, whom I'd fought night and day for, for more than twenty years. Sophie, too, was coming to terms with that reality. In a way, I was happy for her that we would be apart. The independence she had been craving was being forced on us both. This was the beginning of her life as an adult.

As the plane began its descent I looked out at Brisbane's suburbs: swimming pools glinting in the sun, palm trees swaying, high-rise apartment blocks glittering alongside the river. I thought of our new home awaiting us – the balmy air and tropical breezes so welcoming, the easy weather of my childhood. And there was Li beyond the luggage carousel, arms wide, scooping us both up into a bear hug. I couldn't keep the grin off my face.

'Welcome home!' he said.

As we collected our luggage, Li said, 'Come on. I've made dumplings!'

We were suddenly starving.

Li was excited to show Bridie the house. The jacaranda trees out the front were in full bloom with their stunning veil of violet.

We walked through the house and onto the verandah, feeling the breeze. There was that special childhood smell – a tropical smell of flowers and warm, rich earth. Inside, the house was magnificent even without furniture. We only had two beds, bought from the previous owners, and Li had borrowed a fridge from our kind new neighbours. I knew we would be happy here, making this house into our home. Even Bridie looked impressed. I soon felt at home, with all the McKendrys flocking in to nose around and have their say, and the laughter had started already.

Our new life in Brisbane began. A cacophony of birds woke us very early each morning. Li would dive into the pool and do laps before work, which gave him time to think about the many decisions he had to make to implement his vision for the ballet. Bridie's first week at her new school was interesting. 'Mum, where are the Asians?' she asked. She quickly became aware of her 'Asian-ness' and was worried that she didn't fit in.

At last I got to see the Queensland Ballet facilities in West End. Li was excited to show me around and share his grand plans.

'I have hired Greg Horsman as ballet master, and Matthew Lawrence has agreed to come from Birmingham Ballet as a principal dancer,' he told me, 'but if we're going to truly make our mark and stage ambitious productions, we're going to need more good dancers.'

'The facilities are going to need an upgrade as well. And there's not going to be enough toilets,' Li added. I laughed.

I couldn't wait to be a part of the company the following year, and would often go into the studios to watch class and rehearsals to get to know the dancers. Soon they'd be rehearsing for *The Sleeping Beauty*. This would be the departing director François Klaus's last production; thereafter, each program would be Li's. He was determined to make his mark. I could see it pained him greatly to let go of some of the existing dancers who didn't have the skill set required for his new repertoire.

'Mary, I have no choice but to make some tough decisions,' he said. 'I'm not in this job to be popular or loved. I have to do what's best for the company's future.'

~

In that first year, there was an increasingly strong interest in Queensland Ballet. Everyone in the dance world knew of Li and his story. Across Australia, New Zealand and other countries, nearly 1000 aspiring dancers, of varying abilities, turned up for the auditions. And as the Australian Ballet was offering very few contracts that year, Li had the opportunity to take five Australian Ballet School graduates into the company and one scholarship recipient into the pre-professional program.

My coaching work began in earnest. It was hard work and unbearably humid in the studios – a typical Queensland summer – but I loved it. The ceiling fans went at full speed and the windows were wide open. It reminded me of the heat in Miss Hansen's Rockhampton studio, with the cattle trains rolling by. Now we were in Brisbane's cosmopolitan city centre. Things were different, yet the same. I was very happy.

I became totally immersed in my work and loved being in the studio working in tandem with Li. We had been the best partnership on stage all those years ago and now we were creating a new kind of partnership. I was sharing Li's vision for what Queensland Ballet could become and what it could do for the arts, not just in Queensland but in Australia and beyond. We would talk long into the night about how he could realise his vision. That vision – for the company to reach for the stars – was intoxicating.

Our first theatre season was to be in April, with Ben Stevenson's acclaimed *Cinderella* as planned. Ben came to help us stage it for the first time. Even at the age of seventy-seven, he was still so inspiring and dramatic. The dancers had never seen anything like his choreography and worked hard. We were both really touched by Ben's generosity and energy. His time coaching our dancers reminded us again and again just how much he had influenced us as artists at Houston Ballet.

Cinderella was a sellout months before its opening. It was a huge hit. Queenslanders were swept up in the magic and the production was met with rave reviews. It was very special to have friends and family from Melbourne fly up to support us.

When Li had been planning the season and told me he was going to stage an annual production of Ben's *The Nutcracker*, I was excited. I knew Queensland would love it. It was one of the best productions I'd ever danced, because of Ben's flowing choreography and storytelling. Li wanted it to have a brand-new design.

'Can we afford it?' I asked him. 'A new production is going to cost a fortune!'

'I know, but we have to have a beautiful production if we're to have any chance of making it an annual tradition,' he said, his eyes twinkling at the challenge.

First, he had the rest of the year's program to stage. We were still glowing from the public's reception of *Cinderella*, and were further elated when ticket sales for *Giselle* in June, *Elegance* – a triple-bill program – in August, and *The Nutcracker* in December also sold out in advance, breaking all records in Queensland Ballet's history. Queensland was falling in love with Li just as Houston and Melbourne had done.

Sometimes, I worried that he would get sick from exhaustion, as he worked long days and nights and most of the weekend. 'Remember how you told me that this would be a marathon, not a 100-metre dash?' I reminded him one time.

'I know, but the opportunities won't wait. We may have to think that this is a 100-metre dash *as well as* a marathon,' he winked.

Some people thought that Queensland Ballet's phenomenal success was due solely to Li's star power, but they couldn't have been more wrong. Yes, his fame from *Mao's Last Dancer* no doubt helped, but the key to the company's success was his vision and his team's hard work.

'Mary, we're living a dream,' he said. 'I don't want to wake up one day and realise that it remained a dream. We've got one chance to make this dream as big and as exciting as we can.'

That's what kept us going.

~

As for Sophie, she had settled in to her new job and her confidence seemed to be returning.

'I love it at Hear For You,' she told me over the phone one day. 'It's my lifeline, so you mustn't worry about me any more, I'm happy now. I'm with people who understand me. It's so good! I truly believe this program makes a difference in young people's lives, and I just want to keep doing it.'

It was the most passionately I'd heard her speak, and she wasn't done yet. 'That is so good, Sophie!' I said. 'And how's it going in the apartment?'

'Oh, it's fine . . . I must tell you about Meg, though,' Sophie rushed on.

'Who's Meg?'

'Meg Aumann. She is my colleague at work and she's just brilliant. And guess what? She's deaf and doesn't speak, she only signs, and she's so happy signing.'

'I thought Hear For You was only for oral deaf people like you, Sophie?'

'It's both. Her role is the same as mine but for Auslan only, so we basically do the same kind of job. I manage the oral program and she manages the signing one. She's very supportive, not like the people at my last workplace.'

I was thrilled for Sophie. I knew how difficult it had been for her in the previous workplace. She told me Meg had been showing her how to navigate her way through social situations, at work, in meetings and on the phone.

'And I've started learning how to sign properly in Auslan. Meg's helping me. I'm going really well. Remember that Australia Day party I went to with Pip Russell? Maybe I didn't tell you, but it was really great for me.'

'Tell me about it, darling,' I said.

'Well, everyone there was hearing-impaired, and most of them were around my age. All of them could speak *and* sign, and the most amazing thing was that everyone there understood what it was like to be deaf at a party. Lights were on, there was no thumping music, people repeated when someone missed out or asked to repeat what was being said. Pip is the first person to invite me to a party that I didn't want to leave.'

I was delighted to hear the sunshine in her voice, even if a shadow passed across my mind and I wondered where this might lead. But how could I not be happy? Parties in the past had been torture for Sophie. Thumping music always drowned out conversations, jokes and laughter, and lip-reading in the dark was impossible. This party had been a breakthrough for her, and a further boost to her confidence.

The conversation was an awakening for me, too. I realised I'd been becoming increasingly uneasy about Sophie, about how we'd brought her up – how all these years I'd driven her down the oral path, desperately wanting her to be a part of *our* world, and how it was such a struggle for her as she was always an outsider. Could Sophie have communicated better and missed out less with signing? If she had learned Auslan before going to university, would she have fared better? Was she starting to regret that now, not signing earlier, I wondered. Would we lose her to the deaf world if she decided signing was a better way for her to communicate? Had we made a dreadful mistake in imposing our views on her? Had it all been too much for her? Should I have been more sensitive to her feelings?

After so many years, these questions still niggled at me, but despite my misgivings, I said, 'Well, that's wonderful, darling. Whatever makes you happy makes me happy too.' What else could I say?

'You'll have to learn it as well, Mum – and Dad, Tom and Bridie too!'

'Hmm, maybe . . .' I found myself saying. 'For now, just enjoy your life without me on your back!'

We both laughed then, but I couldn't stop brooding about the future. In the end I called Louise for reassurance.

'Mary,' she said, 'this is perfectly normal. Sophie has become very empathetic towards other hearing-impaired people. Her life has been a constant battle. She's been one of the lucky ones, having so much support from you. But it must be a relief for her not to have to listen and speak all the time.'

What Louise said made sense, but that didn't make it any easier for me. 'I fear she's starting to reject speaking and hearing, Louise,' I replied, 'staying there in Melbourne, immersing herself in the deaf world. That's against everything I fought for for her!'

'It's so common, Mary. You've read that book by Paul Jacobs, *Neither-Nor*, haven't you? A similar case to Sophie's.'

'I know. But how could we have all learned to sign? I mean, perhaps if we were living in a different family we could have. But living in the arts world with Li often away, working at night – and there were huge things going on in our lives as well. Just being married to Li, it's like a full-time bloody job, plus I had three kids, and on top of that I was trying to keep my teaching career going. Also, my goal was for her to be able to communicate and survive in the bigger speaking world.'

I knew I was being defensive, but it was all true.

'Don't forget, though,' Louise continued calmly, 'she's also on the journey to becoming bilingual like her friend Alice, who can talk *and* sign. Try to keep an open mind on this, Mary. Be patient. It might be a rocky road for a while but Sophie won't shut you out. She loves you.'

I understood, but I prayed Sophie would not reject speaking. As I hung up the phone, I continued to reflect on the subject. In hindsight, should we have had a tutor teach us to sign in Houston in the beginning? Sign language had always been a last resort in the back of my mind. What also bothered me was that American Sign Language was different to Australian Sign Language and Chinese Sign Language, so how was that ever going to work for our family? *Oh, God*. I was beginning to torture myself with guilt that I was the worst mother ever.

The next time I saw Sophie was when we went to Melbourne during Tom's final year of his Bachelor of Arts degree to see him in a play called *And Then There Were None*. To my surprise, she asked to bring a young man she was dating.

'That's fine, Sophie. Who is he?'

'His name's Patrick, Mum, and I met him at the Australia Day barbecue.'

'Oh!' I said, totally surprised. 'Well, of course he can come. I'd like to meet him.'

It was hard to form a decent impression of Patrick that night since we were all watching the play, and other Melbourne friends of ours – Robin Campbell and her son David – had come along too. Patrick looked nice enough – decent, respectful. He was studying industrial design. I could see that he had a cochlear implant and, like Sophie, struggled in a large crowd. Not everyone saw that, but I noticed. I was happy to meet him and to know that Sophie had someone to care for her.

Sophie was a quick learner and in just a few months she became fluent enough to be able to present a paper with Meg at the World Federation of the Deaf conference in Sydney. Their signed and spoken presentation was on the impact the Hear For You program was having on young deaf teens across Australia and New Zealand. It was well received, but the biggest thrill for Sophie was the realisation that she had fully embraced sign language and deafness as part of her identity. It was a breakthrough for her, and would be a new journey for all of us. I hoped I was ready for it.

Come November, there was more excitement.

'Mum, guess what?' said Sophie when I answered the phone. 'I've just been promoted! My new title is National Communications and Programs Coordinator.'

'Oh, wow, Sophie! That's brilliant! What does that involve?'

'Well, I'm going to be full time here, Mum! I'll still be running the Victorian oral program, but I'll also be managing the training of mentors in other states, and I'll be the main person for media stuff, like Facebook, newsletters and the website. It's exactly what I want to do.'

'That's fantastic, Soph,' I said. 'You'll do a great job. Let me know how it goes!'

'I will, Mum. You know I will never stop talking to you!'

At that moment, tears sprang to my eyes. I was reassured by her words and so proud of her.

We were proud of Tom, too. He completed his Bachelor of Arts and wanted to save for a trip overseas, so he came to live with us and got a job at a cafe in Brisbane. It was fabulous having our son with us again, and he brought a different dynamic to our home. He was lovely with Bridie, played tennis again with his father and swam in the pool.

He also spent time with Coralie, which was very special for both of them. Boys don't always seem to have much time for their grand-parents, but now that Mum was eighty, Tom seemed to realise it was time to make up for that before it was too late. The whole family gathered to celebrate her birthday. We wanted her to know how much she meant to us.

~

The end of 2013 came around quickly. We were barely a year into our new lives with Queensland Ballet and yet here we were on the opening night of the Australian premiere of *The Nutcracker*. Pre-publicity had been amazing and the sold-out theatre was buzzing. Ben had returned to rehearse the dancers and stayed for opening night. The set was sublime – a real traditional Christmas bauble of glitter and colour – and the costumes were a knockout. Valmai Pidgeon and Amanda Talbot, two Brisbane donors, had generously underwritten the new production.

I was backstage as the dancers put the finishing touches to their make-up. Li offered words of encouragement to all. I could see he was nervous. He didn't want to let down a single person who'd been a part of the journey, especially Ben. I knew in my bones that the company would rise to the occasion and give a spectacular performance.

The opening night was exhilarating, and we were floating on air afterwards. Ben and Coralie, Li and I walked across the road, followed by our children and extended family. Bumping into people and being congratulated, we made our way to the Brisbane Convention & Exhibition Centre to celebrate at the afterparty. It was an opportunity for Li to thank Ben and the creative teams, along with Valmai and Amanda. His gamble had paid off: *The Nutcracker* was a triumph!

∼

Greg Horsman's successful world premiere of *Coppélia* kicked off Li's second season. The city was abuzz with talk about the quality and boldness of Queensland Ballet, and Li had much more in store. He had always dreamed of performing Sir Kenneth MacMillan's iconic *Romeo and Juliet*, having worked with and respected Kenneth in Houston before he passed away. Kenneth had been one of the most respected choreographers in the world, with his *Romeo and Juliet* widely considered to be one of the best ballets of all time. Li had also got to know Kenneth's Australian-born wife, Lady Deborah, who now managed his works. He learned that she was going to be in Sydney and arranged to meet her.

'Li, there's no stopping you,' I said. 'If we are allowed, we'd have to be the smallest ballet company ever to perform it. You know this production is usually only performed by companies like the American Ballet Theatre and the Royal Ballet?'

'I know, darling, but I think we can do it,' he said. 'It will take our dancers to another level. I want to bring it to Australia as it's never been done here.'

Li certainly had audacity in spades. He managed to convince Deborah to let us perform it. On his way to the airport after their meeting, he called me excitedly to say, 'Mary, we got *Romeo and Juliet*!'

'What?' I couldn't believe my ears.

'Yes, Deborah agreed. We just have to find another forty-six dancers within a year,' he laughed. I could hear the excitement in his voice.

'God, you're crazy, Li,' I said. 'How did you convince her?'

'Well, I promised her, on my life, that I would have enough people to do justice to Kenneth's work. I also told her that Queenslanders need something special to lift their spirits and help them recover from the devastating 2010 floods. Don't forget she was born in Queensland, so of course she wants to help.'

Excitement aside, I genuinely had no idea just how Li was going to pull this off. Thankfully the company managed to get a grant from the Queensland Government to invite three international superstars – Carlos Acosta, Steven McRae and Tamara Rojo – to guest. The Queensland Performing Arts Centre also came on board as a partner. It seemed that Li's powers of persuasion were impossible to resist. What a coup!

We ended up with twenty-seven company dancers, six Jette Parker Young Artists, thirty pre-professional students, and some final-year students from the drama department of Queensland University of Technology to play guards and other walk-on roles. Li also threw Queensland Ballet artistic staff – including me – into the mix in character roles. I'd been put down tentatively as Juliet's nurse, but I was nervous about getting back on stage – it was an important acting role and I knew that doing both my coaching and that role would take a lot of energy. We would just have to work very hard and put it all together. It would be our *pièce de résistance* for the year, and I could hardly wait.

I was anxious about the first show – not only personally, but for the whole company. It was a huge occasion, with Li's and Queensland Ballet's reputations riding on it. After that first nerve-racking performance I loved it, and often cried with emotion at the end when I lost my beloved Juliet. Li told me, 'You even made *me* cry.'

But the most important thing for me was that Sophie flew in to see me perform. Afterwards, backstage, she was quite overcome.

'I have never seen you on stage, Mum, and you gave up your career for me,' she said, tears in her eyes and giving me a big hug. It was a moment I shall keep in my heart forever.

By the season's end, *Romeo and Juliet* had wildly exceeded expectations and broken an all-time box office record. It was a glass-ceiling-shattering event for Queensland Ballet and for Li. The only way for the company now was forwards and upward. As he said to me more than once, 'Life is made up of journeys, and this is a special one. How lucky we are to be doing it together!'

~

Three months later, we took *Cinderella* on tour through regional Queensland. I was especially looking forward to returning to my home town – to perform at my father's Pilbeam Theatre, no less.

Memories were everywhere. We drove past our old street in Rocky, past the hospital Neil George had designed and where we'd walk to see Mum with the latest baby, past the swimming pool to the river, and there was Dad's theatre. I could see the town had changed very little, although some of the older colonial buildings had been charmingly restored. The Pilbeam Theatre still stood proudly, situated so beautifully among tall palm trees on the banks of the broad Fitzroy River.

I marvelled at the architecture: Neil George had always designed buildings to last. Over the years it had become an iconic civic centre in Central Queensland. I felt enormously proud.

I'd always dreamed of performing for my family at the Pilbeam. Well, having Queensland Ballet perform, with dancers I'd coached myself, was close enough. How I wished Dad could have been there, though. Perhaps he was . . . I could certainly feel his presence. I had a rush of emotion then, thinking of my wonderful dad, the belief he'd had in me that helped shape who I became. He was always his own man, setting his own standards and valuing freedom of thought, and he had put the women in our family on a pedestal, starting with Coralie.

19

Sophie was happy in her Melbourne apartment with two new flatmates, who were also close friends, Alice and Kat. Alice was deaf and together they created a deaf-friendly environment, using captions to watch television, flicking lights on and off to get the attention of someone in the bathroom, and signing in Auslan when their implants were off.

'It's so awesome, Mum!' Sophie gushed in one of our weekly calls. 'Amazingly, it's Alice's and my first time living with another deaf person under the same roof.'

I could see they'd been learning from one another, which was obviously a good thing. I could also see Sophie becoming happier as she moved further into the deaf world, and found myself wondering about my dogged determination to bring her up the way I had. But when I raised these doubts with Sophie, she reassured me.

'Don't worry, Mum. Alice and I have learned that our struggles were similar at the end of the day. It's good to know that I'm not alone. By living together, we're sharing the experience of being deaf. You'll see. It's good, and I'm all right.'

I was encouraged by that.

In the middle of the year, Sophie had landed a new job at Vicdeaf as their social media person, selected from more than thirty applicants. This was a step up from her previous job, requiring more responsibility and being part of a bigger team. Sophie's job was to manage online content and edit the quarterly magazine, *Communicate*. It seemed the perfect role for her. She felt she belonged, and was mixing with more signing people and using her writing skills. Unlike Hear For You, which had focused solely on deaf teenagers, Sophie was learning a lot about support for deaf people of all ages and from all walks of life.

'My life is so much easier now that I can sign,' she would say. 'I can sign at work and with my deaf friends at the beach, in the pool, at night-time at clubs and restaurants. I don't miss out anymore. It's amazing.'

After parting ways with Patrick a year earlier, Sophie had started seeing a new man named Matthew, who was a social worker at Deaf Children Australia. She had met him at a party with deaf friends. He was handsome and very keen on Sophie. He sometimes wore hearing aids but had no implants, could speak a little and was a good lip-reader. I hoped that meant Sophie would continue talking. I was pleased that she had a serious boyfriend. Now she had both work and a social life, and was crossing between the hearing and deaf worlds. I sensed she was beginning to question where she belonged. Although I was happy for her, I had my reservations.

When I told Li my concerns about Sophie, he said, 'You know, Mary, we've given her a hearing world, but it is ultimately up to her to choose. She may choose to be in the deaf world completely – it just might be too difficult for her to navigate the hearing world.'

Li was always more practical about our reality, whereas I was more emotionally invested in Sophie's future. I thought to myself that if she did choose the deaf world over the hearing world, I'd be deeply disap-pointed, as it would definitely limit her options. I even worried she might one day have a hearing baby – how would they communicate? I hoped that she would see the strength of our bond and we would come through this stage of her development as strong as ever.

At this time Professor Clark asked Li if he and Sophie would write the foreword for a new book called *Graeme Clark: The Man Who*

Invented the Bionic Ear, by Mark Worthing. Li happily agreed, but was surprised upon receiving an email from Sophie that said, 'Dad, you should leave my story out of this. I'm sick of being in the public eye. I want my life to be private. Enough is enough.'

Both Li and I were stunned. Professor Clark had always taken a special interest in Sophie and she had always admired him. Her response seemed completely out of character. Had she reached a point where she resented the cochlear implant altogether? Were the deaf world and her boyfriend influencing her thinking about deaf people living in the hearing world? Our influence as her parents didn't count for much any more, it seemed. I felt she was rejecting me as her mother.

In the end Li went ahead and wrote the foreword, including Sophie's journey. I tried to forget about it, but wondered why Sophie had reacted so strongly against doing this.

Our regular phone conversations began to change, too. They used to be weekly, but now Sophie might not call for a couple of weeks and then only for a quick hello. I was anxious to see her in person soon.

The next time she visited, I did try – I really did. But I was so dismayed when I saw that she'd dyed the bottom portion of her beautiful jet-black hair bright purple that I simply said, 'Darling, you should cut your hair to here,' and put my two fingers, like a pair of scissors, just above the point of her purple hair. 'You will look nice with shorter hair.' Not exactly subtle!

'Mum, get over it,' she snapped, and rolled her eyes.

Snappy was becoming Sophie's default position. During dinner that Saturday night, Li told her that one of Queensland Ballet's chosen charities for 2015 was Dimity Dornan's Hear and Say centre. As a family we had been very impressed with what Hear and Say had achieved and all the deaf children they'd helped over the years with the auditory-oral approach.

'Dad, this is not a deaf charity I would support,' Sophie countered quite forcefully. 'If you have to have a deaf charity, please let me choose it for you.'

'What do you mean?' Li asked, taken aback.

'Speaking and hearing is not the only solution for deaf people. There is nothing wrong with deaf people signing. I just would have chosen a different charity,' she replied.

'Of course there is nothing wrong with signing, but it's better to have both options,' I said.

'You're not listening to me!' she exclaimed. 'You're not deaf but I am, so this will reflect back on me! Try to understand where I am coming from.'

'Well, this is a charity that Queensland Ballet has chosen to support. I thought you would be happy about it,' Li said.

I felt desperately bad about this, so sorry and sad for Sophie, and incredibly guilty, too. I'd hung on to the hope that signing would open up the deaf world to her in addition to the hearing world but, as I feared, we were clearly heading the other way, judging from another argument we had just before dinner another night.

'Would you bother to learn Auslan so we could sign as a family?' she asked. 'It would mean a lot to me if only you would try to make a little effort. Is this too much to ask?'

I was stunned by this request, speechless.

'Sophie, it's so good that you can sign,' I started, 'but you know that's not the real world. Everyone speaks and hears and that's what I have wanted for you. Sophie, we are fine for you to learn Auslan and you have learned it so quickly, but why do you want to subject us to learning it if we can communicate well now? Also, we would be very limited at signing compared to you.'

God. On reflection, what I said sounded like none of us could be bothered to learn. No wonder she reacted the way she did.

'Mum, all I ever wanted was for my family and close friends to meet me halfway!' she said vehemently. 'I've worked so hard all my life to fit in to the hearing world, despite the difficulties. And I've never complained, have I? I know you meant well, but you have no idea just how tough it is!'

She paused, clearly struggling to hold back tears with what she was going to say next: 'You were there every time I broke down.'

'Sophie, I do understand how difficult it is for you,' I replied. 'But it's tough for us as well. This is your reality. It would be great if everyone could sign, but that's not—'

She cut me off, getting more agitated. 'If I can learn to speak, why can't you learn to sign? That's all I ask, Mum! Just meet me halfway! Is that too much to ask?'

She continued with a softer tone: 'Mum, you talk so much and so loud that you don't even know if you would be able to actually sign without your voice on at the same time.'

I didn't know whether to laugh or cry. Eventually I said in a dejected voice, 'Yeah, probably not,' and we both burst out laughing. Sophie had said what she needed to say and then cleverly defused the situation. But her anger and frustration surprised and worried me. Our daughter was changing, and I was frightened.

Later I told Li that I felt like we were slowly losing our daughter. 'Please tell me that's not happening,' I said.

'Mary, this may be the next stage of Sophie's delayed emotional development that she never had through her teenage years,' he said reassuringly. 'She's got to reject her parents at some stage. Didn't Louise say that?'

I thought about the times Louise had explained to me how profoundly deaf children rebel when they become young adults and try to figure out where they belong, how often they feel they are neither hearing nor deaf. I hadn't thought this would be a scenario for Sophie as I had been so close to her and felt she had been successful. Inside, I wasn't sure what to think or how to make sense of it any more. I thought my heart might break.

'Mary, everything you've ever done for Sophie has been out of love,' Li offered. 'Sophie knows that. But it *has* been relentless for her for a very long time. She is trying to work out what her future holds.'

'But she's twenty-five, Li! Surely she should be over this "reject-your-parents" phase by now.'

'Remember her social and emotional development has been delayed. You have to think of her still in that adolescent phase where she's sorting out who she is.'

'I know, I know. But God, it's hard having her down in Melbourne with all these other influences.'

'We must trust her, Mary. Have faith in Sophie, and just for a little while, take a step back. Let her find her own way for a bit.'

I knew Li's words made sense, but they were so very hard to hear.

It was a comfort to know that Tom was in Melbourne as well. He had returned after travelling in Europe and working in China. He was quite fluent in Chinese and full of travel stories. He was determined to return to China one day, so it was no wonder he decided to return to Melbourne University the following year to study a Master of Teaching in Chinese and English as a Second Language.

～

It was good to be with Mum that Christmas. Bridie had gone to a host family in Montpellier, France, to learn French, but Sophie and Tom joined us and had fun with their cousins. Coralie was always happiest sitting back listening to our many overlapping conversations. Everyone looked after her, making sure she had a comfy chair in the thick of things and a glass of champagne or Scotch in her hand. We had given up on presents years ago as there were simply too many of us, and were just happy to relax together.

Sophie's boyfriend, Matthew, arrived from Melbourne after Boxing Day. He and Sophie planned to celebrate New Year's Eve with deaf friends at the Gold Coast. I thought he was a very nice man, and it was good to see how much he cared for Sophie. He made an effort to get to know us. By his speech, I could see that he'd had some hearing before he became deaf so I asked him about this.

With his slightly slurred speech, he responded: 'Actually, I was born hearing but then got meningitis when I was two.'

'I see, and that's why you still have some speech?' I asked.

'No, that's because I learned to speak and sign at school.'

Then I couldn't help asking, 'Did you ever think of getting a cochlear implant?'

Sophie shot daggers at me. Matthew had missed my question so he turned to her, and she quickly interpreted.

Matthew answered, 'Oh, well, I don't feel the need to have one. I'm fine. I can speak and sign. I don't really need my hearing and I don't feel anything is missing.'

I could tell my questions were making Sophie uneasy. Perhaps she felt the need to protect Matthew.

'Mum, it's Matthew's decision to not have one,' she told me. I could see that she wanted to say more, but instead she just kept glaring at me to keep quiet.

I nodded, and as the conversation moved on I noticed that Sophie sat opposite Matthew so she could sign for him when required. My heart sank as I realised that she needed to act as his interpreter. Sophie had a big personality and was a people person, and if she was to continue her relationship with Matthew, perhaps this would make her social circle smaller because she'd have to focus on him. Even if we all learned to sign at this point, it would be very limited communication and Sophie would still be interpreting between us and Matthew.

The next day, just before they headed off, Sophie was avoiding making eye contact with me. Although I was happy that she was going out, enjoying life and making new friends, her behaviour unsettled me. I took her aside and asked what was going on. That's when she accused me of being insensitive towards Matthew.

'Sophie!' I responded, quite startled. 'What are you talking about? I'm simply interested, that's all! I don't care whether he has implants or not. I was just curious.'

'I don't think so, Mum,' she replied. 'You want me to stay in your hearing world – just admit it.'

I tried to reassure her that she was wrong, but I could feel an uneasy tension growing between us.

After they left, Li and I went to the Gold Coast ourselves, alone for the first time. It was divine, just the two of us, relaxing and dreaming and planning. I kept my worries about Sophie to myself as I didn't want to spoil this precious time together.

Then Bridie arrived, sharing her stories of the fabulous time she'd had. She loved everything about France, especially the co-ed school. She was about to start her final year of school in Brisbane and looked a little restless and envious of her older siblings' independence, but we reassured her that her time would come.

Tom went back to Melbourne straight after Christmas. He had decided to study through the summer so that he could graduate in June the following year. Once the academic year was in full swing, he especially enjoyed his teaching placements, borrowing our old car to get to the various schools.

~

Back in Brisbane we opened with *La Sylphide*, and then staged the fairytale ballet *Peter Pan*. Just when things were going so well, though, around the middle of the year, we had another upset with Sophie – and this one was worse than before. She and I had hardly communicated in the past few months. She seemed busy and content with work and Matthew, and I had been preoccupied with my work, too.

Sophie came to Brisbane for work and stayed with us for the weekend. During dinner at home, we finally chatted properly about her life back in Melbourne. Sophie and Matthew had been together for almost a year.

'I'm going well,' she shrugged. 'You know, same old. The stories I hear about how difficult it is for deaf people out there with no support make me so sad. If I can help by signing, then that's what I'll do.'

'Well, yes, of course, Sophie—' I began, before she quickly interrupted.

'Also, I'm thinking about Matthew moving in.'

'Oh,' I said, somewhat startled.

'I wanted to let you know. I want you and Dad to be okay about it,' she went on.

'To be honest, Sophie,' I said, 'I don't think he should move in. It's not appropriate.'

'Alice and Kat are fine about it!' she shot back.

Li gently put his hand on my shoulder to quieten me. Nothing further was said until after dinner. Li indicated for me to keep cool, but I couldn't help myself and blurted, 'Sophie, darling, I don't think it's a good idea for a 27-year-old man to move in with three girls. I think you should have your own space.'

'Mum!' Sophie crossed her arms defensively. 'Just stop. I can make my own decisions. I am twenty-five years old, for God's sake.'

'I'm not being unreasonable, Sophie. If you want to live with Matthew, you should move out and rent a place together,' I continued.

Silence. Then a snappy, 'That's fine. Whatever you say.'

I could sense her rage and I felt wretched. I felt things were about to escalate. 'Sophie, what's wrong with you?'

It all came out then. She said, 'You don't know everything. You should have let me sign from the beginning. You should have learned to sign for me, too. Hearing is so hard. And no matter how hard I try to hear in all situations, I still can't hear well! Half the time, I don't know what I am missing. I often felt left out on family holidays – at the beach every morning, then the pool every afternoon – and I'm deaf for the entire day because that's my reality!'

'Sophie, just stop—'

'No, you stop, Mum. Don't interrupt me. Let me finish.' She put her palm up to stop me, and a quick glance at Li silenced me.

Just let her speak, he pleaded with me wordlessly.

'Now that I have deaf friends, I feel like I belong. I don't feel like an outsider anymore. I no longer struggle day in, day out. And God, it was so hard growing up with you!' she said, visibly upset. 'You never gave me a minute's peace. You have no idea how hard it's been, how unhappy I've been. I always felt something was missing. You just wanted me to fit in to your world, and I know now that I can never do that. Anyway, I don't expect you and Dad to understand. You know how hard I've tried. People just think, "Get a cochlear implant and everything is fixed."'

'Sophie—' Li tried to interrupt her. True to his unspoken words with me, I kept quiet.

'Stop!' she interrupted back. 'I still haven't finished. I've said it before, but did you ever think to learn to sign? Did any of you ever consider learning to sign?' She stared at us. I didn't reply.

'Deaf people feel like the hearing world just expects us to fit in,' she continued. 'We don't matter. We have to keep up with your pace. Our opinions and feelings are completely ignored. Why can't you make an effort to learn a bit more about the deaf world for a change?'

'Sophie, that's not true,' Li tried again, calmly. 'We understand—'

'No, you don't, Dad! You think you understand, but you don't. You only want me to listen to you, and I'm starting to think that my opinions don't matter to you. You think I'm doing just fine in your hearing world, right? But I'm not! Every day I struggle. I feel so left out and isolated. Did you know that I was constantly feeling anxious and depressed? I feel happier when I am with deaf people, because we understand each other and our struggles.'

'Sophie, Sophie, listen to me—'

'No, Mum, you listen to *me*. Sometimes I just want to stop wearing my implants, because it doesn't get easier – and I don't think it ever will!'

By this point I had heard enough. I saw so much torment and resentment in her. The thought of her stopping wearing her implants

petrified me. Had all these years of heartbreaking experiences, struggles, sacrifices and hard work come to this? My head was exploding
and I was raging with fear and anger.

'Where do I fit in, huh?' she went on, challenging us. 'I actually
don't fit into either camp! I go to bed deaf, I wake up deaf and I will
die deaf! And I have to live with that and accept that,' Sophie said
with finality.

I was silent because I actually understood. She felt she didn't fit in
to either world, and I couldn't help her.

'That's it, I'm done with this,' were the last words she said as
she pulled out her implants, slammed them on the dining table and
stormed downstairs.

Li and I were utterly stunned. I had never expected this.

I was so shocked that it weren't until much later in the night that
I burst into tears. This was something new. It felt like a great wedge
had come between us. I'd sensed it slowly growing, but Sophie's
bitterness was new. Clearly she felt very passionate about us not
teaching her to sign, and about us, as a family, not learning to sign.
Time and again I had tried to explain the reasons why we hadn't
gone down that path, but apparently this had just made her angrier
and more resentful.

I didn't sleep that night, and when Li woke in the morning, he
was firm with me: 'Please don't bring this up with Sophie, Mary. I will
speak to her. I want you to back off. When you are angry, you might
say things that you don't really mean.'

'But Li, we're losing her! I can't bear it!' I said in despair.

'We won't lose her, Mary. Give her a few days – everything will
be fine.'

'I hope you're right, Li.'

However, Sophie didn't want to speak to us and left early to catch
a flight home. Her implants were gone. My heart was aching with
sadness, just when I'd thought that together we had jumped over all
the hurdles.

A week went by and Sophie still hadn't been in touch. I wanted to call her, but Li stopped me. It was killing me. Each day that passed without hearing from her, my fear that she was moving further away from me increased. But Mothers' Day was coming up. Surely she'd call me then.

Around this time, Bridie told me that Sophie had broken up with Matthew. I was shocked and wondered why Sophie hadn't told me herself, but I must admit part of me was rather relieved.

On Mothers' Day I woke up early, still thinking about Sophie and our fight. Even though my anger had dissipated, my sadness and worries had swelled. I reflected over and over on what Sophie had said that night. How had I failed to sense what she was going through? I had prided myself on knowing my daughter so well throughout her life, and blamed myself for moving away. I felt the urge to move back to Melbourne to be with her. I sensed that Sophie's anger and frustration wasn't just about her past struggles – they were about her future, and that must have been so terribly daunting and frightening for her.

By noon on Mothers' Day, Sophie still hadn't called. It was excruciating and I was so sad. And then, finally, she called in the afternoon. 'Hi, Mum. Happy Mother's Day!'

My happiness was beyond description. Hearing those few words, I felt such relief. That phone call was the best Mothers' Day gift ever.

We didn't have a long conversation. She asked how my day was going, but I couldn't possibly tell her that I'd done nothing but wait for her bloody call. Instead, I told her that I'd had a good day and suggested that we needed to talk about what had happened and I was willing to listen this time. We agreed that it would be best if we could talk face to face, and it was decided that she would fly up again in a couple of weeks' time. I felt much better after that conversation, but I knew, too, that I wouldn't feel good until we'd spoken properly and in person.

I wasn't aware that Li had called Sophie a few days earlier for a chat, telling her that we understood her struggles and loved her no matter

what, and reminding her just what sacrifices I had made for her. It was
he who had encouraged Sophie to call me on Mothers' Day. I was just
glad that she'd listened to her father and that I would see her soon.

A week before her visit, though, she sent us a long email that came
as a real shock and caused us great angst.

1 June 2015

Hey Mum and Dad,

Hope you guys are going well.

*I wanted to wait until I could talk face to face next week, have a
heart-to-heart conversation about what happened last time I was in
Brisbane.*

*However, knowing that Mum will interrupt me again, I'm going
to try writing it down. I'm going to write from my heart. Please listen
with your hearts. That's all I ask.*

*Also, I'll try my best to write this so there are no miscommunica-
tions because I love you guys, okay? I really, really love you both and
I always will. Please don't ever doubt my love for you.*

*I just want to say that I'm finally happy. I'm so happy and I want
to tell you why.*

*It was when I met Meg two years ago at Hear For You. Since she
can only sign, I learned how to sign for her so that we could work
better together. Be a better team together.*

*Meg not only taught me Auslan, she also taught me more life skills:
she taught me how to cope at parties, how to cope with my deafness,
how to manage phone calls, work, noisy situations – basically how to
cope with all things deaf. She unwittingly and openly shared with me a
wealth of information, strategies and skills that I never dared dream of.*

*Because I was working with Meg two days a week, learning and
asking all kinds of questions, my life changed almost within a year.
It was Meg who changed my life – the life that I always dreamed of
but could never achieve until then. To be happy.*

Then I noticed other things: I no longer had breakdowns regularly. I no longer felt isolated and lonely and felt that I had no friends. I no longer dreaded going to parties. I no longer said 'sorry' because I am deaf. And why should I say that when it's not even my fault that I am deaf?

I was twenty-three years old when I finally was at peace with my deafness. Fully accepted it and loved it.

You see, I have to love being deaf because my deafness is going to be there when I wake up, when the batteries run out, when the cochlear implant breaks, when I go to sleep. My deafness is going to be there until I die. My deafness is never going away and my cochlear implants remind me every day. It's a long life to live if I continue to not fully embrace such a permanent and significant part of myself.

When I was twenty-four, I met Matthew. He was wonderful: Matthew showed me more of the beauty of being deaf.

Then I started to worry:

'Will my parents accept me for who I am now?'

'Should I tell my parents that I'm fluent in Auslan?'

'Should I tell them that I'm in love with Matthew and we only use Auslan? Will they love me and Matthew anyway?'

Because of my anxieties about these things, I started seeing a psychologist. Because I was worried about what my parents thought of me now. For the first time in my life, I was worried that my new-found confidence as a deaf person would put a barrier up between my family.

Today, I love being deaf, perhaps because I don't know any different. I have never experienced hearing, so what can I do? Learn to love and embrace deafness, and that's what Meg and Matthew have done for me, and for that, I am so grateful.

My psychologist was incredibly insightful: he said it's almost as if I'm 'coming out'. Like as in gay, but I'm not gay, I'm deaf. He is wonderful – he's been helping me a lot in trying to tell you this in the most loving way possible. Because I love you guys.

So now you know a bit more about me, I only hope that you fully accept me as a deaf person, not a person who can hear with cochlear implants.

I know you are happy that I broke up with Matthew. I just hope it's not because he's deaf and chose not to have cochlear implants. Or that you think he changed me and I'm putting the blame on you. No, I changed my life and I want you guys to be with me on this new journey. It's not about cochlear implants any more: it's about me.

It's my only wish that you can be more accepting of me, and not worry that I will disappear into the deaf community. That's never going to happen. I am now and will always be part of both communities.

Mum, please remember this is not about my past. I don't regret or blame you for the decisions you made. It's okay, I still love you, you did the best you could.

It really hurt me when I found out that my own parents were happy that I broke up with Matthew, but not once did they bring up their concerns with their very own daughter. Why not ask their daughter for answers they need to know? You know, I cried for days. It hit me like a truck a thousand times over when I realised my own parents don't accept me for who I am. Just because I went out with a person who was exactly like me.

I love you Mum and Dad, just please don't put up a barrier between us because of the changes in my life. What it could do to get in the way of our relationship.

I love you both so very much,
Sophie

I felt an enormous guilt descend on me for not knowing the depth of Sophie's unhappiness. Of all the conversations I'd ever dreamed of being able to have with my daughter, I'd never imagined that one email would break me so completely. Both Li and I felt gutted. How had we missed so totally how badly she felt about being torn between her family and her connection with the deaf world?

We could hardly speak about it as we both processed the pain that our daughter had been dealing with.

Neither Li nor I wanted Sophie to resent her upbringing and the fact that she could communicate orally with the speaking world. Neither of us had ever imagined such an outcome. It can't have been *all* our fault, all *my* fault, fighting as I did for her to live in the hearing world. It had to be down to the other influences that had come into Sophie's life. It had to have been largely down to Matthew, I suspected. It was good that he'd helped her to navigate the deaf world, but we felt he was very political about that world and didn't know our family or our situation.

Sophie's email was a huge wake-up call for us, and I waited for her arrival with eagerness, anxiety, trepidation and hope. I couldn't stop thinking about her and her letter. I felt incredibly agitated and emotionally fragile, as though my tears could flood out at any time.

Finally, Sophie arrived from the airport. We hugged each other tightly, for slightly longer than usual. I was relieved that she didn't try to pull away. Li had kept telling me that no matter how emotional we were, we shouldn't lose our cool. And we had both agreed that the most important thing was to get Sophie to understand that our love for her was absolutely unconditional. We could see now that she was crying out for our help and understanding. I loved her even more, if this was at all possible.

Sophie was very calm and composed when we finally sat down to discuss things. Li and I assured her that we understood what she was going through and that she should never feel she was going through it alone. We would always be there for her, loving her.

We talked for hours. I felt that the wall between us was slowly crumbling and we became closer and closer as the conversation went on. I believed that we'd got our daughter back by the end of that evening, even though there were scars that needed time to heal. One thing was clear to me: Sophie knew that we loved her no matter what. And I knew that her love for us hadn't changed either.

~

Later, we sat outside by the pool in the winter sun. Li had made his mother's dumplings as a treat, as we knew Sophie missed them. We'd got through such a lot earlier in the day, but we still hadn't mentioned Matthew. I was curious and asked why she hadn't told us at the time that they'd broken up. Her eyes began to fill with tears.

'I didn't tell you, Mum, because I just couldn't deal with any more at the time.'

'What happened, Sophie?' I asked. She refused to be drawn on it and I could only speculate. After our emotional reunion earlier that day, I guessed that she must have reached a point where she had to make a decision – a life with Matthew or a life with us; it couldn't be both. To this day I still don't know the reason for sure, and perhaps I will never know. I haven't asked her again and we haven't spoken about it. But I did think it was for the best. If *I* could be open to her living in two worlds, why couldn't he, if he really loved her?

'I'm all right now, Mum,' she said, returning from the kitchen with the steaming dumplings. 'Things are much clearer to me now. I think I know how I can make my life work living in two communities. I want to find something that joins them together, or at least find a way where they can be at peace with one another. We need to get rid of the idea that it's either one world or the other. It's so damaging.'

This sounded encouraging. She went on to explain that she'd been talking about her future with her friend Zoe who, like Sophie, was profoundly deaf and could speak and sign. Zoe had suggested that Sophie look into audiology, and this had really piqued Sophie's interest.

'I can't believe there are so few deaf audiologists in Australia, Mum. How can audiologists understand deafness if they are all hearing?' I thought she had a good point. As it turned out, she'd already started to apply for positions at universities.

I could see that Sophie was beginning to take the lead in our relationship, educating me about living independently in both the hearing and deaf worlds that were her reality, and it filled me with joy. I felt that what we'd been through was actually helping our relationship become more equal, which is what we'd both worked for. I believe the mother–daughter relationship is the most important relationship for the happiness of your daughter. And this was happening to us. The conflict between us was starting to dissipate.

I got up and walked over to the frangipani tree near the verandah. The sun was going down behind the hill and I could hear Sophie and Li laughing together. I felt more at ease than I had in a long time. Seeing Sophie's growing confidence in her own beliefs and abilities made me more confident about what lay ahead for her. No one can read the future, but I hoped my instincts were right.

~

We had much to celebrate. Bridie graduated from school, thrilled to be eighteen finally. She was impatient to get out into the world at long last, and we hardly saw her. She was working in hospitality, saving up for a car. She enrolled in a Bachelor of Arts at the University of Queensland but had no idea what subjects to do except for Spanish, having fallen in love with Barcelona two years earlier. Tom would soon be doing the second year of his Master of Teaching and Sophie would start a four-year degree to pursue a Master of Audiology at La Trobe University. The year ahead for the family looked promising, with all three children flying from the nest and finding their own path. I was very proud of them.

But first it was time for a long-overdue family holiday to China over the Christmas break, though it would be filled with sadness as Niang was gravely ill and in hospital. She had had a near-fatal stroke several years earlier and was confined to a wheelchair and was unable to feed herself. Now Niang had contracted an infection. She was eighty-seven. It was important that we make this trip while we could, and that we *all* went this time so we could concentrate on being together with Li's family.

20

On the plane to China, Li was quiet and anxious. I felt sad for him. I looked across the aisle at Sophie, knowing she was longing to see her *nana* again, to feel that warmth, that outpouring of love Niang had for Sophie. Family was what it was all about for us. It always was and it always will be.

Qingdao was freezing when we arrived on Christmas Day. We dropped our bags off at Li's seventh brother Cungui's lovely new house, where the children would be staying, and went straight to the hospital. We found Niang curled up in a foetal position, so tiny there was hardly anything left of her. I let out an involuntary gasp, but Li went straight to her. As soon as Niang saw her sixth son, she immediately cheered up and became her old self, laughing and hugging everyone. Perhaps she would rally now, I hoped.

Her eyesight was very poor. Each of us leant down with our face close to her so she could see us. The children greeted her in order of age, and delightedly she pulled them into big hugs. She hugged Sophie especially long and tight. '*Wo zuomeng ye xiang bu dao ni hui tinjian wo, geng xiang bu dao ni hui he wo shuohua.*' I never dreamed you would one day hear me, let alone talk to me! she said in Chinese. She clicked her tongue and made her signature 'zhi, zhi, zhi' sounds.

Then it was Tom's turn, the precious grandson. He spoke softly to her in Chinese and she laughed heartily.

When Bridie bent down to give her a kiss, Niang gently grabbed her breast, giggled, and cheekily said, '*Oh, Bai La Dee zong da la.*' Bridie blushed. We were surprised but Li burst into laughter and translated: 'She said, "Bridie is all grown-up!"' Bridie thought it was hilarious.

Then it was my turn. I just hugged Niang tight, so grateful to have had this precious woman in my life. We were very emotional, trying to hold back the tears. She was so happy to see us, but obviously struggling with her breathing.

Li held Niang's hands and talked gently to her for quite a while. She clearly missed her cherished son who had been taken from her at such a young age. Looking at Niang's fragile state I felt overcome, and so blessed to have had those happy years with her and Dia in Houston.

We stayed in Niang's apartment for almost a week. Li was very worried about her, but happier now that he was here. We visited her every day after having breakfast prepared for us by Li's fourth brother, Cunsang – dumplings and steamed bread, eggs, pickles and fish. He still lived nearby on the site of the old commune. Qingdao was no longer the same place – so much more modern. The commune had long disappeared and Li's family lived in nice new apartments with televisions and refrigerators.

The hospital was a half-hour walk away. It was fairly primitive. We had to enter via the back stairs, the floor was cement and the bathroom was a shared facility without doors. It didn't look like it was cleaned regularly. Niang was in a room with a window and four single beds, which apparently was one of the best rooms in the hospital. The family had paid for a full-time carer to help Li's parents at home, and now the carer was here twenty-four hours a day, sleeping beside Niang. There were few hospital staff and Niang needed help with toileting and feeding. The family took meals to her because the hospital food wasn't good. Despite her condition, she could still eat ten dumplings with gusto. This brought smiles to our faces, but Li and I both felt she would not be with us for much longer.

'She wants to be with Dia now,' Li said to me quietly. 'She keeps saying that he's waiting for her in another world and she wants to go and be with him. I think she knows her time is near the end. She told me today that she can go to Dia now, as she has seen me. She's been waiting four years since Dia died to be together again with him.'

It was heartbreaking to hear Li say this, but I knew he was right. 'I know,' I told him. 'None of us can bear to see her suffering like this. It is so cruel for her to suffer such indignity. I hope she will go peacefully and soon.'

Before long, it was time for us to return to Brisbane. As always, we visited Dia's grave to pay our respects. Li also knelt sadly at his oldest brother, Cuncia's, grave. He had died suddenly of a heart attack, not long after Dia. I remember him vividly. He was such a gentle soul, and so handsome. True to tradition, Li's brothers organised for paper money, alcohol and food to be placed on the top of Dia's marble gravestone. The alcohol was poured and paper money lit. Then, one by one, each of us knelt down and kowtowed to Dia by touching our head on the ground three times. The children had become accustomed to this traditional way of showing respect to the elderly. Seeing Niang's empty plot next to Dia's gravestone brought even more emotion to the ceremony. On our next visit, we would most likely be kowtowing to both Dia and Niang.

We went to the hospital one last time, each of us getting close to Niang's face again and kissing her gently on the cheek. We tried to hold back our tears, knowing that this could be the last time we'd see her. Niang was openly crying, though trying hard not to, so that we wouldn't be too sad. '*Buyao danxin wo, buyao dnaxin wo.*' Don't worry about me, don't worry about me, she kept saying to Li in her croaky voice. They hugged for a long time.

The car ride to the airport was quiet as we each reflected on our own relationship with Niang. I remembered how painfully sad it had been when she and Dia left Houston all those years ago – what they had given up in order to do the right thing for Sophie.

Farewelling Niang made me desperate to spend more time with Coralie. After all, my mother was eighty-one. I was happy that we would be going almost immediately to Coolangatta for our annual holiday. She was already there, staying with Ger and Marlene in their apartment in the complex. It was a special time spent playing cards together, chatting and sharing meals. I treated Mum to lunches at a restaurant downstairs: a few oysters and a glass of champagne were her favourite. But after she returned to Brisbane and Brig confided, 'Mum is not quite right,' I knew what she meant. Coralie was frailer and less energetic.

Not long after we returned to Brisbane I made a quick trip to visit Sophie in Melbourne, determined not to allow space for another rift to open up. We enjoyed a couple of days together in the hot Melbourne sunshine, going out for lunch and shopping for Sophie's first car. With much excitement she was planning to go to a global deaf conference in America.

I headed home feeling more positive about our relationship, but when the plane touched down there was a phone message from Brig: 'Mary, Mum's had a stroke. We're at St Andrew's. It's pretty bad.'

I rushed straight to the hospital emergency department. Beloved Coralie looked very pale and frightened, her mouth drooping to the left side. She was speaking but it was slurred. She recognised Brig and me, so I felt things might not be too bad. I couldn't really take it in. Apparently Dom's partner, Clive, had gone to visit Coralie early that morning to fix her television. The door was locked and Clive knocked, but when she didn't answer he called out to Brig, who was just next door, to come and let him in. Coralie was in bed, unable to rise.

It turned out that Mum's stroke was significant, affecting her whole left side. It was a shock to us all. None of us could believe it. Jo even flew in from the US. Coralie had been able and independent, and this would change now. While she was able to recognise everyone and tried to rally as her children and grandchildren visited, it was clear that she was very unwell. The Coralie we'd known and loved forever was no longer the same. We were beside ourselves with grief and anxiety. What did it mean for the future?

I wanted to be there all day, every day with Mum, but Li told me to prepare for 'the long game'. He had seen his own mother linger for years after her stroke. 'It can be a marathon, Mary,' he reminded me gently.

Mum was in hospital for six weeks. It was devastating for us all. It took a few weeks before the nursing team and physios could get her into a wheelchair. Her left side, including her eyesight and mouth, still had not recovered and she had some trouble swallowing. Thank God she could still communicate, even though she slurred her words a little. As time went on, we could see she was also confused, and the doctors told us the stroke had caused vascular dementia. This was when we knew that she would never be able to go home and live independently: she needed full-time care.

Brig, always the organiser, found the best aged-care place for Mum. It was a nice facility where she had her own spacious room with a bathroom. The staff were caring and friendly. When she arrived, her brain couldn't process what was going on and it was very traumatic. She became bed-bound and couldn't be taken on outings. But her beloved family rallied round her, with everyone visiting as often as they could.

~

As we struggled to adjust to the impact of Coralie's stroke, there came another blow. We'd only been back at work for two weeks when we got the news from Li's fifth brother, Cunfar, that their beloved Niang had passed away. Li called me into his office and shared the shattering news. He looked broken but resolute, and set about booking flights for himself and his third brother, Cunmao, who was in Melbourne visiting Lulu. I just gave him a hug, then quickly called the kids.

Even though he'd been mentally prepared for her death, Niang's passing was still a huge blow to Li. Of the seven brothers, he was the closest to her. He called me from Qingdao as soon as he and Cunmao arrived the next day. Niang's body was already in a coffin in the hospital's cooling room – 'the Peaceful Room', they called it – where she would lie for three days. It was opened so Li could see her face and farewell her spirit for the last time.

'Niang looked peaceful and serene,' he told me on the phone.

'That's good, darling,' I replied gently.

'After we left China, she apparently caught a virus and her health quickly deteriorated,' Li explained. 'Her cough got worse and she had to wear a mask to help her breathe.'

'Poor Niang. I'm so sorry, Li!' was all I could say.

I listened with a smile as he said, 'Cungui told me that on the morning of her death she drank an entire bowl of rice soup and ate half an egg pancake. She maintained her good appetite until the end. Before her last breath, she asked when her third and sixth sons would arrive. But we were too late.'

'You did your best, darling.'

'The doctor then told everyone that they should prepare her clothes, so they knew it was time.'

Li was referring to the local tradition of special clothes for dying people to wear for their afterlife: shirt, pants, socks, shoes and a wooden comb. No metal or plastic objects – only old-world stuff.

'Oh, Mary, on the way to the Peaceful Room, one of the wheels of the mobile bed dropped off,' Li continued. 'Can you imagine? It should have been a peaceful journey to the Peaceful Room.'

'Oh God, Li.'

'One of the nurses said, "Your Niang doesn't want to go." Then Cungui's wife, Xiao Zhu, remembered Niang's last words and said, "Niang, don't worry, your third and sixth sons are on their way. They will be here tomorrow to say goodbye." Once they fixed the trolley, she was wheeled into the Peaceful Room without any more trouble.'

'So Niang can finally be with Dia, then,' I said.

It was very cold on the day of Niang's funeral, Li told us afterwards. It snowed, which is a rare thing in Qingdao these days. All of the family members, relatives, friends and village people came to farewell Niang. There were flowers and wreaths surrounding her simple coffin, and a funeral director who recited loving and lucky words to the crowd of over a hundred people. I could only imagine their howls and cries of grief filling the cold funeral hall: no one would have held back. Then, after the surviving sons' names were called, Li and his five brothers knelt in front of Niang's coffin and kowtowed three times. It was the very last time they would kowtow in their beloved Niang's presence before her body was cremated.

Although we couldn't be there with Li, I was comforted by the thought that we had seen Niang only a few weeks earlier. I felt so lucky to have had a mother-in-law like her. Her generosity and larger-than-life personality would never leave me. Her love and kindness for me and our children, especially Sophie, would always live in our hearts. The legacy she and Dia had left behind was immense. What a special woman! What a life she lived. I will never forget her.

~

It was the end of an era – and the end of an era is always marked by feelings of loss combined with a view to the future. I wanted to spend more time with Coralie and was determined to do so. It was unbearable seeing her unable to move, but I chatted with her about our growing up in Rocky in that crazy house with our boisterous family, about Dad and his enthusiastic support for all of us siblings, and that often brought a smile to her face – and mine.

I wanted to be there for Sophie, too, but it was time to try and properly let go. *I can do that too, now*, I thought to myself. *Truly I can. Even though uni will remain challenging, she's really on her way now at La Trobe University. She will make a great audiologist, I just know it.*

I was coming to see that with her improved signing capabilities, Sophie's language, pacing of speech, clarity and nuance were also improving. It seemed that learning to sign had helped develop her vocabulary even as an adult. Back when we had first decided on the oral path for her, we had been told that signing would be a hindrance to her speech and hearing development. I was proud of her resourcefulness now and could only stand back and observe, support and hope. Just like Niang had taught me, really. No use moping – just get on with it.

With Sophie and Tom sorted and Bridie settling in to first-year uni, Li and I decided to move house for a fresh start, to mark the beginning of the next phase of our lives. Admittedly it was just up the hill, but we swapped our Queenslander with its cross-breezes and tumbling vines for a larger, architect-designed modern house that we had fallen in love with. It had a fabulous aspect beneath the wide sky, large gracious spaces with lots of glass to let in the light, a wide staircase, a terrace with a lap pool and a low-maintenance garden. It was perfect for holding the increasing number of ballet parties that Li liked to host.

In May 2016 Sophie left Vicdeaf to concentrate on her studies. After passing first semester at La Trobe, she applied to Melbourne Uni to complete her Master in Audiology. Tom graduated in August and took up a teaching position at a language school in Shanghai. I was truly thrilled for him even though I was going to miss him.

We decided to go to Shanghai to spend Christmas with him in that amazing city. Luckily Sophie would be able to join us. The visit would allow Li to return to Qingdao and respect the tradition of kowtowing before Niang's grave on the one-year anniversary of her death, as well as to pay his respects to Dia and, importantly, for all of us to be together.

We left after the final performance of our annual *The Nutcracker* and were with Tom and his flatmates the next evening. He lived in the French Concession area and knew his way around already. It was great fun to spend a few days together away from our responsibilities, enjoying the hustle and bustle of this megacity with its old colonial buildings and futuristic skyline, shopping in the markets and dining in smoke-filled restaurants, where it was a thrill to hear Tom ordering in Chinese. It was mind-boggling how China had developed in recent years.

The days raced by, and before we knew it we were heading home to prepare for another year of work and uni. But first there were Li's connections – always his connections – and a dinner. A dinner that would open a new door, this time a door that would lead Sophie to another journey altogether. A journey that would make my once impossible dream become a bigger reality than any of us could have imagined.

We were all invited to dinner at the swish Ritz-Carlton by an acquaintance of Li's, Richard Yan, and his Taiwanese wife, Tina. The hotel was right on the Bund and the views over the Huangpu River from the seventieth floor were stunning. Food and wine flowed in abundance and everyone chatted happily in a mix of Chinese and English. Richard seemed particularly interested in Sophie and how she was managing her disability. She was being her usual impressive self when he surprised us by suggesting that she come and work for him in Shanghai. He owned an international leather manufacturing business and said he could see she had a lot to offer.

'I think you can do more than you think, Sophie,' he said. 'I can see you have a good business mind, and I think audiology will only limit you.'

His proposal took my breath away. We didn't know how to react, but Sophie quickly thanked him politely and simply reaffirmed that helping deaf people was her priority. Richard pointed out that she could still help deaf people even if she wasn't in the profession, given the good people skills and strong work ethic she evidently had. If she ever changed her mind, he added, he had a job waiting for her.

This was most unexpected, and needed a bigger conversation at home in private. For now, Li and I merely showed our appreciation to Richard.

On our return to Brisbane, we were glad to be back at work but there was a lot to think about with Sophie. In fact, she brought up the topic herself.

'Mum,' she started, 'maybe I should just chat to Richard to see what he has in mind for me? I mean, it wouldn't hurt to go to Shanghai for a year and then return if I still want to do the audiology degree in Melbourne.'

I looked at my daughter and marvelled at just how much she was like Li in this aspect – always open to opportunities. I nodded and said, 'That's not a bad idea, Sophie, if that is what you want to do. Just do it. It's your life. I did the same thing at your age, and look where it took me!'

Sophie smiled and said, 'I'll talk to Richard.'

Some weeks later, when she was FaceTiming with us, she said, 'Dad, the more I think about Richard's offer, the more excited I am. This is a rare opportunity for me. I'm a bit scared but also excited.'

'What are you scared about, Sophie?' Li asked.

'Well, my Chinese isn't very good. I wish I'd kept it going through uni, to be honest.'

'Sophie, I reckon what you have learned in high school will get you off to a good start – and there are plenty of people there who speak English,' I said.

'I guess so. But, Mum, this is an opportunity for me to improve my ability to speak Dad's language. I already fit into two worlds – oral and signing – and maybe I can fit into a third.'

'What are you saying, Sophie?' I asked, knowing the answer already and looking at Li's very proud-father face.

'Mum,' she began, 'like you said, you went for it when you were sixteen and flew to the other side of the world, and look what happened. I'm going to go for it. It's what I want more than anything right now. I don't know where it will lead, but if I don't take this opportunity I never will know, will I?'

'I'm so proud of you, darling' was all I could say. Here, now, in front of us on our little phone screen, was our daughter having the most meaningful conversation with us. And here was I, lost for words.

~

With the decision made, Sophie blossomed. She said she had never been happier. Nor had I. Straight away she deferred her university course, sold everything in her rented apartment and came to Brisbane to live with us while she waited for her visa application for Shanghai to be approved. This could take a few weeks, but that was fine by me because it was just sublime to spend a bit more time with her. She was a joy to be with, and we adored having her around, coming to the studio with us, hanging out with Bridie, cooking dinner, sometimes on her computer keeping up with her friends.

Sophie was searching for a career that would be fulfilling. She knew her passion was working within the deaf community, but after four years of working and volunteering, she was starting to get burnt out and the responsibility was heavy. I think perhaps the opportunity to live in Shanghai was a way out or, dare I say, an escape that Sophie had never thought to take before. Even though Shanghai may not offer her the job of her dreams – she still didn't really know what kind of work she wanted to do – it certainly appealed to what she needed in her life right then: a fresh start.

A month later and still with no visa, Sophie was beginning to have second thoughts. 'If the visa doesn't come through, should I go back to Melbourne where there are more job opportunities?' she asked us.

Li kept saying, 'Just be patient, Sophie! It's China. The visa will come.'

Then one night he suggested, 'Actually, maybe you could start writing down your story?'

I looked at him. What a great idea! I thought Sophie's story would be so inspirational for young people. And I think she liked the idea too, because just like her father, she loves a project and she was getting restless not having anything to do. I just sat back and sipped my wine.

'And Sophie, it's funny,' I said. 'When I think about it, I always knew that if I was ever to write my story, I wouldn't be able to do it without you.'

'What do you mean, Mum?'

'Well,' I revealed, 'back when Dad's book was published, Julie Watts suggested I write my story too. She said readers wanted to know what happened to me after your diagnosis, that the few articles and interviews about me didn't tell the full story. But I told her that I wouldn't write it unless you wanted it, too.'

I looked at her as I said this. I meant it. Being a mother to Sophie was one of the toughest challenges but also one of the most rewarding experiences of my life. If there was ever to be a second book about our family, it had to come from her – I just wouldn't do it otherwise. And all that work. Writing! It would be my worst nightmare if I had to do anything with writing.

Sophie nodded. 'Thanks, Mum. I really appreciate that you didn't want to write your story without me.'

I was delighted that she wanted to start writing. Her story needed to be shared. I only wished that a similar book had been available when I discovered she was deaf. I would have found such comfort and hope in reading something like that.

Sophie got started as soon as she woke up the next morning, sitting in Li's home office typing bullet points. That evening, she came to me and asked a few questions about her early childhood. It developed into an interesting conversation. Once I began to talk about how things were back then and how I'd felt, I could see a change in her face. I realised that now she was a young woman, I could explain things – such as my feelings during that tumultuous time, and the choices Li and I had made – in a fuller way. Before long we also began touching on the recent years of her life, when she had started to become part of the deaf community. I recognised that not only was this going to keep Sophie busy, it could also be just what she and I needed.

Even though I'd dreamed of one day sitting down with her to talk about our shared experiences, I'd never expected it to happen this way. She was taking the lead and was the one pushing me to tell her about the hard decisions we had made about her life. What surprised me most was that she started to share some very vivid memories of her early childhood with me. I had always been aware of her 'dark moods', but I could never have imagined the real depths of her suffering and despair. She questioned me about some of the decisions we had made, such as her cochlear implant and changing schools. Writing the book was giving us the opportunity to open up to each other. She was coming to terms with the things that troubled her, and I was gaining a more profound understanding of and compassion for our daughter's plight. I think she was also gaining insights into my perspective and the decisions I'd made. We were becoming even closer.

So far, she was just making notes in point form. Then Li fished out, from his dusty mountain of paperwork, some points I'd written when giving a talk about my life at All Hallows' School in Brisbane when we had first arrived. Sophie became fascinated with my childhood in Rocky. We were sitting at the kitchen bench watching Li cook dinner when she began pestering me to write down something about it. I kept saying that I'd answer any questions, but there was something amiss. What was it that Sophie was really asking of me?

Suddenly, I looked at her in confusion and shock. All this time, I'd thought that she was writing about *her* life. I raised my eyebrows at her.

'Sophie, what's this sudden interest in *me* about?'

'Mum, I actually think it should be you who is writing this book,' she stated.

Ah. The cat was out of the bag.

'Sophie. You know I am not a writer!' I bluntly told her as I got up to refill my wineglass.

'Don't worry, Mum. I can help you. You just have to talk and I'll write it down for you.' she said. Then, giving me a dreamy look, she continued, 'Or this can be a book that we write together.' She suddenly whipped out her phone and pressed something. 'Mum, talk a bit about something that has happened in your life. Just talk into the phone and it will record and I will transcribe it.'

I immediately responded, 'Oh, Sophie! No, I can't do it.'

'Why not, Mum?'

'Because I know what a huge project this is. I lived through the writing of your father's book!'

I panicked, remembering the relief I'd felt when Li's writing fever was finally over. 'And Sophie, I can't put pen to paper. Who would want *me* to write?' I put my hand to my chest, earnestly.

'But Mum, you just have to talk. You know you never shut up anyway,' Sophie deadpanned. We both started laughing.

We moved on to dinner, with me hoping deep down she'd forget all this nonsense. But no, the next morning she popped her head in at the bedroom door and charmingly said, 'Coffee, Mum?'

I looked at her and from that moment knew what I was in for, whether I liked it or not. I threw some clothes on and we walked to the cafe nearby. It was a sunny winter's day and we could sit outside with Nala at our feet. As soon as we sat down, she took out an A4 notebook and pen, put them on the table and said sweetly, 'I'll get the coffee, you write.'

I looked at the pen and paper helplessly.

'Just write anything, Mum.' Sophie called from the counter. 'What about a paragraph about your brothers in Rocky? What were they like growing up?'

I was silently fuming. I hastily scribbled some rubbish over a page and tossed back the notebook, saying I was done for the day. Sophie smiled but didn't say anything more; she just put the notebook and pen away.

That night, she ran down from Li's office and said, 'Mum, this is brilliant! You need to write more.' She had somehow typed up my scribbles from earlier that day.

'How could you even read my scrawl?' I responded with surprise.

'Oh, it was difficult, Mum,' she said, laughing out loud, 'but can you please write more, a bit more, and write more clearly, please?'

I had to admit that it was fun to work on a project together. Sophie's happiness and her sense of humour gave me such joy. Later that weekend, after more coffee and scribbling fiascos in the mornings, I would hear her laughing as she typed up my scrawl. She was laughing at my stories. How wonderful! How could I refuse her? That's why I wrote – I could not refuse my daughter.

Over the next few weeks, Sophie was tenacious. She continued to wake me up with her charming coffee agenda and off we would go. Her visa still had not come through, and while she was concerned, she was excited about our project and also somehow managed to find a couple of casual jobs to keep her going. One was assisting teachers of deaf students at a local high school, and the other was teaching weekly Auslan community classes for Deaf Services Queensland. What a go-getter!

A few weeks later, Sophie said, 'Mum, I've been in contact with Julie Watts. She's interested in our story.'

'She is?' I asked, panic starting to rise. Julie was still waiting for me, even after all these years?

Julie was working for herself now but was keen to help us get started and, if possible, to remain involved.

'Sophie, I told you before, I cannot write!' I continued to protest. 'I mean, I am already *bored* writing about myself!' I dramatically put my hands up to my face in mock despair.

Sophie laughed. 'Mum, don't worry. I have a plan. We'll just keep doing what we've been doing and not worry about the book. We don't have to publish it if you don't like it. It will just be nice for your grand-children to read one day.'

Over the next few days, Julie contacted Penguin Random House, as they were now, and they were very quick to put in an offer for our story. I was very surprised and also worried. I had reservations, as we still had to write the bloody book! As it turned out, Julie's own daughter, Ali Watts, was our publisher there. The lovely mother–daughter serendipity was not lost on me.

Sophie kept pushing me, every morning. She was turning our interviews into a collection of conversations. Conversations! *Conversations with My Daughter* is what she was calling the book. I marvelled that she had thought of a working title that echoed my impossible dream from all those years ago.

And then there we were a couple of months later, a few sample chapters done and a publisher's contract on the table. I was in shock. Just from our daily coffee dates, we had somehow amassed 160 000 words! Along the way we had also come to the conclusion that the conversation format was probably not the best vehicle for our story, and perhaps it should just be my own memoir . . . Was *I* to be a published author? Really? Could I do it on my own?

Sophie's visa still hadn't come through and we were able to continue our coffee mornings until we had most of my story down. Yes, it is ultimately my story, but without Sophie and her disci-pline, there would be no story. When I thought of writing about my life I was immediately overwhelmed, but her tenacity was just like her father's.

I was working full time at the ballet and wrote when I could. Sophie had all but given up on the visa. Though Li kept reassur-ing her, she wasn't so sure. However, she agreed to give it a few more months, to the end of the following summer break. If it hadn't come by then, she would let it go and move on, but in Brisbane instead of Melbourne. She would not pick up with her masters after all. I had started to wonder if the delay was meant to be so that Sophie could help me write. I wanted China for her, but it was a relief to me and our writing project that she wasn't going anywhere just yet.

Life continued to be hectic, juggling my commitments at Queensland Ballet, whether in the studio or on tour, and finding time to expand on my story, not to mention visiting my poor mother in her nursing home. Some days were really testing. I tried not to think too much about it, reminding myself how when I was raising Sophie alongside two other children, I had simply taken it one day at a time. That's what I had to do now.

When I sat with Mum I explained the book project Sophie and I were working on. She looked at me with knowing eyes, saying that she understood. 'That's lovely, darling,' she said. I know how proud she was, in her quiet way, to learn that I was writing my story. After all, it was Coralie and Neil George who had allowed me to go through that first open door at Miss Hansen's at such a young age, which was what made possible everything that followed. How lucky I was to have such amazing parents! I wanted her to know I was writing about her, Neil George, her family, and Rockhampton too.

But would I ever finish it? And in time? Because that wasn't all. December was fast approaching and there were some surprises in store as we revisited Li's story again.

There was to be an exhibition of Li's life at the Brisbane Museum. I was sceptical at first. Hadn't I chucked out all of his junk over the years? But when I walked in to the opening of *Mao's Last Dancer the Exhibition: A Portrait of Li Cunxin* and saw the display of memorabilia that the curators had found around our house, I was blown away. Not only were there many artefacts – from Li's father's handmade wooden stools to reproductions of Dia's kites and old family photographs and stills from his ballets – but there were also mannequins wearing dance costumes, including some fabulous swan outfits; his copious hand-written manuscript notes; and everything in between, including the rarest of rare film footage of Niang and Dia chatting proudly about their son some ten years earlier in Qingdao when Sophie and Tom were in their teens. I was overcome with emotion. A snapshot of Li's journey was happening before my eyes. As I walked around, taking my time to look at each display, I thought the exhibition was incredible.

Bridie and Sophie came to the opening, along with a few of our dear friends from Melbourne, and my family. Tom would catch it later at a private viewing when he came to visit later that month. I could see how special the exhibition was for our daughters. Sophie was struck hard when she saw the footage of her grandparents. Niang was laughing cheekily and Dia was doing a lot of talking, which was unusual as he was a man of few words. I could see the girls were very proud of their father and their family.

It was especially hard for Li to watch the film footage of his parents, but it was also an opportunity for us all to remember them and be reminded of how dear they were to us.

~

Queensland Ballet's funding depended very much on donors, corporate partners, government funding and ticket buyers. Ever since Li's retirement from dancing, he had often been asked to go back on stage and he had always declined. But Queensland Ballet was facing a challenge to meet its budget this year. Furthermore, with its principal partner, Suncorp, it had a successful initiative called Wishing Upon a Ballet Star, which each year enabled one child from regional Queensland to perform with the company in *The Nutcracker*. It would mean a lot to Suncorp if Li would agree to perform a comeback dance at that performance.

I knew something was up when Li came to me with a strange look on his face. 'Mary,' he said, 'Dilshani has asked me to do something in *The Nutcracker* so we can turn it into a major fundraiser. Just one performance.' Dilshani Weerasinghe was the executive director of Queensland Ballet and Li's partner on the corporate side of the organisation.

'What do you mean, just one performance? Do you mean going on stage?' I asked, incredulous.

'Yes,' he said. 'I would only be acting in the role of Drosselmeyer. What do you think?' Drosselmeyer entertains guests at the Christmas party with magic tricks and hands out presents to the children.

'Well, that would be fine,' I said, relieved.

The media went into a frenzy, both in Australia and abroad. We had celebrities, politicians, donors, corporate partners and even a former prime minister wanting to get hold of tickets. But the 2000 tickets sold out in less than thirty minutes! People were hugely disappointed when they missed out.

Li received many messages from people exclaiming how excited they were at the prospect of seeing him dance again. He was confused and shocked, because he wasn't going to be dancing, just acting – as would I, in a comic role as one of the parents. Yes, Li and I would be on stage together again after twenty-six years, and in the same ballet for which we'd danced our final *pas de deux* as the Sugar Plum Fairy and the Prince. Talk about full circle! Everyone thought it was terribly romantic – and so did I, to be honest, even though we wouldn't be partnering.

But it was a dilemma for Li, who said, 'Darling, I don't want people feeling cheated if they are expecting to see me dance. I think I have to do *some* dancing.'

'Are you crazy, Li?' I exclaimed. 'You're running a ballet company – how can you have time to get into shape to do that as well?'

'Not sure,' he murmured.

'How many years has it been since you retired from dancing?'

'Eighteen,' he replied.

'That's a long time, darling.'

'I know. I'll need to think about it a bit, won't I?'

I rolled my eyes.

'Can I do it, though, Mary?' There was real doubt in his voice.

'It'll be difficult, but I think you can – as long as you don't go overboard!' I said.

'It won't be easy.'

'No, but I will help you. Haven't I always been your best coach?' We both laughed.

So Li threw himself into training, doing classes with the company dancers three and four times a week. I could see the fierce concentration in his eyes and kept telling him to slow down.

'You don't want to get injured,' I said one night during the first week.

'I know, but I don't have much time to get myself back into decent shape – and otherwise I'll disappoint the audience,' he replied.

'No, you won't!' I said, knowing that he always gave more than 100 per cent once he was committed.

Over the following weeks he worked with diligence and focus, not only in classes, but on weekends and evenings too. His body got sorer and sorer.

Of course he had to ask Ben Stevenson for permission to include some dancing in the role of Drosselmeyer, and he also asked Greg Horsman to help him with the choreography. One day I peeked in to see how they were going. I couldn't quite believe my eyes: Li was doing *pirouettes*, high leaps and split *jetés* around the studio like a madman. What was he thinking? Hadn't I told him not to go overboard?

But discipline was part of Li's DNA, and he put himself through a rigorous twelve-week training regime, gradually building up his strength. He had to get his body used to dancing again and not be dizzy turning. On top of that, he needed to continue his busy role as the company's artistic director. What he hadn't realised was that none of his old injuries had gone away – they had simply lain dormant. Out came the heat pads and ice buckets. Off he went for physio and massages. Sophie massaged his left calf every night to keep the soreness at bay. I felt sorry for him but never heard him utter a single word of complaint.

The whole company was abuzz about Li dancing on stage again. Some of our young performers hadn't even been born when he retired, and only knew about his legendary career because of his book and the film. He was under so much pressure to perform well. And everyone seemed happy for me, too. Although our roles now were hardly the same as before, the chemistry was still there and I felt very lucky.

On the day of the full-run rehearsal, a few days before Li was due on the stage, his left calf – which was his turning leg and the one he had torn before – started to become extremely sore and tight. He had been practising rising on his left foot while whipping fast turns, and now he couldn't even walk properly without pain. I was worried that he would re-tear his calf. What a disaster if that happened in the actual gala performance! I told him to slow down, but we both knew the next few days were the most crucial and it would be very difficult for him to ease back.

I had my own role to think about. I wanted to enjoy being in the dressing room, in front of the mirror, putting on my make-up and having time to prepare for going on stage. That hour beforehand, getting into the zone, was always special.

Then, catastrophe! On the morning of the performance, Li woke up and said, 'Darling, my calf is cramping. I can't put weight on it.'

Oh God, this was exactly what I'd been worried about. 'Li, you could re-tear your calf muscle,' I said, concerned.

'I know. It feels like it's already torn.'

'What do you want to do?' I asked.

'There's nothing I can do now. The show has to go on.'

I knew he was right. Just imagine the disappointed fans and sponsors!

'Li, just don't rise on *demi pointe*,' I suggested. 'You could just do your hop-turns instead. No one will know as long as they're fast. But if you pull your calf and start to limp around, everyone will certainly notice a crippled Drosselmeyer instead of a dancing magician.'

Li saw the humour in what I was saying, and started chuckling.

And then, our ballet of all ballets was upon us. We were unbelievably excited – and a little terrified. As we took our places behind the curtain, in the wings and backstage, everyone was slightly hysterical. I was playing the role of the Fat Mother and Greg Horsman was my fat husband. We were having a ball together, cracking up just looking at each other.

A full house of over 2000 people, including the Queensland premier, Annastacia Palaszczuk, were waiting with great anticipation and excitement. Hearing their voices and the musicians in the orchestra tuning up, and feeling the warmth of the lights above, added to the heightened sense of occasion.

The acclaimed Australian actor David Wenham, a good friend of ours, had graciously agreed to introduce this rare performance. From the minute he appeared in front of the curtain, the audience knew it was going to be a special experience. Their expectation and excitement were at fever pitch, and the nervousness and adrenaline among the dancers were palpable. I only needed to see the focus on Li's face to know that he was in the zone. He was no longer Li my husband: he had turned into Drosselmeyer the magician, and there was a sense of magic in the air.

The wonder of *The Nutcracker* had something extra that night. You could sense the anticipation of the audience waiting for Li to appear. And there he was, in his black flowing cape. The audience erupted, clapping and cheering. The cheering grew louder when he did his dazzling turns and *jetés*, flying around the stage. If he was in pain, he didn't show it; if his calf was cramping, I couldn't tell. Li was leaping and flying like the star of old. The dancers filled the wings to watch him.

It was an electrifying show, and at the end there was a spontaneous standing ovation. My heart was full and I was relieved that Li was still standing.

After many curtain calls we returned to our dressing rooms, exhausted but so alive. All the staff clapped and smiled as we walked by.

We felt very special! Bridie came backstage in tears, completely overcome – she had never seen either of us dance before. Sophie just said, 'Dad, it was great, but please don't do that again!'

Afterwards there was a splendid gala function. Tributes flowed, as did the champagne, and state government minister Kate Jones gave a speech about Queensland Ballet's future plans and announced that we would receive a grant of $10 million to invest in Li's dream of a new state-of-the-art ballet academy. The crowd gasped and clapped and cheered. How long had it been since anyone had heard of such support for the arts? And it was for Queensland Ballet! Li was gracious in his thank-you speech and expanded on his plans for the company's future. The whole experience had been exhilarating!

That night, when we finally made it home, Li said with a sense of relief, 'We did it, Mary!'

'No – you did it, Li.' I gave him a tight hug. This was the man I'd fallen in love with all those years ago.

What a night of nights it had been, I thought to myself the next morning. Such joy and love all around. Yes, Li and I were exhausted but we were riding high, and on the cusp of something new. With Queensland Ballet's future assured and Sophie about to bravely embrace a new kind of independence, I couldn't possibly ask for more, especially when I had my beloved siblings around me too. My life, with its ups and downs had come to its natural resting place, I felt. I was content, replete with happiness.

All we needed now, before Sophie left us, was one more Christmas together, and that meant flying to Shanghai to be with Tom and his Texan girlfriend, Mikala. We were thrilled to be back. We rugged up to go shopping again, stuffed ourselves with dumplings, and checked out where Sophie would be going to work. She was in a good space now, and the dark days of the last couple of years were fading from memory. You can never be sure of anything, but I hoped it would stay that way. Her visa came through while we were there – at last! – and Li took all of us to a Chinese hotpot

restaurant to celebrate. We raised our glasses to Sophie: '*Gongxi!*
Gan bei!'

Then before we knew it we were back home in Brisbane to prepare
for the start of another exciting year at the ballet, spend some time
with Coralie and the rest of the clan, and for Sophie to pack her bags
and book herself a flight back to Shanghai after the Chinese New Year.

It was all very real now, but I was ready.

21

It is Sophie's last night with us and we're having a farewell dinner at home with just the family. We are sitting at the long table with the dining-room glass doors folded back, looking out across the pool terrace. The sun is going down and I'm sitting opposite Sophie. I can see how beautiful she is, bathed in a soft glow after being at the beach during the summer.

Amid the happy chatter and laughter, I don't have any appetite. I try hard to hide my ambivalence and unease about Sophie's big trip. In no time at all, my daughter will be gone. I know she will be fine in Shanghai with Tom close by, but I am not feeling fine about writing my book without her.

'Ask Marlene to help you,' Sophie says with a grin.

What a good idea. My sister-in-law is a former journalist and a fast typist. If I can dictate the rest of my story while she types, that will be even better. To be honest, this is the only way I could do it anyway. Having brought Sophie up as I did – talking, talking, talking from the minute she was diagnosed – it has become the only way I know how to communicate!

I look at Sophie's excited face full of curiosity and adventure. How can I possibly believe that our deaf daughter is leaving us to forge her own path far away? It wasn't so long ago that I was too fearful to dream I would one day be able to have a mother–daughter conversation.

I sit here now, listening to her chatter, full of confidence about her future. A swell of love and adoration for her overcomes me. I know just how much she has endured already in her relatively young life.

At this moment, I feel so lucky that we have Sophie as our daughter. In an ironic way, her deafness has made her a stronger and more endearing person. Her deafness has taught me and our whole family so much humility and gratitude. She has made us better and more compassionate human beings. Her challenging but miraculous journey has enriched our lives. The reward and satisfaction we have gained, and are still gaining, from her achievements are far more meaningful to us than any of Li's or my own achievements.

Of course we will always worry about Sophie and her struggles ahead, and we have no idea how tough her future challenges might be, but one thing we know for sure is that she will be fine. Her strength of character, resilience, generosity and maturity will get her through rough patches, and I'm sure there'll be many. I'll always be there for her, no matter what. But I know that she is her own person now and on her way to making her own exciting discoveries and living the life of her dreams.

I wonder if my father, Neil George, is looking down on us and remembering how he and Coralie sent me off to London all those years ago, knowing that his belief in me, his eternal 'Hello, beautiful!' and Mum's quiet faith, too, allowed me the confidence to go out into the world and become the person I am. Is he watching me doing the same now for my daughter? Does he trust me putting that same faith in Sophie despite the challenges she will face?

I feel sure that he does, and I know the move to Shanghai is right for Sophie. Only an experience like this will teach her that she can navigate the world on her own. I look around at the rest of my family and feel blessed.

It is still dark when my phone buzzes on the bedside table. The birds are not yet singing. As I head downstairs, I realise that for the first time in my life it is not *me* boarding a flight halfway across the world to start a new chapter: it is my daughter. My brave, resilient, beautiful daughter is taking the next step in her own life's journey. My heart is bursting with pride and tears are threatening to spill.

I turn to her proud father and we don't need to say a word. We are just so thrilled that this journey to China is finally happening for Sophie. She is more than ready to go. It is 5 a.m. and we are all in the hallway to kiss her goodbye. She steps through the door. She is now on her own. *Go well, my darling girl – the world awaits you. I love you more than you'll ever know.*

Li puts his arm around me and pulls me to him. As always, he knows just how I am feeling. I see tears in his eyes, but his words are nothing but positive.

'Don't worry, Mary,' he says. 'Remember we're taking Queensland Ballet to China in eight months' time. We'll see Sophie then. Right now, though, let's focus on what we have to do. And you, Mary . . . *You* have to finish your book!'

And that is what I did.

For Sophie.

Acknowledgements

I would like to thank my daughter Sophie, for pushing me to write this book.

To Julie Watts, for being my guiding light.

To my sister-in-law Marlene McKendry, for tirelessly helping me throughout the editing process.

To Li for all his encouragement and shared memories.

To Rachel Scully and the wonderful team at Penguin Random House, especially my publisher Ali Watts, for believing in my story.

And finally, to my parents Coralie and Neil George, for instilling the sacred family values in me.

Discover a
new favourite